D0049421

FROM THE FILES OF <u>TRUE DETECTIVE</u> MAGAZINE

THE CRIMES OF THE
RICH AND
FAMOUS

Edited by ROSE G. MANDELSBERG

PINNACLE BOOKS
WINDSOR PUBLISHING CORP.

The editor wishes to express her sincerest thanks and appreciation to Lieutenant Ronald E. Peragine, Commanding Officer of the Brooklyn Homicide Squad, for his efforts and cooperation, and whose only "crime" is that he has yet to be rich or famous, but there's still time . . .

PINNACLE BOOKS

are published by

Windsor Publishing Corp.
475 Park Avenue South
New York, NY 10016

1-55817-630-6

Printed in the United States of America

TABLE OF CONTENTS

"STRANGLED HEIRESS IN THE PINK NIGHTIE!"

by Joseph L. Koenig

For the last 22 years of her life Marion Mavrougenis, of Salem, Massachusetts, was part of the annual migration of winter snowbirds from the northeastern states to Florida's Gold Coast. Although her southern nest was a costly two-bedroom oceanfront condominium in the exclusive Marl-borough House on the 5700 block of Collins Avenue, her tastes in life were simple. For padding around the house, she preferred the white mules that cost $1.39 a pair at the discount store where she bought them. Her white Mercedes Benz rarely left the garage, and then only for infrequent trips to Nieman Marcus or Saks Fifth Avenue in the Bal Harbour Shopping Center, or to mass each Sunday. In outward appearance, the woman was a plain-living widow. Her late husband, Dennis, had been a Salem deputy until he tired of police work. He then retired from the department and turned to real estate investments, where he demonstrated unsuspected brilliance in making his fortune.

"Dennis was a wonder when it came to speculation," a friend of the Mavrougenises would remember. "After a lifetime of being a cop, he just up and started a second career and the money never did stop rolling in. He could have been worth two million, he could have been worth five times that. Who knows? But wealth never turned Marion's

7

head. Right up until the end, she was basically the same unaffected woman she always had been."

In 1970, Dennis Mavrougenis died unexpectedly. Several years later, with no experience in real estate or in managing the great sums of money that were now her responsibility, Mrs. Mavrougenis retained a young Salem man to be her sole financial adviser.

"He did everything for her, looked over all of her finances from A to Z," the woman's lawyer would recall. "He went down to Florida a couple of times a year. He was always talking to her on the phone."

Many of those conversations, as it turned out, concerned how Marion Mavrougenis wanted her not inconsiderable fortune dispersed upon her death. Childless, and with few relatives other than a number of cousins she rarely visited, Mrs. Mavrougenis decided that she would divide her holdings among a number of charities that interested her and among the friends and acquaintances who had made her golden years exactly that.

Early on the bright Thursday morning of May 8, 1986, some house painters who had been engaged by Marion Mavrougenis to redecorate her sixth-floor apartment notified Marlborough House security officers that no one was responding to their persistent knocks on the 77-year-old woman's door. The guards thanked the painters for their concern and hurried to the Mavrougenis apartment. When they received the same lack of response to their persistent pounding, they decided to open the door.

Behind the door, the security men found a strangely still apartment, tastefully decorated with French Provincial furniture. It was not until they entered the living room that they discovered why no one had come to let them in. Curled up on the couch in a pink nightgown was Marion Mavrougenis. There was a blanket thrown around her body and a telephone cord wrapped around her throat.

Immediately, Miami Beach police, led by Detectives Nick Lluy and Michael Bower were summoned to the Marlbor-

8

ough House. A hasty check of the posh condominium produced a number of surprises for the homicide investigators. Whoever had slain the elderly woman did not seem to have been especially interested in her riches. Left behind were $33,000 in cash in a bureau, diamonds and pearls valued conservatively at $70,000, and $50,000 worth of ceramic Hummel figurines, prized sculptures that Marion Mavrougenis had been collecting for decades.

As Lluy and Bower were taking inventory inside the apartment, the phone rang. The caller began asking the homicide investigator who answered about the "disposition of her property."

"Who is this?" the detective asked.

The caller identified himself as an acquaintance of Marion Mavrougenis from Salem. What the caller was unable to answer, however, was how he knew that the wealthy widow was dead when word of her killing had not yet been made public on newscasts or in newspapers.

Hoping for a quick break in the case, the probers huddled with the night doorman at the Marlborough House. Just a couple of weeks before the slaying, the doorman told them, on Thursday, April 24th, he had seen a strange man hanging around the parking lot at 2:30 in the morning. Later, using his own key, the stranger had entered the building through the front door.

When the doorman had asked the stranger who he was, the man had responded that he was visiting a woman on the seventh floor. However, when the doorman buzzed the apartment the tenant had told him she was not expecting anyone.

The doorman went on to say that he had summoned Miami Beach police, but by the time they arrived, the stranger had fled.

Working with a Miami Beach police artist, the doorman helped put together a composite drawing of the man who had quickly emerged as their prime suspect in the troubling case. The drawing was that of a black man with short hair, a mustache and silver-framed eyeglasses. The description accompanying the drawing portrayed the man as carrying some 180 pounds on a 5-foot, 10-inch frame and wearing a brown leather jacket.

Because the other significant lead in the case was the phone call from Salem fielded by detectives at the crime scene, copies of the composite drawing were sent to Massachusetts where Salem Detective Richard Howell began showing them around. Soon, he had a name to go with the picture. A witness said that the portrait reminded her of 41-year-old Baren C. Van Alstyne, a $24,000-a-year night shift officer with the 80-man Massachusetts Capitol police in Boston. Van Alstyne, the witness said, was the father of two children and currently estranged from his wife. In recent months he had been making his home on Chatham Street in nearby Lynn, Massachusetts.

Now Salem police began pushing the investigation at their end. A check of Van Alstyne's work record at the Massachusetts statehouse indicated that he had not reported to his job on April 24th, or on May 7th or May 8th, the dates on which the Marlborough House doorman claimed to have seen him in Florida. On the strength of the information they and the Miami Beach probers already had gathered, the Salem detectives obtained a search warrant for Van Alstyne's Lynn apartment. It was there that Salem Detective Richard Urbanowicz discovered the most damning piece of evidence so far, a key ring containing eight keys, one of which was found to open the front door of Marion Mavrougenis' Miami Beach condominium apartment.

Baren Van Alstyne, when questioned by the Salem homicide probers, denied ever having been to Florida. But he had no handy explanation for what he was doing with the key to a Miami Beach apartment. When the detectives asked why he had recently shaved off the mustache that he had worn for years, Van Alstyne told the lawmen that, in fact, he had been going clean-shaven since early April.

Other witnesses, however, reported that Van Alstyne had remained hirsute at least until May 9th, the day after the Miami Beach slaying.

On Thursday evening, May 29th, Baren C. Van Alstyne was taken into custody on first-degree murder charges at his Lynn apartment. The suspect was a quiet, bespsectacled man who once drove buses at the United States Military Academy at West Point, and was the possessor of an unremarkable 12-year record in law enforcement work. The following day, Friday, Van Alstyne entered an innocent plea to the charge of being a fugitive from Florida justice at a brief hearing in Salem District Court.

During the proceedings, Salem Police Detective Sergeant Richard R. Howell and State Police Staff Sergeant John J. O'Rourke testified that they had obtained an employment photo of Van Alstyne and sent it to Florida. There the night doorman at the Marlborough House positively identified it as the man he had seen in the building on April 24th and early on the morning that Marion Mavrougenis' body was discovered. Reportedly, a brown leather jacket similar to the one worn by the Florida suspect had been seized by police during the court-authorized search of Van Alstyne's apartment.

But the arrest of Baren Van Alstyne hardly signalled the end of the investigation into the killing of Marion Mavrougenis. A number of sources close to the case believed that it was just the beginning. Assistant Essex County District Attorney Frederick B. McAlary declared to reporters that Van Alstyne was a "contract killer."

Major Fred Wooldridge of the Miami Beach police department told newsmen: "The theory is that there was a conspiracy between the officer (Van Alstyne) and other persons to kill this lady for money."

Wooldridge went on to explain that the leading suspect was Marion Mavrougenis' 38-year-old financial adviser, Harvey Cronican, who, sleuths learned, had been a longtime friend of Van Alstyne's.

11

One investigator related that, "Cronican and Van Alstyne (had been) friends for about a dozen years, since they both were employed as security guards at a condo development over in Swampscott. We're still looking into reports that at one time or another Cronican hired Van Alstyne to do maintenance work on Mrs. Mavrougenis' Lynde Street properties."

"We're taking a look at him and anybody else with a possible motive," Wooldridge said.

About the motive there could be little doubt. It was money — and lots of it, although no one yet was certain exactly how much the victim was worth.

"I heard it could be as high as $11,000,000," said Assistant District Attorney McAlary. "More likely, it's about $2,000,000."

Digging deeper, investigators would learn that, although Marion Mavrougenis left the bulk of her fortune to charity, Harvey Cronican stood to inherit the wealthy widow's sixth-floor apartment in the Marlborough House upon her death as well as all the personal property that she kept there and her private parking license.

On Monday, June 2nd, Salem Police Chief Robert M. St. Pierre announced that he was assigning an additional detective to work on the Miami Beach murder case. St. Pierre also stated that Harvey Cronican, who made his home next door to the slain heiress' Salem residence on Lynde Street, had been questioned over the weekend for the third time concerning the events in Florida.

St. Pierre also told reporters that Cronican had called the police station on Saturday and asked to speak with the detectives working on the case. The detectives, glad to accommodate him, had questioned him at length about his long-standing friendship with Baren Van Alstyne.

From other sources close to the probe came word that, in addition to Cronican, detectives were focusing on his reputed girlfriend, 38-year-old Linda E. Ellis, a former waitress who made her home at the same Lynde Street address

12

as Cronican, in one of two apartment buildings on that street that had been owned by Marion Mavrougenis.

Newsmen were told that Cronican was the executor of Marion Mavrougenis' estate and was believed to hold the power of attorney to manage her properties. In a codicil to her will dated September 17, 1982, the elderly widow had left her condominium and its contents to Harvey Cronican with the stipulation that if he died before she did, the condominium would go to Linda Ellis.

For the past several years, investigators said, Cronican had driven Marion Mavrougenis to Florida for the winter and chauffeured her back to Salem, where she spent her summers. At the time of her death, the woman was believed to be making arrangements for her return trip north. Detectives theorized she might have told Cronican that she planned to make some changes in the management of her financial affairs when she got home, changes that effectively would reduce the younger man's control over her money.

In Florida, meanwhile, homicide investigators were poring over airline manifests and rental car company records on the chance they might find some evidence that Baren Van Alstyne had taken two trips to Miami Beach in the weeks prior to the killing.

On Friday, March 20, 1986, just three days before he was due to go on trial in Dade County, Florida, on charges of first-degree murder, 42-year-old Baren Van Alstyne entered a guilty plea to the reduced charge of second-degree murder and was sentenced to a term of 20 years to life in prison.

Less than a week later, on Thursday, March 26th, Harvey Cronican and Linda Ellis were formally charged with hiring Van Alstyne to kill Marion Mavrougenis. After surrendering themselves to authorities in Salem, the couple was ordered held without bail as fugitives from Florida justice. During a brief hearing in Salem District Court, the couple waived rendition to Florida. Miami Beach police who had come to Salem to handle the legal formalities said that Baren Van Alstyne had agreed to testify against the couple at their trial in exchange for being allowed to plead guilty to the lesser murder count.

Assistant District Attorney McAlary told reporters that the couple had worked out a "contract murder" plot with Van Alstyne because they believed Marion Mavrougenis was going to cut them out of her will.

"This is nothing more than a cold, calculating, premeditated murder on their part," McAlary said.

It was McAlary's contention that the couple believed they were in line to inherit Marion Mavrougenis' $3,000,000 estate. But after Cronican withdrew about $100,000 from a joint account that he held with the elderly widow, she became suspicious and her friends had urged her to exclude her financial adviser from the will.

Harvey Cronican and Linda Ellis had known Baren Van Alstyne for years before they introduced him to Marion Mavrougenis. In 1985, the couple reportedly approached Van Alstyne to ask him if he knew someone who would kill the woman. Subsequently, it was alleged, Cronican offered Van Alstyne $10,000 plus some stock and property if he would take on the killing himself.

It was Linda Ellis, according to D.A. McAlary, who purchased airline tickets for the men to go to Florida in April 1986, so that Van Alstyne could commit the slaying. An initial attempt was aborted when Van Alstyne heard noises in the Mavrougenis condominium. He then went back to Salem. On May 8th, he allegedly returned to Miami Beach. This time he entered the apartment. The elderly woman was asleep on a couch because her bedroom had just been painted. Van Alstyne carefully approached the sleeping victim and strangled her to death with a phone cord.

"It was a classic contract killing," said Essex County District Attorney Kevin Burke.

Other sources close to the investigation said that Harvey Cronican and Linda Ellis had become acquainted when he managed a Salem restaurant where the woman worked as a waitress. It was Linda Ellis who introduced her boss to the wealthy widow.

At the murder trial for Harvey Cronican and Linda Ellis in Miami during the summer of 1987, the state's star witness was Baren Van Alstyne. He told the jury that he had been friends with Cronican for 16 years when, in April of 1986, the defendant asked him to kill Marion Mavrougenis "because she was getting cranky and was starting to look more closely into where her money was going."

"I said it would be no problem," Van Alstyne testified, adding that on a previous occasion he had torched a house to help out a friend of Cronican's.

Van Alstyne's story continued: It was April 23rd, when he left work early to fly to Miami with Cronican. After taking a taxi to Miami Beach, his friend showed him the Marlborough House and pointed out the floor Marion Mavrougenis lived on. Then, as Van Alstyne was checking into a motel, Cronican flew back to Boston to establish an alibi.

Using keys that Cronican had given him, Van Alstyne entered the Marlborough House that night. But as he was about to let himself inside the wealthy widow's apartment, he heard her say, "Let's see who's at the door."

Van Alstyne told the jury that he fled the building and flew back to Boston, where he informed Cronican that there was someone staying with his intended victim.

"He said she always talks to the cats," Van Alstyne testified, "that there wasn't anybody else in there."

Less than two weeks later, Van Alstyne returned to Miami. At four o'clock on the morning of May 8th, he said, he entered Marion Mavrougenis' apartment and strangled her as she slept on a couch.

"She never stirred," Van Alstyne recalled. "So I went over to the telephone, doubled the telephone cord, slid it over her neck and strangled her."

Van Alstyne went on to say that Cronican had instructed

15

him to take whatever cash he found in the apartment, but that he was too scared to steal anything from his victim.

"I just wanted to get out of there," he said.

Courthouse observers noted that in a June 5th deposition, Van Alstyne had given another reason for having left the apartment empty-handed.

"I was taking a person's life," he had explained then, "which is not actually my cup of tea."

Although he had been promised $10,000 for the hit, Van Alstyne said, Harvey Cronican and Linda Ellis had paid him only $2,400, explaining that the big money was supposed to have come from what he took from Marion Mavrougenis' apartment.

Under cross-examination, Van Alstyne conceded that Harvey Cronican had never used the word "kill" when they spoke about Marion Mavrougenis. Nevertheless, he insisted that his friend had made himself clear.

"I assumed from the amount of money I was going to be paid, and other things we had talked about, that it wasn't for mowing the lawn."

During the course of the trial, the jury was never informed that, shortly before the proceedings got underway, Harvey Cronican had taken a lie detector test in which he flunked every question put to him. Because the state had rejected all along Cronican's offer to take a polygraph exam, the state was not allowed to use the results as evidence.

On Thursday, August 15th, after 200 hours of deliberation over three days, the jury found Harvey Cronican and Linda Ellis guilty of first-degree murder, burglary and conspiracy to commit first-degree murder and burglary. Circuit Judge Arthur I. Snyder sentenced the couple to terms of life imprisonment with 25 years to be served before eligibility for parole.

"PLEASE SAVE ME!"
by Olga Kogan

Tuesday, July 26, 1988, was supposed to have been a day of relaxation for wealthy Mississippi socialite Annie Laurie Hearin. The 72-year-old woman had invited several friends over for luncheon and an afternoon game of bridge. Some Southern-style vittles, pleasant chitchat, and a few hands at cards—such was the intended agenda. There was, however, an unexpected addition, and before the afternoon was over, Annie Laurie Hearin would become the object of attention of much of the Jackson, Mississippi, police force, the FBI, and the State Police Patrol.

The invited guests found their hostess in good spirits when they arrived at her stately home on Woodland Drive in the exclusive Woodland Hills area of North Jackson. The tree-shaded mansion, exuding the charm of the Old South, befitted the wife of reputedly the richest man in the state.

The luncheon and subsequent card game passed with all the cordiality for which the hostess was well known. At around 2:30 in the afternoon, the guests bade a happy goodbye to their hostess on her doorstep, then drove away as Annie waved and closed the door behind her.

Annie Hearin spent the next quarter of an hour supervising her housekeeper, who dutifully cleared away the lunch-

17

eon and card party accoutrements. Then, her duties done for the day, the housekeeper left her employer at around three o'clock. At that point, Annie Laurie Hearin was alone in the large house. Her husband—still putting in full workdays at the age of 70—was not expected for another couple of hours or so.

When Annie's husband returned home at about 4:30, he found that his wife was absent. It was unusual, but not immediately alarming. Although she had not mentioned anything about going out that day when they spoke on the telephone earlier in the morning, it was possible that his wife had gone on some unexpected errand and would be back soon.

Annie's husband, therefore, proceeded to take a short nap in the upstairs bedroom. He felt secure that his wife would return by the time he got up and prepared for dinner.

When he arose an hour or so later and went downstairs, there was still no sign of Annie. Naturally curious as to her whereabouts, he called the housekeeper at home, hoping that Annie might have mentioned where she was going after the scheduled card party. The housekeeper did not, however, have any news to offer. As far as the housekeeper knew, Mrs. Hearin planned to stay at home all afternoon.

Mr. Hearin then called some of his wife's bridge partners, hoping she might have gone to one of their homes for some additional socializing. Here, too, he could find no news.

It was now becoming evening and Hearin felt growing concern for his absent wife. His worry was shared by a close relative whom he called as a last resort. The relative agreed to come over and help search the house grounds for some sign of Annie.

As seven o'clock passed and a search revealed no clue to the woman's whereabouts, Hearin took the only step he felt was adequate under the circumstances: he telephoned the police. At the same time, he came across the explanation he had been seeking for the last few hours. It came not from

18

the police, but in a one-page message typewritten on a piece of paper that had lain unnoticed until then in the foyer of the main entrance to the house.

The message confirmed the wealthy man's worst suspicions.

In poorly written English, the message spelled out that Annie Hearin had been kidnapped and was being held for ransom. At least, that was what the message appeared to be saying. It was so incoherent that even the detectives who arrived in answer to Hearin's call were somewhat puzzled by the message's demands.

The note mentioned one obvious link to Mr. Hearin—a photography service called School Pictures of Mississippi, Incorporated. It was a franchise business that specialized in sending photographers to schools to take yearbook pictures and the like. Although Hearin was the company's largest shareholder, he took no direct acting role in the firm's operations. Hearin's real source of wealth lay in his insurance and gas companies, not in a relatively minor business like School Pictures.

Suddenly, however, School Pictures became Hearin's prime concern. The ransom note listed the names of about a dozen people who had "got mixed up with School Pictures" and lost money when the company ran into management problems. It demanded that Hearin reimburse these people for their losses, but without telling them why they were being reimbursed. The total amount requested was a round one million dollars. The note added bluntly: "Do this before ten days pass."

The School Pictures connection was quickly investigated. It was true that several years earlier, Hearin had sold the company to some investors who subsequently brought it to the edge of ruin. Hearin had successfully sued to have the company returned to his management, winning damages from the investors for the mysterious loss of much of the company's equipment. It had been strictly a business affair, common enough in entrepreneurial circles.

19

Someone apparently thought otherwise. The kidnapping of Hearin's wife took on the earmarks of a revenge action as detectives carefully took note of the 12 people listed in the ransom note. One or more of them had to be linked to the abduction, since they were logically the only ones who would benefit by Annie Hearin's return for ransom.

Raising the ransom money did not pose any problem to a man of Hearin's vast wealth, not even within the 10-day time limit. Conservative estimates put his holdings at 100 million dollars; more speculative estimates put it at twice that.

It was not the amount of the ransom money that worried the victim's husband and detectives on the case, but the unusual, even bizarre fashion in which the money was supposed to be distributed. Kidnappers as a rule want all the money for themselves, yet here was a kidnapper prepared to give the ransom away to virtual strangers. The notion that all 12 people in the ransom note were in on the kidnapping together was dismissed as too improbable. The most likely theory was that one person had engineered the crime out of a combination of hatred and bitterness. The question was, which one of the dozen people was it?

The victim's husband had further cause for concern: his wife suffered from a disease known as ileitis, an intestinal inflammation that required her to take daily medication. Without daily treatment, ileitis leads to dehydration and eventually to death. Whether or not the kidnapper considered doing his victim any harm, he automatically put her life in jeopardy by separating Annie from her source of medicine.

And there was still another sinister turn in the case. Detectives found what looked like blood spatters on the front door of the Hearin house. The marks were almost unnoticeable and were the only signs of violence found during the lawmen's extensive search of house and grounds, but slight as they were, the marks looked ominous. Subsequent testing of the blood by crime laboratory specialists revealed that they were the same blood type as Annie Hearin's, but it could not be determined positively whether the blood grouping, Type A or Type A positive, was the same.

As Hearin awaited further word from the kidnapper, police contacted the local FBI office in Jackson and alerted Mayor Dale Danks about the case. Mayor Danks took more than an official interest, since he was a personal friend of the Hearins. On the advice of lawmen and in deference to the best interests of the kidnap victim, the mayor requested the cooperation of the local media in keeping a lid on the crime until further notice. Although rumors of the wealthy woman's disappearance were already filtering through Jackson's gossip grapevine, the media agreed to maintain silence.

Meanwhile, lawmen pushed forward with their investigation on all fronts. As checks were made on all the people in the ransom note list, interviews were conducted with friends and neighbors of the Hearins, as well as with service industry personnel working in Woodland Hills. The latter group fell under a particular suspicion, since a service van would be just about the ideal vehicle in which to approach the house unnoticed in order to transport an unwilling captive.

So it turned out. Diligent detectives interviewing everyone they could find came up with not one but three separate sightings of a white van parked near the Hearin mansion. The first sighting came three months earlier in April. A deliveryman noticed a white van near the house and recalled that it had Florida license plates. Then, just a little more than a week before the kidnapping, a local resident observed the van parked near an intersection of Woodland Drive. Finally, a scant three days before the abduction, the white van was again spotted by a repairman working at a site about two blocks from the Hearin home. This witness saw the van's driver get out of the vehicle, but could not tell police where the driver went.

Two days after Annie Hearin's kidnapping, the media

21

were given the go-ahead to release the story. It hit the city of Jackson and the whole state of Mississippi with the impact of Hurricane Camille. Annie Laurie Hearin was a well-known figure, a patron of the local opera and symphony, and an advisor to the state arts festival. Her abduction and her present fate contained the elements of high drama.

While waiting for further word from the kidnapper, the victim's husband went ahead with the ransom instructions. Twelve separate checks were made out in various amounts to the individuals whose names were on the payment list. All of the checks were posted within the 10-day time limit. In only one case was the name on the check different from that on the list, since the listed name belonged to someone who had died. The kidnapper, apparently aware of this, had included in his instructions that "if any is dead, pay his children."

When all the payments had been sent out, Annie's husband appeared on television to make the announcement and to plead for some word on his wife's fate. Then came the anguishing moments while the Hearin family and their friends waited for the telephone to ring or for a letter to be delivered that would tell them where to find Annie Hearin.

They waited for two long, painful weeks before news came. It was a letter written in the kidnap victim's handwriting and dated August 10th, five days before it was delivered. The postmark on the envelope indicated it had been sent on August 12th from Atlanta, Georgia.

The note made for difficult reading. In a single sentence, the elderly woman asked her husband to do as the kidnappers wanted or else she would be locked up alone in the basement of a house. Her last words were "Please save me," followed by her signature.

It was a cryptic, disquieting letter. Beyond the fact that it had been written several days earlier and posted from a city in another state, its plea was not for anything that had not already been done. Hearin had already cooperated with the

22

kidnappers to the fullest possible extent. What more could he do to satisfy them?

Then another curious slant to the case occurred: the checks sent to the people on the ransom note list started to come back! Just about everyone returned the money. Those few who did not were checked out thoroughly by the police and determined to be incapable of anything remotely resembling a kidnapping.

Veteran lawmen working the case shook their heads at this perplexing turn of events. It was the first time they'd heard of kidnappers returning the ransom money. Nonetheless, they were convinced that someone on that list of a dozen people was somehow involved in the mystery. It was the only conclusion that made any sense at all in their investigation. Yet everyone on the list, in one way or another, failed to pan out as a viable suspect. All were respectable businessmen. All had verifiable alibis for the time of the kidnapping.

More weeks passed, and with each additional day, the string that held the life of the kidnap victim appeared to stretch closer and closer to the breaking point. Detectives made thorough checks of all the local drug stores to see whether any purchases of the victim's crucial medicine had been made recently. Although two such purchases were discovered, both were legitimate prescriptions for individuals known to be suffering from the same affliction as Annie Hearin.

By the end of that month of August, the unspoken but ever-present fear was that the kidnap victim had already succumbed either to her lack of life-saving medicine or to the kidnapper's violence.

Her husband stoically appealed again through the media for any word on his wife's fate. He posted a reward of $100,000 to anyone who could provide information that might lead to her safe return. But more days passed, and still the kidnapper made no contact of any kind. Perhaps, after all, the kidnapping and the ransom demand had been nothing more than a ruse. Perhaps tormenting Annie Hearin's husband was the real motive behind the crime.

Detectives again looked closely at the list of investors in the ill-fated School Pictures venture, searching for the one person who might have reason to seek revenge on Hearin. Their investigation finally centered on Newton A. Winn, a 64-year-old lawyer who worked out of St. Petersburg, Florida. He'd provided a good alibi at the time of his first police interview, but certain circumstances surrounding him suggested a possible reason why he might harbor a grudge against industrialist Hearin.

Simply put, Winn's participation in the School Pictures enterprise had just about cost him his shirt. After Hearin bought back the company to save it from total ruin at the hands of the 12 investors, Winn filed a lawsuit claiming, among other things, that he had been misinformed concerning the company's chances of financial success. The court ruled against Winn, however, and he ended up owing Hearin a considerable sum—$153,883.

As a consequence, in October 1986, much of Winn's property was seized and sold to raise the cash to pay off his court-imposed penalty. In the last few years of his working life, Newton Winn suddenly found himself on the brink of ruin—not a bad start for a revenge wish, however unfairly motivated.

The problem with Winn as a suspect was twofold. First, he was among those who had returned Hearin's checks and second, he had an alibi that put him in Florida at the time of Annie's kidnapping. Lawmen decided to investigate Winn's alibi a little more closely.

According to Winn, on July 26th, he'd been with a woman of doubtful morals who demanded that he pay for his pleasure with her. Finding himself without the required cash, Winn called a worker in his law office to come around with the needed sum. The worker, a paralegal by the name of John Spain, corroborated Winn's story. The alibi looked as ironclad as the Merrimac.

A follow-up visit to Spain by FBI agents garnered the same story: he'd brought money to his employer at an address on the south side of St. Petersburg, then left directly after. FBI agents thanked the witness a second time for his cooperation, but their suspicions about Newton Winn still wouldn't go away.

Using their wide network of contacts, detectives learned that Winn had made three separate trips to New Orleans in April of that year. Each time, he rented a van from a local car rental agency. On two occasions, the van had been white.

The coincidence of Winn renting a white van during the same month that a white van was spotted near the Hearin residence was not lost on the sleuths. Just why would a Florida lawyer rent a Louisiana van three times in the same month?

But there was more to the van story. In June of that year, a van was bought in Tampa, Florida, under the name of John Spain, Winn's employee. When sleuths asked him about the purchase, Spain mumbled a lame explanation that he had bought the vehicle as a favor to his boss, but Winn had paid for it, and it rightfully belonged to him. Detectives decided that Spain was either an unusually accommodating employee or a liar—perhaps both.

The investigative noose then tightened around another acquaintance of Newton Winn's—an intimate one. The woman—who was half Winn's age—had had an affair with him the previous year while she was still married to another man. Both her marriage and her affair with Winn came to an end before 1988, but her contact with Winn, detectives learned, still continued.

It was a contact fraught with intrigue.

Informed by detectives about the nature of their visit to her, the woman soon began to tell what she knew. For each piece of the puzzle she provided, sleuths provided one of their own from their previous investigations.

At the end of July—five days after the Hearin

25

kidnapping—Newton Winn had come to her to ask a favor. She didn't know what he had in mind until a few days later, when he phoned and arranged to meet with her at a motel in DeLand, Florida. She agreed to come.

At the meeting, Winn pulled out a large brown envelope from which he took a smaller letter with a warning not to look at the letter's address. It sounded very cloak-and-dagger, but the woman said Winn spoke and acted in deadly earnest. He said he would pay her $500 if she would fly to Atlanta in five days and mail the letter from there. He offered no explanation for the errand, but she figured that since Winn was a lawyer, he might have some need for such a cryptic mission.

The woman did as she was asked, later collected her $500, and then put the incident out of her mind—until news of the Annie Hearin kidnapping and the "letter from Atlanta" made Dixie headlines. That's when she put two and two together and came up with a frightening four. The detectives' visit to her did not come unexpected.

With this additional circumstantial evidence pointing the finger of guilt toward Newton Winn, detectives returned yet again to Winn's paralegal helper, John Spain. He proved a tougher nut to crack, but in the end he, too, opened up to the police.

He'd been lying, Spain now admitted. He had not seen Newton Winn on the night of July 26th and did not, in fact, know where Winn had been. Winn had asked him to tell police that story as a personal favor. Spain went along with it not only because Winn was his employer, but because Winn had given him a helping hand a few years back when he was down. He figured he was just paying him back.

Spain's confession was the explosive testimony that lawmen needed. On March 11, 1989, Newton Alfred Winn was arrested by federal agents as he crossed a parking lot in De-Land, Florida. He was subsequently charged with extortion and perjury in connection with the Annie Hearin kidnapping—but not with kidnapping itself, since the victim had not been found even after so many months.

On March 12th, FBI men searched Winn's home and office, seizing what looked like more telling evidence—aerial maps of Jackson (one with the Hearin home circled in red), two handguns, and an old Royal typewriter. Forensic technicians had already determined that the ransom note was typed on a Royal typewriter manufactured in the 1920s. Winn's machine fit the requirements to the incriminating letter.

Despite the evidence, the accused man continued to protest his innocence. A trained attorney, he fought every legal attempt to have him extradited from Florida to Mississippi, but his efforts, though they brought several months of delay, proved in vain.

On January 29, 1990, jury selection began in Hattiesburg, Mississippi, and one day later, January 30th, Newton Winn found himself facing 12 of his peers in the courtroom of Federal Judge Thomas Lee. Winn unwisely chose a fool as his lawyer—himself.

Prosecuting attorney James Tucker called both John Spain and Winn's one-time lover to testify. Further testimony came from a Jackson repairman who identified Winn as the man he saw driving a white van one day before the Hearin kidnapping. The incriminating evidence found in Winn's home and office further sealed the Florida lawyer's fate.

On February 7th, Newton Winn was found guilty as charged. Two months later, on April 20th, Judge Lee sentenced the convicted man to 19 years imprisonment—virtually a life sentence for the 65-year-old prisoner.

Winn took the sentence defiantly, addressing the court in a lengthy harangue in which he maintained he was innocent. He left the court hobbling on a cane.

The kidnap victim, Annie Laurie Hearin, has still not been found, and given Winn's silence, it is doubtful that her final fate will ever be known. Should Winn one day decide to tell the full story of her abduction, he would be open to new criminal charges, and it is not likely that he will want that. For now, Annie Hearin's fate is not known, but lawmen feel it is more than likely that she is dead.

EDITOR'S NOTE:
John Spain is not the real name of the person so named in the foregoing story. A fictitious name has been used because there is no reason for public interest in the identity of this person.

"I NEED SOMEONE TO KILL FOR ME!"

by Bill G. Cox

The security guard expected nothing more than routine duty when he started his rounds of the wealthy residential neighborhood in Houston, Texas. It was the hot summer afternoon of Wednesday, September 2, 1987. The Pine Shade subdivision in west Houston is made up of elegant mansions. The prosperous neighborhood is a natural target for burglars and thieves. With this in mind, the private security patrol officers stay on the alert for strange vehicles or strangers who show up along the tree-shaded streets.

The unexpected is what plays hell with normal patrol routine. It can quickly ruin a security guard's day.

That's why the mental alarms went off in the guard's head when he spotted the maroon Cadillac cruising slowly along the street. It wasn't the car, but the driver who seemed out of place. He was wearing a white baseball cap and a dark sweatsuit. Big cars are a dime a dozen in the neighborhood. Sometimes they are driven by hired help, but there was something about the driver's actions that drew the security guard's attention.

The guard watched closely as the car made another slow swing along the block.

It was about 4:30 P.M. when a gold Jaguar drove into the neighborhood. The security man saw the Cadillac fall in

29

behind the Jaguar. The guard recognized the Jaguar as one of the fancy vehicles owned by the Saragusas, millionaires who lived in a palatial home on Green Tree Street. The guard walked down the street to the driveway of Saragusa's neighbor, looking to see where the maroon Cadillac had gone. He saw both of the automobiles parked at the Saragusa residence. The guard moved closer so he could see the license tag on the Cadillac. Then he started to walk away.

He had gone only a few steps when he heard the unmistakable sound of a gunshot. It came from the area of the Saragusa mansion. As the guard turned back toward the house, he saw the maroon Cadillac leave the Saragusa home. The man in the baseball cap was at the wheel. Only seconds had passed since he heard what sounded like a shot, and as the guard watched, the Caddy left the neighborhood.

He quickly radioed for a backup from the security service. When the assistance arrived, the security men entered the Saragusa home through an unlocked door after getting no response to ringing the door bell.

Quickly checking through the first floor rooms, they walked up the spiral staircase and entered a large master bedroom. They stopped in their tracks at the sight of the fully clothed woman sprawled on the floor in the northwest corner of the bedroom. Blood from an apparent head wound oozed onto the floor. A quick examination revealed the woman was dead. The patrolmen immediately notified their office and the Houston Police Department.

Uniformed patrolmen arrived first, followed quickly by homicide detectives alerted by the uniform men. A search of the huge home determined that no one else was inside, except the body in the bedroom. The victim, who officers saw had been shot in the temple, was identified as Judy Wood Saragusa, 37, the attractive wife of one of the city's leading wine and liquor distributors and a millionaire several times over.

On the scene were Homicide Lieutenant Richard Hol-

30

land, four homicide detectives, and several crime-scene unit investigators. The medical examiner's office was also notified.

It's been the experience of veteran crime investigators that spectators swarm to a crime scene like flies, and the exclusive neighborhood was no exception. Though they hung back some distance from the growing contingent of black-and-whites, detective cars, ambulance people, and officers, neighbors gathered to watch. They stared in stunned disbelief as the investigators combed the grounds and the stately home for clues to the killing.

Inside, the detectives' examination of the body revealed a single gunshot wound in the temple. Blood had pooled beneath the woman's head and also stained the baseboard behind her head. The detectives observed a spent shell of small caliber, apparently fired from a .22-caliber pistol, on the floor near the body.

The victim's jewelry had not been removed. On her left hand were two rings, one of gold and the other containing a setting of clear stones. The detectives could find no evidence of a struggle in the bedroom, nor any signs that the house had been ransacked, which seemed to rule out burglary or robbery as a motive for the fatal shooting.

Valuables in the house appeared to have been untouched, the officers noted.

The woman's clothing appeared undisturbed, indicating that no sexual motive was involved in the slaying. In fact, after grilling the security guard who had seen both the maroon Cadillac and the gold Jaguar arrive in the neighborhood, the investigators surmised that the killer probably had entered the residence after Judy Saragusa came home. In the large kitchen the detectives saw a woman's purse, a set of car keys, and a glass containing partly melted ice on the table. Glancing inside the purse, the lawmen saw a .38-caliber handgun with five unfired cartridges and some personal stationery besides the usual effects.

The detectives wondered about the gun in the purse and

why the victim was carrying it, though it wouldn't have been unusual for a wealthy woman to want some protection in the city that was infamous for its violent crimes. But more firepower was found in the home, including a .22-caliber automatic pistol and a shotgun with a pistol grip found upstairs. There were no signs that any of the small handguns had been used to kill Judy Saragusa. A search of the bedroom and the rest of the big house failed to turn up a weapon that might have fired the deadly shot.

The gold Jaguar the victim had been seen driving earlier was still parked in a covered parking area. Forced entry by the killer was ruled out after the officers checked doors and windows.

Directing the search for physical evidence at the murder scene was Sergeant Russell Dunlap of the homicide division. A color videotape was made of the mansion's interior, the camera panning through the lavishly furnished rooms on the first floor and up the long, brass-coated spiral stairway and into the master bedroom, where the body lay in a corner alcove. Throughout the night, the crime-scene investigators would be busy dusting the rooms for possible fingerprints and looking for other clues.

But as far as the homicide men were concerned, the most promising lead was the information on the maroon Cadillac furnished by the private security guard. He remembered the car's license number, which police immediately put on the air with a description of the vehicle.

Within a short time, the license number was traced to a Jane Ada Callaway, who had a Houston address. But in this instance, it turned out to be a case of the car owner coming to the police instead of detectives seeking her to ask questions about the car.

Shortly after police had been summoned to the Saragusa home by the private security firm, the victim's distraught husband arrived. He had been called at his office and told of the tragedy. He was accompanied by his executive secretary, Jane Ada Callaway.

In addition to his grief over the violent death of his wife of 17 years, the mustached, dapper business executive was at a loss as to why anyone would have slain her. And Jane Callaway, when told that a Cadillac traced to her ownership had been seen apparently fleeing the shooting scene, said she was equally baffled by this news. She had no explanation as to why a man might have been driving her automobile. The shocked secretary, who also had been working at the office when word of Judy Saragusa's death was received, told the detectives she had loaned the vehicle to a woman relative from Lubbock, Texas.

As investigators continued to question the husband, the secretary, and the security guard, other officers fanned over the neighborhood to see if neighbors had seen or heard anything that would throw light on the daylight slaying. They found that the nearby residents knew little of the Saragusas' background or activities—other than the couple had moved into the mansion about three weeks ago and had been remodeling it.

Neighbors said the couple kept a low profile. Mrs. Saragusa had been seen driving various expensive automobiles and would wave in a friendly manner, the residents told police.

The investigators learned that Judy Saragusa and her husband had moved to the new address from another palatial residence only a few blocks away. Their former home had been built by movie actress Gene Tierney and her oilman husband.

Although the neighbors knew little about Judy Saragusa, she was not unknown to the public—at least to readers who kept up with the lifestyle pages of the local newspapers. She raised and trained horses and was recognized as a horsewoman of some stature. Before her marriage, she had been a commercial artist. More recently, she had designed boats for a marine company. She belonged to several equine organizations.

As the probe moved into the evening hours, Detective

33

Lieutenant Holland told reporters he feared the investigation might be a lengthy and complicated one. And Detective Dunlap told reporters, "I believe the murderer was there to kill her. He wasn't just going door to door. He was looking for her specifically. It appears it almost was an execution style type of murder. It gives the impression almost of being a hit. There are a lot of directions this could go."

Since officers found no signs of forced entry, they could only theorize how the killer had gotten inside. He might have pretended to be a delivery or service person.

Or, the gunman might have rung the bell and then forced his way inside when the door was opened, they speculated. After the victim's husband had regained his composure and was able to talk, detectives quizzed him about his wife's demeanor and activities that day. There hadn't been anything out of the ordinary to indicate she had been worried or scared, the grieving spouse related. But there had been a strange incident involving a frightening encounter his wife experienced two months before her death. It had happened on June 22, 1987, he recalled.

As he had heard the story, his wife and his secretary, Jane Callaway, had gone to lunch together. After lunch Jane had asked Judy to drive her home. When the women entered the Callaway residence, they were confronted by a tall, slender, elderly man wearing thick glasses and brandishing a small caliber handgun. Gesturing in a menacing manner with the gun, the intruder ordered the women to walk to another room.

At that point, as the story was recounted, Judy had pulled a pistol from her purse and fired at the gunman, who dropped to his knees and then fled from the house. He apparently had been surprised and frightened by the woman's gunfire but not wounded. Judy hadn't reported the incident to police because she feared she would be in trouble for carrying the pistol.

The women hadn't known what the gunman's intentions

34

had been or how he had entered the house, said the victim's husband.

The businessman said he had noticed that Jane seemed to be nervous and upset earlier on this day, the day his wife had been slain. The secretary had blamed it on pills prescribed by her doctor. He also had noticed that his secretary's Cadillac was missing from its usual parking spot at the office. When this was mentioned, she had commented she loaned the car to one of her relatives.

Continuing their search for leads, the detectives contacted the maid who had been on duty in the Saragusa home that day, but she had left apparently before the slaying. Shocked by news of the killing, the maid recalled one bit of information that raised the interest of the investigators.

The maid remembered that Jane Callaway had phoned about 1:30 P.M. that day to remind Mrs. Saragusa of a 4:00 P.M. appointment with a burglary alarm company. The secretary had asked what time Judy was expected home, said the domestic worker. Following up this information, a detective called the alarm firm mentioned by the maid.

After checking the company records, an official with the firm said he could find no record of a Wednesday appointment at the Saragusa residence.

Had the woman's killer gained access to the home by posing as an alarm company representative, the detectives wondered? And if such was the case, just how much did Jane Callaway know about the slaying—considering also that the killer seemingly had been driving her car? The investigators turned their attention to the pretty secretary in hopes of getting answers to the puzzling questions.

Though badly shaken by the violent death in the big home, the 35-year-old secretary was composed enough as she talked with the officers. She denied any knowledge of her car having been at the murder scene with a young man at the wheel. She also gave a different version of the pur-

35

ported call she had made to Judy's house about the alarm company appointment.

She claimed the company had contacted her at her office to say the appointment at the Saragusa residence had been cancelled. Thus, Jane had relayed the message to the maid, she said. However, when the alarm company was again called by a detective, the company official said no one had called to cancel an appointment because there hadn't been one for that day.

It was shortly before 9:00 P.M. — with crime-scene technicians still busy processing the mansion for possible clues — that the homicide detectives asked witnesses to accompany officers to the police station to make statements. The witnesses included the security guard who had seen the Cadillac leaving the scene, and Jane Callaway.

At police headquarters, Detectives Jim Ramsey and his partner, Detective Bill Stephens, conducted the interrogation of the secretary. She replied to questions in a flat, unemotional tone of voice. She hardly even blinked, the detectives noticed. But she strongly denied having any information about the circumstances surrounding the shooting death of her employer's wife.

When asked if she knew anyone who might have been driving her Cadillac, Jane Callaway insisted that she had loaned her automobile to a relative from Lubbock, Texas, a young woman relative. The detectives placed a phone call to the woman named by Jane and put the call on a speaker phone in the homicide office.

When asked if she had borrowed the Cadillac owned by Jane Callaway, the Lubbock woman replied she didn't know what they were talking about. She certainly hadn't borrowed the car, she answered.

Jane Callaway's only comment was, "That sounded like her voice." The secretary added she didn't know what was going on, sticking to her story of whom she had loaned the vehicle to.

Confronted with the conflicting stories about the car and

36

the phone call to the Saragusa home about the alarm company appointment, the unruffled young woman told the sleuths, "I know it doesn't look good. I just want to stay here until we get this worked out."

The detectives agreed it certainly didn't look good for the attractive secretary, but the long question-and-answer session was wearing them down. They marvelled that Jane Callaway showed no signs to weariness or any desire to end the talk. She remained calm — and talkative.

Then, at 4:20 A.M. on Thursday, she suddenly started changing her story.

Detective Ramsey had just helped her to her feet and placed handcuffs on her wrists to take her to a cell to await further questioning, when she exclaimed, "O.K. I'll tell you what you want to know about Menard Adams."

Adams, the detectives learned, was a young college graduate whom Jane Callaway had known through his late uncle while both were employed at a real estate firm. She had worked at the firm before taking her present job.

In a two-page statement she made to the detectives, the secretary said Adams had done odd jobs around her home while looking for a job after coming back to Houston from a college he attended on a basketball scholarship. She said that he had asked to borrow her car about 2:30 P.M., Wednesday to run some errands.

"I don't know anything else concerning what he was going to do with my car," she added.

She also told the detectives that Adams had a "crazy relative" named Leon, "who was capable of doing anything." Furthermore, Adams was being blackmailed by a dope dealer named "Gene." But the main point of her statement was that she knew nothing about or had anything to do with the killing of Judy Saragusa.

She related that she had first learned of the murder about 5:30 P.M. when she received a phone call at work.

While the grilling of the secretary continued, other detectives — having obtained a search warrant — had gone to

37

her home to see what they could find. On a nightstand in a bedroom, Detective Sergeant Dennis Gafford spotted a loaded .380-caliber Walther PPK automatic pistol. It would later be identified as one given to Jane Callaway by a friend after the elderly gunman had menaced her and Judy in the residence.

As the investigators pursued their search, they spotted several photographs affixed to the refrigerator door in the kitchen. Among the photos was one that showed Jane Callaway and a woman friend dressed in cheerleader costumes and sitting on the back of a Corvette. Judy Saragusa was sitting beside her husband on the front seat. As the detectives would learn, the picture would be of critical significance to the murder probe.

Running a background check on Jane Callaway, homicide investigators learned she had grown up in the little town of Cameron, near Waco, Texas. After graduating from college, she had lived in Austin; then Houston. Friends said that the young woman had kept in close contact with her relatives, sometimes calling home several times a day.

She devoted most of her time to her job and much of her spare time to working with her church, where she was a member of the choir. Friends told officers she liked to sing. Frequently she would sing along with a radio she kept at her desk in the office.

Jane was described as a highly intelligent young lady, who had a sterling reputation and the voice of an angel. Detectives couldn't help but wonder if it was the voice of an angel of death as they continued to dig up information that made things look dark for the secretary who steadfastly claimed her innocence.

At one time, the investigation revealed, she had been married to a man much older than herself. She had later divorced him. He, incidentally, had been the director of a church choir, the detectives learned. Checking further, the detectives discovered that the ex-husband's description closely matched that of the elderly gunman who had accosted Jane and Judy Saragusa on June 22nd. Detectives were assigned the job of locating and interviewing the ex-spouse.

Meanwhile, other investigators found Menard Adams at a Houston video store. He was working there as a clerk. He was given a ride to headquarters for questioning.

Confronted with Jane Callaway's earlier statement that she had loaned her Cadillac to him on the afternoon of the murder and that a young man about his age had been seen by a witness driving the vehicle from the slaying scene, Adams soon was telling the detectives what he knew about the homicide. It turned out to be a great deal. After he was given legal warnings, Adams made a statement to the officers that was recorded on video tape.

The 23-year-old suspect related that Jane Callaway had first contacted him in July 1987. She expressed regrets over the recent death of his uncle, whom she had known at the real estate company. She also said she needed some work done on her driveway.

She mentioned she wanted "something else" done but didn't elaborate, Adams recalled. She told him to expect another phone call from a person she described as "a friend." It was a few days later that Adams received a phone call from someone "who sounded like an old guy," Adams related. The elderly caller soon made it clear just what Jane Callaway wanted: She wanted to arrange the death of a woman, whom the caller didn't name, Adams said in his statement.

When he again talked to Jane, said Adams, he told her of the call from the old man.

"She asked me if her friend had called, and I told her I didn't appreciate that guy calling me," said Adams. "She said she was sorry."

But he said the calls from the secretary persisted. She called to ask whether he had found a job. Adams told her he hadn't and asked for a loan of $257 to make a payment on his Camaro. She agreed, Adams said, and he went to the office where she worked to pick up the check.

At that point, according to his story, Adams was a man on a hook.

"The next day she asked me would I find someone to kill a lady," he continued. "She said she would pay someone to do the job."

She never named the intended victim, but Adams said he figured that the "bitch" Callaway kept referring to was Judy Saragusa.

"I told her I didn't know anything about anything like that," Adams told the detectives.

But the secretary continued to call him daily—sometimes four or five times a day, at his home or at his job, said Adams. She eventually asked about a man named "Gene," whom Adams identified as one Eugene Stewart. Stewart was an acquaintance of his, according to Adams, and he agreed to get the man's phone number for Jane Callaway.

Adams related that he met Stewart in a Houston park to get the phone number and tell him that a woman would call him about a proposed job.

"You know what she wants me to do?" Adams quoted Stewart as asking.

"I don't know, and I don't want to know," Adams said he replied.

Then, on August 7, 1987, Adams stated, he followed Jane's instructions by going to a specified bank and picking up $20,000 in cash, for which the woman had made the arrangements. Several days after that, said Adams, he gave half of the sum to Stewart and kept the other $10,000 for himself.

According to Adams, Stewart told him after taking the money he wasn't going to do anything—meaning presumably that he wasn't going to harm anyone for the money.

Later, Jane had become increasingly angry that Stewart had not carried out his end of the deal, Adams said in his statement.

As a result, said Adams, he had told Stewart to "watch his back" after Jane had declared, "He'll get his." She obviously was upset that the killing had not been done, but Stewart had answered he wasn't worried.

Late in August, Jane again called Adams about Stewart's failure to go through with the hit. While talking to him on the phone, she had heard someone else in the background laughing, said Adams. When she asked who was laughing, Adams said it was his stepbrother, Leon Hawkins Jr.

"Well, hell, I'll pay him," he quoted the secretary as saying.

"No you won't," Adams said he responded. "You're not getting him involved."

But Adams admitted he had relayed the conversation to Hawkins, who then wanted to know what the lady would give him.

Next, the talkative Adams told of an August 28th meeting at the Callaway home. There, said Adams, while he and Hawkins were seated in the living room, Jane brought out two pistols on a serving tray and asked Hawkins to pick one.

She then showed Hawkins a photograph in which she pointed out Judy Saragusa, the intended victim. It was the same photograph that detectives later found posted on the refrigerator door in Jane's home—the one in which Judy was seated beside her husband in the front seat of the Corvette with Jane and her friend perched on the back.

After giving Hawkins the pistol and displaying the photograph, Jane had driven him and Adams in her car to point out the Saragusa home to the hired gunman.

Hawkins told him later that Jane had offered him $50,000 and a Nissan 300ZX as payment for the contract job. Adams related he had told his stepbrother that he was a fool and "to get the money and not to do anything."

"He said that's what he was planning to do," said Adams.

Adams continued that on September 1st—the day before

41

the slaying—he took Hawkins to the office building where the secretary worked. They went inside to talk to her, and he saw Jane give his stepbrother the keys to her Cadillac parked on a lot at the office.

She also handed him an envelope, according to the statement.

The next evening, Hawkins phoned Adams and told him, "Man, I've done something, and I'm scared," said Adams.

Following up on Adams' taped statement, the detectives put out a bulletin for Leon Hawkins Jr. to be picked up for questioning. Next, a team of detectives went to the bank where Adams said Jane Callaway had made the arrangements for him to pick up the $20,000 in cash. Ushered into a bank official's office, the lawmen asked to see the records of the financial transactions by Jane Callaway.

They discovered that they were more than in luck: The bank official informed them that all verbal money transactions are tape recorded.

While the tape recordings were being brought to the office, the official also explained that records showed that three persons from the wine and liquor distributing company where Jane worked had authority to call and make a change in the firm's accounts with the bank: Jane Callaway, the company's owner, and one other company employee. Funds sometimes were shifted from one account to another to keep the money in the accounts bearing highest interest.

But it was Jane Callaway, with seven phone calls over a period of time, who had transferred about $138,000 in all from the company accounts to another account she had set up under her own name, the bank spokesman disclosed. The secretary appeared to have been embezzling funds from her employer.

With still another call to the bank from the scheming secretary, part of that money had been turned over to Adams, the apparent middle-man in the murder-for-hire plot, as the growing evidence indicated to the detectives.

One tape recording listened to by the investigators had been made when Jane opened the new account on August 3, 1987, transferring money from the company account to another bank in Houston. A loan officer at the second bank told investigators that Adams had been in on the new account set up by Jane from the start because he came to the bank to pick up the necessary documents for her to sign and later returned the signed papers.

The bank official told the detectives that Jane phoned the bank on August 7th, saying that she was having $30,000 transferred to her account. She said Adams would come to the bank to pick up the money in cash. Though the banker advised against this procedure, Jane had insisted.

"She said she really needed the money, and she had to pay the workers (for remodeling work being done on the new Saragusa mansion)," the bank official said. Jane had said the new account was to be used for that purpose to expedite the project.

When the banker suggested to Jane that she get the money in cashier checks, she balked, explaining that the construction workers were aliens who didn't have checking accounts that would enable them to cash their pay checks. The secretary further explained that Menard Adams was the architect for the remodeling job, and that was why he was picking up the money.

But she did finally agree to drop the cash withdrawal to $20,000, which subsequently was picked up by Adams, the investigators confirmed.

On Friday, September 4th, the Harris County District Attorney's office filed formal complaints against Jane Callaway and Adams. She was charged with capital murder in that she allegedly hired Adams to arrange the killing of Judy Saragusa. Adams was charged with conspiracy to commit murder.

Both suspects were ordered held in county jail with bond denied.

The day saw other developments in the sensational case.

43

The maroon Cadillac owned by Jane and apparently used by the killer was found in a parking garage at Houston International Airport.

In the meantime, a city-wide manhunt for Leon Hawkins Jr., sought as the suspected triggerman in the murder, had failed to locate him. It was thought that he probably had taken a plane to an unknown destination. But on Friday night, the elusive Hawkins walked into Houston police headquarters to surrender voluntarily.

As he was being led down the hall from the homicide offices, the murder suspect told waiting reporters, "They made me do it," but didn't elaborate on the cryptic remark.

In the complaint filed against Jane Callaway, Hawkins was named as the actual killer of Judy Saragusa. Though it would not be made public until later, police investigators had learned that Hawkins had used a plane ticket—which Jane had bought under another man's name—to fly to San Francisco after the shooting.

It was not explained why the suspect had returned to Houston and given up to police.

Hawkins was scheduled to appear in a police lineup on Saturday to be viewed by the witness who had seen the man driving the Cadillac leave the scene. The shooting suspect was charged with capital murder on Saturday and denied bond, but police did not immediately reveal whether an identification had been positively made by the witness.

A Harris County grand jury moved fast after the district attorney's office presented evidence in the case. An indictment charging capital murder was returned against Jane Callaway on September 8, 1987.

Prosecutors recommended bond of $100,000, but acknowledged that the defendant had a good reputation in the past and no criminal record. A state district judge set her bond at $50,000, which the secretary later made and was freed from jail to await trial.

Later, the grand jury returned a capital murder indictment against Hawkins, the alleged triggerman. Adams also

44

was indicted for his part as alleged middleman in the murder for hire plot.

Police also arrested Eugene Stewart, 26, the man who Jane was accused of first hiring to make the planned hit. He was charged with conspiracy to commit murder.

Police announced that the gun thought to be the murder weapon had been found and traced from the time it was purchased until it fell into the hands of the accused triggerman. They declined to give details at that point in the investigation.

Later, because of extensive news coverage given to the banner headline case in the Houston papers and on TV and radio, Judge Michael McSpadden of 209th State District Court, who would try the murder case, ordered a change of venue for Jane Callaway. The trial was moved from Harris County to Amarillo in Potter County, some 600 miles away in the upper part of the big state.

The secretary's lead defense attorney was famous criminal lawyer Richard "Racehorse" Haynes of Houston. Selection of a jury to hear the case began in Amarillo on April 6, 1988. The trial was to be held in the old but recently remodeled 47th State District courtroom. The legal lineup, in addition to presiding Judge McSpadden and Attorney Haynes, included as prosecutors two Harris County assistant district attorneys—Chuck Rosenthal and Lyn McClellan.

Houston Attorney Dan Cogdell was the other defense lawyer representing Callaway.

It took nearly six weeks of individual examination of the jury panel before a jury of five women and seven men was chosen, along with two alternate jurors.

The trial began with opening remarks by both sides on May 16th, 1988.

The prosecution told the jury that the woman on trial had designs on her boss's wealth and envied the position of his wife in upperclass society. She had dreams of replacing

Judy Saragusa in the event of the wife's death, the state contended.

The prosecution said it would prove that Jane Callaway plotted Judy's death over a period of time and furnished the murder weapon and the getaway car for alleged hit man Leon Hawkins Jr. The secretary embezzled money from her employer to pay for the hired assassin, the prosecutor told the jury.

The state also said it would prove that the defendant set up a phony appointment purportedly with a burglary alarm company repairman to make sure that Judy would keep her "appointment with death."

The defense contended that Jane Callaway was taking the rap for someone else, and that the state had tailored its case to fit her.

As the trial progressed, light was thrown on the mystery of the June 22nd, 1987, incident at Jane's house during which the aged gunman wearing thick glasses and waving a pistol confronted Jane and Judy when they went there after lunch together.

Out of the presence of the jury, for the purpose of determining whether it would be admitted as evidence, Prosecutor Rosenthal told the judge that Jane had her ex-husband, who then was in his 80s, to pose as an armed intruder to frighten Judy as part of the murder plot. The assistant D.A. also said that the weapon brandished by the ex-husband, a .22-caliber pistol, was the gun later used to kill the victim.

Rosenthal said the elderly ex-spouse would be called later in the trial as a state's witness, and that he earlier had given a statement to police admitting that he had been the armed intruder and that he had bought the pistol that eventually took Judy's life.

The state called to the witness stand Menard Adams, who testified about Jane's stubborn efforts to have him hire someone to kill Judy Saragusa. This included Eugene Stewart, the first prospective killer who hadn't

46

followed through on the job after taking money, he told the jury.

It was also made known to the jury that Adams was testifying as part of an agreement with the district attorney's office concerning his own fate. He had agreed to plead guilty to the charge against him in exchange for a 10-year prison sentence.

Adams testified that Jane had persuaded his stepbrother, Hawkins, to make the hit. She had promised him money and a sports car, given him a .22 pistol in her home a few days before the killing, pointed out the targeted victim in a photograph, and had loaned him her own car the day before the murder.

But the witness related that he had only wanted to con Jane out of her money when he accepted it to ostensibly employ a killer. He called his plan a game and said he didn't think a murder would ever be carried out.

Also presented as witnesses were two fellow employees of the secretary. One testified he had seen two young men get into Jane's car at the office and drive away on the afternoon before the murder.

Next to the stand, a woman secretary who worked in Jane's office related that Jane had been in a bad mood on September 2nd, the day of the murder, until she received a phone call about 5:00 P.M. The witness said she noticed that Jane's mood improved considerably when she hung up from the call. She had commented cheerfully to her and another employee who was walking out of the office, "You ladies have a good evening. Ta ta." She was smiling, the witness said.

The witness also told of having heard part of another phone conversation earlier that day, in which Jane had said, "You better do it. This is my final warning." She had slammed down the receiver, the witness recalled.

Under cross examination by the defense, the secretary admitted she had disliked Jane Callaway from the day she came to work for the firm.

The state also entered as evidence and played for the jury tape recordings made by the bank of the verbal account transactions and transfers made by Jane Callaway.

The Harris County Medical Examiner testified that Judy Saragusa's death had been from a gunshot fired from a .22-caliber pistol held no more than 10 to 24 inches from her right ear.

Another witness testified that a man, identified as Jane's elderly ex-husband, had purchased a .22-caliber pistol from her store on June 14th. The prosecution contended this was the gun wielded by the old gunman on June 22nd and the same weapon that killed Judy Saragusa.

The state's plans to call the elderly man who had been married to Callaway were blocked when he had to undergo surgery in another state. It was thought he wouldn't be available to testify for at least another month.

The state filed a motion that attorneys be permitted to videotape the state's prospective witness' testimony in an out-of-state hospital, but the motion was denied when the defense objected.

Winding up three weeks of testimony, the state presented a videotape taken by a concealed security surveillance camera in the lobby of the office building where Jane Callaway worked. The film showed two shadowy, out-of-focus figures entering the lobby shortly before noon on September 1st, the day before the murder. A few minutes later, the same two were shown leaving the building with Jane.

Recalled to the stand, Adams identified the two men as Leon Hawkins and himself. It was the afternoon when they had gone to her office to pick up her car, he testified.

After the jury had viewed the 33-second tape, the state rested its case.

When the defense called the defendant to the witness chair, a murmur ran through the crowded courtroom. For the next few hours, the defense attorney would take her firmatively, the judge would be mandated by law to sentence her to death.

If both or even one answer was "no," then the sentence would be life under the state law.

The state did not push for the death penalty in its punishment arguments before the jury. The jury deliberated only two hours this time to reach a verdict.

The verdict was life in prison. Jane Callaway turned and smiled at her family when the lesser sentence was read by the judge. Defense attorneys announced the verdict would be appealed to the Texas Court of Criminal Appeals.

Leon Hawkins Jr., who faces a capital-murder indictment in the shooting death of the Houston woman, had not been brought to trial at the time this was written. He must be presumed innocent unless found otherwise by a jury of his peers.

As part of the agreement with the state, Menard Adams is expected to testify for the state in Hawkins' trial.

Eugene Stewart, the man who had taken money to kill the intended victim but hadn't done the act, entered a guilty plea to the charge of conspiracy to commit murder and was given a 10-year probated sentence and fined $1,000 by the state district judge.

EDITOR'S NOTE:
Menard Adams and Eugene Stewart are not the real names of the persons so named in the foregoing story. Fictitious names have been used because there is no reason for public interest in the identities of these persons.

question by question over the fatal events of the past summer that had led to the capital murder charge.

With hands folded in her lap, she answered the questions in a poised and confident manner. She looked straight at the jury and held her head high.

She told the jury that Judy Saragusa had expressed concern that if she ever divorced her husband, the only property she would get would be the newly purchased mansion on Green Tree Street that was in the process of being remodeled.

"She was going to try to spend as much money on items and things that went into the house as she could," said the defendant.

Although Jane's name appeared on the account that she had transferred money into from company accounts and hers was the only authorized signing name for the account, all of the transactions for the account had been made at the direction of Judy, Jane testified.

It also had been Judy who instructed her to pay Adams the $20,000 from the account, the witness said. She claimed she had no idea why he was paid that amount. Asked about her own financial status, Jane related that she received a salary of $2,500 a month. She also received about $10,000 a year in dividends from $1.3 million worth of stocks that had been given to her by her family, and her family frequently sent her extra money to help with her needs, she testified. She also said that Menard Adams had lied when he said he and Hawkins came to the office on September 1st. In fact, Jane said, she had never seen Hawkins.

When asked by her attorney if she had anything to do with the murder of Judy Saragusa, Jane replied definitely, "As God is my witness, I did not." The only change in the former secretary's confident appearance occurred during cross examination when one of the prosecutors showed her a picture of Judy Saragusa's body. Tears started to stream from her eyes as a defense attorney leaped to his feet to object.

Otherwise, Jane explained away questions put by the prosecution with the explanation that the state witnesses had lied. She said she had no idea how her .22-caliber pistol became the weapon used in the murder. Adams was lying when he testified he saw Jane give the pistol to Hawkins in her home, she said. She claimed she was having dinner with her parents that night, and they spent the night in her home.

She admitted having loaned small amounts of money to Adams. She said he did yard work around her house. She flatly denied having given him large amounts of money to hire a hit man.

Furthermore, she didn't give her car keys to Hawkins on September 1st, as Adams claimed, the witness said. She said Adams borrowed her Cadillac on September 2nd. She also denied she was pictured with the two men in the lobby of her office building as Adams had testified about the surveillance camera videotape.

Under cross examination, Jane said she didn't know she had Hawkins' phone number in her address book until the day she was arrested. The prosecutor asked her to look under the numbers for Adams in the book. One of these numbers was that of Hawkins, and it had the letter "L" beside it. She said the "L" stood for the "last" number to dial for Adams and not for "Leon."

In all, Jane Callaway testified that at least nine state witnesses lied when they gave testimony involving her in the murder-for-hire plot.

Following Jane's six hours on the stand, the defense called 11 character witnesses who testified she had a good reputation and no previous criminal record.

During summation arguments by both sides, the state told jurors that if they took Jane Callaway at her word, then Judy Saragusa had arranged her own murder by set-

50

ting up a bank account to which $138,000 was transferred and much of it later paid to the middleman and hit man in the slaying. But the state argued Jane Callaway was lying. "She lied so gracefully and so brazenly," said one assistant D.A.

But in its final arguments before the jury, the defense contended that the state's witnesses were not telling the truth, and that Jane Callaway was taking the fall for someone else. The state had merely tailored its case to fit the secretary, said the defense lawyers.

It didn't make sense because Jane had no reason to want Judy Saragusa dead, argued the defense. She wasn't seeking a wealthy status because she had over $1 million in stock of her own, given to her by her family in addition to supplemental sums that relatives sent her regularly.

If the secretary had done all that the state witnesses said she did, she might as well have taken out an advertisement in the local newspapers, one of the defense attorneys told the jury.

But an assistant prosecutor told the jury, "I'm sure she never considered she'd be caught."

After deliberating for 17 hours, the jury returned its verdict. The jury found Jane Callaway guilty of capital murder.

The defendant displayed no outward emotion except to turn and look over her shoulder at her relatives seated in the courtroom. She was wearing glasses, and court observers noted she didn't have the well groomed appearance of the earlier days of the trial.

Now, the same jury was faced with answering two issues that would determine whether the convicted killer would be put to death by lethal injection or sentenced to prison for life.

The key questions that the jury had to decide was whether the defendant had deliberately caused the death of Judy Saragusa and whether she would be a continuing threat to society. If the jury answered both questions af

51

"WHY DID THE WIDOW WILL HER KILLER $250,000?"

by Olga Kogan

The penthouse party aboard the luxury ocean liner Royal Viking Star was in full swing. San Francisco socialite Muriel Barnett was setting off on a cruise to Alaska and her well-heeled friends had assembled to toast her, "bon voyage." When finally it was time for all visitors to go ashore, the guests tossed down their last champagne cocktails and reluctantly filed out, once again bidding the 80-year-old widow a pleasant trip. But while Muriel happily contemplated the glorious two weeks ahead, someone else on board was grimly contemplating how to murder her.

The Norwegian liner's smooth white hull glided out of pier 35 into San Francisco harbor on August 10, 1985, and headed north. Muriel Barnett was standing on her cabin balcony, watching the city slip by. She could easily pick out her own residence commanding a panoramic view of the bay from the best part of town, a stately residence reflecting wealth and social standing.

Muriel had lived there many years, choosing to stay on even after her husband, prominent attorney Philip Barnett, had died the year before. But the ensuing time had not been lonely, for her loving husband had ensured that Muriel would be left in good hands.

Her faithful entourage included employees of long-

53

standing—the dignified doorman who stood at the entrance to the Barnett home, often helping Muriel into her car; a pretty Salvadoran woman whose job was to open Muriel's mail and answer the phone; and Robert Frisbee, Muriel's 59-year-old personal secretary and traveling companion, who had assured his good friend, Philip Barnett, that he would always care for Muriel after his death.

Muriel and Robert had been looking forward to the trip to Alaska for some time. In the spring, they had been set to go off on an extended trip to Europe, but the plans fell through when Robert, a slight, frail man, became ill. Now that he was in better health, the trip to the Alaskan glaciers seemed like the perfect adventure, especially aboard such a beautiful ship.

When Muriel Barnett traveled, she traveled deluxe-class, and her penthouse suite on board the ship—at $2,000 a day—provided her with the best: a private balcony, her own maid and butler, several rooms and all the caviar she could eat. Thirteen small bottles of champagne stood chilling at all times in the refrigerator.

As suited their employer-employee relationship, Robert Frisbee slept on one of the twin beds in the bedroom.

Every amenity, it seemed, was provided for Muriel. The Austrian maid kept the suite tidy as a pin, the Cypriot butler popped the champagne and served the caviar, and Robert tended to Muriel's other needs, escorting her to the elegant dining room, propping up her cushions on the deck chairs, and diverting her with humorous stories and the occasional sad reminiscence of her late husband.

One afternoon, an Arizona woman and her husband casually complimented Muriel on her jewelry—a gold elephant encrusted with precious stones—and this led to a pleasant shipboard friendship between the two couples.

Another day, the butler amused Muriel when he mentioned that she was sleeping in the same bed that Elizabeth Taylor had slept in when she had been a passenger.

The whole trip was turning into one delight after another

and the port cities glided by—Seattle, Vancouver, Ketchi-kan, Juneau. At Skagway they reached the halfway point, and the ship turned its bow and headed south.

When the ship docked at Victoria on Vancouver Island, Canada, its last port before returning to San Francisco, Muriel Barnett was already thinking of her trip as a period of uninterrupted joy.

That day, Robert took her on a tour of Victoria, a "small English paradise offering a charming Victorian salute to the past," he told her.

Late that afternoon they reboarded the ship, both of them tired and in need of a rest. They had a date for cock-tails with their Arizona friends early that evening, and were invited to attend the captain's farewell reception later on.

Muriel changed into a light robe and lay down for a nap while Robert laid out his tuxedo, cufflinks and collar stud. He then mixed himself his favorite drink, a French 75—three ounces of vodka in five ounces of champagne. He also took a mild sedative, changed into his robe and mixed himself another French 75 before finally lying down to sleep.

In the meantime, the Royal Viking Star was pulling out of Victoria harbor and steaming into the Strait of Juan de Fuca on a course for San Francisco.

At 6:45 P.M., the Cypriot butler came to serve the couple's usual order of caviar. With professional aplomb, he lightly tapped on the door and waited patiently. A few seconds later, the door opened. Robert Frisbee, in tuxedo pants and formal shirt, was holding his head in his hands. His voice shook: "She's dead."

Through the door, the butler could see Muriel Barnett ly-ing on the bed, face up, her head awash in blood. More blood was soaking into the two pillows. The butler hurried away, returning minutes later with two stewardesses as-signed to the luxury suites.

With great self-control, the stewardesses contained their shock. Blood continued to pour from the elderly widow's

55

head. Her head and trunk lay on the bed, her knees on the floor.

One of the stewardesses tended to Robert Frisbee, who sank to a couch, sobbing in grief. The butler, meanwhile, summoned the ship's doctor and the captain. But nothing could be done. Muriel Barnett was dead. Apparently, someone aboard the vessel had entered her cabin unseen and bludgeoned her mercilessly.

While the ship's officers performed their duties, Robert Frisbee performed his — telephoning ship-to-shore to inform people in San Francisco of his employer's death. "She's dead," he kept repeating. "She's dead." He repeated the phrase yet again when the Arizona couple called to ask why he and Muriel had unaccountably broken their cocktail date.

When the ship berthed in San Francisco on August 21st, a seven-member investigating team including homicide detectives, crime scene specialists, deputy coroners and the city medical examiner, Dr. Boyd Stephens, went aboard.

In penthouse suite number six, they found a heavily bloodstained bed, blood on the head board, and blood on the wall and ceiling above the bed. "Like having salad dressing dropped on your shirt," Dr. Stephens remarked grimly.

With a professional eye, he assembled the facts of the crime scene, rolling over in his mind the events of the murder as well as he could.

It appeared from blood patterns on the two pillows that the victim had been lying on her back when the attack occurred. The assailant had struck her on the left side of the forehead at least four times, sending blood splattering on the wall and ceiling and likely on himself. The victim had bruises on her front knuckles, but these were more likely caused when Muriel's hands were raised in reflex action, rather than in trying to ward off blows.

After the pathologist had finished his task, the homicide team took over. Again, professional eyes examined and selected the salient facts. Among the many details, two stood out.

The victim's blood marked a good part of the penthouse bedroom, including a bottle of Famous Grouse highland whiskey on a table near the bed. Strangely, the blood on the bottle appeared diluted. Had the killer tried to wash or wipe it after the attack?

Secondly, it was clear from comparing the butler's and the stewardesses' accounts that the victim's body had moved from lying prone on the bed to a kneeling position after the blows were inflicted. The blood patterns further suggested this. The sleuths supposed the victim was still alive and might have moved herself, but pathologist Stephens said it was more likely that someone else had moved the corpse.

The obvious person to have done this, since he was also in the room, was Robert Frisbee. But detectives weren't about to put the cart ahead of the horse. Frisbee was timid, physically frail and a longtime friend of the victim. With Muriel's death, he also lost his employer. As a suspect, he left a lot to be desired.

The probers decided to check out all the passengers on the ship's roster, including Frisbee only as routine. But the information they obtained on Frisbee couldn't easily be ignored.

Reluctantly, the detectives put out an arrest warrant for Robert Frisbee, knowing that by doing so they faced the indignation of a lot of his high-society friends. Consequently, within a day of stepping out of a luxury cruise ship penthouse, Robert Frisbee found himself in totally unfamiliar quarters, staring through the bars of a city jail.

Wealthy friends assured him it was all a mistake. They knew he was incapable of murdering Muriel Barnett. "Dear old Muriel," he had called her. But if friends thought Frisbee was being held on trumped-up charges, they were soon disillusioned.

Authorities charged Frisbee with first-degree murder and

set a trial date. Weeks and months passed while he waited in his jail cell, scribbling notes and observations into a notebook. Even in jail, he was the consummate secretary.

Then he received some news: The trial had been called off. Frisbee naturally was elated. But it was short-lived euphoria. For months, legal experts had been wrestling with the problem of dealing with a murder at sea. The crime had occurred about 90 minutes after the Royal Viking Star had left Victoria harbor. According to the captain, the vessel had been exactly five and a half nautical miles off Point No Point in the Strait of Juan de Fuca. That put jurisdiction in the hands of Canadian authorities in British Columbia.

Had Frisbee been tried in San Francisco, there would have been an automatic acquittal. As it now stood, his trial would take place in Victoria, Frisbee's "quaint Victorian town."

But the testimony that would be heard at his trial would have made Queen Victoria herself turn over twice in her grave.

On December 3, 1986, Frisbee's long-awaited trial opened before Justice Lloyd MacKenzie in a wood-paneled courtroom thickly carpeted in crimson. Dressed smartly as always in a tweed suit, with a silk handkerchief in his breast pocket, Frisbee appeared confident as he seated himself beside his lawyers. The three-man defense team lent a further touch of status to the classy proceedings. Lead defense lawyer was William Deverell, the noted crime authority whose best-selling mystery thrillers contain their own intricate death plots and weird murders.

Squaring off with him for a long legal battle was no less than the province's second-ranking lawman, Assistant Deputy Attorney General Dennis Murray.

On their very first day, the two legal eagles squabbled over a minor procedural point, prompting Murray to comment wryly, "In all points of interpretation of the law, I defer to Mr. Deverell."

"Very good of you," Deverell replied.

In his long opening address, Murray accused Frisbee of bludgeoning Muriel Barnett to death with complete awareness of his heinous action. The motive? Barnett was planning to cut Frisbee out of her will as soon as they arrived home in San Francisco.

As the will stood, Frisbee would inherit two-thirds of the Barnett millions. Once they docked, he would be out of the picture.

But that, Murray declared, was only the tip of the iceberg, as far as motives were concerned.

The prosecution quickly began to show that Robert Frisbee was not the shy wallflower everyone thought, but a complex man harboring a hatred as cultivated as the tailor-made suits he wore.

Called to testify, the Barnett housemaid related that Philip Barnett first met Robert Frisbee in 1964, and later hired him to be a driver, valet, secretary and companion, all for an initial salary of $50 a month. But Frisbee's duties did not end there. When the prominent San Francisco attorney was 78 years old, he called Frisbee into his room one evening and asked him: "Robert, do you think you could arouse me sexually?"

The maid testified that she once saw Frisbee fondle Barnett and kiss him on the mouth as the lawyer sat in a chair with his feet on a stool. On another occasion, she saw Frisbee fondle and kiss Barnett while bathing him naked in Barnett's pink bathroom. Muriel's bathroom, she mentioned, incidentally, was colored blue.

The two men would often kiss and make up after the lawyer verbally abused him, the maid testified. She said the two men were very close, although Barnett could be "very nasty" if Frisbee made a mistake in his duties.

Frisbee's salary was eventually raised to $500 a month, but if he was expecting any big inheritance from the lawyer for his 21 years of service, he was deeply disappointed. Although Philip Barnett had amassed a fortune, all he left his faithful "companion" was a pair of cufflinks.

Frisbee's disappointment was profound, but for a long time after the lawyer's death he was known to look at his picture and cry. And not to be forgotten, there was the matter of Frisbee's death-bed promise to "care for Philip's bride." It was a promise that Frisbee would keep—at a price.

After the maid finished her testimony, the prosecutors declared they had a surprise witness who would show that Frisbee had been milking the wealthy widow for all she was worth. As the courtroom waited impatiently to see who this might be, bailiffs wheeled in a videotape machine.

The "witness" had declined to come voluntarily to Victoria, preferring this method to give his testimony. He appeared as a fuzzy image on the screen, a 65-year-old man in clerical attire.

Describing himself as Frisbee's lover for 10 years, he said that he and Robert had been pooling their incomes to take care of their living expenses. He had been one of those whom Frisbee had called ship-to-shore minutes after Muriel Barnett was found dead.

The man chuckled and giggled as he described Muriel Barnett's "selfishness," describing Frisbee as an underpaid slave to her and her husband. But all that changed one afternoon at a luncheon party.

On that occasion, the mystery man said he witnessed Muriel's signature on a codicil to her will—a codicil that the mystery man himself apparently encouraged. He and Frisbee, he said, planned to slip the codicil into Muriel's papers, fully aware that it gave Robert Frisbee an inheritance worth more than $2 million.

Still more clout then came into Frisbee's hands. Muriel gave him power of attorney over the Barnett funds, a veritable key to the candy store. To be sure, Frisbee wasn't shy when it came to money, and he took full advantage of his windfall. He signed two big checks to the mystery man, one totaling $100,000 to "help him open a gift shop," and the second amounting to $20,000, to assist the mystery

60

man's son's religious work in Australia.

Was it shady dealing or simply a natural gesture of affection that prompted the generous gifts? Defense Attorney Deverell maintained it was just another example of Frisbee's kind nature. He called to the stand the manager of the apartment where the two homosexuals lived. The witness testified that the two men were "excellent tenants." Frisbee, the manager said, was a "very loving, very caring human being," who had a "mother-son" relationship with Muriel Barnett.

The manager's sincerity shone through, and jury members began to feel a little sympathy for the frail-looking defendant.

One by one the witnesses told their stories — the ship's butler, the stewardesses, the ship's captain, homicide detectives and coroner Boyd Stephens. All had come voluntarily — they could not be subpoenaed — traveling from France, Jamaica, Norway, Cyprus and Denmark.

At last, on December 15th, the man at the center, Robert Frisbee, stepped to the stand, dapperly dressed, relaxed, as confident as ever. He began with a few words about his life before he had met the Barnetts.

Frisbee was born Robert Dion in 1927 in West Springfield, Massachusetts. He remembered he'd always been afraid of his father, trembling whenever he appeared. At school it was no better, being teased and ridiculed because of his effeminate nature.

He admitted he never did well at school, mainly because he spent most of his time daydreaming, casting himself in the latest romantic novel he was reading — as the heroine.

Frisbee said things got worse in 1945, when he was drafted into the army.

"The sergeant always became angry with me," Frisbee recalled, "because I threw hand grenades underhand and closed my eyes on the firing range."

After his army fiasco, Frisbee found himself involved in one homosexual liaison after another, always with older men. In between such affairs he had a brief marriage to a woman who bore his child, only to see it die in infancy.

Then he came to San Francisco, where he found new passion in the figure of charming, wealthy attorney Dwight Frisbee, who was married and socially prominent—an earlier version of Philip Barnett. For sixteen months, Dwight and Robert carried on a torrid homosexual affair until one day Dwight made a surprise announcement. Henceforth, he said, there would be no more trips to the bedroom. He was adopting Robert, he said, so sex with his adopted son would naturally be incest and inappropriate.

From that time on, Robert Dion took the name Frisbee, staying with his adoptive father until his benefactor died of alcoholism. Unlike Barnett, Dwight Frisbee was generous to Robert, bequeathing him $160,000.

Accustomed now to wealth, Robert Frisbee hobnobbed with the carriage crowd, plagued by the uneasy knowledge that his inheritance would not last forever.

In 1967, he met the mystery witness in the clerical collar and began a love affair with him. Their affair continued even after Frisbee went to work for the Barnetts.

Over the next 15 years, Frisbee said, he became a kind of court jester to the regal Barnett couple, accepting their taunts and abuse as the price he paid to be a member of their select social set. Perhaps mindful of the inheritance he once received, Frisbee was resentful when Philip Barnett passed away leaving him nothing. The bitter pill was made even harder to swallow when Muriel Barnett "gleefully proclaimed" that all of the Barnetts' millions would go to her.

When the prosecutor asked how he felt knowing that Muriel Barnett was planning to cut him out of her own will, Frisbee shrugged. Was it not motive enough to plan and execute her murder on the day before she was going to change her will? the prosecutor asked.

"No," replied Frisbee. "She already did that two months before we embarked for Alaska."

The reply visibly shook the prosecutor's case and the jury

began to have further second thoughts about the prosecution's position.

"C'est la guerre," commented Frisbee, who added that he'd been disappointed but not resentful of Muriel Barnett's decision.

But the prosecution wasn't letting up on this side of the motive.

"Were you written entirely out of Mrs. Barnett's will?" the prosecutor asked.

"No," the defendant replied.

"Then if you didn't stand to collect two million, how much did you expect?" Pros. Murray pressed.

Frisbee paused. "Only one quarter of a million."

Not quite an Arab shiekdom, but still motive enough, the prosecution maintained.

Murray then entered into evidence a manuscript written by Frisbee in shorthand that the Royal Canadian Mounted Police had seized from him when he was extradited from San Francisco to Vancouver.

Entitled "A Demented Parasite," the 200-page manuscript was written while Frisbee was being held in a San Francisco jail. It was intended to be a fictional novel loosely based on Frisbee's own life, but the prosecution made more of it. Reading aloud from the manuscript, Murray suggested that Frisbee considered his homosexual lovers to be "johns" while he was just another hooker..

"That's not true," Frisbee denied. "I was never promiscuous."

Then Murray read out loud the last passage in the novel: "A calumnious act to perform as promised . . . Tonight she must die . . . The shocking realization . . . When, how, where?"

The prosecutor stared at the defendant. "That's the real ending, isn't it, Mr. Frisbee?"

"No. You're misreading my notes," the defendant replied.

"I had the passage transcribed by a business college here

in town," the prosecutor shot back.

Again the defense was on the spot, but they knew how to take a punch and throw a few themselves.

"That sentence, 'Tonight she must die,' does not appear in Mr. Frisbee's manuscript," declared a shorthand expert from Victoria, put on the stand the next day by the defense. "I studied the manuscript for three hours and could not discern the word 'she' or 'die' in the closing passage."

The expert then used shorthand textbooks to show the jury that Frisbee's symbols did not conform to the phrase alleged by the prosecution.

That round's points went to the defense, which now wound up with a power punch—its main defense argument.

Questioned about the sort of mood he was in shortly before the Royal Viking Star left Victoria, Frisbee replied, "Very gay, if you'll pardon the expression."

Frisbee and Muriel had had a perfect day in Victoria, and were awaiting more fun to come that evening with their Arizona friends and at the captain's reception. The Arizona couple had already testified that both Frisbee and Muriel appeared charming and affable that evening, as they had during the entire cruise.

"It's absolutely incredible that Mr. Frisbee would kill Mrs. Barnett just minutes before the butler was scheduled to bring in the caviar," declared Defense Attorney Deverell. "Not only that, but the chambermaid was also due in to turn down the beds."

Then, pointing to his client, he said, "Mr. Frisbee is too sweet, too besotted and too servile to have planned such a gruesome crime."

The defense then called a psychiatrist to the stand. He said he had interviewed the defendant and concluded that Frisbee could only have carried out the bludgeoning while in "sleep-related automatic behavior." The psychiatrist pointed out that there were documented cases of people committing suicide or murder while in this state of "sleep-walking" or "sleep-drunkenness."

As a rule, he said, this person's action has a purpose, but it occurs without his conscious participation, as when a person finds himself in the kitchen at home and can't remember why he went there.

The psychiatrist concluded that Frisbee, in his normal nonviolent state, would have been incapable of killing or even forming an intent to kill.

With that, the defense rested.

The prosecution repeated its contention that Robert Frisbee planned the crime and then killed Muriel Barnett to secure his fortune in her will. They also declared the crime to be a particularly brutal one, since Frisbee allegedly first hit the widow over the head once with a wine bottle, then bludgeoned her again with a whiskey bottle when he saw she was still alive.

On January 10, 1987, after three long weeks of testimony, the jury was allowed to retire to begin its deliberations. They passed nine hours in seclusion, then the jury members filed back into the courtroom to announced their decision.

Frisbee, dressed in a dark blue suit, blue shirt and maroon tie, stood to hear the verdict.

His reaction when found guilty of first-degree murder was like a man struck by a fist to the groin. At most, he'd been expecting a verdict of second-degree murder or manslaughter.

Justice Lloyd McKenzie asked if the defendant had anything to say before he passed mandatory sentence.

"Oh, not a word, your lordship, not a word," Frisbee replied.

"I have no choice but to pronounce the severest sentence under Canadian law," Justice McKenzie said. "You are sentenced to a life term without eligibility of parole for twenty-five years.

Frisbee's carriage-crowd days were over, and everybody in the courtroom knew it. But the judge, apparently out of compassion, gave a word of hope to the convicted man. A section of the criminal code, he said, allowed a provincial chief justice to consider shortening the period to be served before parole. Frisbee nodded slightly. It was a small consolation for a man who'd once lived so well.

More bitter still, at the very instant that Robert Frisbee stumbled pale and shaken from the courtroom, his long-time lover with the clerical collar lay sunning himself in Palm Springs. Prosecutors admitted they were highly suspicious of the man's role in the murder plot, but without sufficient evidence against him, their hands were tied.

Three days after the verdict, Muriel Barnett's will was read in San Francisco. Robert Frisbee, the man condemned to a slow death behind bars, was bequeathed $250,000 tax-free, by the woman he brutally killed. The University of San Francisco law school got the rest.

"THE MILLIONAIRE WAS INTO MARIJUANA & MURDER"

by Jack G. Heise

The handsome man in his early 30s stood before Cherokee County Judge Daniel Brewster in Columbus, Kansas, on the Friday morning of October 8, 1982. He had entered a plea of guilty and had asked the court for leniency.

Judge Brewster was aware of the defendant's background. He had heard it in a preliminary hearing. He had literally pulled himself up by his bootstraps, parlaying a restaurant he bought with borrowed money in Miami, Oklahoma, into a million-plus in various enterprises, including bars, a recording studio, a motor home rental business and used car lots. His biggest success had been promoting rock music concerts.

He had a luxurious home, several expensive cars, a beautiful wife and a hundred grand in cash. It wasn't enough as he strove to become a multi-millionaire and sought greener pastures to multiply his wealth. He made his mistake in finding them in marijuana fields.

Judge Brewster was also cognizant of the crimes. He had heard the testimony of Cherokee County Sheriff Chuck Sharp who had described the murders of two men as "the most horrible, gruesome torture deaths of humans that could be imagined."

The man waiting to be sentenced very likely wouldn't

67

have been there if it had not been for the dogged perseverance of the rural sheriff and his deputies, along with some
expert investigation that consumed every waking hour of
Sheriff Sharp for more than a year.

It all started with a call from Cherokee City Marshal Joe
Burns to Sheriff Sharp on the morning of September 18,
1980. "Guess I'm going to need your help," Burns said. "A
couple of people spotted a car in the water at the old abandoned strip mine west of Weir. I checked it out and it hasn't
got a license. Figure it must be stolen but we got no report
on a blue 1978 Chev."

"How deep is it in the water?" Sharp asked.

"Nosed in about up to the windshield," Burns said. "If it
had gone all the way in, it's deep enough in the pit to have
covered it and probably wouldn't have been seen."

Sharp said he would come out with a tow truck to re-
trieve the car. He met Marshal Burns at the intersection of
K7 and K103 and went to the mine. There was nothing inside the vehicle or trunk when it was pulled out to indicate
the owner. Sharp had it towed in to his office and obtained
the serial numbers. He called them in to the state motor vehicle registration bureau.

A call came in later in the day reporting the abandoned
car was registered to Keith Arthur with an address in Pittsburg, Kansas.

It seemed strange, if someone had stolen the car, that Arthur wouldn't have reported it. It was even more strange
when Sharp checked with the police in Pittsburg and talked
to Chief Investigator Al Locke and learned that the 22-
year-old man, who lived alone in an apartment, hadn't
been seen in several days.

Arthur's parents lived in Pittsburg so Sharp, Donaldson
and Locke called on them. They were aware that their son
was possibly missing and were deeply concerned. They had
been about to go to the police to file a missing person report when the officers came to see them.

The reason they hadn't gone to the police earlier, they

68

said, was because Tony's (the name Arthur preferred to Keith) close friend Doug Ashby was also missing. The pair had been nearly inseparable since high school days.

"They were both here for dinner on Saturday," Arthur's father said. "They didn't mention going anywhere or doing anything special. Tony usually comes by every day or two. When we couldn't locate him we were worried, but didn't want to embarrass him by going to the police if he and Doug had just gone off somewhere."

One thing was for sure, his parents told the officers, if Tony's car had been stolen and nothing had happened to him, he would have reported it. His car was his pride and joy.

Sharp called his office to direct Deputies Pat Collins and Bill Richardson to check with Marshal Burns and start a search around the strip mine. He contacted the state police with a request for divers to probe the deep, murky water for possible evidence or bodies.

Both missing young men had been raised in Pittsburg, so it didn't take Locke long to locate their friends. The officers learned that the last they had been seen was at a card game on the previous Saturday night. They had left together shortly after midnight.

After questioning the person who had been at the card game, Sharp had a feeling that he hadn't been told everything that went on or what might have been known about their disappearance.

He cornered one of the players and laid it on the line. "Look," Sharp said, "if they won big or something happened, I'm going to find out about it sooner or later. If you're covering up for someone and what happened . . ."

"No, no . . . it isn't like that at all," the card player interrupted.

"Okay, let's have it — and straight," Sharp demanded.

Reluctantly, the man related that while Arthur and Ashby had been at the game they had talked about ripping off a marijuana field they had spotted. The reason the other players hadn't mentioned it was that they didn't want to get their friends involved if they were doing something illegal.

The plans Arthur and Ashby had, according to the informant, had sounded pretty fool-proof. They would sneak into the field at night, cut as many of the big plants as they could haul and then let the marijuana dry, process it and collect a bundle peddling it.

The sweet part of the plan, Arthur had told them, was that whoever was growing the grass couldn't go to the police. He had likened it to hijacking during the prohibition days.

"Did they say where this field of marijuana they were going to rip off was located?" Sharp asked.

The informant shook his head. He had gathered from what had been said it was somewhere south, where the state lines of Missouri, Kansas and Oklahoma meet, possibly not far from where the car had been found at the strip mine.

Deputies Collins and Richardson with Marshal Burns hadn't located anything in a search around the mine that could be linked to the abandoned mine.

Skin divers covered the deep mud and rock bottom of the water filled pit and came up empty. They were positive if there had been any bodies in the pit, they would have found them.

It left the investigators with two possible theories of what might have happened to Arthur and Ashby. They could've ripped off the marijuana field and then ran into the law. They had unloaded their illicit cargo, abandoned the car and fled someplace to avoid arrest. Or, they could have run into the owner or guards at the marijuana field and there had been swift retribution.

Sharp checked with the Kansas Bureau of Investigation and the Federal Drug Enforcement Agency. Neither had a report on suspects being chased or sought in the area.

He asked if they had any information on cultivated fields of marijuana in the section.

Both agencies, along with law enforcement officers from the other states, were aware of the lucrative business of growing marijuana in the remote sections where the fertile fields had once grown corn. They estimated it as being a multi-million dollar operation, but they didn't have the manpower to root out all of the fields.

One DEA agent explained, "They plant the stuff everywhere. It's a crop easily grown and doesn't take much care. The investment is almost nil, since they don't own the land on which it is grown. The take in dollars is fantastic, once it's harvested and distributed. By the time we locate one field and make a raid, they've got another crop growing somewhere else. It's like bailing a sinking boat with a sieve."

The search for Arthur and Ashby around the strip mine continued. It turned up nothing. If the pair had been slain, it was not where the car had been driven into the water. It could have been at the marijuana field, or almost anywhere. And the chances of locating the corpses, without some kind of a break, appeared remote.

The break came on September 20th. A man walking the railroad tracks, a couple of miles from the strip mine, was alerted by a putrid odor. Investigating the stench, he found the decomposing bodies of two men who had been dragged into a wooded area.

There wasn't any identification on either corpse, but it was safe to assume from their ages and appearances that they were Tony Arthur and Doug Ashby. Dr. Gary Dean Zuck, a forensic dentist, confirmed it from dental records.

A postmortem conducted by pathologist Dr. James Bridgen at the Shawnee Mission Hospital revealed each of the men had been shot twice in the backs of their heads with a fairly large size caliber weapon. There was evidence they had also sustained head injuries and had been beaten about the bodies and faces.

71

"It adds up to they must have run into the owner or someone guarding the marijuana field they intended to rip off," Sharp reasoned. "They must have kicked hell out of them and then blew them away."

But how to locate the field and whoever committed the murders?

KBI agents Harvey Harris and Don Windsor, along with DEA agent Mel Ashton were assigned to assist the sheriff and his deputies with the investigation. Jasper County Sheriff Leland Boatwright and Ottowa County Sheriff Floyd Ingram also lent a hand.

The KBI sent a plane with spotters to fly over the fields to try to locate the marijuana fields. They put in a couple of days, but it was tough going. The cagey growers often locate their illicit crop in the center of corn fields so that they are almost impossible to spot from the air.

Sharp and Donaldson made another trip to Pittsburg for a chat with Locke. "I've got a hunch that some of the guys around here who knew Arthur and Ashby, particularly those who were at the card game, may not have told us everything they know. I think it's time we leaned on them a little to jog their memories."

His hunch proved correct.

It didn't take much leaning for one of the card players to fold. He said Arthur and Ashby had invited him to join them to hijack the marijuana field because he had a pickup truck and they could haul a larger load than they could in Arthur's car. He said he thought it over but declined because he had a good job and didn't want to risk losing it in event there was trouble.

"But you know where they were going?" Sharp persisted.

The informant hesitated, indicating he knew. Sharp prodded him. The man said, "Jeez! I didn't say anything before because if those guys blew away Tony and Doug and they find out I've fingered them, they may come after me."

Sharp assured him that the information would be kept confidential and his identity protected. He told them the field was located in a rural road near the small town of Opolis in Jasper County, just across the Kansas line in Missouri.

Sharp called the KBI and DEA agents and they conferred with Jasper Sheriff Leland Boatwright. They drew up plans for a raid on the marijuana field. It would take place early in the evening with the hope that whoever was guarding the field would be there.

When the officers were stationed completely around the big field so that no one could escape, Sharp, Boatwright and Agents Harris and Windsor moved in toward a farmhouse. The lights were on, indicating someone was there.

They had gone only a short way when they were met by snarling guard dogs. Sharp used a bullhorn. He called out to those inside the house to call off the dogs and come out with their hands up or the officers would move in shooting.

Two men came out of the house with their hands in the air. They called to the dogs and chained them. The officers went inside with them where Sheriff Boatwright informed them they were under arrest for the illegal possession of marijuana.

They were read their legal rights and Sharp asked, "Okay, do you want to tell us about the two guys who were out here about a week ago and turned up dead over in Cherokee County?"

The two prisoners eyed each other for a few moments. One of them nervously licked his dry lips and then blurted out, "Hell, I don't mind taking a rap on a charge of growing grass, but I ain't going to take a bust for murder. I told those bastards they were crazy to blow them away."

The man was again read his legal rights and asked if he understood anything he said could and would be used in a court of law against him. He said he understood.

He said that he and his partner had been hired to stay at the farmhouse and guard the marijuana field. They were to split 10 percent of the take after the crop was harvested.

He related that sometime after midnight of Saturday,

they had been awakened by the guard dogs that were allowed to roam free in the field. The dogs had two young men cornered when they came out with guns and herded them into the house.

They used some nylon packaging tape they had for wrapping the marijuana plants damaged by wind and bound the feet and hands of the men.

"We accused them of trying to steal our grass and they admitted it," the man said. "They seemed like fairly nice young guys who were just out to pick up what seemed to them to be easy money."

"And then what did you do?"

"I called Dick Adams over at another of the farms and told him we'd caught the guys and asked him what we should do with them."

"Who is this Dick Adams?" Sharp asked.

The man said Adams had a reputation as a gifted grower of marijuana. He had been hired to plant and cultivate four large fields of the illicit plants.

Later, investigators said Adams' reputation was well earned. The single field that Arthur and Ashby had intended to rip off held plants 15 feet tall, with many of the stock the size of small trees. It took a chainsaw to fall some of the plants, when destroyed by DEA agents, and if they had been allowed to ripen and be cured, would have had a street value in excess of $1 million.

The man making the statement said Adams and Virgil Fox, the owner of the fields, came to the house.

The DEA and KBI agents didn't need to inquire about the identity of Fox. They knew him well from his reputation.

Fox lived in Joplin, Missouri, in a luxurious home. He had a half-dozen business enterprises and was considered to be a millionaire. He had acquired much of his money as a promoter of rock concerts in Missouri, Kansas and Oklahoma.

Earlier in the year, before the fields he had planted were

74

ready to harvest, Fox negotiated with a smuggling group in Texas for the purchase of 1,500 pounds of Columbian marijuana to be delivered in Oklahoma City. DEA agents got wind of the transaction and planted an undercover agent. They nailed Fox.

He was indicted and put up a $150,000 bond to be released, pending trial.

"After Adams and Fox got here, what happened?" Sharp asked.

"This guy Fox has a real nasty disposition," the man making the statement said. "He started screaming at them and then began kicking and beating on them with his fists. That was okay by me because they had some lumps coming, but when he picked up a two-by-four and began pounding on them, I said it was enough."

There was a discussion of what should be done with the hijackers. It was decided they would be taken somewhere and let loose, with a warning they'd be located and killed if they went to the police or revealed to anyone else the location of the marijuana field.

The pair, still taped hand-and-foot, with gags in their mouths, were placed in the trunk of Arthur's car. Fox drove the car and Adams followed him in a pickup truck.

What took place after that was hearsay from what Adams had told the man later.

He said Fox told him to meet him at the abandoned strip mine where he was going to leave the men. When he got there, he said Fox was standing at the edge of the water filled pit cursing and the car was half-submerged.

According to the witness, Adams said Fox told him he had planned to push the car into the water where it would have gone to the bottom of the pit with the two men in the trunk. Somehow, the front wheels had struck a rock or something and the car was stuck in the mud.

He claimed he helped Fox drag the two men out of the trunk of the car and Fox had pushed them into the water, thinking they would drown. The men, although bound

75

hand-and-foot and gagged, managed to keep bobbing around in the water.

Fox was infuriated. He went to the pickup and got a hammer. He tried hitting the men on the head, but couldn't make a solid contact as they bounced around in the water.

"I finally talked him out of killing them," Adams was quoted as saying. "I told him it wouldn't get us anything to have them dead and after the beating they had taken, it wasn't likely they'd try to rip off anyone else or go to the police."

Arthur and Ashby were fished out of the water and the tape around their ankles removed. After more threats, they were allowed to walk down the railroad track.

"Both of them were bleeding like stuck pigs, but I thought they could make it," Adams had told the guards.

He related they had driven the pickup to another of Fox's marijuana fields. Fox was still fuming about punks trying to rip him off. At the field, he borrowed a .357-magnum from a guard and they left.

"I thought we were going back to his car and he was going home," Adams said. "Instead, he was driving and went back to where we'd let the two guys go. He spotted them up the track a mile or so and jumped out of the car. The next thing I heard were the shots."

Adams said Fox had shot each man twice in the back of his head. He helped Adams drag the bodies into some brush and they left.

With the guards at the marijuana field taken into custody by Sheriff Boatwright, the other officers located Adams. Confronted with the story they had heard from the marijuana field guards, Adams confirmed the account, insisting he hadn't known Fox intended to kill the men and hadn't taken part in it, other than help dispose of the bodies.

"And I figured I didn't have much choice about that," Adams said. "Virg had that damn gun and had just killed two guys. I wasn't too damn sure he wouldn't kill me so that there'd be no witnesses."

The officers hurried to Joplin, but neither Fox nor his wife was at the house. Neighbors said they hadn't seen the couple in several days.

The officers returned to question Adams about where Fox might have gone.

"I don't know, but I think you're going to have one hell of a time finding him," Adams said.

Adams related that after Fox had killed Arthur and Ashby, he'd asked him what they should do if the bodies were found and they might come under suspicion of murder. He claimed Fox had told him not to worry and if he was questioned to lay all of the blame on him.

He said Fox said, "I've got that Fed rap coming in Oklahoma City. I'm not going to do any time in any lousy jail. I've already got things started, this is just going to speed it up. Where I'm going there won't be anybody who can find me."

Investigators attempting to locate Fox on a charge of first-degree murder learned that what Fox had said about disappearing appeared to be true.

For several months he had been secretly converting as much of his holdings as possible into cash. He had obtained loans on his property and businesses and sold as much as he could for cash. They estimated he might have as much as a million dollars in cash.

Fox walked away from his luxurious home, left behind several expensive cars, a motor home and his business. He and his wife vanished without a trace.

"He's one smart cookey," a federal agent grudgingly admitted. "He didn't take a damn thing with him that can be traced. You've got to have guts to walk away from what he left behind."

A warrant charging Fox with being a fugitive was issued. A wanted bulletin was put out by the National Crime Information Center. They had his fingerprints and mug shots from the Oklahoma City drug bust. If he got into trouble

77

anywhere, they'd have him.

Attorneys for Adams went to Cherokee County Attorney Ron Boyer with a deal. They pointed out the state had no evidence nor eyewitnesses that Adams had killed, or assisted in killing, Arthur or Ashby. By his own admission, he had helped kidnap them. They offered Adams to plead guilty to two charges of kidnapping in exchange for his testimony naming Fox as the murderer.

Recognizing that it was Fox who had borrowed a gun from one of the marijuana field guards, and the two other guards had stated it was Fox who was infuriated and had beaten on the men while they were being held captive, Boyer accepted the deal. Judge Charles Sell sentenced Adams to two concurrent 10-year-to-life sentences on the guilty plea to kidnapping.

But where was Fox?

There was speculation he had fled to Mexico, Canada, South America or Europe. He had plenty of money to go to any of the places and live very comfortably, so long as he stayed out of trouble.

Searching for Fox became an obsession with Sheriff Sharp. He spent all of his free time trying to come up with a lead as to where he had disappeared when he and his wife vanished from Joplin.

While others thought Fox had fled the country, Sharp wasn't convinced. He had studied Fox with the intensity to compile a complete biography from the time of his birth until he disappeared. He was certain that Fox, who had been an aggressive, ambitious man, would surface sooner or later.

Sharp spent his free time away from the sheriff's office tracking down and talking to anyone he could locate who had been associated with the fugitive. He talked to employees, business associates, friends and relatives.

Fox, he reasoned, had planned his disappearing act prior to the time of the murders in order to escape a jail sentence for the federal narcotic charge. It meant that he had some plan in mind as to how he could completely elude his pursuers.

"The guy is shrewd and has guts," Sharp said. "I've been trying to think that if I had been in his position, how I would have pulled it off. So far the thing's got me stumped."

It was nearly a year after the murder that the perseverance of Sheriff Sharp paid off. He was questioning an associate of Fox when the man said that he and Fox had been discussing what should be done if Fox was sentenced to prison if convicted on the federal drug charge.

"He told me that he didn't intend to spend any time behind walls," the man explained. "I asked him how he was going to manage that and he said the cops wouldn't be looking for a dead man."

"A dead man," Sharp repeated the statement. "I think I know the guy well enough so he wouldn't have planned on killing himself, so that means . . ."

Sharp broke off vocalizing his thoughts in mid-sentence. He exclaimed, "I think I've got it. It's the kind of thing that would fit him to a T."

Hurrying back to his office, Sharp pulled the voluminous file he had compiled on Fox. In it was information he had collected that a relative of Fox's wife had been killed in an automobile accident. He reasoned that Fox could've taken the dead man's identity, and as long as he kept out of trouble and was not fingerprinted, he'd be safe.

Sharp had a name, but how to find it? With the assumed name of the dead man, Fox might be anywhere in the country or have gone to Canada, Mexico or abroad. Looking for a man with only a name and a description would make looking for a needle in a haystack a very easy task.

Sharp mulled it over for days. Too much time had passed for any hope of tracing him through airline passenger flight records, and he was fairly certain Fox had simply boarded a plane and gone somewhere when he left Joplin.

He went back to studying his file on Fox, asking himself

where Fox might be and what he was doing.

Then it hit him.

Fox was the kind of guy who liked the good things in life. He had lived lavishly in Joplin. He had the money to continue with that kind of life style. Wherever he was, he was going to be living it up. But where, and how to get a line on him?

Sharp had a hard time containing himself when he finally dropped the last piece in the jigsaw puzzle.

"Cars," he exclaimed to himself aloud. "The guy was nuts about big, fancy cars. Wherever he is, he'll have at least one."

Sharp contacted the NCIC. He gave them the name of the dead relative of Fox's wife. He requested a special bulletin to every state, asking for the vehicle bureaus of registrations to check on the name, particularly for expensive cars that had been purchased within the past year.

The payoff came with information from California that a man using the name had bought a new Lincoln Continental giving an address in an affluent community near Los Angeles called Running Springs.

Sharp passed his information on to the FBI. Agents located Fox and took him into custody as a fugitive from the federal drug charge in Oklahoma. He waived extradition.

The charges of murder against Fox in Kansas were held in abeyance until Fox faced the federal drug charge. He entered a guilty plea and was sentenced to serve eight years at Leavenworth.

A preliminary hearing on the murder charges was held in Columbus, Kansas, with prosecutor Boyer presenting the evidence and witnesses to support the charges. Fox was ordered held for trial.

The trial was scheduled to begin on Monday morning, October 11, 1982. On Friday, October 8, Boyer and the defense counsel for Fox requested a private hearing before Judge Brewster. He granted it and they appeared with Fox.

Boyer related to the court that the defendant offered to

enter a plea of guilty to two counts of aiding and abetting a murder in exchange for the state to drop the charges of first-degree murder.

Asked why the state was willing to agree to the plea bargaining, Boyer explained that there was only one witness to the crimes and he was serving time in prison. He felt, even with the evidence, it would be difficult to obtain a verdict with the death penalty. The charges to which the defendant was willing to plead guilty carried the same life sentences as a first-degree murder conviction but without execution.

"I feel the end results would be the same," Boyer said. "And it will save the state and taxpayers the expense of a lengthy trial."

After questioning Fox if he fully understood the consequence of his guilty plea, Judge Brewster accepted the plea.

At the sentencing, Fox asked the court to show him leniency. Judge Brewster imposed two life sentences to run concurrently.

Sheriff Sharp watched the proceedings. He left the courtroom with a smile. The long hours he had put in on the case he felt had finally been rewarded.

"MURDER MYSTERY OF A MILLIONAIRE"

by Andrew Lowen

The yellow light from the car's headlights flooded the gravel drive ahead. Trees swayed in the stiffening October breeze, like night prowlers suddenly making their move. Pockets of beefy clouds ganged up to keep the moon blindfolded. The driver shivered in the overbearing eeriness. She couldn't wait to be indoors, warming herself in front of the log fire, doors and windows bolted, her husband sipping his usual nightcap brandy and the television filling the house with easy-listening noises.

Even the children in the back of the car were silent, as if muted by a miserable night bristling with hidden demons.

Now the headlights splashed on the majestic mansion, which somehow, in that cold, artificial light, seemed more of an austere fortress than a blissful home.

At that moment, the spidery outline of a human figure was lanced by the headlights as it staggered into the drive.

The driver hit the brake and twisted the wheel. Her Lancia Gamma Coupe 2500 slithered sideways to a halt, kicking up a blinding cloud of dust.

The children shrieked. Nothing moved outside the car. *My God, I've hit somebody!* the driver thought. She went to open her door, then hesitated. What if the person she'd hit was a prowler or burglar and was merely feigning injury? she warned herself.

But she had to find out for sure. "Lock the door behind me," she instructed her eldest child. "I want you kids to stay in the car. Don't move, you hear me."

By the time the driver reached the front of her car, a man was dragging himself to his feet, using the hood as a crutch. Blood was pumping from wounds on his face and head. The sleeves of his jacket were tattered, and his arms appeared to have been crushed.

And now the car's headlights smeared the man's face with a sickly, ghost-like hue.

"Michael!" the woman screamed, looking into the dying eyes of her millionaire husband — Michael Robertson, aged 43.

Michael Robertson tried to speak, but collapsed before he could utter a word.

The ambulance arrived within 20 minutes. Mr. Robertson was rushed to Southampton General Hospital, some 30 miles away along the English south coast. His family travelled with him in the ambulance. The journey took 35 minutes.

An intern noted the time of arrival at the hospital. It was 10:25 P.M. The date: October 27, 1984.

A young uniformed constable reached the hospital some 10 minutes later. He introduced himself to the victim's wife, then had a brief word with the intern in the casualty unit. By this time, a senior surgeon was on the scene, surrounded by a team of brisk nurses.

The rookie cop then took the briefest of statements from the distraught wife and went off to his car to radio headquarters.

Coffee and orange drinks were plied to Mike Robertson's family by a junior nurse who replied to all frantic questions about the victim's condition: "I'm sorry, but I can't tell you anything. Sister or doctor will be out to have a word with you any minute now."

83

The minutes multiplied into an hour . . . and longer. Finally, a doctor emerged from the emergency unit, grim-faced and frosty.

"You say you knocked down your husband when he stepped in front of your car?" the doctor queried.

"Yes, that's right," she replied. "He seemed to come from nowhere. How is he? Is he going to be all right? Please tell me."

The physician answered guardedly. "I'm having him sent down to X-ray. He has many severe injuries, the extent of which I'm not yet sure. I'm positive he'll have to undergo surgery as soon as possible.

"Your husband's condition is critical. It would be wrong of me not to be frank with you. I cannot make any promises."

The truth was worse than the suspense of no news.

It was one A.M. when a bleary-eyed Detective Inspector Mitch Gregory walked through the doors of the hospital, having been roused from his bed by a duty sergeant at the Southampton City Police Headquarters. The victim's wife had no way of knowing at that moment that the new arrival was, in fact, one of the top cops in homicide.

Gregory went straight into the emergency unit, but, in passing, he *clocked* the Robertson family, missing nothing.

Half an hour later, he was questioning Mike Robertson's wife in the deserted waiting room. "I have to tell you," he stated, "that your husband has 13 very deep cuts to his face and head, a fractured skull and some brain damage, plus severe damage to his arms."

"But is he going to be all right?" the wife pleaded.

"I can't help you on that score," the inspector retorted. "You'll have to speak with the doctor again. My interest is how he came by his injuries."

"I told the doctor. I told the constable who spoke with me earlier. What more is there to tell?"

"I think we should go back to your place and take a look at your car," suggested Gregory.

84

"But I can't leave here, not until I know."

"There's nothing you can do here," Gregory stated firmly. "You'll be notified if there's any change in your husband's condition."

Mystified, the victim's wife allowed herself and the children to be driven home. Her Lancia was where she'd left it, outside the door to her home. After finding her husband, she'd driven to the house to call the ambulance.

Inspector Gregory shone his flashlight along the fender of the Lancia, then around the front wheels and over the hood and lights. "You say he appeared from nowhere in front of you?" Gregory recapitulated.

"That's right," she answered. "You can ask the children."

The sleepy kids, almost snoozing on their feet, nodded in agreement. "That's how it happened, just like Mom says," asserted the elder of the two.

"OK, let's take a look at the spot where it happened," said Gregory, allowing himself to be led.

He was careful not to rearrange treadmarks and other configurations in the gravel at the scene of the alleged accident.

"Did you hear a bump when you struck your husband?" the inspector asked.

"No. He was there one second and gone the next. You know, like I hit him, and he fell."

"Did you know who it was at that stage?"

"No. I didn't see his face. I didn't even know it was a man, though I guessed . . ."

"Why do you say that?"

"Well, he sort of appeared to be staggering; wavering a little."

"As if drunk?"

"As if he'd had a drink."

"And your husband had been drinking?"

"He went out for a drink in the village pub. Please, Inspector, will you tell me what this is all about?"

"Let's go to your house. I want to make a phone call.

85

Then I'll explain. This will take all night. You'd better get the kids to bed."

While the children were put to bed, Inspector Gregory contacted the duty officer at forensics. The inspector explained that he wanted a car collected for examination. He also requested a team of science detectives to comb the grounds for clues. "A daybreak start," Gregory ordered.

When the woman returned from upstairs, Gregory explained to her: "We have a problem. You see, the senior casualty officer on duty at the hospital—you spoke with him—is adamant that no way has your husband been involved in a car accident."

Their eyes locked. The victim's wife was speechless; aghast. Her face was a true reflection of her mind.

"The injuries, according to the surgeon, are consistent with your husband having been viciously attacked, not run down by a car. What's more, there don't appear to be any marks on the front of your car.

"If you had caused those injuries with your car, there would be considerable damage to your vehicle. Believe me. No, there's much more to this case, I'm afraid. I must know about your husband's movements last night."

According to his wife, Mike Robertson had gone to the village pub in Hayling Island, Hampshire County "around eight o'clock." This was his Saturday night ritual. Sometimes he would be out for a mere hour. Another night, he might stay until the pub closed at 11:00. "It all depended on his mood—and the company."

His wife had taken the children to visit relatives some five miles away. "There's no school tomorrow, so it didn't matter their being up late."

"You saw your husband leave?" Gregory inquired.

"I did."

"How did he go?"

"In his own car."

"Which is?"

"A Volvo."

86

"Where is it now?"

"Parked round the side. I saw it as we drove up to the house."

The pair of them went out to the Volvo. Again using his flashlight, Gregory was able to establish that there didn't appear to be any damage whatsoever to the husband's vehicle either.

They returned to the house, and Gregory continued with his questions. "Okay, so your husband left and that's the last you saw or heard of him until you discovered him at the foot of your car, when you thought you'd run him over?"

"Yes."

"Did he knew where you were going?"

"Of course."

The team from forensics were at the Robertsons' home— Pond Head in Saltens Lane, Hayling Island—at first light on Sunday, which came late, about eight o'clock.

By this time, Mike Robertson was in intensive care, having undergone emergency surgery during the night. His wife hadn't been to bed and was still answering police questions at her home. The kids, understandably, slept on.

Just before 10:00 A.M., photographs of Robertson's injuries were shown to a police surgeon at the hospital. He was unable to examine the actual wounds because Robertson was encased in bandages. However, the police doctor was also shown X-rays, and he had no hesitation in backing the original medical opinion.

Mike Robertson, a high-flying executive with a computer company, was no accident victim. Certainly he hadn't been struck by any car. However the injuries had been inflicted, they had been done so very deliberately. "Attempted murder," the police surgeon assured Gregory. "I'll lay my reputation on the line."

Before Gregory had a chance to speak, the surgeon was adding: "When you catch the perpetrator, the charge won't be attempted murder, however. It'll be murder."

"You mean you don't think Robertson's going to

87

make it?" Gregory asked.

"He hasn't a chance."

A round-the-clock bedside vigil was mounted in the intensive care unit at the Southampton Hospital.

Meanwhile, forensics had information on the Lancia. "This car hasn't hit anybody recently," Gregory was told. "It hasn't been involved in any kind of accident. No marks, no blood."

Gregory was only having confirmed officially and scientifically what he already knew from his own experience and judgment.

The victim's Volvo had also been given the works by forensics, just in case there had been any switch of cars before the cops arrived on the scene. The verdict was the same. "Neither vehicle has been involved in a recent accident of any kind, inspector."

From this moment, the cops began casting their net much wider. The wife's account of events on the night of the "mystery" were put to the test, and that tallied. The landlord of the village pub, barmaids and customers were interrogated. They all remembered Mike Robertson drinking there on the Saturday night between "about eight and 9:15 to 9:30."

"Was he alone?" asked Gregory.

"No," replied the landlord. "All his friends were in. They're regulars, especially at weekends."

"But did he arrive alone?"

"Oh, yes."

"Did he leave alone?"

"As far as I know. Mind you, we were pretty busy. We always are on a Saturday night."

"Was he in mixed company?"

"Mostly men, but I think there were a couple of women. Wives of a couple of men in the group."

The barmaids were quizzed specifically about their recollections of Robertson leaving the premises. Gregory wanted to know for sure whether the victim had left alone.

Only one of the three barmaids could be certain about Mike Robertson leaving the pub alone, and she told Gregory emphatically: "He called out 'good-night' to me as he went. The bar was crowded and I didn't see anyone with him when he went out of here."

"And no one appeared to follow him out?" Gregory pressed.

"Sorry, I wouldn't know about that. In any case, there are several doors. Anyone could have slipped out the back, for instance, at around the same time."

The pub staff was also questioned about Robertson's mood and behavior that fateful night. In particular, the cops wanted to learn of any arguments, feuds or fights in which Mike Robertson might have been involved.

Every witness scoffed at the idea that there could be anyone who wanted to deliberately harm Robertson. "He's a man of peace," one witness stressed. The landlord of the pub emphasized: "He's no fighting man. He's a real gentleman. It's absurd to suggest he could be mixed up with people who go in for violence."

Robertson's wife was asked the usual questions about her husband's possible enemies from his business or social life. The reply was the biggest cliche of them all: "He hasn't any enemy in the world. Everyone loves and respects him. You can forget that line of inquiry."

On the contrary, Inspector Gregory knew only too well that he could not afford to dismiss any possibility.

The people Robertson had been drinking with that Saturday night were rounded up during the next couple of days. They all confirmed the statements of the pub landlord and barmaids: Mike had arrived alone and had departed the same way. What's more, he had been in high spirits, telling stories and polite jokes.

"He was the life and soul of the party," commented one of the women. "He's an intelligent man, very soft-spoken and not at all malicious. It's impossible not to like him. He's a doll. A real sweetie."

His fellow executives at work knew him as a man of honor and someone with considerable technical expertise. "One of the best in his field," commented the company chairman.

Next stop for Gregory was Mike Robertson's accountant. "No financial worries," said the accountant. "He has the usual kind of bank overdraft, but there's no pressure on him. He has more than enough money coming in every month to meet the outgoings. As you can see from his life-style, he's a man of considerable substance."

"And he isn't involved in any business deals at present?" Gregory wanted to know.

"Certainly not that I know about," was the answer. "Of course, he's dealing every minute of the day on behalf of the company which employs him, but I don't think that's the kind of business involvement you were referring to."

The accountant was right in his reading of the inspector's question.

During this time, detectives from forensics had been conducting an inch-by-inch search of the grounds of Pond Head, Robertson's palatial home.

Just before noon on Tuesday, Detective Roy Bannister, probing on his hands and knees, armed with a giant magnifying glass, came across a blade of grass darkened by stain. Investigating further, he found more dark grass which was incongruous among the light-green lawn. Much of the grass in that area had been trampled flat.

The head of the forensics unit was immediately called over by Bannister to take a look. Minutes later, Gregory was being informed over the phone: "I think we've found the spot where Robertson copped it. The place is about 200 yards from where the wife says she found her husband."

"Within the grounds of the house?" Gregory demanded.

"Oh, yes, on one of the lawns, almost under a tree," came the answer.

Blades of grass were cut and dropped into a plastic bag; the kind that forensics use for storing exhibits. The bag was then taken to the laboratory at headquarters and the blades of grass were subjected to a series of scientific tests. It was soon established that the dark stain on the grass was human blood. A call to the hospital also confirmed that the blood on the grass matched Robertson's blood group.

That night, Mike Robertson's pulse weakened dramatically. The emergency team at the hospital went into action, trying every trick known to the medical profession: the patient was already on a life-support machine. Thirty minutes later, Mike Robertson was dead. And with him went the grim secret of that fateful Saturday night. He hadn't regained consciousness, not even for one second, not even to utter one word. The one word which would have been enough — the name of his attacker.

Could robbery have been the motive for murder? How much money had the victim been carrying?

Thirty-five pounds had been left untouched in the victim's wallet. Neither had the attacker bothered about Robertson's considerable collection of credit cards or checkbook. His wife didn't know exactly how much money her husband had been carrying that night, but she couldn't imagine that he would have gone out with much more than was found on him. "He tried to avoid carrying large sums of money on him," she explained. "There's no need when you have all the credit cards."

What about burglary? Could Robertson have arrived home and disturbed a burglar, gave chase and was pole-axed to death? Maybe as he drove along the gravel drive, he spotted a prowler and, after parking his car, went to investigate?

Certainly there was no evidence of an attempted break-in. The possibility that Robertson had pursued a prowler seemed far more plausible. There were valuables in the house, and someone could well have been casing the place.

The autopsy showed that Mike Robertson had died as a result of brain damage, including a fractured skull and a cerebral hemorrhage. The injuries had been caused

91

by something long, round, fairly narrow and very hard.

"An iron-bar?" Gregory asked the police pathologist, who replied: "Almost certainly, I'd say. The injuries to his arms were caused, in my opinion, by his trying to defend himself from a frenzied attack. This was the work of someone who intended to bludgeon him to a pulp. My only surprise is that he lived so long. He must have had the constitution of a warrior."

The medical evidence tended to kill the theory that Robertson had stumbled across a prowler. A professional burglar or peeping Tom would have done just enough—and no more—to escape, Gregory reasoned with his men. And everyone agreed with him. They were still very much stuck up blind alleys.

Every member of the staff at the mansion had been interviewed. There was a gardener, a cook, a kitchen maid, a nanny and a daily help. None of them lived on the premises, and they had all been off duty at the time of the crime.

Gregory wondered if Robertson might have been having a long-running dispute with any member of his domestic staff, but this idea was quickly dispelled by the victim's wife and all the staff.

Nevertheless, Gregory decided to check out their alibis for Saturday night. The gardener, Timothy Smith, aged 41, was a bachelor. He lived with a relative at the Sea Front, Hayling Island and had worked for the Robertson family for almost five years.

"He's a real gem," said the murdered man's wife. "A magnificent worker and so reliable and helpful."

Gregory and his partner interviewed Smith at the Robertson mansion. "I was drinking on Saturday night," Smith claimed. "In a pub."

Gregory, for a moment, wondered if it could have been the same pub that Robertson had visited, but it wasn't.

"What time did you leave home?" the inspector asked.

"Around seven."

"What time did you leave the pub?"

"Not until about 11:30."

"You were there the whole time?"

"Definitely."

"Who were you drinking with?"

"Lots of people. I don't know their names."

"Then you went straight home?"

"I did."

"How did you get on with Mr. Robertson?"

"He was the best boss any man could have."

"Did you kill him?"

"Don't be daft! Of course I didn't."

"Do you know who might have done it?"

"No idea. Must be a lunatic. Someone insane; that's all I can think of."

A relative of Smith's vouched for the time he had left home on Saturday night. She couldn't, however, remember the time he'd returned. "I was in bed almost asleep," she explained. "It was late. Well, late for me. I'm always in bed by ten."

The landlord of the pub confirmed that Smith had been in his pub on Saturday evening, but he couldn't guarantee that he'd been there all night. "When you're busy, it's difficult to be certain about something like that," he explained to police.

There was no real reason to suspect the gardener, but Inspector Gregory decided to probe further. He applied to a magistrate for a search warrant for the house where Smith lived.

And in the rafters of the garage at the Smith home, the cops discovered a three-foot-long iron pipe. As a matter of routine, it was taken to the science lab for tests. The result: human bloodstains matching the victim's blood group, plus latent palmprints.

"Find the hand that fits those prints and you have the killer," declared the head of forensics triumphantly.

Gregory and his men went to pick up Smith, but by now he was missing. News of the iron pipe and the palmprint

93

was leaked to the press. The following day, after reading of the developments in the newspapers, Smith phoned Gregory.

"I'm ready to give myself up," said Smith miserably. "Please come and fetch me."

He was in a country pay phone some 10 miles away, having slept rough on a frosty night. He was arrested within 15 minutes and charged with murder that evening.

When Timothy Smith appeared before Winchester Crown Court in March 1985, he spoke only two words: "Guilty, sir." This was when the charge was read to him. Throughout the whole investigation, committal proceedings and trial, the accused refused to offer any explanation for the homicide. The trial itself lasted only a mere 40 minutes.

Smith made a thin, pale figure in the dock. He wore a dark-blue blazer, a blue shirt and matching tie. Sentencing him to life in prison, the judge, Mr. Justice Tudor-Evans, commented: "Whatever your motives were, this was a brutal murder for which the sentence is prescribed by law. It is one of life imprisonment."

The motive for the slaying remained a mystery.

Clearly, it was not a spur-of-the-moment killing. The court was told that Smith had taken great care in trying to establish an alibi for himself. Then, during the evening, he left the pub, drove to Pond Head and hid in the grounds, waiting for his boss to return. Obviously, Smith knew all about Robertson's weekend routine. After committing the crime, he'd returned as fast as possible to the pub, suspecting that on such a busy night his absence for an hour wouldn't be noticed. And he was right.

After the case, Gregory commented: "It's a satisfactory conclusion, but I'm not satisfied! I'm sure everyone would like to know the reason for the killing. Whenever Smith is ready to talk, I shall be only too pleased to visit him in prison and listen. I like everything tidy. I'm sure every policeman knows exactly what I mean."

"BLOODY HOUR OF THE WOLF!"

by Bud Ampolsk

It's been more than a quarter of a century now. A whole generation has grown up since those terrible days. Still there are those who can never forget what it was like. The horror is so indelibly etched into their memories that the sands of time will never wear it away.

To come to grips with the bloody saga, one must turn the clock back to the early morning hours of February 2, 1959. One must not only travel back in time, but must journey half a world away. The destination is a model city where crime — violent or otherwise — while not completely unknown, is not a daily fact of life.

The city of Perth, Australia is proud of its half million residents. Whatever its origins as a penal colony for the felons of the mother country, Australia has become a land of enlightenment and progress. Perth reflects the strides being made everywhere in the continent down under.

Perth is a good place to live. It is not a place in which to die violently . . .

Certainly, lovely Pnena Berkman was not preoccupied with thoughts of death on that sultry warm summer night. The soft breezes blowing in from the sea filled her opulently furnished suburban apartment. They brought

95

thoughts of romance and a joyous life ahead to the socially prominent 33-year-old divorcee.

It had been a lovely evening. The party was filled with sparkling conversation and sophisticated good will. Her extremely handsome escort was courtly and attentive. The taste of his goodnight kiss lingered warm and sweet upon her own soft, full lips as she gracefully slipped out of her party clothes, slid into bed and gave herself over to the type of drowsy thoughts that were a fitting climax to the events of the day.

It will never be known whether the thoughts and dreams which followed were blasted by the stealthy step of the intruder. Did Pnena awaken as he approached her bed and gazed down on her nubile body, feasting on the sight of her firm flesh, so warm and vibrant under its gossamer covering? Did the cold steel of the sharp knife point touching that warm flesh bring her suddenly awake? Did she in fact feel the torturing agony of that knife blade slicing into her vital organs? No one can say for sure.

All that is known is that on the morning of February 2nd, a devoted neighbor came to call on Pnena and found the young divorcee's bloody corpse lying amid the gore-soaked bedclothing.

The assailant had done a fearful job on Pnena. Deep, thrusting wounds had ripped into her in a number of places. The knife punctures ran all the way from the divorcee's head to her feet.

Not remaining in the room long enough to determine for sure whether there was still the breath of life in Pnena, the neighbor raced from the Berkman apartment to summon those who would know what to do under such circumstances.

In a matter of minutes, Chief Inspector Cecil Lamb of the Criminal Investigation Bureau of Western Australia was on the scene. The universally respected criminologist watched closely as his detectives and forensic specialists under the command of their medical expert went about their macabre task of trying to deduce what had actually occurred in the Bergman flat.

A number of primary questions begged for quick answers: How had the murderer gained entry? Had the victim in any way tried to defend herself? Had the killer's motive been personal? Had it been robbery? Had it been sexual?

If the answer to any of these were affirmative, it would give the detectives a leg up on solving the killing. When at least some aspects of a case make a modicum of sense, it gives law-enforcement officers a chance to think along with the perpetrator. They can pit their own sense of logic against his in a sort of investigative chess game.

The condition of Pnena's body and the apartment were to give Lamb scant comfort, however.

From the fact that there were no signs of struggle, it was apparent that the killer had probably been someone unknown to his victim. Obviously the intruder had operated with a degree of stealth that had not alerted his victim nor given her an opportunity to defend herself.

There was no sign of forced entry. The killer probably had found an unlocked door. (Many residents of Perth, lulled as they had been by their feelings of security, were neglectful about such mundane things as locking doors and securing windows.)

Robbery couldn't possibly have been the reason for the intrusion. This was made obvious by the fact that Pnena's bag had been in plain sight and had been open. But not one pence had been stolen from it.

Then a sexual attack had to be the motive. But the autopsy, which was carefully carried out, proved this not to be true.

What it all added up to was that Inspector Lamb was dealing with the most frustrating of all criminal cases — a random killing with no apparent motive and the strong possibility that victim and slayer had been completely unknown to each other prior to the murder itself.

The public reaction to Pnena's violent death was immediate and almost hysterical. Citizens of Perth did not have the same framework of criminal reference as do residents of our megalopolises. They did not have violence served up to them with their morning tea, blasted at them from their "tellies" nor screamed at them frequently in blazing headlines. Reverting to the frontier ways which were so much a part of their heritage, the Western Australians quickly armed themselves with handguns, sought the services of locksmiths, visited kennels to buy large guard-dogs and generally took on the coloration of a populace under siege.

By late December of the same year, some of those who had gone all-out in their security campaign were beginning to feel slightly chagrined. Another summer had come to Perth and nothing had happened of a murderous nature since Pnena Bergman's slaying.

Then, just five days before Christmas, the stricken community was to learn that Pnena's death had not been an isolated atrocity, after all. This knowledge came to them as word of the murder of beautiful 22-year-old Jillian McPherson Brewster, heiress to an Australian chocolate fortune, quickly spread.

The facts were stark. On Sunday, the 20th, Jillian had had a date to play golf with her fiance. The young man, full of happy thoughts of how the two would spend the day, arrived at her home some time around 9 A.M. Leaving his convertible parked at the curb, the caller rang Jillian's bell several times. The only response was the whimpering and barking of the heiress' pet poodle.

Using a key Jillian had given him, the man let himself in.

His head swam with the horror of what awaited him inside the house. Jillian's body was stained red, as was her bedding. There was no doubt that the young woman had been hacked and stabbed to death.

With Detective Sergeant Owen Leitch among the first to arrive at the murder scene, the forensic work got under way immediately. There were a number of similarities between the conditions around Jillian's slaying and that of Pnena

98

Bergman. The killer had entered surreptitiously, beginning his assault on the woman as she slept. The blows, probably of a hatchet, had rendered her unconscious and allowed him to go about his grisly handiwork at his leisure.

Jillian's body bore numerous hatchet and stab wounds. As in the case of Pnena, nothing had been stolen. Also, there were no indications of a sexual attack. As in the case of Pnena, the murder had taken place in the early hours of the morning. (Jillian's fiance had been with her until midnight of the 19th. He had returned bright and early at 9:00 A.M., to keep his golfing date with Jill. The killer had been there at some time in between.)

Sergeant Leitch was quick to call in Inspector Lamb. The internationally known and respected Criminal Investigation Bureau chief was forming his theories even as he entered the second murder house. A short conversation with the grieving fiance told Lamb that the man was in no way a suspect in the case. Fighting back the tears that welled up in his eyes, the bereaved fiance cooperated fully with the authorities.

His story was simple and to the point. He and Jillian had spent an uneventful evening together. Nothing untoward had happened. There had been no forewarning when he said goodnight to his fiancee around midnight that this would be the last time he'd see her alive.

A thorough search of the apartment turned up a bloody pair of scissors that might have played a part in the fatal stabbing. As the detectives widened their physical probe of the grounds, they discovered one piece of evidence that was very significant. It was a blood-covered hatchet which had been hidden behind a wooden fence.

Now came the task of talking to the unnerved and mourning neighbors of the lovely 22-year-old victim.

Lamb was particularly interested in what a woman who had lived next door had to say. The woman recalled recently having seen a man hidden in the undergrowth and staring intently into Jillian's bedroom. The woman said that Jill had not been in the habit of pulling her window shades down because she thought the remoteness of her home was enough protection against voyeurs.

The woman was staunch in her assurance that a Peeping Tom had indeed invaded Jill's privacy. She went so far as to describe how, when she had opened her own door on one occasion, the man had "melted into the shadows." The woman described him as slim, youngish and dressed in dark clothing. She could not give him details as to facial characteristics or hair coloring.

The neighbor's daughter added some pertinent facts. She revealed that at about 2:00 A.M., on the fateful morning, she had heard a door slam. A man answering the description the older woman had given had walked rapidly away from Jillian Brewster's home and disappeared into the darkness.

Lamb was almost convinced that the man he sought was a killer of opportunity. Women became his victims for the sin of being in the wrong place at the wrong time.

Rather than being gratified by the crystalization of the manhunt — at least the police knew pretty well what kind of perpetrator they had to find — Lamb felt a chilling depression invade his own fatigued body. He was aware that he would have to demand that his detectives go out into the field to find the proverbial needle in a haystack.

Files on every known sex offender in the area were carefully checked. In addition, orders were given that any suspect arrested on any sex charge at all should be questioned closely on the Berkman and Brewster murders.

Despite their diligence in following their chief's directives, detectives assigned to Perth's precincts were to spend an agonizing year of making no progress whatsoever on the baffling cases.

Then on April 7, 1961, more than a year and a quarter after the discovery of the heiress' blood-drenched body, there seemed to be an important development.

On April 7, 1961, a young man was picked up on a morals charge.

He was accused of having taken a number of small girls into nearby parks and abused them sexually. Although the man had used no force in persuading the youngsters to do his bidding, he was never the less considered enough of a sexual psychopath to be interrogated in the Berkman and Brewster killings.

Questioning was easier said than done: the suspect was a deaf mute. He was also mentally defective.

Lamb exercised the greatest amount of patience. Working with an interpreter who relayed his questions and the suspect's answers through sign language, the inspector zeroed in on the Brewster murder. He kept hitting away on the events of that pre-Christmas night when someone had stolen into Jillian's room and wantonly hacked and stabbed her to death in an orgy of blood-letting.

Suddenly, the deaf mute's face crumbled. He collapsed in a series of wracking sobs. The man admitted with gestures that he was the slayer of Jillian MacPherson Brewster. He even volunteered to accompany police officers to Jill's late home. There, in writing, he answered questions and enacted portions of the crime that convinced Lamb the right man was in custody.

However, if Inspector Lamb had hoped for a simultaneous break in the Berkman case, he was to be terribly disappointed. The suspect was able to come up with an iron-clad alibi in the February 2, 1959 knifing of Pnena Berkman.

Prosecution of the mentally and physically impaired suspect would have to be limited to accusations linking him to Jillian Brewster.

At his trial, which got under way in August, 1961, the suspect startled the courtroom by repudiating his confession. He stoutly insisted, in writing, that he had nothing to do with the December 20th hatchet attack and stabbing. The defense annotated the suspect's claim when they produced witnesses who placed him at other sites on the fatal night of Pnena Berkman's death.

However, the tide of public opinion was running against the suspect. Perhaps the original revulsion at the barbarity of the Jillian Brewster murder, or a continuing fear that unless something was done quickly, lightning would strike again, motivated the jury. Whatever the reason, the suspect was convicted and sentenced to be hanged at a later date.

Defense strategy was to seize on the man's impaired mental capacity. They used this as the wedge for opening a series of appeals that delayed his execution.

The public soon lost interest in the case. The fact that there were no further homicides that compared in any detail to the slayings of Pnena Berkman and Jillian Brewster during the ensuing months indicated to them that the right man was behind bars.

Then, on January 27, 1963, the false sense of security that had lulled Perth residents was shattered.

It all started in what psychiatrists call "The Hour of the Wolf" at 2:30 A.M. (This is the time, the alienists report, when mental aberrations take on their most deadly form.)

The scene was a quiet suburb of Perth known as Cotteloe. Little-used Napier Street had become a favored trysting ground for Perth couples.

The love idyll between a middle-aged business executive and a young and beautiful barmaid was ripped asunder by a single bullet. The slug tore through the car on the passenger side. Its path was through the woman's hand and into the neck of her lover.

Although not seriously wounded, the couple were treated at Fremantel Hospital. Having calmed down from their devastating experience, the couple submitted to an extensive interview by interested police personnel.

They were able to give a detailed description of their assailant. The man, they reported, had been in his 20s, slightly built and of medium height. His actions had been furtive in the manner of a Peeping Tom. The male victim of the gunman's assault was sure that the perpetrator had been spying on him and his girlfriend.

An immediate dragnet was stretched across the neighborhood. Police cars criss-crossed the streets in hopes of intercepting the night stalker who was said to be dressed in dark clothing.

Meanwhile, within the hour, an officer assigned to communications was to receive a call from an hysterical young woman. The caller reported that her father had been shot and was dying. The woman begged for an ambulance to be dispatched to her house. Her address was only a mile from the site of the lovers' lane shooting.

Racing to the latest violence, officers found 55-year-old George Osmond Walmsley, a retired grocer, lying on the floor of his vestibule. The pajama-and-bathrobe-clad middle-aged man was bleeding profusely from a gunshot wound in the forehead.

The wounded man died minutes later while being treated in the emergency room of Royal Perth Hospital.

Pulling herself together as best as she could, the distraught daughter told police that the family had been awakened from a sound sleep by somebody ringing the front doorbell. Her father had donned his bathrobe and gone to the door. Upon opening it, he had been greeted by the blast from a small-caliber weapon. The family had rushed to the father's aid too late. They had seen a shadowy figure running down the street away from the house.

Investigating officers immediately relayed this latest intelligence to Inspector Lamb. In a matter of minutes, he was fully dressed and on post, directing an all-out search for the gunman.

The early morning of blood had just gotten underway. At exactly 4:13 A.M., the third complaint came crackling over the phone wire. This one was from a woman who lived in a boarding house close by the Walmsley home. Alerted by the police sirens screaming through the area, the woman had raced to tell a male boarder that a killing had taken place. The boarder had been taking advantage of the warmth of the Australian summer to sleep on an open veranda.

The young man, 19-year-old John Sturkey, a student at the University of Western Australia, was in no condition to listen to accounts of another killing. He, too, had been shot in the head. The victim was semi-conscious and bleeding profusely from his wound. He'd been shot at point-blank range by an intruder who had walked up to him out of the early morning darkness and fired a small-caliber slug into the student's skull.

John Lindsay Sturkey was the second man to die in the Royal Perth Hospital emergency room that morning.

And still the senseless carnage went on. At 8:10 A.M., a third report was received from the Cotteloe district. This time it concerned a 29-year-old accountant. The man was rushed to the hospital, where he was judged in extremely critical condition. Doctors thought there was an outside chance of saving his life. They worked frantically to do what they could.

The exact moment of the assault on the accountant could not be pinpointed, since he'd been alone when it had occurred. Best estimates of physicians was that the shooting had taken place within the last six hours. This was within the time frame of the original lovers' lane shooting.

As news of the early morning blood-letting swept through the city, residents felt the same numbing panic that had gripped them in 1959. Once again a maniacal killer was stalking Perth's quiet streets, leaving behind a fearful toll of dead and wounded. Once again there seemed to be no defense against his murderous rages.

Now Inspector Atholl Wedd was put in charge of the widening investigation. His first move was to cancel all police leaves. The department would remain on emergency status until a suspect was brought in.

With infinite patience, Wedd went over everything that was known thus far.

All of the shootings had been carried out with a .22-caliber weapon. On the surface, this might have ruled out a linkage with the knifings of Pnena Berkman and Jillian Brewster.

Yet there were similarities that could prove more than coincidences.

The most important of these were: First, the hours in which the killer struck. They were invariably between midnight and dawn. Second, the fact that the killer appeared to be a voyeur. In each case the man had apparently spied on his victims for some time before dispatching them.

Wedd went public with his findings thus far. He issued urgent appeals for civilian cooperation in the manhunt. Everybody within the area was asked to contact authorities immediately upon seeing suspicious activity of any nature—especially should that activity take place at night.

Once again there was a run on locksmiths and stores selling firearms. Perth became a city under siege for a second time. The public thirsted for news of the wounded accountant. By now it was certain that the man would survive. But he would remain brain-damaged.

Six and a half months were to pass without any new development. Australia was deep in the chill of its down-under winter. The date was the wind-swept and drenched evening of August 10, 1963.

A young couple returned to their home on Wavell Road in Dalkeith. They were chattering happily about the fine party they'd attended. They were anxious to get inside the warmth and comfort of their house and to be with their eight-month-old baby. They were aware of the late hour— 2:00 A.M.—and were concerned as to whether they had kept the attractive 19-year-old baby sitter, Shirley McLeod, up too late. However, the college science student was a happy girl and probably would have no feelings of having been taken advantage of.

Cheerfully the couple called out, "Hello, Shirley. We're back."

The only sounds that greeted them were the whimpered mewlings of their infant child. This was totally unlike the baby—especially when Shirley McLeod cared for him.

Entering the living room, the husband found the sophomore seated on the couch, her head lolling to one side. She appeared to have dozed off.

Moving closer, the baby's father gasped in horror. The rivulet of blood that ran down Shirley's face from a gunshot wound in her head told him all he needed to know. The sophomore had been shot to death.

There was the, by now, all too familiar gathering of forensic experts and plainclothes police officers. There was the same preliminary report as in the past. Shirley McLeod had been slain with a small-bore weapon—probably a .22.

Making a search of the premises, Inspector Fred Douglas discovered the path the killer had taken through an inadvertently unlocked side door from the built-in garage of the house into the living room. The killer had spied on the girl from a position behind the double doors of the dining room before shooting her.

Neighbors had heard no sounds of a struggle. A check into the dead girl's background showed there was nothing in her personal life that could have led to her slaying. From every indication, it appeared that the Peeping Tom sniper's self-imposed vacation was over. Once more he was back at his grisly work.

Lamb once again made a public appeal. He covered much of the same groundwork he had in the past. This time he specifically asked Perth residents to be on the lookout for any man who owned a .22-caliber weapon and acted the least bit odd. He tried to calm the jitters of the public by reminding them that the police would not rest until they had apprehended the random killer. He pointed out that 50 detectives were working full time on the case. He asked anybody with any information to contact authorities over a 24-hour hot-line which had been set up to handle communications on this case alone.

The public jumped to. Soon the hot-line was flooded with calls. Most of the information given by well-meaning callers led to blind alleys. Still, the bone-tired detectives remained alert. There was always the hope that the next call would prove of some value.

Then, on August 17th, it came. An elderly man reported that while he and his wife had been gathering wild flowers near the Canning River, they had come upon a new-looking .22-caliber rifle, partially covered by brush. Knowing the importance of not disturbing potentially valuable evidence, neither the man nor his wife had touched the weapon. Instead, they had raced to the phone to relay news of their discovery.

Inspector Douglas rushed to Mount Pleasant where the couple waited to point out the gun to him. Handling the rifle gingerly, Douglas made a preliminary judgement that the weapon was in good working order. In fact, it had been fired recently. The owner had not bothered to clean it after the firing.

Ballistics experts assembled immediately at the police department range. A test-firing of the .22 brought electrifying results. Striations on the fired bullet matched exactly those on the one which had been taken from the skull of Shirley McLeod.

At last, after so many long months of agonizing frustration, Inspector Lamb now felt that he had the murder weapon. (This despite the fact that a match could not be made with other slugs which had been taken from the bodies of other victims because of the poor condition of those bullets.)

Lamb speculated at length.

Why had the killer left the .22 in the bushes rather than having thrown it into the nearby river?

The answer that evolved in exhaustive discussions between Lamb and Douglas seemed logical.

The killer had meant to hide the gun rather than destroy it. This because the cunning sniper had

107

reasoned that he would have further use for the weapon.

A plan was hatched. The critical .22 was impounded under lock and key. Then, a second gun, closely resembling the first one, was placed in the very same bushes where the couple's discovery had been made. To insure that should the killer show up for the weapon he would not be able to move quickly, it was decided to wire the rifle to a bush to impede its removal. Then a round-the-clock stake-out was set.

The discomforts endured by the teams of detectives as they hunkered down in their improvised and camouflaged blind would have been too much for less dedicated men. But these law officers were goaded by the memories of innocent victims who had paid with their lives because of a cunning killer's maniacal need to destroy human life.

Without protest, the detectives went about their agonizing vigil, mindless of the bitter late-winter winds and torrential cold rains that chilled them.

Their dedication paid off.

At 1:20 A.M. on the night of September 1, 1963, with Detectives William Hawker and Peter Skehan on watch, it happened.

A car moved slowly into view. It stopped and the driver cut the headlights. Could this be it, or was this just another couple looking for privacy on a deserted road?

The answer came after long minutes. Hawker and Skehan felt every nerve in their cramped bodies come alive. The lone occupant of the car, a slim man dressed in dark clothing, got out. He moved quickly toward the waiting bush. He bent down and began tugging at the .22.

The two detectives moved silently forward. They came up behind the suspect and took him from either side. There was a brief struggle. But the suspect was no match for the burly detectives.

There was the click of metal handcuffs being clamped to wrists. The suspect was firmly in tow.

At Criminal Investigation Bureau headquarters, the man

identified himself as Eric Edgar Cooke. He said he was 32 years old and gave his occupation as a truck driver. The suspect, slightly built and only 5 feet, 4 inches tall, told the officers that he was married and the father of seven children.

Chief Lamb headed the intensive questioning of the suspect. He was assisted by Detective Sergeants William Nielson and A.J. Parker. Complying with Australian law, the police kept Cooke's answers secret pending trial. But the announcement that a prime suspect was being held in the shooting death of Shirley McLeod electrified the public. A large group of citizens gathered outside headquarters in hopes of getting a look at the man.

Cooke was formally charged in Shirley's murder the following morning. However, in a far-ranging press conference with impatient reporters, Lamb reported that the .22 used in Shirley's murder was not the same gun fired in the killings of John Sturkey and George Walmsley.

On September 3rd, Cooke was taken to the Nedlands-Cotteloe district for further questioning.

On September 4th, he was taken aboard a launch in the Swan River near Perth. Two police divers were among those on the boat. They found a rifle.

While maintaining their veil of secrecy concerning the field trips, the police were ready on September 5th to charge Cooke with the murders of Sturkey and Walmsley.

All Perth was breathless in anticipation of the revelations that the populace was sure would come at Cooke's trial. At this point all they knew was that an ugly, diminutive man had been charged in three separate killings.

The trial finally got under way on November 25th. A jury of eight men and four women assembled in the Perth Criminal Court and heard Mr. Justice Virtue call them to order.

With R.D. Wilson, Queen's Counsel, conducting the prosecution, the packed courtroom heard Detective

Nielson recount Cooke's statement to him concerning the murders of Sturkey and Walmsley.

Nielson testified that Cooke had told him that following a drinking session in a Perth hotel, he'd broken into a house and stolen a .22 rifle and some ammunition. He had also "borrowed" a car from a nearby garage.

Feeling restless, he'd driven around until he'd come upon the couple parked on Napier Street. He'd spied upon them, but had become enraged when the middle-aged man had thrown a whiskey bottle at him. He'd fired twice at the car, wounding the man and woman.

Detective Nielson quoted the defendant as saying that he had no reason to shoot, but "just wanted to hurt somebody."

Cooke had felt a surge of power following the lovers' lane episode. This emotional outburst had led him to shoot Walmsley while the victim slept on his own premises.

Once again Nielson quoted Cooke: "He was on his back and I walked up to about four feet from him. I pointed the rifle at him and shot him. I do not know why. I did not have the slightest reason for harming him. He was a complete stranger to me."

The same line of reasoning followed the rendition of the other shootings in which Cooke had been implicated.

The defense, headed by K.W. Hatfield, based its entire case on the horrors that had beset Cooke in the little man's own life. Hatfield hit away at the fact that Cooke had been deformed as a child because of a harelip and cleft palate. He'd also been rejected and abused by his parents. Schoolmates had mocked him because of his physical abnormalities and his personality.

He'd become accident-prone as a young man, having suffered a number of industrial injuries while employed as an unskilled worker. Among these were several traumas to his head.

Hatfield contended that the humiliations and physical pain his client had undergone had led to sexual aberrations—not the least of which were voyeurism and housebreaking. He had also engaged in arson. He'd served 18 months in prison for having set fire to a church where he'd been rejected after auditioning for the choir. He'd also torched a movie house.

To his surprise, he'd successfully courted and married an attractive young woman. But his joy had been short-lived. This because his first-born child had been mentally retarded and another had been born with only a stump for a forearm. (The other children had been normal.)

Under the friendly questioning of his attorney, Cooke took the stand to review the feeling of power he had experienced prior to and at the actual time of the shootings and the remorse he had felt afterward.

"Were you able to prevent yourself from doing this shooting?" Hatfield asked.

"No, sir," came the defendant's reply. "The power was so great that I could not stop myself. It was not until afterward when I read the details in the papers, that I fully realized the dreadful things I had done."

To the jury hearing the evidence, Cooke's remorse had been much too little and too late. They found him guilty as charged of willful murder, with a mandatory death sentence.

On October 24, 1964, Eric Cooke was hanged.

Until this day, he remains a prime suspect in the 1959 killings of Pnena Berkman and Jillian Brewster, as well as for the lethal shootings of which he was convicted. But he was never brought to trial in the knifings.

"THE CASE OF COLORADO'S
MILLIONAIRE BREWER COORS"

by Ellery Queen

As nasty and useless as was the abduction-murder on or
about February 9, 1960, of Adolph Coors III of Morrison
and Golden, Colorado, to the gourmet of such crime fare
the case becomes a triumph of man's ingenuity in pursuit
of man. Not often does a criminal act result in so many of
the forces of human indignation collaborating to corner
and trap a taker of human life.

In the Coors affair the manhunt, pursued for nine
months, was continent-wide and bi-national. It began with
the deputies, assistants, horse posse and jeep patrol of a famous and battle-scarred Colorado sheriff, who were soon
joined by the Colorado State Patrol and the FBI. Before
their man was run down, these were augmented by a district attorney, another sheriff, and a coroner from the same
state; various penal authorities in California entered the
field; the police of Atlantic City, New Jersey, made an important contribution; and a magazine of international cir-
culation performed a public service, the result of which was
to draw to the chase first the Toronto Metropolitan Police,
then the Royal Canadian Mounted Police, and finally the
local officers as far away as Vancouver, British Columbia.

And throughout the hunt, like the counterpoint in a
Bach fugue, ran the motif of citizen cooperation, as per-

sonified by various ordinary joes with good luck, good memories, and a simple affinity for justice. For all the professional patience and cunning exhibited by the law, two of the three most important breaks in the Coors case must be credited to the so-called unglamorous public.

The FBI, of course, was the great coordinating and investigatory agency; and the purely detective story of the search for Adolph Coors III's killer is largely the story of the FBI's activities in the case.

In this context the Coors investigation is exceptional. Seldom indeed do the bread-and-butter facts of an FBI investigation become public knowledge; J. Edgar Hoover's Bureau prefers to work in anonymity and darkness. But in this case "a detailed summary of information developed by the Federal Bureau of Investigation during our extensive investigation" was sent by the FBI special agent in charge to the district attorney of the county of jurisdiction, for his official use pending prosecution; and an almost verbatim account of this summary was published in a prominent newspaper the following day, "with only confidential material deleted."

For once, then, we can follow an FBI job step by step in its brilliant work.

Adolph Coors III was one of the three sons of a wealthy Colorado businessman. With his brothers, Joe and Bill, Ad ran the Coors enterprises—the Coors Brewery, one of the nation's largest, located in the town of Golden; and the Coors Porcelain Company, a huge ceramics plant which not only made pottery, but also held government contracts for the manufacture of nose cones for guided missiles.

Ad Coors was 44, married, had four teenage children, and lived in a rambling mountain ranch house in nearby Morrison—a rather shy, agreeable man who was one of the most popular citizens of Jefferson County.

As the FBI Denver agents and Sheriff Art Wermuth of

Jefferson County were soon to establish, Adolph Coors III stepped out of his Morrison ranch home shortly before eight o'clock on the overcast morning of Tuesday, February 9, climbed into his green-and-white station wagon, an International Travelall, and set out on his daily drive to the Coors plant some fifteen miles away.

About two hours later Daniel Crocker, a young driver for a Denver dairy, found the Coors Travelall parked on a little wooden bridge spanning Turkey Creek, some three miles from Morrison. The engine was running, the radio was on, and the car was empty. The milk driver waited for the owner to come back and unblock the narrow bridge; but when fifteen minutes passed and no one appeared, Crocker drove the station wagon a few yards off the bridge, got back into his truck, and proceeded on his isolated milk route.

Returning later, the milk driver saw the Travelall standing just where he had left it, still unoccupied. Disturbed, he drove into Morrison and telephoned the Colorado State Patrol Headquarters in Denver. Within minutes a patrol cruiser, alerted by radiotelephone, was inspecting the deserted station wagon beside Turkey Creek bridge. Then the state patrolman, George Hedricks, stepped onto the bridge to the spot where Crocker had reported finding the abandoned car originally parked.

Spotting some fresh-looking scarlet stains on the bridge railing at that point, Hedricks hastened to report by radiophone to his Headquarters, where through the license plate number the car's ownership was immediately established, and the officer was instructed to get in touch with the Coors family.

Hedricks sped to the nearest house in the foothills and phoned the Coors Brewery in Golden.

Adolph Coors III was not in Golden. In fact, Joe and Bill Coors had been worrying for some time over their brother's failure to arrive at the plant at their usual early-morning executive meeting; they had already telephoned

114

Ad's wife Mary in Morrison, only to be told that Ad had left home before eight A.M. The brothers had even checked with the Denver offices of the company, but no one there had seen or heard from Ad.

Patrolman Hedricks phoned in the grim information, and the hunt was on.

The Jefferson County Sheriff, Art Wermuth, an eight-times-decorated World War II hero and one of the best known lawmen in the modern West, took immediate charge, aided by the chief investigator, Captain Harold Bray, his assistants, his deputies, his renowned horse posse and jeep patrol, and a small army of Colorado state patrolmen under personal command of Chief Gilbert Carrel.

One of their first discoveries was the headgear Ad Coors had been wearing when he had left home that morning: a light tan baseball cap. It was found along with a mysterious pecan-brown felt hat, unidentified, at the edge of the creek on its south side, below the east end of the bridge.

There was a floodgate upstream, which was ordered closed. As the icy waters receded, a pair of plastic rimmed eyeglasses became visible in the creekbed. They were identified as the eyeglasses of Adolph Coors III.

The Travelall was taken into Golden for a going over.

Sheriff Wermuth and Chief Carrel agreed that the disappearance was beginning to look like a kidnaping.

"But I don't like those glasses in the creek," the Sheriff muttered. "And that blood."

"Bungled?" the State Trooper Chief suggested.

"Could be." And Wermuth made a steely little speech to the more than 100 deputies, possemen and troopers assembled for orders. "Men, this is a manhunt. We are looking for Ad Coors. He may be dead. Or badly injured. Or being held prisoner in these hills. And we're looking for another man—men—who may have assaulted him and abducted him. Let's go!"

115

Men on horseback explored cavernous gullies, dark and scrub-clogged gulches. Jeeps labored like bugs along old cattle trails or sank hub-deep into swampy roads. Climbers bellied on to rock ledges, peered into caves. Darkness fell. And at the Coors house family and friends waited for some word, some sign that Ad was alive—if only from a kidnaper. But there was nothing.

Undersheriff Lew Hawley, one of Wermuth's most trusted assistants, took a section of the Turkey Creek bridge railing showing the bloodstains, and some blood-spattered dirt found just beneath the railing, along with Ad Coors' baseball cap, and stepped into a plane bound for Washington and the central laboratories of the FBI.

And a team of FBI agents from the Denver office of Scott J. Werner, laconic Special Agent in Charge, came quietly into the case.

On that Tuesday they let it be known that they were merely "observers." But on Wednesday morning the FBI entered the case officially and clamped the tight-fitting lid of FBI secrecy over it.

The Bureau's "detailed summary of information" seven months later revealed why.

On that Wednesday morning, February 10, 1960, 24 hours after Adolph Coors III vanished, a special delivery letter addressed to his wife at her Morrison ranch home arrived to announce that her husband was being held for ransom.

The kidnap letter, from its postal markings, had been mailed in Denver the previous afternoon, probably before 1:45 P.M.—within a few short hours of the snatch. There was no handwriting on either envelope or enclosure; both were typed. The letter said:

"Mrs. Coors: Your husband has been kidnaped.
His car is by Turkey Creek. Call the police or F.B.I.:

116

he dies. Cooperate: he lives. Ransom $200,000 in tens and $300,000 in twenties.

"There will be no negotiating.

"Bills: used / non-consecutive / unrecorded / unmarked.

"Warning: we will know if you call the police or record the serial numbers.

"Directions:

"Place money & this letter & envelope in one suitcase or bag.

"Have two men with a car ready to make the delivery.

"When all set, advertise a tractor for sale in Denver Post section 69. Sign ad King Ranch, Fort Lupton.

"Wait at NA 9-4455 for instructions after ad appears.

"Deliver immediately after receiving call. Any delay will be regarded as a stall to set up a stake-out.

"Understand this: Adolph's life is in your hands. We have no desire to commit murder. All we want is that money. If you follow the instructions, he will be released unharmed within 48 hours after the money is received."

There was no signature.

The FBI findings regarding this ransom letter are characteristic of the Bureau's attention to detail. Paper, watermarks, typing were categorized and pursued. The machine on which the message and address had been typed was identified as either a Royalite or a Hermes, probably the former. The Royalite is an inexpensive portable manufactured by the Royal Typewriter Company in Holland; and it has been on sale in the United States for about three years.

Further: From its neat and correct appearance the letter was presumed to have been the work of an experienced typist. From the facts that "not a single error or spelling" occurred in the text and—except for the profuse use of colons—that the punctuation was "practically perfect," it was concluded that "the author is reasonably well educated and writes well."

So minute was the FBI scrutiny that the summary even noted an odd fact about the ransom note's use of colons: "While the writer double spaces after each period, he single spaces after use of a colon." Since in common typing practice two spaces are used after colons, this was an idiosyncrasy of the ransom note typist—therefore of possibly high value to a prosecutor as evidence against the kidnaper if and when he should be apprehended and tried!

Sources of the notepaper and envelope were narrowed down to two Denver department stores—the Denver Dry Goods Company and the May-D and F Company.

But all this went on in a complete blackout. That Wednesday the FBI had nothing to say for publication, and Sheriff Wermuth was constrained to state to newsmen that there had been no demands for ransom.

The hunt for Ad Coors and his abductors intensified and broadened. Out-of-the-way ranches, hundreds of remote mountain cabins, were searched. The Alpine Rescue Team, a Jefferson County mountain-climbing group, went into action. An Air Force helicopter from Denver's Lowry Field took the air. There were now hundreds of searchers in the field—not only Sheriff Wermuth's men and Chief Carrel's troopers, but volunteers from among Colorado's aroused citizenry.

Meanwhile, the parents of the missing man, hastily summoned from a Hawaii vacation, arrived home by air. And now a queer coincidence was recalled. Adolph III's father over a quarter of a century before had himself been the target of a kidnap plot that, fortunately, had proved unsuccessful.

The elder Coors told the lawmen simply, "I am dealing with crooks who . . . have something I want to buy—my

118

son. The price is secondary."

While Sheriff Wermuth sat on the news in the interests of the younger Coors' safety, the Federal men went silently and thoroughly about their business.

Several witnesses were turned up who claimed to have noticed, on various occasions in the period just prior to February 9, a 1951, yellow Mercury four-door sedan parked in the neighborhood of the Turkey Creek bridge. A caretaker and a maid at the Coors ranch home mentioned having seen, several times before the fateful Tuesday morning, a yellow sedan hanging about the vicinity. All the witnesses said the yellow car carried Colorado plates, and one of them stated emphatically that the license number began with "AT 62—."

The job, then, had been carefully cased and plotted. Confirmation of this arose from S.C. Nielsen, a school bus driver, who had driven across the little Turkey Creek bridge twice that Tuesday morning, first at 7:35 A.M., and again about ten minutes later. At neither time had Nielsen seen a car on or near the bridge. Since Ad Coors had undoubtedly reached the bridge at just about eight A.M., it must have been blockaded to stop him there on a tight time schedule by someone who had studied not only his daily routine but the morning traffic conditions about the bridge as well.

Thursday passed; Friday. So far as newsmen covering the case were concerned, nothing had developed except that Mary Grant Coors had collapsed and was under a doctor's care.

But undercover activity was considerable. At Mrs. Coors' plea Sheriff Wermuth withdrew his guards from the premises to give the kidnaper, if he were watching, a clear field and a chance for safe contact. An ex-FBI kidnap expert, A.S. Reeder, now Denver undersheriff and warden of the Denver County Jail, was surreptitiously called in to act as liaison between the frantic family and the kidnapers.

The instructions in the note were followed precisely. The advertisement was placed in section 69 of the Denver *Post,* the ransom money was put together in the amounts and denominations designated, and the family waited.

No word came from the kidnaper.

No word ever came.

Had he been scared off? Had he cut and run, leaving his victim behind? Perhaps helplessly trussed up in a lonely cave — or mine shaft somewhere, to die of thirst and starvation?

The efforts of the searchers multiplied. On Saturday the Sheriff alerted volunteer fire departments in mountain areas, calling on them to check all cabins and shacks in their districts. Deputies were ordered to visit outlying grocery stores in the back country on the trail of any unusually heavy purchases of food supplies that might have been laid in to stock a hideout. Scores of tips and leads were checked and found false. No trace of Ad Coors or his abductors turned up.

Nevertheless, progress was being made. The FBI determined that during 1960 four Mercury automobiles were registered in Colorado with plate numbers beginning "AT 62 — ." Only one of these four was a yellow 1951 four-door sedan!

License plate "AT 6203" was registered to one Walter Osborne of No. 1435 Pearl Street, Denver. The serial number of Osborne's car was 51LA38766M, and his license-bureau record showed a clear recent photograph, as required by Colorado's new license procedure. And to a copy of his license application was affixed a print of Osborne's right index finger.

The fingerprint was rushed to Washington for processing.

Meanwhile the Federal men swiftly descended in force on Denver's 1435 Pearl Street. In the plain apartment building

120

at that address they learned that, while Osborne had lived in Apartment 305 there since April 1, 1956, he had suddenly decamped . . . on February 10, the morning after Adolph Coors III's disappearance!

Mrs. Viola Merys, manager of the building, praised Osborne as an "ideal tenant." "About eight A.M. he rang my buzzer," Mrs. Merys said. "He told me he was leaving, going back to school at the University of Colorado at Boulder."

There was no Walter Osborne in Boulder. There never had been.

Then on Wednesday evening, February 17, at 9:30, the police of Atlantic City, New Jersey investigated a burning automobile at the city dump. The car was thoroughly gutted before the fire could be put out, but enough remained to lead police to the conclusion that the fire had been deliberately set. The car was a yellow 1951 Mercury four-door sedan, serial number 51LA38766M. The license plates were missing.

As a matter of routine, the Atlantic City police notified the FBI of their find.

With Osborne's car in custody undergoing scientific examination, his hurriedly abandoned Denver apartment available for fingerprinting, as well as the last known place in which he had been employed—a Denver paint manufacturing firm, Benjamin Moore and Company—the FBI was now able to pinpoint the missing owner of the Mercury. On being processed at FBI Headquarters, the print on his Colorado license application, the prints from the Pearl Street apartment, and some raised at Benjamin Moore and Company, as well as his driver's license photograph, all revealed that Walter Osborne was not his name at all. It was an alias for FBI Number 605-861-A . . . one Joseph Corbett, Jr., born in Seattle, Washington on October 25, 1928.

And who was Joseph Corbett, Jr.?

An escaped killer!

121

On December 11, 1950, while attending the school of letters and science at the University of California in Berkeley, Corbett had shot to death a hitch-hiking Air Force sergeant he had picked up during an auto drive. Corbett's story had been that the sergeant had pulled a gun on him and, grappling to defend himself, Corbett had managed to turn the weapon on his assailant. Just the same, Corbett had pleaded guilty to a lesser charge of second-degree murder and had been sentenced in San Rafael to five years to life imprisonment. He had been sent first to San Quentin, then to Terminal Island, and finally to the California Institution for Men at Chino.

On August 1, in 1955, Corbett had managed to escape from the Chino prison and he had been at large ever since.

On March 23, 1960, the FBI disseminated 100,000 "Wanted" circulars on Joseph Corbett, Jr., naming him to its Hall of Infamy list of the "ten most wanted" criminals in the United States.

The flier, stating that Corbett was wanted for "inter-state flight—murder," did not mention the Coors case; but during the following week the Denver FBI chief, Werner, sent a letter to all typewriter firms and pawnshops in the area, seeking information about a Royalite typewriter with a specified serial number; some Denverites who owned Royalite portables were visited by FBI agents for a check of their machines, and to these people had been shown police "mug" shots of a young man; and then Corbett's photograph was published in the newspaper. A lot of people put two and two together to arrive at the Coors case connection.

Very quickly it became common knowledge that Joseph Corbett, Jr., was wanted by the FBI and the Colorado authorities in connection with the disappearance of Ad Coors.

As a result, the tidal wave of "Helpful Henry tips" that inundates all such investigations descended on the heads of the manhunters. Corbett had been "seen" near Pike's Peak; holed up in a Laguna Beach, California, seaside shack; across the U.S.-Mexico border. Motel people, diner attendants, hot-dog-stand operators claimed to have seen him or served him food on February 9, the crucial date. The yellow Mercury, too, was "remembered" by many—its reputed path stretched across the map of Colorado in all directions. Each claim was patiently checked out by the Federal men and Sheriff Wermuth's by-now haggard deputies. Each came to zero.

Two months after Ad Coors stepped off the little Turkey Creek bridge into oblivion, the FBI took a rare step. It broadcast a national plea for all citizens to help in solving the Coors mystery.

What the FBI did not broadcast was the scope of its circumstantial findings in the case.

As a partial sample of a very long and involved *precis:*

They had squeezed a great deal out of the mysterious, brown-felt, snap-brim hat found under the bridge beside Ad Coors' tan baseball cap. It was size 7³/₈; in January, 1951, while Corbett was being held in California for the Air Force sergeant's murder, a size 7³/₈ hat found in his room was placed on his head by police and it had fitted him perfectly.

Moreover, the brown snap-brim had been purchased at the May Company department store in Denver between mid-1956 and mid-1958. "Walter Osborne" had rented the Pearl Street apartment on April 1, 1956.

Also, one of the witnesses who had reported seeing a 1951, yellow Mercury sedan parked near Turkey Creek bridge in the "casing" period before February 9, was sure that the man sitting behind the wheel had been wearing a brown, snap-brim hat. And two persons who had known Corbett in Denver had stated that on numerous occasions they had seen him wearing a brown, snap-brim hat. When a hat identical with the one found under the bridge was shown to these people, they identified it as similar in style and color to the hat worn by the driver of the Mercury and by Corbett.

An employee of the May-D and F Company, on viewing photographs of five different men, including one of Corbett, picked out that of Corbett as being most nearly like the man who had purchased a Royalite portable typewriter on October 8, 1959 . . . just such a machine as the ransom letter had probably been typed on. (The efforts of the FBI to locate the exact Royalite were, of course, directed toward scientifically connecting the machine on which the ransom note had been typed with a machine which could be identified as Corbett's.)

Internal evidence in the ransom letter had indicated that the kidnaper was "reasonably well educated" and "an experienced typist." Not only had Corbett attended college in the state of Washington and California, but the FBI determined that in 1946, while a teen-age physics major at the University of Washington in Seattle, Corbett had operated a student typing service; and in 1955 (presumably after his escape from Chino), he had been employed in California by the Adams Rite Manufacturing Company as a typist.

The Federal Bureau found itself in a curious position: While it had developed a mass of circumstantial evidence, it had been unable to turn up the two prerequisites of most successful homicide prosecutions: the dead body of the victim and the living body of the killer.

Where was Adolph Coors III—dead, or even (conceivably, though most improbably) alive?

Where was Joseph Corbett, Jr.—also either dead or alive? For some close to the case were beginning to speculate that Corbett might be as cold turkey as they presumed poor Ad Coors to be. Most American kidnapings for ransom, they pointed out, were traditionally the work of several confederates. Corbett may have goofed his part of the job, they said, or chickened out at the last moment, and was therefore killed by an accomplice for his ineptitude or lack of moxie.

But if the FBI and the Jefferson County Sheriff's office held such a notion, they did not permit it to impede their official efforts. The hunt for a clue to Corbett's whereabouts was pressed harder. The foothill and mountain area around Denver, where Adolph Coors III had vanished, was gone over, section by section, again and again, for some trace of him.

None was found.

Spring passed; summer came. Colorado is popular with summer vacationers, and there was hope that some tourist might stumble upon a clue when the hills and woods were swarming with pleasure-bent folks. None did.

September . . . and the night air of the Colorado Rockies was beginning to nip. The Summer people, the out-of-staters, began their outward trek. With Fall around the corner, the hopes of the lawmen fell.

And then, as if this were a bad play written by a clumsy playwright who knew no cleverer way of springing his dramatic surprise . . . then came September 11, and a young man named Edward Green, who drove a delivery truck for, of all things, a Denver pizza company.

On that day Green went out target shooting alone. On this sun-drenched and winy-aired Sunday he drove southeast from Denver, heading for the mountains. On a lonely road in Douglas County Green parked, took his gun, got out, and strolled whistling into the woods.

On what looked like a game trail young Green ran across a pair of men's brown shoes in what appeared good condition, although when out of curiosity he picked one up he found it full of spiderwebs. Walking on, he stumbled on a pair of men's dark-gray flannel slacks with a brown belt in its loops. He kicked the trousers and, hearing a jingle, explored the pockets. He found 43 cents, a silver key chain holding eleven keys, and a small silver penknife bearing the engraved initials "AC III."

"It was then I realized," Green later told police, "that all this must be connected with the Ad Coors case. I hightailed it out of there!"

Green hightailed it back to Englewood, where he lived, and reported his discovery to a friend on the local police force, Patrolman Charles R. Riddle. Riddle leaped for a phone; within seconds he was announcing the electrifying news to Denver FBI Special Agent in Charge Werner.

Green guided the Federal men and deputies of Douglas County Sheriff John Hammond to the scene of his find; they worked like demons against the lengthening shadows in the woods to lay hands on all they could root out. Some scattered bones were found. There was an isolated dump nearby, and below it a ski-shaped tie clasp with the initials "AC III" was turned up, as well as a man's navy-blue nylon zippered jacket, a white shirt with a faint green check, underwear, tie, socks and a blanket.

All the clothing was positively identified as having been worn by Ad Coors on the morning he vanished.

The nylon jacket had been eloquently pulled inside out. The green-checked white shirt was torn and bloodstained, as was the undershirt.

During the next three days the entire area of the trail and dump was gone over inch by inch. Numerous other bones were found. And a silver wrist watch with a brown leather band inside which was the inscription, "A. COORS, III."

On September 14, the bones, which had been turned over to Douglas County Coroner C.D. Andrews in Castle Rock, the county seat, were identified as those of "a mature human male approximately six feet tall." Ad Coors had been a little over six feet tall.

126

But this was still legally indecisive. Until the next day, when Coroner Andrews himself made the definitive find about 200 yards from where most of the other bones had been located. It was a human skull. Doctor Arthur A. Kelly, Adolph Coors III's dentist, identified the dental work in the skull as "identical to that which had been performed previously on Coors."

From laboratory examination of irregular holes in the jacket, shirt and undershirt, and two holes in a right scapula bone found in the dump area, the FBI technicians were satisfied that Coors had been shot twice in the back, almost certainly at close range. Since the slugs were not found, they could conclude nothing about the caliber of the death gun.

Poor Ad Coors had been found at last, and his fate made specific. There was a deposition on file by a Mrs. Rosemary Stitt, who lived near Turkey Creek bridge. On Tuesday morning, February 9, she had heard loud voices coming from the vicinity of the bridge, and "a cracking which sounded like lightning hitting a tree or possibly a shot from a gun."

"It was about eight o'clock," Mrs. Stitt had stated, declaring that she was sure of the time "because I had just sent the children off to Bear Creek School."

It was likely, then, that Ad Coors had been ambushed that morning at Turkey Creek Bridge. Perhaps he had put up a battle, or had gamely refused to cooperate; in either event, the abductor had lost his head and shot the man he had intended and painstakingly planned to hold for ransom. He must then have driven with the body to the lonely dump in Douglas County and flung it there; wild animals in the intervening months had done the rest. The killer had then calmly returned to Denver and posted the ransom letter to his victim's wife.

The remaining question now was: Was Joseph Corbett, Jr., alias Walter Osborne, that man?

The FBI summary, of course, does not make this allegation. It merely records its findings.

They are impressive. Soil and mud scraped from the undercarriage of Osborne-Corbett's yellow Mercury found ablaze in the Atlantic City dump have been analyzed and compared with samples of soil and road-surfacing materials in the area where Ad Coors' bones and clothing were found.

Three pieces of metal chain were discovered in a gray pail on the Pearl Street, Denver, premises where Osborne-Corbett had his apartment — a pail which yielded an unmistakable fingerprint of Corbett's. This seems to link up with another FBI finding: on February 24, 1959 — a full year before the Coors kidnap-slaying — Corbett had purchased a postal money order in the amount of $15.80 payable to Kline's Prince Enterprises. Kline's Prince Enterprises, according to the Bureau, "handles only one item, a U.S. Navy surplus combination hand and leg iron." The price of a single pair of these unusual implements is $3.95. $15.80, the summary points out, would be exactly the price of four pairs.

In the incinerator at 1435 Pearl Street the remains of four black handcuff cases were dug out. On April 25, 1959, Osborne-Corbett had purchased a money order in the amount of $38 payable to the Big Three Enterprises, Inc. The records of this company disclosed that on May 1, 1959, they had shipped four pairs of handcuffs in four black handcuff cases to one Walter Osborne, and a receipt dated May 5, on the handcuffs' delivery bore the signature "Walter Osborne." The Osborne signatures on the money orders and receipt have been identified by FBI handwriting experts as being in the known writing of Joseph Corbett, Jr.

While nowhere in the report does the FBI make a point of it, the implication of these findings is plain. A man planning to hold another man for ransom would find hand and leg irons and handcuffs excellent means of securing his

128

prisoner. Corbett bought such items as early as a year before the actual kidnaping. This coincides with the other indications of long-range planning on the part of the kidnaper.

And those indications are spelled out without comment by the FBI. A "close associate" of Corbett's had revealed that Corbett had spoken frankly to him of considering a Denver bank robbery, but that a bank robbery would net him only $5,000 to $10,000; therefore he was planning "one big job" from which he, Corbett, expected to make a haul of from one half to one million dollars. Corbett had boasted to this associate of having taken two and a half years to plan this job. He had indicated that he planned the big job for the summer of 1958, but "something had happened" to postpone it.

The FBI points out that in the summer of 1958 Adolph Coors III suddenly moved his family from their Denver home to the ranch house in Morrison. Had the Coors kidnaping been "the big job" of which Corbett had spoken, such a move would have upset his plan, and the new home and new habits which living there made Coors develop would cause Corbett to plot a new plan and timetable.

The Federal Bureau was able to develop also the evidential fact that on June 8, 1957, Osborne-Corbett had made a mail-order purchase of a K-32 Smith and Wesson Combat Masterpiece revolver. It had been delivered to him on June 10, and he had signed a receipt for it. Other information indicates that Corbett had displayed to acquaintances a .22-caliber Woodsman or Hi-Standard pistol, a nine-mm. Llama automatic, and a .38-caliber revolver. What appeared to have been high-powered rifle cases were observed in Corbett's possession as well. And he had once told a friend that he owned a sleeping bag and tent which he hauled about in his car.

An aluminum picnic set and Coleman camp stove found in unopened cartons in Corbett's hastily evacuated Pearl Street flat were traced to a Denver shop, where a salesman stated that he had sold identical items to a man during the Christmas-New Year week in 1959—some six weeks before the Coors kidnap-slaying. This salesman recalled having asked the customer why he was buying camping equipment at such a time of year, and the customer replying that he "intended to camp during the Winter in the mountains."

It all added up to a man preparing a hideout in some out-of-the-way mountain or woods spot. The fact that the plan blew up in the planner's face at the very inception of his crime did not invalidate the evidence as to his intent.

With the discovery and identification of Ad Coors' remains, the FBI for the first time in the case released the ransom note. It was pointed out that the $500,000 demanded in the note coincided with the "one half to one million dollars" Corbett had bragged to a crony he meant to get out of his "one big job;" further, that he had once told some prison pals he hoped to net that exact amount in one great haul, after which he would flee the country to some place from which he could not be extradited.

And then the FBI announced that, in view of the kidnap victim's apparently not having been taken across a state line, it would seek Corbett merely on a charge of unlawful flight to avoid prosecution. At the same time District Attorney Barney O'Kane of Jefferson County (who has since lost his post in the November elections to Ronald J. Hardesty) filed a formal murder charge against Corbett.

With State and Federal warrants out, the manhunt for Corbett at the end of September took a new lease on life. Once more tips poured in which proved as false and unproductive as all their forerunners. Still, the lawmen continued to give the case publicity.

"The more publicity Corbett gets," one investigator said, "the sooner he'll be nabbed."

The FBI had two good recent photographs of Corbett, the one from the Colorado driver's license file, the other snapped at a company party given by the Denver paint-manufacturing firm for which he had last worked. Canadian newspapers had run these photos late in August without result. But then, in its November, 1960 issue, out in late October, *Reader's Digest* ran an article entitled "The FBI Wants This Man," written under a pseudonym by Blake Clark, one of the magazine's perambulating editors. The article was illustrated by the FBI photographs.

The results were instantaneous and sensational. No sooner did the *Reader's Digest* issue reach Canada than a Canadian citizen who had worked beside Corbett in a Toronto warehouse disclosed his information to the Toronto Metropolitan Police, who promptly notified the FBI. (J. Edgar Hoover himself is authority for the information that there was another significant tip from a *Reader's Digest* reader. In a letter of thanks to the magazine's editor, Mr. Hoover wrote, "The apprehension of Corbett was the direct result of two leads received from your readers, either one of which would have led to his capture." Of the 131 most wanted fugitives from justice caught by the FBI since the "top ten" list was first conceived and published, the FBI claims that no less than 53 criminals were captured as a result of citizen cooperation through leads attributed to newspapers, magazines, radio and TV broadcasts, and "Wanted" circulars.)

At the Toronto warehouse, other employees identified Corbett's photo as that of a "Walter Osborne" who had worked there as a laborer. The local address he had given the company proved spurious, but on another company record Corbett had made a bad slip. He had written down an address, then attempted to destroy it in order to write over it the false address. The all but obliterated address was deciphered, and the lawmen descended on it.

The bird had flown. He had moved out, the landlady there said, on August 31 — the very day, one investigator

131

pointed out, that his picture had been run in the Toronto papers.

"But I have some of his things stored in my basement," the landlady said. "He forgot to take them in his hurry. Would they help?"

The detectives swooped down on Corbett's effects. Among them were his Colorado driver's license, a Denver library card, and a possibly significant four-foot length of heavy chain with two padlocks attached.

Of the fugitive himself there was no trace.

But digging soon revealed that Corbett, using the Osborne alias, had arrived in Toronto late in February—very shortly after his decampment from Denver. The FBI agents were not to be denied so close to their man. A letter of recent date in Corbett's abandoned effects, inquiring about a bad check he had written on a Toronto bank, was from a bank in Winnipeg. To Winnipeg sped the FBI agents, accompanied by members of the Royal Canadian Mounted Police.

Here they learned two things: A man answering Corbett's description had rented a fire-engine-red car from a Hertz agency on October 6. And he had inquired about the best route to Vancouver, 1,100 miles away in the Canadian Far West.

The scent was now visibly smoking. More FBI agents were flown in. Plans were quickly formulated with Canadian authorities for the expected showdown.

On Saturday morning, October 29, a Vancouver constable, John Marshall, recalled having seen, about ten days earlier, a fire-engine-red car parked beside a West End apartment building. Quietly he drove his police car there and talked to the manager, a Mrs. Mary Bell, showing her the FBI circular on Corbett with which he had been supplied that morning.

"That man?" Mrs. Bell said, staring at the circular. "Why, he's still here, Constable, registered as Thomas Wainwright. Shall I call him?"

"No!" Marshall almost shouted. "Just sit tight, please!"

He swiftly notified his office and then drove to a small nearby hotel, where he was joined by Detectives Harry Gammi and Sam Fowlow and a squad of FBI agents.

A dozen unmarked cars threw a stranglehold around the West End building. FBI Agent Al Gunn and Detectives Gammi and Fowlow went noiselessly to "Thomas Wainwright's" door.

One of them knocked.

The door opened.

And there stood Joseph Corbett, Jr., alias Walter Osborne, at long last . . . staring into the muzzles of three unwavering guns.

"Okay," Corbett said coolly. "I give up."

A nine-mm. Llama automatic, fully loaded, was found in his bag. On a table were two books, "How to Speak Spanish" and "How to Fly," a foreshadow perhaps of his intentions.

Corbett waived extradition, and D.A. O'Kane, Sheriff Wermuth, and Captain Bray flew him meekly back to Denver from Vancouver.

And that was the beginning of the end of the Coors case. Or was it?

At this writing Corbett has been in custody four weeks. Veteran lawmen have questioned him again and again during that period without the slightest success; not only has he not confessed to the kidnap-slaying of Adolph Coors III, he has admitted nothing whatever and has shown no slightest sign of weakening. He is very polite, using "sir" in his completely unresponsive answers. He smiles frequently with a sort of sad resignation.

What is his point, if any?

It might lie in this: While Colorado law maintains capital punishment in murder cases, it bars the death penalty unless the defendant signs a confession or there is an eyewitness to the slaying.

Corbett has signed no confession, and so far as it's known there was no eyewitness to the slaying.

As a prisoner at San Quentin and Chino, he had a reputation as a "jailhouse lawyer," a guy who figured the angles. The original fugitive bulletin put out on him by the FBI in March described him as "calm, aloof . . . superior general intelligence but possibly having fantasies of omnipotence."

What Corbett may be figuring on is a mere prison sentence and another escape. After all, he made one break from stir, in Chino, and got away with it.

Why not again?

"BIZARRE CASE OF THE LAUGHING GAS KILLER"

by Joseph L. Koenig

In 1981, a year after the death of her husband, Margaret Benson, the heiress to the Lancaster Leaf and Tobacco Company fortune, moved from the eastern Pennsylvania city that had lent its name to her family's business to Naples, Florida, a new enclave of power and wealth on south Florida's Gulf Coast.

"In Lancaster," an acquaintance would recall, "the Bensons lived like they really might have everything that money could buy, everything and then some. Their house was a 17-room stone mansion in School Lane Hills with 14-karat gold fixtures in the bathrooms, an Olympic pool and manicured lawns and gardens that required the care of a small army of housekeepers. They toned it down some when they moved to Florida. What brought them here, in large part, was Margaret's adopted son, Scott, who was a gifted tennis player and who trained in Naples. Often, you'd see his mother sitting in a lawn chair at courtside, pleased as punch as she watched him practicing his strokes."

Scott Benson, a handsome, dark-haired boy, was the youngest of Margaret Benson's three children. There was a daughter and another son. Steven, an electronics wizard and the entrepreneur of a raft of small business outfits headquartered north of Naples in Fort Myers.

Although the Bensons were the wealthiest people in Lancaster, among the heavy hitters in Naples their new home in the Port Royal section hardly stood out. Margaret had plans, however, to construct a 28,000-square-foot mansion with separate kitchens and dining facilities for all her children and grandchildren. When her neighbors balked at those plans, Margaret, in October, 1984, relocated to Quail Creek, in scrubland away from the coast, where homes began in the $400,000 range and where there was a security guard at the gate at all times to screen visitors.

Although she enjoyed her new house, Margaret Benson still spoke often of building the home of her dreams. She already had purchased the site—three lots which, when combined, would provide the room for the immense residence that she had in mind. By the summer of 1985, the 63-year-old woman was prepared to make her plans a reality. On Tuesday, July 9th, along with her three children, she was going to visit the future site of her new home.

That Tuesday morning dawned seasonally hot and rainy in southwestern Florida. By 9 A.M., Margaret Benson, her daughter, and her sons were awake and breakfasted and ready to start out on the short drive to the new homesite. By 9:18, the family was seated in their brown and white Chevrolet Suburban station wagon when an incredible explosion rent the morning stillness of Quail Creek.

A friend of Margaret Benson's, who was about to tee off from the third hole of the nearby Quail Creek Country Club golf course, heard the blast.

"We thought, at first, it was some sort of construction," he would recall, "but then we saw the cloud of black smoke rising from her driveway."

The man threw down his club and, along with his golfing partners, raced to the Benson driveway. There he found Margaret Benson's body sprawled beside the burning wreckage of her station wagon.

"The car was completely engulfed in flames," her friend would say. "And you couldn't see anyone or anything in it,

136

it was so filled with flames."

Despite the danger to himself, the golfer ran to his friend's side and attempted to pull her away from the burning vehicle.

"I hoped there might be some life in her," he would remember. "As I pulled her back, I slipped on a mound of dirt and . . . fell back, just as the second explosion occurred."

That blast, which came barely 45 seconds after the initial one, tore apart what was left of the station wagon and sent a piece of shrapnel into the chest of Margaret Benson's courageous friend.

"I didn't notice it until five or ten minutes later, when they pointed out that there was blood all over my shirt," he would recall. "I've thought since about the luck of slipping when I did."

Another member of the golfing foursome would say that when he reached the vehicle, Margaret Benson lay sprawled on the pavement. Because it was plain to him that the woman was dead, he had focused his attention on attempting to aid her daughter.

"The car was an inferno," he would say later. She was screaming, 'I'm hot, I'm hot!' " It was as he was pulling the woman away from the vehicle that the second blast went off, knocking him back and putting a small piece of metal through his shoulder.

When Naples police and firefighters arrived on the scene, they would learn that Margaret Benson and her daughter were not the only people inside the station wagon when it exploded. Margaret's adopted son, 21-year-old Scott Benson, had been killed in the blast.

"This was no accident," said one of the first Collier County, Florida, investigators to reach Quail Creek. "This was definitely not a case of a car blowing up on its own fuel."

Before the morning was over, agents from the Federal Bureau of Alcohol, Tobacco and Firearms would be called into the case and would make a quick diagnosis of the cause of the blasts as an "explosive device."

Among the first witnesses to speak with investigators was a construction worker who had helped pull the injured daughter from the wreckage. The woman had told him that her brother Scott "just turned on the key and it blew up."

By late morning, homicide probers had arrived en masse in exclusive Quail Creek. After retrieving debris that had been sent flying 200 feet from the car, the probers covered the wreckage with large sheets of plastic to protect it from the rain.

"We've never had anything like this around here," Collier County Sheriff's Lieutenant Eric Daniels told reporters.

As news of the blast spread throughout Naples, it was followed by the first perceptible indications of panic.

"We still don't have the motive for what happened," one prober said. "And if, indeed, it was a bomb, we don't know who rigged it up. Until we have the answers to both those questions, I'm afraid a lot of people here are going to be afraid to start their cars.

"A guy'd come up and say, 'Hey, I don't really know what's happening, but maybe somebody went to the wrong house, or put bombs elsewhere,' " said Collier County Sheriff's Captain Curtis Mills. "He'd ask us if one of our policemen could go down and start his car for him. We told him to start his car himself."

Some officers, though, had been assigned to have a look at the cars of Margaret Benson's closest neighbors.

The case, Mills said, "is more of a mystery than most investigations are. We don't have the good leads we normally have in a murder case."

On Thursday, July 11th, the homicide probers developed their first broad avenue of investigation when they learned that Margaret Benson had left two wills dictating how her fortune should be disposed of. In the first, dated May 11, 1983, she had expressed the wish that a trust fund be established to provide income for her children. The second will, filed January 29, 1985, made no mention of a trust, and all three of her children were to share equally in her estate, which was valued in excess of $10,000,000. Under Florida law, the second will took precedence over the first.

On Sunday, July 4th, funeral services for Margaret and Scott Benson were held at St. James Episcopal Church in Lancaster, Pennsylvania. At the close of the ceremony two bronze caskets were driven to Woodward Hill Cemetery— the resting place of James Buchanan, the 15th President of the United States—and the site of the Benson family's gray granite mausoleum.

In Lancaster, acquaintances of the family would recall that Margaret Benson had grown up in the lap of luxury and had remained there for the rest of her life.

"The family had a number of homes, here in Lancaster, one in Canada where they liked to go skiing, and another one at an oceanside colony in New Jersey. Once, Mrs. Benson's husband bought her a three-story warehouse, just because she needed someplace to store ten antique cars."

Scott Benson, the family acquaintance said, was something of a playboy, an indifferent student whose life revolved around fast cars and his desire to make it as a professional tennis player.

"He was a bit on the wild side. He'd been picked up for speeding three times in Florida, and once for reckless driving. Another time, he was charged with fleeing an officer."

Margaret, a tobacco industry executive would recall, "was very protective of Scott. Once she had the police in Lancaster warn one of Scotty's friends to stay away from the family, because she distrusted the young man."

For all his effort to become a successful tennis player, though, Scott Benson never developed into an outstanding athlete.

"He could never put the strokes together," his former tennis coach would say.

Family friends also spoke with newsmen about Steven Benson, Margaret's oldest son. The 34-year-old man was described as an electronics wizard who once had built a plumbing system for the family greenhouse.

"He had a very bright mind as far as mechanics and engineering were concerned," the tobacco executive said.

As a businessman, though, Steve Benson was less successful. After moving to Fort Myers, where he had set up a burglar alarm firm that made a great deal of money by offering a wide range of electronic security equipment, Steve Benson had formed a group of about a dozen corporations, none of which had prospered.

As the only member of the family not injured in the blasts, Steve had come in for some questioning by the homicide probers, although he had not provided them with a detailed statement.

According to Homicide Lieutenant Harold Young, Benson had been about to join the rest of the family in the station wagon when, at the last moment, he returned to the house.

"From what we can gather," Young said, "Steve walked away from the car."

Moments later, Scott slipped behind the wheel, his mother sat beside him and his sister got into the back seat.

Young went on to say that his men were checking into a lot of hearsay they had heard concerning drug involvement on the part of young Scott. Usually, it was Scott who drove the Suburban, and officers were eager to find out if he had had any problems with Florida's not insignificant drug underworld.

But the probers were looking at everyone who might have stood to profit from the deaths of Margaret Benson and her son.

"Money and everything else is a motive," Young said. "That's the way people usually get killed. We're going to have to be looking at everyone in the family business."

On Tuesday, July 16th Collier County Chief Deputy Ray

140

Barnett told reporters that detectives had located a Naples plumbing supply firm that recently had sold a section of four-inch galvanized pipe similar to that used to construct the bombs that triggered the fatal blasts. Investigators had obtained a receipt signed by the purchaser, but the signature was illegible.

"We're going to check the handwriting against the handwriting of everyone involved in the case," Barnett said.

The following day, Steve Benson's attorney informed investigators that his client would answer no more of their questions.

"That's his constitutional right," commented Chief Deputy Barnett.

Although Benson's decision will "slow us down a bit," Barnett said, ". . . I think we will still get where we're headed for."

Benson, other probers said, had arrived at his mother's house around 7:30 A.M. on July 8th, after the half-hour drive from his own place in Fort Myers. Prior to the blasts, he had driven the Suburban to a convenience store for some coffee and doughnuts and then had returned to the big house in Quail Creek. Just before the deadly explosions, he had walked away from the vehicle, returning to the house to pick up a tape measure that he said he had forgotten.

Barnett said that his department had sent the plumbing company receipt to the FBI labs in Washington, D.C.

"We're hoping we can get some latent prints off it," he said.

In early August, homicide probers reported that the man who had purchased the section of galvanized steel pipe was a man of medium build wearing glasses. The clerk at the supply firm where the sale was made had said that the purchaser stood out in his mind because a one-foot length of pipe was a very unusual order.

On Wednesday, August 21st, newsmen learned that although the signature on the purchase receipt had not been

141

deciphered, a latent palm print had been discovered on the slip of paper, a palm print that had been identified as belonging to Steven Benson.

At 10:00 on Thursday morning, August 22nd, detectives from Collier County joined by Federal ATF agents arrested 34-year-old Steven Wayne Benson at his Fort Myers home on two counts of first-degree murder and one count of attempted first-degree murder. At his arraignment, Collier County Circuit Judge Thomas T. Trettis ordered Benson held without bond at the Collier County Jail in Naples.

According to the warrant authorizing his arrest, Benson had been seen in the days before the blasts carrying a length of pipe with fuses in it. Allegedly, Benson had obtained some $2,000,000 from his mother for unauthorized purposes, and in the days before her death Margaret Benson had summoned her attorney to Florida to relieve Steve from participating in a number of businesses that she owned and operated. The warrant also alleged that plans had been made to drop Steven from his mother's will.

Sources close to the case reported that when Steven arrived at his mother's house at 7:30 on July 9th, he chatted briefly with the others and then announced that he was going to take his mother's station wagon to a nearby convenience store for coffee and doughnuts. Steven explained that he didn't want to take his own van because he wanted to save gas.

Although the convenience store was no more than a five-minute drive away, an hour and 10 minutes went by before Steven returned. Steven explained his lateness by saying that he had run into someone from an area construction company at the store and had talked business for about an hour. However, a check with officials of that firm indicated that none of its employees was in the vicinity of the convenience store at the time Benson said that he was there.

When the family went out to the station wagon between 9:10 and 9:15, police said, Scott Benson slipped behind the wheel with his mother in the passenger's seat and the daughter in the left rear seat. Steven got into the right rear seat, but when Margaret Benson told him to give the keys to Scott he left the vehicle, walked around to the driver's side and then, suddenly, said that he had to go back inside the house for a tape measure. Steven was running toward the house, police said, when the first explosion went off.

The police went on to say that on the afternoon of July 5th, Steven had asked employees of one of his firms, Meridian Security Network, if they had a hat that he could borrow, or if there was one somewhere in the office. The incident had stood out in the minds of Benson's employees because they had never seen their boss in a hat before.

Around 3:25 on the afternoon of July 5th, the police said, a man described as carrying some 200 pounds on a six-foot frame and wearing a baseball cap bought two four-inch galvanized pipes and caps from a local construction supply outfit. The purchaser had asked for four end caps, but was told that only two were in stock. The same man, whose description seemed to match that of Steve Benson, returned to the supply company one day before the bombings to purchase a couple of foot-long lengths of the four-inch galvanized steel pipe and two more end caps.

Additionally, investigators said, pieces of an electronic circuit found in the wreckage of the Benson station wagon matched equipment used by Steven Benson in his security business.

Investigators said that in recent months Steve Benson had bilked his mother out of about $2,000,000 that he had withdrawn, in large part, from her account with a Naples brokerage, money that he deposited in his personal checking account and the account of his burglar alarm company. On other occasions, he was believed to have misused blank checks that his mother had given him. When his mother discovered what he had done, the police said, she contacted the family lawyer in Philadelphia with a request to come to Naples to draw up a new will that would exclude Steven from her estate.

143

Later, the homicide probers would reveal that on July 23rd, in Lancaster, Collier County Sheriff's Investigators Michael Koors had spoken with a former employee of the Benson estate in that Pennsylvania city, and that he had said that while working on the roof of the main house in 1982, he had seen Steven Benson walking away from the structure with three lengths of copper tubing and wires protruding from the tubes. Benson, the witness recalled, walked toward the tennis courts and disappeared from view. A few moments later, three separate explosions rocked the grounds and the employee hurried down from the roof to find Steven on one of the tennis courts holding a small black box "the size of a remote control garage door opener" with two push-button switches, one of which was red and the other white.

The witness, police would report, "stated that Steven Wayne Benson was laughing about what he had just done and walked away . . . without saying a word."

In the second week of September, a Collier County grand jury handed down a nine-count indictment against Steven Benson. On Friday, September 13, Circuit Court Judge Hugh D. Hayes denied bail for the young inventor.

At Steven Benson's murder trial, which got underway in Fort Myers in July of 1986, Prosecutor Jerry Brock described the defendant as a man caught in a family squabble over money that ultimately led to death.

Defense counsel, on the other hand, said that "the evidence will show that Steven Benson was the loving son of Margaret Benson—the peacemaker in the family . . . the only one who did not fight physically, tooth and nail, drawing blood."

It was part of the defense strategy to put in the minds of jurors speculation that it was Scott Benson, rather than his older brother, who had the motive to murder their mother. On Wednesday, July 30th, the attorneys called the defendant's psychiatrist to the stand. In the absence of the panel, he testified that he had been shocked by the youth's appe-

144

tite for nitrous oxide, a drug which he believed had triggered a violent outburst on Scott's part in 1983.

The youth was addicted to the laughing gas, the doctor said, so much so that he used to keep an enormous tank of the drug at his bedside.

"He wanted more, more . . ." the witness said. "So what I'm saying to you is that he inhaled nitrous oxide like you might drink Diet Pepsi."

In 1983, the witness went on, he had treated Scott Benson after two Naples police officers brought the 19-year-old boy to a hospital because he had threatened his mother during a quarrel over his attack dog, Buck. He described Scott's violent reaction as temporary, and attributed his hasty recovery to his condition as an athlete.

"His mother was terrorized by his huge tank of nitrous oxide," the psychiatrist said. "It was a shocking experience."

A former employee of the Bensons told the court that because of the youngster's wild behavior, Margaret had grown to fear Scott. Margaret had had a deadbolt lock installed on the outside of the boy's bedroom door and a special key-lock placed on her own bedroom because of her fears that Scott, or his friends, would come into the house and cause problems. Scott, she noted, had an outside entrance to his bedroom.

In his closing argument on Wednesday, August 6th, defense counsel said that, "In a family that had no reason to do harm to one another, we had one poor unfortunate man who was running amok, threatening to kill his mother, dragging his mother across the floor, beating his sister . . . with his fists and consuming such quantities of narcotics as to create the probability of behavior consistent with that kind of violence, who would do anything to get more drugs."

Defense counsel said Steven, in contrast, was a loving son, who took over when his father died, who never said a cross word to anyone, who was the peacemaker, who only got angry when Scott abused his mother.

On Thursday, August 7th, after 11 hours of debate, the jury of ten women and two men found Steven Wayne Benson guilty of two counts of first-degree murder and seven lesser counts.

"He was just a young man who wanted to be a millionaire," commented Lieutenant Young after the verdict was in, "but wasn't making it."

During the penalty phase of the trial on Friday, Prosecutor Brock asked the panelists to sentence Steven Benson to death in Florida's electric chair.

"He put a pipe bomb in an auto between his mother and brother—not to mention putting his sister on top of a bomb," Brock said. "Do you recall how Judas sold out Jesus for thirty pieces of silver? That was nothing compared to what this defendant did."

Defense counsel, in a brief address to the panelists, pleaded for his client's life.

"I suggest to you that there has been enough killing," he said. "I suggest to you that you can spare three little children the horror of knowing their father has been executed."

The jury took 81 minutes to announce that it was split six to six as to whether or not Steven Benson should pay for his crimes with his life. Under Florida law, the vote was one shy of the number required to send Steven Benson to the electric chair.

On Tuesday, September 2nd, Steven Wayne Benson returned to court to hear Judge Hayes formally sentence him to two life terms in prison without the possibility of parole for 50 years.

"KIDNAPPED COED SAVED FROM LIVING GRAVE"

by Glenn W. Thomas

It was nearly four A.M. on Tuesday, December 17th, eight days before Christmas of 1968, as Mrs. Robert F. (Jane) Mackle sat talking on a bed with her daughter, Barbara Jane, in their two-room suite at the Rodeway Inn Motel off Clairmont Road in suburban Atlanta, Georgia. Mrs. Mackle had flown to Atlanta to be with her daughter, a junior economics major at nearby Emory University, because Barbara Jane had fallen ill with the flu bug which had been sweeping the nation as she was taking her final quarter examinations.

The girl's mother was attempting to nurse her back to good health so the two could return to their plush home in Coral Gables, Florida, just outside Miami, for the holidays. Barbara Jane had left school in the midst of one of her exams the previous Saturday, December 14th, and checked into the motel with her mother. They intended to fly home later that Tuesday.

As the mother and daughter sat talking quietly on that chilly early morning of December 17th, there was a knock on the door of Room 137. "Who is it?" Mrs. Mackle asked.

A man's voice said he was a police officer and that he wanted to check out some information he had on a wreck involving a young man driving a white Ford.

A young male friend of Barbara Jane's, also a business school student at Emory, who had visited them just a few hours before and taken them for a brief ride, drove such an automobile, and Mrs. Mackle feared he had been in a wreck. Thus she made the near-fatal mistake of opening the door to their first-floor rooms, inadvertently setting off a sensational true crime tale of two cities which grimly proved to be stranger than fiction.

For as Mrs. Mackle opened the door, a young, heavy-set man, wearing a black leather jacket and cap and brandishing a "long-barreled gun," pushed his way into the room and thrust a cloth saturated with what she thought was chloroform into her face. The man then ordered her to turn around and a second person, wearing a ski-type mask, whom the dazed woman at first took to be a small boy, entered the room, roughly bound her hands and feet, and slapped strips of adhesive tape over her mouth. The two intruders then quickly ordered Barbara Jane to accompany them. They left the room with the 20-year-old coed, who was wearing only a red-and-white-checked flannel nightgown.

Although dazed, Mrs. Mackle soon managed to work her feet free from their bindings and staggered out the door to a car parked nearby. She worked the car door open, fell inside and frantically blew the horn with pressure from her face. A motel clerk attracted by the noise ran to the scene and untied the shaken woman, who hurriedly told him what had happened. The clerk called DeKalb County police.

Detectives M.E. Glover and R.L. Glosson quickly answered the call and began trying to fill in the details. What they learned caused them to call in more help, including detectives from nearby Atlanta and agents of the Federal Bureau of Investigation.

The abducted girl was a member of one of the most prominent real estate development families in Florida, and indeed in the nation.

148

Her father, Robert F. Mackle, was secretary-treasurer of the $65 million Deltona Corporation, with headquarters in Miami; president of the Farrand Corporation which owns the Key Biscayne Hotel, and of Westwood Lakes, Inc., a development company in Dade County.

Mackle and his brothers, Frank and Elliott, inherited a construction firm from their father and turned it into one of the largest home building firms in the country during the post-World War II building boom. They pioneered in building large pre-planned communities attracting retired families from the north to buy their low-cost "Mackle-built" homes. They formed the giant General Development Corporation in 1965, developing such projects as the 90,000-acre Port Charlotte community on the Florida west coast, but sold it in 1961 and formed Deltona. They also were among the principal developers of the prestigious Key Biscayne community, where President-elect Richard Nixon, a close family friend, was soon to buy his "winter White House."

Robert Mackle's only daughter had come back to his native Atlanta two years ago to attend Emory, a Methodist church-related four-year liberal arts college, after graduating from the exclusive Everglade School for Girls in Miami. She had made her debut at the Cotillion Ball at the exclusive Bath Club in December 1966.

As one of the FBI agents later remarked about the kidnap case, "We've got a big one here."

Mrs. Mackle described her daughter to the police as a brown-eyed brunette who was five feet 10 inches tall, weighing about 120 pounds. That description and a bulletin on the abduction was flashed over police networks in the area.

DeKalb Detective Captain J.L. Smith said no mention of ransom had been made to Mrs. Mackle during the kidnaping, but added that she "was told what to do" by those who snatched her daughter, and that the hour of noon that Tuesday was considered significant.

149

Witnesses at the motel told the investigators that they had heard what sounded like a struggle in the Mackle suite, followed by a car speeding away from the area. The FBI agents, in a routine check, began poring over motel guest records and checking out stolen car reports for the past several weeks.

After hearing of the abduction, the young student friend of Barbara's came to the motel and told the investigators about being there the night before.

He said he took Mrs. Mackle and Barbara Jane for a ride on Monday evening, and at one point thought his car was being followed by a man driving a blue Oldsmobile. He said he made a turn which caused the other driver to get close enough so he could see the man, and he was "staring at us."

FBI agents also went to the Emory University campus to see what else they could learn about the kidnaped girl. Friends at her Delta Delta Delta sorority and in the dormitory, McTyerie Hall, described Barbara Jane as publicly reserved, but "very warm when you get to know her. Anything Mackle was involved in was usually fun," one said.

They also said that she did not flaunt her family's wealth and many actually were surprised to learn of her background. Some said she had expressed herself as being tired of Emory and thinking of transferring to the University of North Carolina. Emory officials said Barbara Jane was a good student and that she had been excused from a test because she was ill. They explained that juniors and seniors are not required to sign out and they had thought she had gone home for the holidays.

Meanwhile, Mrs. Mackle telephoned her husband in Coral Gables to give him the shocking news, and he immediately made arrangements to fly to Atlanta in his company's private plane. He was accompanied by his son, Robert Jr., a 22-year-old business student at the University of Pennsylvania, who had attended Georgia Tech in Atlanta, and by Billy Vessels, the former All-American football player and Heisman Trophy winner at the University of Oklahoma, who worked as a public relations man for the firm. Robert Mackle Jr. was home for the Christmas holidays.

Shortly after they departed Miami, the telephone rang at the Mackle home at 4111 San Amaro Drive in an exclusive section of Coral Gables. It was about 9:10 A.M., five hours after the abduction. William O'Dodd, a Deltona official who had rushed to the home to help out, answered the phone.

A male voice curtly said to him: "I'll give you this one time."

The caller told O'Dodd to look underneath a tree in the northwest corner of the back yard, where he would find a rock. Buried six inches under the rock, he continued, he would find a note giving detailed instructions, which must be followed to the letter if Barbara Jane were to be returned safely.

After the caller hung up, the family friend's first move was to call the FBI, and agents rushed to the home. The spot identified by the caller was found, near a golf course which backs up to the property, and a three-page note apparently buried there in advance of the kidnaping, was dug up.

The note, according to reports, described how the kidnaping would be conducted, demanded $500,000 ransom and warned that each detail must be carried out minutely. It instructed that the ransom was to be paid in old $20-bills, wrapped in packets of 500 each, placed in a suitcase of specified width, length and depth. A classified ad was to be placed in the Thursday morning editions of the Miami Herald indicating that the family was ready to cooperate, after which further details would be forthcoming.

Mr. O'Dodd telephoned Mr. Mackle in Atlanta at about 12:30 P.M., telling him of the note and its instructions. The distraught father asked that they be carried out, and his

151

two brothers began moving. They telephoned First National Bank President Robert W. Druce and found him having lunch with a group of the bank's executives. Mr. Druce instructed Ray Basten, executive vice president to begin putting the bills together.

A search was launched for a suitcase to fill the kidnaper's specifications, but one could not be located until a bank official remembered his wife had one which sounded similar. He called her to measure it, and it fit exactly. The bag was rushed to the bank. Working all afternoon and into the night on the secluded third floor, a group of top bank officials gathered the money, carefully recorded the serial numbers of the notes, and packaged them as ordered.

Meanwhile, FBI agents went to the Miami Herald office about 3 P.M. Tuesday to place the classified ad as ordered. It read: "Loved one—please come home. We will pay all expenses and meet you anywhere at anytime. Your family."

Back in Atlanta, Mr. and Mrs. Mackle and their party, heavily guarded by FBI agents, were ushered from the Rodeway Inn about 7 P.M. An agent told waiting newsmen they were being taken elsewhere to rest because "they just need a little peace and quiet. We're getting them away from the motel." But actually they were escorted to the Atlanta Airport, where they boarded the family plane and flew back home to await further word from the kidnapers.

Amidst rumors of a possible break in the case, the Mackle home was a beehive of activity during the night and next day, with FBI agents, local police, close personal friends, doctors and ministers coming and going. Mrs. Mackle reportedly was suffering from shock.

Numerous FBI agents, whose leaves had been canceled for the duration of the investigation, were working on the case from Washington to Miami. One FBI source said they were proceeding on the theory that the kidnaping had been well planned for some time in advance. They pointed out that the abductors had indicated they knew a lot about the Mackle family and their activities.

The agents were busy checking out numerous reports of suspicious persons reportedly seen around the Emory campus and the motel for days prior to the abduction, but despite a nationwide alert for the kidnapers, nothing firm had been turned up by Wednesday, and the focus of the case had been shifted to Miami.

The Reverend Father John Mulcahy, assistant rector of the Church of the Little Flower, attended by the devoutly Catholic Mackle family, who had visited them, said the family "have reason to believe their daughter is alive and unharmed," but he did not elaborate.

A representative of the Mackle family picked up the suitcase packed with the half million dollars in ransom money from the bank about 11 A.M. Wednesday and took it to the home to await further instructions.

The center of attention now became the telephone in the Mackle home, and callers were asked to hang up quickly to leave the line clear for a contact from the kidnapers. Later in the day another call did come, and Mr. Mackle was instructed to have one of his cars gassed up and ready to move, and to wait for other orders. The vigil continued throughout the day and night and into the early hours of Thursday, December 19th.

Finally, at 4 A.M., two days after the kidnaping, the phone rang again. Mr. Mackle answered. An anonymous caller gave him detailed instructions to follow to make the payoff. He was ordered to move instantly.

Taking the suitcase packed with the half million and telling no one where he was going, Mr. Mackle entered his car alone and drove away. He proceeded slowly to a point about five miles from his home to the dark corner where Bayshore Drive meets Fair Isle Street near the bayfront. Pausing only briefly, he turned east toward Biscayne Bay and drove one block past a group of homes to a roadblock barring the way across a causeway to Fair Island, sitting 800 feet out into the bay. He parked his car in the darkness, got out and picked his way to the nearby sea wall, and lowered the money-laden suitcase over the water side of the concrete wall. The tide was out, and he set it on the dry beach. Mr. Mackle then hurried back to his car and drove back home to await word of his daughter's hoped for release.

Meanwhile, an incredible tragedy of errors began to unfold which was to strike terror into the hearts of the Mackle family. For after Mr. Mackle got back to his home, a resident of the Biscayne Bay waterfront near where the drop was made heard the unmistakable sounds of a motor boat passing near his property at about 5 A.M. Bert Galbraith of a Brickell Avenue address looked out the back of his house and saw a white boat being beached at the far corner of the property owned by his neighbors, Lance Corby and his sister. At about the same time, the sister was awakened by their dog barking, at the paper boy, she thought. Galbraith called their residence and Corby answered. Galbraith told him of the boat, and asked if he would call the police. But Corby said he had turned in numerous such reports before, and it just meant he had to fill out a bunch of papers. Galbraith decided to report the matter himself, and called the sheriff's office.

Meanwhile, Deputy Sheriff Paul Self, assigned to patrol the Key Biscayne area across the bay via the Rickenbacker Causeway, had driven back to the mainland to get some food and was enroute back to his post with a sack of hamburgers when a call came from the radio dispatcher to check out a "suspicious persons" report on South Brickell.

At that time Self was approaching the causeway at the Brickell Avenue extension. He glanced down the street, normally deserted at that time, and saw a car parked there with some activity going on around it. But a roadblock prevented him from entering the street at that point.

The officer was forced to drive around by way of South Bayshore Drive and Vizcaya and approach the car from the south. He drove up to the parked car and stopped. What he took to be two men jumped out of the car and ran. One was carrying a suitcase and what looked like a carbine rifle, and the second lugged a duffel bag.

Deputy Self radioed for help, then jumped out and started chasing the pair. The man with the gun dropped the suitcase and opened fire on him with the rifle, and Self pulled his revolver and returned the fire. The second person dropped the duffel bag and the two fled on foot in different directions.

At about that time, Miami Patrolman William Sweeney arrived on the scene, followed quickly by Patrolman Matthew Horn. Deputy Self followed his man through a residential section leading toward the intersection of South Dixie Highway and the north-south expressway, but lost him in the early-morning inky darkness. He did not know if one of his bullets had found its mark. The second person, described as smaller, also escaped in the opposite direction.

Other policemen and FBI agents swarmed onto the scene and it was not until then that the unwary deputy and policemen learned that they had unwittingly broken up the attempted ransom payoff for the missing Mackle heiress.

"I just happened on this whole thing," the deputy said. "I saw this car that just didn't belong there." But they also were to learn that their accidental action was to provide the first major break in the sensational kidnaping case.

Meanwhile, Mr. Mackle had returned to the scene of the money drop about two hours after his original visit and found that the bag had been removed. He returned to his home, hoping soon to get word of his daughter's release, only to find that the payoff had been accidentally bungled. After 48 sleepless hours worrying about the safety of his daughter, he broke down and wept. But he recovered quickly and asked the FBI to put out a statement for him assuring the kidnapers he was innocent of the unfortunate events and that he still wanted to cooperate for his daughter's safe return.

"I had nothing to do with the action Thursday morning

155

of the Miami police who tried to arrest you and recovered the money which I had left for you," his statement, which he hoped the kidnapers would receive, said. "I regret that you did not get the money because my only interest is the safety of my daughter. I pray that you have not harmed my daughter. I did everything you told me to do, and I had nothing to do with the accidental appearance of the Miami police on the scene. Please contact me again through any channel. I will do anything you ask so my daughter will be freed."

FBI agents, who said the payoff instructions had come so swiftly that they had no time to warn local police to stay out of the area, said, "A girl's life is at stake" and added, "Mr. Mackle doesn't care anything about the money, just his daughter's safety."

The Mackle plea was widely printed and broadcast in the hopes that the kidnapers would receive it, believe him and make a new contact to arrange another payoff. The agonizing wait began again.

Meanwhile, FBI agents and police officers swarmed all over the area where the kidnapers had been spotted, and helicopters, airplanes and bloodhounds were pressed into the search. They found that the suitcase dropped by one of the fleeing persons contained the ransom, all intact. The duffel bag was stuffed with skin-diving gear, apparently to be used to recover the money had it become submerged in the water. The suitcase and money were dry, however.

The abandoned car, a blue 1966 Volvo station wagon with Massachusetts license plates, was parked near an old estate which had been bought by the City of Miami, eventually to be turned into a park. Checking the waterfront, the investigators found a 13-foot Boston Whaler type outboard motor boat beached at the end of the sea wall between the Corby property and the estate. They theorized that the kidnapers had parked the boat there, walked on land along the seawall to a point between the estate and an adjoining, heavily overgrown piece of property between it

156

and the causeway, and followed a 20-foot path through the thick mangrove trees and underbrush to Brickell and their parked car. The point where the boat was beached was about a mile and a half north of the area where Mr. Mackle had dropped the money.

Meanwhile, the caretaker of the old estate arrived for work and saw the Volvo being towed away. He told officers he recognized the car. He said that just the previous afternoon, about two o'clock, a couple drove up to the estate and asked if they could look around. He told them they could.

He described the pair as a stocky man who "looked like one of them football players," and a slender, attractive, dark-haired girl who appeared to be of Latin descent. While "I didn't look at them too close," he added, they spent considerable time looking around the grounds, including about 20 minutes on the waterfront. The man then came back and asked the caretaker what time the place closed. "I said 3:30. Then they got in the car and rode away."

In the meantime, investigators traced the serial number of the abandoned boat and found that it had been stolen during the night from the University of Miami's Institute of Marine Science, located on Virginia Key three miles across the bay from where the payoff was made. James Gibbons, an official at the Institute, said the boat was missing when he reported for work that morning. It had been taken from a boat trailer parked on the beach in the rear of the Institute's boat shop. He said also that a padlock on a gasoline storage shed had been sawed off and some gasoline taken. He added that whoever did it must have been very familiar with the Institute grounds.

Tight security was placed around the area where the kidnapers had last been spotted, and all major exits from Miami were plugged in an attempt to prevent their escape. One veteran lawman said the city was "the tightest cage I ever saw."

Some two hours after the bungled payoff, the FBI traced the Massachusetts plates on the abandoned car to a man named George Deacon, 23, who had been employed as a technician at the Massachusetts Institute of Technology in Cambridge for 18 months until the previous June. At that time he had gone to work at the Institute of Marine Sciences in Miami.

Further checking showed Deacon to be an alias for Gary Steven Krist, an escaped convict from the Deuel Vocational Institution at Tracy, California, where he had been serving a sentence for auto theft. He escaped, in November 1966, by scaling a wall. During the break a companion of Krist's was shot and killed by a guard. Krist, using the Deacon alias, obtained employment at MIT as an electronics specialist in December 1966. He had been sought by the FBI on a federal warrant charging interstate flight since December 1967. Krist was born in Aberdeen, Washington, but had graduated from high school in Sitka, Alaska, in 1963.

Evidence found in the impounded Volvo and subsequent checks also led the FBI to another student-researcher at the Miami Marine Institute—26-year-old Ruth Eisenmann-Schier, who claimed to be a native of El Hatillo, Honduras. Miss Eisemann-Schier was described as being slight but athletic and sometimes dressed in masculine type clothes. She was a brunette who sometimes dyed her hair blonde, according to reports.

Investigators learned the woman held a master's degree in chemistry, pharmacy and biology from the National University in Mexico City, and had worked from October, 1967 to June, 1968 as a biology researcher in the Department of Scientific Affairs of the Pan-American Union in Washington, D.C. She had enrolled in the Miami Institute for the fall semester. Miss Eisemann-Schier was fluent in Spanish, German and French and had taken a crash course in English after getting her job in Washington.

Krist got his job in Miami in June and moved his wife and two children into the Al-Ril Trailer Park on

NW 14th Street at 84th Street.

He and Miss Eisemann-Schier apparently met at the Institute and, officials there said, became friendly when they went with other school officials on a two-week scientific cruise to Bermuda in September. They spent time riding around the island together on a motor scooter, friends said. Since that time, according to one of her professors, Miss Eisemann-Schier, who had been an excellent student and "a nice, friendly little girl," began to seem uninterested in her studies.

"She seemed to be preoccupied," the professor said. "She wasn't studying. She wasn't doing her work, ever since that cruise. She did so poorly in class that it was obvious she was preoccupied with something. I talked to her about it and she said she was going to study harder. Every student says that."

Dr. F.G. Walton Smith, director of the Miami Institute, said that the fair-haired Deacon, as he was known there, was a technician working in submarine geology, both at sea and in the laboratory. He said that while he did not know the fugitive personally, he understood he was a good worker. Deacon had been on Christmas vacation since the Monday before the kidnaping.

But at the trailer park where Deacon had lived, his neighbors gave further insight into the man. They said Deacon, who had worn a heavy beard until the previous Monday, was a man who did not have much to say. He was, in fact, "very close-mouthed, not very friendly," one man said. He also was described by his neighbors as a man who resented having to live in a trailer with his wife and two children, one of them a baby, and who was envious of the wealthy.

The trailer park residents said Deacon's family had left the park about two weeks before, his wife saying she was returning to her family's home in California. But Deacon, they thought, was there late Wednesday, because the air conditioning unit in his blue and white trailer was running, and his Volvo wagon was parked in its spot.

159

The FBI quietly issued federal kidnap warrants against the two on Thursday afternoon, but withheld public notice of them to see if the kidnapers would again contact the Mackle family, offering the safe return of Barbara Jane in return for the ransom money. But as the day wore on and no word came, Mr. Mackle prepared to approve public announcement of the warrants so the information could be flashed around the world and nationwide lookouts posted for the suspects.

Just as this was about to be done a "hold" order flashed through from Miami to Washington. Contact had been made again. This time Father Mulcahy was chosen by the kidnapers as the intermediary. They called him at his rectory late that Thursday afternoon and told him to warn the Mackles to be ready for another payoff. The clergyman rushed to the Mackle home and told them the news, and again the agonzing wait for further instructions began anew. The wait stretched through the night, while the FBI secretly transferred the money recovered after the original payoff attempt, which had been held in their Miami office, back to the Mackle home to be held in readiness for the second try.

Finally the notice came, and shortly after midnight an unnamed close family friend left the house with the money. He drove some five miles northwest of the Mackle home, out the Tamiami Trail to the Coral Park Shopping Center at SW 97th Avenue. The drop was made there, this time without a hitch. The friend drove back to the home and the tense wait began anew for word that Barbara Jane would be released unharmed.

The promised deadline was noon that Friday, December 20th. But noon came and passed, so FBI Director J. Edgar Hoover announced the warrants in Washington, flashing a lookout for the wanted pair around the nation. Hoover also warned that Krist should be considered "armed and very dangerous," and placed the fugitive's name on the FBI's 10 Most Wanted list.

But ironically, at about the same time, the FBI office in Atlanta received a call from an anonymous source giving terse instructions on the general location where the missing heiress could be found. The call sent scores of agents scurrying out of the city to a point about 20 miles northeast of town, near the rural Lake Berkeley community, just across the DeKalb County line in Gwinnett County. Near the Buford Highway and Indian Trail Road, they fanned out to begin an inch-by-inch search of the wooded area there. For hours they stomped through the rugged, hilly countryside, and as the minutes dragged on and an early winter sundown approached, their spirits sagged.

But about 4:15 P.M., as one of the agents cautiously made his way over a small hill through a forest of pines and sweetgum trees about 150 yards off Lake Berkeley Road near a trash dumping ground, he heard a thumping noise almost under his feet. Glancing down, he saw what looked like two small pipes protruding slightly from underneath the earth. The agent bent over and called out, and again heard the thumping. The excited agent sounded an alarm, and other FBI men came rushing up.

Together they frantically began digging in the spot with their hands or anything else they could find. And after they had dug about 18 inches into the loosed, damp red Georgia clay, they discovered a wooden, coffin-like box buried there. The pipes, which later proved to be skin diver's snorkels, were protruding from its top, which was fastened on with screws. One of the agents quickly found something with which to remove the screws, and they raised the plywood top and peered inside.

Stretched out inside the box, still wearing her flannel nightgown and a sweater, Barbara Jane Mackle stared up incredulously at the agents, blinking against the winter light which filtered into her "grave."

"When they opened it, there were faces all around, looking," Miss Mackle later told Miami Herald reporter Gene Miller in a copyrighted story. The girl, after days in the buried box, could not walk at first, so the agents gently lifted her out.

"How are my parents?" she asked them immediately. Then she looked closely at the men, all veteran FBI agents who had seen more than their share of human misery. "They were all crying," she said.

The FBI agents found that Barbara Jane's living coffin contained a small battery unit, which operated a ventilation fan and a light that was burned out. There also obviously had been a small amount of food and water left inside the box to help sustain her.

In the newspaper interview later, Barbara Jane said that after she was abducted from the motel by a man and woman, she was forced to take a tranquilizer as the car sped away.

"I was woozy, but I knew what was happening," she told reporter Miller. "I tried to talk them out of it." But they would not listen, and she said that before she was placed in the box underground, she was forced to lie sprawled on the damp earth while her abductors placed a sign lettered, "kidnaped," near her, then snapped a picture.

Then the man took her ring and watch, and ripped the buttons from her night gown, apparently for identification purposes, Barbara Jane said.

"The girl gave me a sweater. They told me they would be back and check on me in two hours."

Then she was placed inside the box and covered over with earth. But the kidnapers never returned. About two and a half hours after she was buried, she said, the light in the box burned out. And the box started leaking, and "it was cold."

As the hours dragged on, Miss Mackle tried to pass the time by attempting to recall every word of every song she had ever sung. "You don't know what time it is in the dark."

Then, after a seeming eternity, she heard footsteps approaching her grave. "I thought it was the kidnapers com-

162

ing back for me," she related, "but I had been there so long I really didn't care. One of the ventilation fans made a zang-zang sound and I turned it off so I could hear better. I couldn't see. I had no conception of time."

After the FBI agent spotted her ventilation tubes and began hollering for help, she said she heard him and "I kept rapping" on the cover of her wooden prison.

Miraculously, despite her 80-hour entombment under the chilly Georgia ground, the girl seemed to be in relatively good shape. Doctors later said that she had managed to survive despite the freezing night temperatures because the earth on top of the box provided enough insulation for her body heat to maintain a temperature of about 50 degrees inside the close confines of the box.

After the agents lifted her out of the box, they rushed her to an Atlanta hospital for a checkup. Meanwhile, the word was flashed over the radio back to their Atlanta office, and sent on to Washington, where FBI Director Hoover personally telephoned the good news to the girl's jubilant family in Coral Gables. Mr. Mackle immediately made arrangements to fly to Atlanta to recover the daughter he had never been sure he would see alive again.

While waiting for her father to arrive, Miss Mackle talked over long distance to her mother, her Uncle Frank and her brother Robert. "How are you, Barbara?" her anxious uncle asked.

"Fine, Uncle Frank," she assured him, adding that her abductors had not mistreated her.

Frank Mackle later said that her only concern was about her family, and how much they had worried. Speaking calmly, she told them her kidnapers were "very considerate" and a woman had especially taken good care of her.

"This will be the best Christmas we've ever had," young Robert Mackle said.

Meanwhile, Mr. Mackle arrived in Atlanta and was rushed to the hospital, where his daughter had been given a thorough check, for a tearful but joyous reunion. Then, assured that his daughter, despite her ordeal, was capable of traveling, he and Barbara Jane were given an FBI escort back to the airport where they took off for home at 10:55 P.M. that Friday night, December 20th, more than three and a half days after her nightmare had begun.

As they boarded the private twin-engine Beechcraft, Miss Mackle, dressed now in a white, fur-collared, dark blue coat over a plaid suit and white blouse, at first leaned heavily on her smiling father's arm, but she seemed to walk under her own power without difficulty as she mounted the steps to the aircraft.

Even before Robert Mackle and his daughter arrived back in Miami, where she was rushed to the Miami Heart Institute for further observation and rest, the FBI intensified the search for her kidnapers, throwing out a dragnet which they hoped soon would land their quarry and recover the half million dollars in ransom money which had bought back the life of Barbara Jane Mackle.

That ransom represented the second largest ever paid to kidnapers in the United States. Only the $600,000 paid for little Bobby Greenlease 10 years before topped it. But Bobby later was found murdered.

It was learned that FBI agents had ordered a lookout for a lime green Ford Fairlane, bearing the Florida license plates 1E-24848, which had been rented late Thursday in Miami by a man suspected of being one of the kidnapers. The agents also were borrowing boats and planes from the Coast Guard to search the Intercoastal Waterway between Miami and Palm Beach to the north.

Then a break came. Late Friday afternoon the FBI got a call which sent them scurrying to the D and D Marine Supply in West Palm Beach, Florida.

There one of the owners of the boat sales firm, Dix Oliphant, told them a man fitting the description of Gary Steven Krist, but using the name Arthur Horowitz, had come to his place about noon that day to look for a craft. He picked out a 16-foot outboard with an 85-horsepower

164

motor, and asked Oliphant for a "test run." The owner obliged by launching the craft at nearby Currie Park and, after giving him a turn around Lake Worth, the man pulled out two paper bags and counted out $2,300 in $20-bills, handing it all to Oliphant.

"Count it and make sure it's right," he told him.

Oliphant said later, "I didn't think it was peculiar" at the time because "this is a screwy business. People pay you all kinds of ways. He was quite a smoothie." The man also vaguely mentioned that his wife would be joining him "from up north in two or three days" and he asked for travel directions to Bimini.

The man left the boat works for about 20 minutes to go park his car. Oliphant left him at the dock. But a couple of hours later, Oliphant and his son were discussing the sale and the son suggested "that guy could be one of the kidnapers." So he decided to call the FBI.

The agents checked the cash the man used to buy the boat, and impounded it as part of the ransom money. Checking the area, they found he also had bought $400 worth of supplies from the nearby Spencer Boat Company, including an extra gas tank, a compass, directional signals and a flashlight. Again he paid with twenties.

Also in a nearby parking lot, the agents found the rented green Ford, which one said was "loaded with fingerprints." The car also was impounded.

But where had Krist gone from there? He could have cruised out to sea, or headed north up the coast or back down south toward Miami. And he had several hours head start. So the painstaking search began. Working all afternoon, through Friday night and Saturday morning, FBI agents and local officers checked every possible route.

Finally they discovered that a man identifying himself as Art Horowitz of Fort Lauderdale had entered the St. Lucie Canal lock about 5:10 P.M. Friday. The lock, located down the St. Lucie River just southwest of the Atlantic coastal town of Stuart, north of West Palm Beach, is the entrance to the cross-Florida route known as the Okeechobee Waterway. Lock attendant Lawrence Shrout said the man, who left the lock at 5:25 P.M. headed west, told him he was going from Miami to Lake Okeechobee, 22 miles to the southwest in central Florida, to cruise around the lake on a vacation trip.

But it was believed that from there he took the southern route around the lake after entering it at Port Mayaca on the eastern edge, probably gassing up enroute. At any rate, he arrived at the Moore Haven Lock entrance to the Caloosahatchee River, which he entered at 9:40 that night, heading west again 20 minutes later.

But the locks are closed from 10 P.M. until 6 A.M., so the fugitive was forced to stop and spend the night between there and the Ortona Lock, about halfway between the lake and the Gulf Coast, which he passed through about 7:15 A.M. Saturday morning. He arrived at the Franklin Lock about 12 miles east of Fort Myers at 8 A.M.

Finally the boat was spotted just before noon Saturday as Krist brazenly cruised through the heart of Fort Myers, near the end of his 150-mile, cross-state, high-speed flight to avoid the ever tightening dragnet. A Lee County harbor patrol boat gave chase just as the big boat swung out of the canal and into the Gulf, heading north.

As the patrol boat closed to within 100 yards of Krist's craft, it sprung a leak and the fugitive pulled away again. But with the other vessels and planes, which had been alerted, closing in, he ran the boat aground, ironically at the junction of Captiva Pass and the Miakka River, which leads inland to Port Charlotte. A helicopter pilot spotted him leaping from the boat, lugging a briefcase and other gear, and saw him disappear into a nearby mangrove swamp.

An army of FBI agents, coast guard, state patrolmen, deputy sheriffs and other officers converged on the area from all directions. Agents swarmed over the beached boat and quickly discovered a duffel bag crammed with $20-

bills, which they later said proved to be $480,000 of the ransom.

They began an inch-by-inch search of the jungle-like area, at first centering around the tiny fishing village of El Jobean, within sight of Charlotte Harbor. From there the search shifted to nearby Deerfly Bay and finally to a tiny bit of mucky, mangrove-covered land known as Hog Island, sitting out in the river from the Lazy R Fishing Camp.

As the night of Saturday, December 21st, approached, search headquarters was set up in the fishing camp. All through the night boats shuttled a strange array of lawmen back and forth to the tiny island. They ranged from business-suited FBI men lugging submachineguns to shotgun-armed deputies dressed as hunters.

While the island was only one mile long and a few hundred feet wide, it was heavily overgrown and, as Charlotte County Sheriff Jack Bent said: "Man, you can't see five feet in front of you in there, even in daylight." The jungle island was home only to alligators, rattlesnakes and mosquitoes, with small sharks swimming in nearby tidal waters.

Through the night eerie lights illuminated the area as helicopters dropped flares and coast guard boats crisscrossed the search area with beams from their powerful search lights. Bloodhounds used in the search bayed over the waters. The lawmen hacked their way through the thick underbrush, or waded around the edge in a careful search for the elusive Krist. But the hours dragged on and he still had not been sighted.

At about midnight that Saturday, Charlotte County Deputy Sheriff Richard McLeod and part-time Deputy Milton Buffington stationed themselves on the El Jobean side of the island, because, as McLeod said later, "I had an idea he would head for the lights and probably steal a car." Staying ahead of the search lights, the two men inched their way stealthily, trying not to make any noise, and listened intently for any sign of their quarry. Finally, they heard something on the north side, about 100 yards away from them.

"He'd wade awhile and stop and listen, so we knew we couldn't make any noise at all to get near him," Deputy McLeod related. So they went out waist deep into the water and waded slowly in the direction of the noise.

"Every time a boat would crank up or come back and forth, he'd stop. Then, I presume, he would go in the bush on the sly."

McLeod and Buffington proceeded to where they had last heard him and quietly waited. Some 30 minutes passed as they occasionally heard a noise in the underbrush. Finally they heard him come out, directly in front of them. "The underbrush was thick, and when we heard him step in the water, we knew he was close to us.

"We turned the light on him and there he was, crouched down on a log, just sitting there."

McLeod leveled a shotgun at the fugitive and ordered, "Put your hands on your head."

Buffington threw handcuffs on Krist, and McLeod searched him, finding a hunting knife in his hip pocket. He carried a briefcase containing $18,000.

"He didn't do anything," McLeod said. "He just obeyed what we said."

At 12:25 A.M. that Sunday morning, December 22nd, almost five days after Barbara Jane Mackle had been kidnapped in faraway Atlanta, an exultant FBI agent radioed back to the fishing camp: "We've got our man, and we're bringing him in."

A few minutes later, Krist, soaking wet, mud-smeared and exhausted, was brought to shore kneeling on the prow of an airboat, closely guarded by his captors. The exhausted prisoner was rushed to Lee Memorial Hospital in nearby Fort Myers, where he was sequestered in a heavily guarded upper room and treated for exposure. Later that Sunday, Krist was arraigned by U.S. Commissioner George

T. Swartz on the federal kidnaping charge. He waived a preliminary hearing and right to counsel and his bond was set at $500,000, the amount of the ransom. Later that day he was secretly hustled out of the hospital and taken to the Dade County jail in Miami.

Now the spotlight switched from the captured Krist to his alleged companion in the kidnaping, Ruth Eisemann-Schier. No trace of the petite researcher had been found since the original payoff attempt, on which she was believed to have accompanied Krist. But the search went on.

Meanwhile, that Sunday afternoon, Miss Mackle made her first public appearance since her rescue. She held a brief press conference at the Miami Heart Institute, where her doctor said that although she had lost some 10 pounds, she was in remarkably good condition.

"I feel wonderful, just wonderful," the girl said. "I just want to thank everybody for their prayers."

Her father, standing at her side, was obviously shaken, but said, "This is truly a day of thanksgiving. Our first and deepest thanks—those of myself and Mrs. Mackle, our son and daughter, Barbara—are to Almighty God Who in His infinite mercy has seen fit to return our beloved daughter safely to her family." He also thanked the thousands who had sent expressions of sympathy, and the FBI for their work in helping to bring her back alive. He described the four-day ordeal as "simply a waiting game—an endless period of helplessness."

During a preliminary hearing for Gary Krist on Monday, during which federal extortion charges were added to the kidnap charges, U.S. Attorney William Meadows revealed that Barbara Jane had identified the accused pair as those who abducted her, but he did not reveal the circumstances.

The attorney said the kidnap charges may have to be dropped since it appeared that Miss Mackle had not been taken out of the state after she was abducted. But the State of Georgia stood ready to file kidnap charges, carrying the death penalty, against the pair if the FBI furnished them with their evidence. The new federal charges accused the pair of extortion by use of the telephone, mails and travel in interstate commerce.

As Christmas Day came and passed, celebrated with a special emphasis this year by the Mackle family, the search for Miss Eisemann-Schier went on. Finally on Friday, December 27th, she made history by becoming the first woman to be placed on the FBI's 10 Most Wanted list in its 19-year history.

The FBI bulletin, which said she also goes by the names of Mrs. Johnson Rarik and Mrs. George S. Price, added that the fugitive "is thought to be armed and should be considered dangerous."

Meanwhile, President-elect Nixon, spending a Christmas holiday at Key Biscayne, visited for about an hour with Miss Mackle on Christmas Eve. He told her he had kept in constant touch with FBI Director Hoover during the search for her.

A family spokesman said Mr. Nixon told Barbara Jane, who had worked in his headquarters during the GOP national convention in Miami, that she should write a book about her experience.

EDITOR'S NOTE:

The names Bert Galbraith and Lance Corby, as used in the foregoing story, are not the real names of the persons concerned. These persons have been given fictitious names to protect their identities.

"20 GRAND FOR A DOUBLE MURDER"

by Walt Hecox

The driver dropped the killers off a short distance from the residence. They left the car and walked to the house from the ditch which transports high water through a large culvert that crosses Seventh and Idaho Avenues during Hanford, California's short, and sometimes non-existent rainy season.

There was some trouble getting in. According to the best information available, the garage door should have been open. It was not. Inside they could see Ray and Gayle Yocum. The woman was reading a newspaper and the man either watching television or snoozing. Ray Yocum was a farmer. A wealthy farmer, yes. But a farmer. He had earned his right to catnap just as he had earned the callouses on his hands, the Mercedes in the garage and his money in the bank.

Somehow the killers managed to hold their weapons and force open the garage door with sufficient stealth not to be noticed. The gunmen squeezed past the big van and the Mercedes 450 sedan parked side by side in the garage. They found an entrance which opened to the game room that connected the main portion of the Yocum residence to the garage. They eased through it, grim and silent shadows on

171

a chilly winter night, and opened the door to the family room.

Guns leveled, the killers moved inside, advancing several steps into the light before Gayle Yocum, engrossed in her newspaper, was distracted by their approach. A small dog, sitting beside her, barked loudly several times.

Mrs. Yocum opened her mouth, perhaps to scream, when confronted by the two rifle-bearing intruders. Whatever sound she might have made was drowned by the roar of a 30.06 Marlin, a weapon known to destroy the deer it was intended to kill and which promptly demolished Mrs. Yocum's features.

The killer was conscious of flesh and bone and brain matter splattering against the wall behind the woman in the wake of the speeding bullet. He moved his hand to lever a second projectile into the firing chamber, but the gun jammed. Ray Yocum, wide awake now, was rushing across the room, his face a mask of fury, to defend his shattered wife. He was met by the bark of the .22 held by the second gunman, a toy compared to the powerful weapon which had just started Mrs. Yocum on her journey into eternity. But the weapon was sufficiently powerful to stop the rancher when one of the slugs it fired entered his surging chest.

Ray Yocum staggered and swayed, the rage and anger his face had mirrored suddenly converted to surprise, confusion and perhaps some fear.

He threw his hands up over his head and said, "Please don't shoot me."

The killer holding the .22 wasn't listening. He had come to the house with a mission in mind. Pleas for mercy from a middle-aged rancher were not going to help.

Flame spouted from the barrel of the .22 as one barking little report followed another while the killer virtually emptied the gun into Ray Yocum. The rancher twitched, jerked, struggled and tried to fight back, his body reacting convulsively as one bullet after another entered his arms,

172

his chest, his neck and eventually his head.

Ray Yocum could not have died easily. His killer unleashed a virtual fusillade of bullets to bring him down. Eventually he crumpled to the linoleum floor of the kitchen, adjoining the living room, where he had finally stumbled. His convulsions stopped and silence settled over the Yocum residence at last.

The killers moved through it quietly, their progress marked only now and then by the sound of overturning furniture, opening drawers and closet doors. They paused at a small safe long enough to remove a set of gold Krugerrands, then continued their stealthy rampage. After a few moments they left.

Three centuries ago, when Captain Juan Bautista de Anza led his small expedition from Sonora, Mexico, through Arizona and across the blazing Mojave to San Gabriel, thus establishing his little used "land bridge" to California, he ignored the long, dust-dry San Joaquin Valley. It was, in his mind, little better than the Mojave and not worthy of his attention.

Some 150 years later when Jedediah Smith, a giant among the mountain men, followed somewhat the same route to California, he too ignored the long valley.

Fifty years ago, Hanford, the county seat of Kings County, California, was a dusty cowtown ignored and bypassed by travelers struggling through the summer heat or winter fogs between Fresno and Bakersfield on United States Highway 99.

Today, Hanford is a submetropolitan jewel in the heart of the land ignored by deAnza and Smith—the dusty acres which had lain fallow for centuries and which late arrivals to the Gold Rush settled on would produce four crops a year of some staples and booming single harvests of fruit or cotton.

By the 1980s, people who owned large acres of land in the southern San Joaquin were among the elite and wealthy. Ray and Gayle Yocum were among those people.

On December 20, 1983, a young woman, a psychology major on the University of California campus at Davis, was just beginning her holiday visit to her home town. Christmas was right around the corner. Her official residence was at Davis, the place where she spent nine months a year, but Hanford was the place she was raised and she was, at the moment, staying at the Yocum residence on Idaho Avenue there.

Early on the evening of December 20th, the student went to visit a pair of young friends, a recently married couple, both of whom she had known for years. They were chatting happily when, at 8:30, the telephone rang and the call was for her. The caller was Kevin Yocum, a youthful relative of the young woman who told her he would visit with her for a while. He was a couple of years younger than she, but the pair had been close for years and enjoyed each other's company.

Within a few moments, the student met the young man, according to their arrangement, at a convenience market on 11th Street in Hanford not far from 12th and Hanford-Aroma, a major thoroughfare. The next couple of hours passed rapidly. The youthful relatives chatted, exchanged experiences, enjoyed a snack at a fast food restaurant specializing in hamburgers, and shortly thereafter she left Kevin, dropping him off at a street corner not too far from the restaurant. It was a little later than 10:30 P.M.

The house was quiet, almost eerily so, when the young woman entered, although the lights were on. As she stepped through the front door she noticed the front room had been disturbed, although the damage didn't appear to be excessive. A table was overturned and a chair was upset. She entered the family room and was advancing toward the kitchen when she saw the woman sitting on the couch.

At first it appeared to the student that her relative was just sitting there, quietly, reading. Then, as the young woman drew closer, she saw the blood and the shattered features and human tissue splattered on the walls. Gayle

174

Yocum was not reading. The speeding 30.06 projectile had reached her so fast she had died without ever changing position.

The student uttered a little cry of horror, then a choked sob as the enormity of what she had discovered sank into her numbed senses. She took a step back, turned toward the kitchen, and saw Ray Yocum on the floor. He had not died fast or easily. Blood from at least a half dozen wounds oozed from his body onto the linoleum floor.

Almost sick with fear, grief and horror by then, the student found the telephone, picked it up with trembling hands, dialed the operator and asked for the police.

"I want to report a murder on Idaho Avenue," she said, squeezing the words through sobs as she spoke. When she hung up, she remembered young Kevin. Less than five minutes earlier, she had dropped him off at a street corner. The news of what had happened to his parents would devastate him. She wondered how she could contact him. He had mentioned he was meeting some friends.

The holidays had suddenly become a nightmare for the student from Davis.

Deputy Sheriff Randy Leach responded to the call from his dispatcher and headed for Idaho Avenue, reflecting that no one gets used to murder, not in Los Angeles, not in Oakland, where blood and bullets stain the lives of homicide investigators almost daily. Certainly no one gets accustomed to bloodshed in Hanford, where most of what violence there is occurs on summer Saturday nights when farm laborers are converting their wages to the fermented product of grapes, hops and a variety of grains.

Hanford is not such a large city that Deputy Leach didn't recognize the address on Idaho Avenue as that of Ray and Gayle Yocum, one of the community's wealthier and best-known couples. He wondered what had happened there, how someone had managed to be murdered in one of the city's finest neighborhoods. Off the beaten track and with few escape routes readily available to bandits, the munici-

175

pality is generally avoided by experienced holdup men and burglars.

The deputy eased his brown and white patrol car to the curb in front of the house. He followed the short walk through a carefully manicured yard to the front door. The place, he noted, was located at the southwest corner of Idaho and Seventh Avenue. The house was not unknown to him.

Deputy Leach tried the door and it was locked. He knocked and rang the doorbell, but there was no reply. He then followed a walk to the side of the garage where he found an unlocked, partially open door. He walked in, passed the Mercedes and the van, and moved into the game room.

Almost subconsciously, with senses honed by years of experience, Deputy Leach noticed the garage was undisturbed except for a door leading into the residence. The portal was slightly ajar. He walked through it, ignoring, for the moment, signs that the room had been ransacked, continuing to the kitchen. There he found Ray Yocum on the floor.

He was, the deputy noted, lying on his back, his head nearest the east wall of the room, his feet to the west. A large puddle of blood had gathered under the murdered man's head. He was, the officer saw, shoeless.

Deputy Leach moved on, into the large family room which was connected to the kitchen. As he advanced, he saw Gayle Yocum still in a sitting position on the couch, the newspaper still in her lap. Had not her features been almost destroyed by the bullet she would have appeared to be cat-napping.

The woman was wearing a reddish colored robe, liberally stained with blood, when the deputy entered the room. He saw that a television set in the room had been turned off but that a VCR attachment atop it was still turned on ready to record or play.

Behind the couch, occupying most of the south wall of

176

the room, Deputy Leach saw a large, plate glass window. The east wall, to the murdered woman's right, was chiefly occupied by a big fireplace.

The drapes over the picture window were drawn. A large opening connected the living room with the linoleum floor of the kitchen and it was at the opening between the two rooms that the body of Ray Yocum was lying close to an overturned table.

Deputy Leach was aware of the sound of almost soprano whining somewhere in the house. He followed the sound to a door just north of the kitchen and there found that a small dog, unhurt but unhappy, had been locked in there. The officer wondered about the dog. The killers had displayed a strange, selective kindness. The little animal must have tried to protect his mistress in some way, at least by barking. Killers, burglars and robbers are not normally so solicitous of the family pets of their victims. If they get in the way, they are killed, particularly if the other occupants of the house are being murdered. Yet the little animal at the Yocum home was not only unharmed, it had been carefully shut up in the bathroom.

The person who put the dog in the bathroom had apparently not been completely clean. There was a large quantity of blood on the floor of the bathroom.

What kind of a dog, the deputy wondered, would let his mistress's killer pick him up with bloodstained hands and drop him in an adjoining room? The little animal was young enough to be active, agile and alert. His behavior just didn't make any sense.

The deputy moved through the house while he waited for help to arrive from sheriff's department headquarters at the county administration complex across town. He saw that many rooms had been ransacked, drawers pulled out, closet doors open, the little safe open and apparently emptied. Somehow the picture wasn't quite right. It was something he almost sensed. The situation was not exactly normal.

Of course, the situation was not normal in any sense of the word. It is not often one of the wealthier and most influential couples in the area are murdered in a city the size of Hanford. The Yocums were known and respected by almost everyone in town and, of course, perhaps envied by some.

Ray Yocum was the kind of man that even those who envied him would have admired. He had worked, as a young man, with his father and three brothers developing extensive farming land southwest of Hanford.

Later he had parlayed 64 acres of his own land into a highly successful independent operation. Known as Ray Yocum Farms, his business had incorporated and included vast acreages. It included everything from spray rigs and cotton pickers to trucks for transporting produce to market.

Still, Yocum remembered how to enjoy life. His possessions included a water ski boat, beach buggy and a variety of recreational machinery.

Deputy Leach found two sets of footprints in the house, bloody impressions left by the stained bottoms of tennis shoes, and the deputy followed them back through the game room, or "den" as he thought of it, into the garage and out into the street.

The footprints followed the walk out to Seventh Avenue. There they revealed some indecision on the part of the people making them. One set traveled south to the intersection of Seventh Avenue and Idaho and ended at the dirt shoulder there. A second pair of prints followed the pavement to a drive immediately south of the residence and ended abruptly. It seemed obvious that the two people responsible for the footprints had been picked up by an accomplice driving a car or truck at the places where the two trails ended.

Deputy Leach's report of the murder had brought a

178

small platoon of King's County sheriff's deputies to the crime scene by the time he concluded his examination of the murder scene. With them were Detective Chris Mullin, veteran homicide detective for the King's County Sheriff's Department, and Detective Larry Orth, another experienced homicide investigator.

Patrol deputies were directed to begin a canvass of the neighborhood which, on the outskirts of town and beyond the city limits, was rather thinly populated. Detectives Mullin and Orth listened to Leach's account of his activities and inspected the crime scene carefully. Photographs of the interior of the house and the murder scene were taken by the investigators themselves and by technicians summoned from the California Department of Justice Crime Laboratory in Fresno.

From the beginning, the detectives agreed with Deputy Leach: there was something strange about the crime scene. Although the house had apparently been ransacked, the attempt appeared to be half-hearted and, with the exception of the emptied safe from which they would later learn the gold Krugerrands had been stolen, little of value appeared to have been taken.

The behavior of the dog puzzled them. Even the friendliest of animals don't allow themselves to be locked up unless they know their jailer.

Beyond that, the murder of Ray Yocum appeared to be the act of both a frantic and vicious person. The small caliber weapon which killed him, obviously a .22 from the size of the entry wounds, had been fired again and again. On the scene, the detectives didn't get an accurate count of the number of wounds the wealthy rancher had absorbed before dying. They estimated the count at about a dozen.

Whoever had murdered Ray Yocum appeared to be determined to kill him but was not very efficient at this task. The rancher had been savagely and sickeningly butchered.

Gayle Yocum had obviously died instantly. The heavier caliber bullet which struck her head had been swiftly effi-

179

cient, although the effect was macabre and grim. Her head and features had been partially destroyed by the wound.

The bullet, which had buried itself in the wall above the couch on which the woman was sitting, was recovered and appeared to be in decent enough shape to be used in ballistics tests. Also, the investigators found several shell casings on the floor of the living room, some from the .22 and a larger one which had fired about a .30-caliber bullet.

Early in their investigation the detectives located the young woman who had found the bodies and who had taken refuge in a friend's home after her grisly discovery. She had recovered enough to be able to tell them she was a psychology major at the University of California at Davis, that she was visiting her home town over the winter holidays and how she spent the evening. She detailed the time she had spent with young Kevin Yocum, told about leaving him on a street corner across town, going directly to the home of his parents and finding them dead.

The young woman also was able to examine the house later and inform the detectives about the Krugerrands missing from the family safe.

"Do you have any idea how much the Yocum family was worth?" she was asked.

She said she had reliable information that Ray Yocum had amassed a fortune worth about three and a half million dollars.

Asked who the principal heirs to the fortune were, the young woman said they would be Gayle Yocum—who had been murdered with her husband—herself and young Kevin.

"Then Kevin stood to inherit almost two million dollars when his parents died," the detectives observed.

The young woman told them that was not quite the truth. Kevin would inherit a sum approaching that figure when he was 25 years old. In December of 1983 he would be 18, almost seven years from any inheritance. To this the young woman added that Kevin could hardly be responsible for his parents' death. He had been with her since early that evening; she had left the Yocums in the company of someone else at the time she departed from the house. Plenty of people had seen the two of them together in the interim.

The detectives explained that investigators are always inclined to look at the family and close friends during murder investigations, particularly when the victims are wealthy.

Early the next morning, Dr. Armand Dollinger, a King's County forensic pathologist with headquarters in Hanford, verified the investigators' assessment of Ray Yocum's murder. The wealthy land-owner had been shot many times. There were, the pathologist reported, at least 12 gunshot wounds. He had been hit several times in the left arm, the right shoulder area and the right chest.

Dr. Dollinger said he could not tell exactly how often Ray Yocum had been hit in the head. The hard bones of the skull had reduced the bullets fragments and multiple entry holes in a small area made it impossible to determine exactly how many there were. There were at least four such holes, possibly more.

The pathologist used blue knitting needles to show the trajectory of the projectiles which had killed the man, helping the detectives determine about where the killers were standing during the murder. Enough bullets were recovered in good enough condition for the investigators to be sure they were .22 caliber and to use them in ballistics tests if the weapons were found later.

News of the murders occupied much of page one in the Hanford Sentinel and nearby newspapers. The detectives, meanwhile, searched for possible witnesses who might have seen strange automobiles pulling up in front of the Yocum residence between 7:00 and 10:30 P.M. on the night of the 20th, or had perhaps heard the gunshots. They spoke to the guest at the Yocum house who had been there when

181

the young woman found the bodies left early in the evening. She said she left shortly before eight o'clock. No one had heard the shots, nor could anyone identify whatever automobiles approached the Yocum home between the time she left and that when the bodies were found. Dr. Dollinger set the time of their deaths at about between 8:30 and 10:00 the night of the 20th.

Friends and relatives were questioned while the detectives sought a motive for the murder. Robbery was the obvious motive, a little too obvious, the investigators decided. The "ransacking" of the Yocum residence was half-hearted, incomplete, and could have been a ruse to throw suspicion off the real motive. The behavior of the dog indicated he might well have known the killers.

There were, the detectives learned, people who might not like Ray Yocum. No man acquires the kind of success in any business he had without making some enemies along the way. There might be employes who had been discharged; people who believed he had bested them in business deals. The detectives began a tedious check through the murdered man's business life, searching for anyone who might believe he had reason to murder Ray Yocum.

They also launched an all-out effort to find the murder weapons. Reasoning that the killers might have sought to dispose of the weapons, they enlisted the public's help in the search. They also believed that at least one of the killers, and possibly both, had been splattered with blood. There was no question in their minds that at least two people had been involved. The two sets of footprints supported that theory. Irrigation ditches and canals, which abound in the area where the runoff from the Sierra Nevada snowpack is the chief water supply, were cited as likely places for the weapons to have been hidden.

At the Yocum residence, technicians were combing the property for latent fingerprints and possible clues.

The search for the killers might have been long and difficult had not the murderers been uncommonly careless. Laborers at a residential construction project adjoining an elementary school found two pairs of blood-stained athletic shoes, a .22 rifle and a Marlin 30.06. These were turned over to the investigators, who compared the treads of the athletic shoes with photographs of those found at the murder scene and discovered they were identical.

Ballistics tests for the deer rifle and the .22 were scheduled, as were laboratory examinations of the hammer and chamber markings on the expended shell casings.

Later in the day, the investigators learned that several .22 shell casings had been found along 7th and 12th Avenues and Parsons Way in Hanford.

The weapons, the detectives learned, had been purchased by a woman living on Parsons Way. The investigators were spared a long check through sales slips. The woman and her husband returned from a holiday trip early on the 22nd, discovered their house had been burglarized while they were gone, and that the .22 and the 30.06 were among the items stolen. In fact, they were the only items stolen.

Asked who might know about the weapons and where they were kept, the woman told the investigators that a young man named John Cox, who lived just three doors down the street, was a friend of her son's, and no doubt had all the information needed. With a little digging, they learned that Kevin Yocum often spent long periods living at the Cox residence.

John Cox, the detectives noted, was among the close associates listed for Kevin Yocum. He was not home when the investigators visited his residence. Probing farther into young Kevin's associates, the detectives discovered that Cox, a youth named Mark Lawson and another named Larry Spanke had been close friends. Probing into the background of that trio, the detectives learned that a rumor they might be involved in the Yocum murder was growing in some sections of Hanford.

Early in the morning, armed with a search warrant, the detectives visited the home of Larry Spanke. They indicated they wanted to question Spanke and to search the property. During their visit they searched young Spanke's car, that of one of his relatives, the house, the garage and the basement. When their search was completed, they took Spanke into sheriff's department headquarters, and after reading him his Miranda rights, questioned him.

Late that afternoon, Spanke admitted he had driven John Cox, 18 at the time, and Mark Lawson, also 18, to the Yocum house for the purpose of killing Ray and Gayle Yocum.

Spanke explained that Kevin Yocum had promised John Cox $10,000 from his insurance money to pay for this part in the crime, and $10,000 for a helper. He said the duo had first planned to shoot the couple through the window, then decided that was risky and too noisy. Moreover, such an attempt might not be successful.

Spanke said the trio had returned later for a second attempt, after being promised by Kevin that the garage door would be open. They had managed to enter, shoot the couple and escape.

Because part of the faked robbery had included plans for Lawson and Cox to take the Mercedes and van, and abandon them later, Spanke had simply dropped them off a short distance from the house, thus completing his participation in the crime, or so he thought. But later that night he had received a frantic telephone call summoning him back to the scene.

"Something's gone wrong," he was told.

When he returned in his Oldsmobile 88 to pick up the pair, he was told they had not been able to find the keys to either the Mercedes or the van.

Spanke's confession triggered a chain reaction. He told the officers first about Kevin Yocum's offers to John Cox. Later, in prison, Yocum, Lawson and Spanke all talked with a fellow prisoner, telling him about the crime bit by

184

bit. The prisoner turned his evidence over to the detectives and helped secure murder convictions.

The prisoner said he had asked Yocum why he wanted his parents killed when he would get no money until he was 25. Yocum said he believed his parents didn't care about him and that, if they were dead, things were set so that he and his buddies could live in the Yocum house and do whatever they wanted until he inherited his fortune.

He had set up the other Yocum heir, the UC Davis psychology major, as an alibi for the night of the murders.

Ballistics tests, blood tests and the bloody shoeprints all helped convict the quartet of murder, but the testimony of Mark Lawson, Larry Spanke and the cellmate in whom they all had confided were devastating as far as Kevin Yocum was concerned.

On May 7, 1984, Yocum was found guilty of the murders of his mother and father. At that time, Judge William Fernandez of Santa Clara County, where the trial was moved because of excessive publicity in Hanford, said he would, on June 13th, sentence Yocum to life in prison without the possibility of parole.

Mark Lawson, 20 at the time Yocum was convicted, pleaded guilty to first-degree murder and was awaiting sentence at the time Yocum was found guilty.

John Cox was found guilty of first degree murder and sentenced to life in prison without possibility of parole.

Larry Spanke, the driver, 19 at the time of Yocum's trial, testified for the prosecution and pleaded guilty to second-degree murder.

"OVERKILL MURDER OF THE RICH PLAYBOY"

by Olga Kogan

Werner Hartmann was the type women would vote for as the man they'd most like to go out with on a date. In the looks department, he had a lot to brag about: thick, carefully coiffured locks of hair, bedroom eyes, and an aristocratic aquiline nose, finished off with fine, sculpted lips and a strong, masculine chin. He might have kept those looks right into old age if murder hadn't interrupted his life permanently in his 38th year.

Police in the North Chicago suburb of Northbrook received an alert on Werner Hartmann's death at an early hour on the morning of June 9, 1982. The sun had yet to peek above the edge of the horizon when the desk officer at the Northbrook headquarters looked up to see a sultry blonde looking at him, her eyes full of fear. At any other time and in any other place, her willowy figure and full-lipped pout would have seized any man's attention. But she was clearly distraught, and the words she was speaking were pure police business.

"My husband . . . I think it's suicide. His body's covered with blood in the bathroom . . ."

As the woman spoke, a teenage girl stood watching a few feet away. She'd apparently come in with the older woman, who looked to be in her mid-20s.

The frightened blonde was directed to Deputy Police Chief James Wallace. She gave her name as Debra Hartmann. Just a few minutes before and scarcely a mile away, she said, she'd returned to her home following a night of club-hopping with her stepdaughter. When she went upstairs, she was startled by the figure of her husband, Werner, lying on the floor by the bathroom of the master bedroom. He was naked and his skin was marred by long streaks of blood.

In panic, Debra had grabbed her stepdaughter's hand and hurried to the police station. She'd been too shocked by the sight of her dead husband to think clearly enough to just grab the telephone and call the police. The few minutes needed to come to headquarters had given her time to collect her thoughts.

The deputy police chief accompanied the two women back to their house. The Hartmanns, he observed, lived well. Shade trees framed their large two-storied home and in the driveway stood two convertibles — a Mercedes and a Rolls-Royce. Even in that well-to-do area, those were extravagant trappings.

Inside, the same wealth permeated the elegantly furnished, richly carpeted suites. It was only upstairs in the master bedroom that the lawman found a note that jarred the harmony.

Werner Hartmann's strongly built, medium frame was sprawled half in the bathroom, half in the adjoining bedroom. There was no doubt that he was dead, but suicide was definitely not the cause of his death. Even a superficial glance told the experienced eyes of the veteran lawman that Hartmann had taken several bullets above the waist. This was murder, pure and deliberate.

No one among the homicide team that began investigating Werner Hartmann's brutal death suspected that eight years would go by before the case finally saw its end. At the outset, however, their attention was focused on the current task: to gather as much information at the crime scene as

187

possible. This the team did with professional dispatch.

As the crime scene technicians combed through the house, a detective questioned the victim's widow. She had little to add to what she'd already reported. The previous day, she recounted, she'd left the house during the early evening to go to dinner with some friends in a nearby suburb. Her 14-year-old stepdaughter had accompanied her.

After dinner, the group drove to a fashionable cocktail lounge in still another suburb. It was the start of an evening of club-hopping that would draw to a sleepy close at four o'clock the next morning.

Meanwhile, at some point during those nighttime hours, someone had ambushed Werner Hartmann, defenseless as he stepped out of the bathroom, toweling his naked skin.

The Hartmann home contained many objects to interest a burglar, but a thorough check of all the doors and windows showed not the slightest sign of forced entry. Like other wealthy homeowners in the area, the Hartmanns had installed a burglar alarm system to protect their property. The system was bought only after the house had been "hit" a few times. Unfortunately, the occupants sometimes forgot or didn't bother to turn the system on, especially when someone was at home. On the night of Werner Hartmann's murder, the system had been off.

What made the burglary angle a bit hard to swallow, however, was that nothing of value in the house appeared to have been stolen. It's a rare burglar who can make his way to a second-floor bedroom, shoot the homeowner in cold blood, and then flee without one dime of loot. And it was almost definitely not a professional burglar. Pros don't take weapons with them on the job, because the penalty of armed burglary is far more harsh than a mere breaking-and-entry rap.

The murder began to look more and more like a deliberate hit job. Someone had wanted Werner Hartmann out of the way. As the detectives delved into his life and activities, they discovered that there were more than a few people who

188

might have had reason to want to do away with Werner Hartmann.

The source of Hartmann's prosperity was his car-stereo business in Franklin Park, a West Chicago suburb. By all appearances, it was a good operation, patronized by many a local notable, including a few officials and lawmen.

Hartmann relied strongly on his family to keep the business running. His wife, Debra, and another close relative were employed by the firm. And, surprising to detectives, Hartmann's first wife was also an employee, handling the company's books.

It was a surprise with a double whammy, for not only were both wives working under the same roof, but they were also living in the same house!

The unusual arrangement had been set up about a month earlier. The first wife had been living in Florida with their two daughters. Hartmann had contacted her with a request that she return to Chicago to help him out with the accounting, a job she'd performed—and performed well—during their marriage. The first wife agreed to come if she could bring along the younger of the two daughters. The two women eventually moved into Hartmann's house, an arrangement apparently proposed by Hartmann's current wife, Debra.

Two wives living under the same roof seemed to spell trouble. Although Debra Hartmann insisted that she and "the ex" got along extremely well, the detectives' natural reaction was skepticism. Inquiries into the nature of the breakup of Hartmann and his first wife revealed that he had filed for divorce, charging prolonged mental cruelty. Divorce had been the probable outcome of their union ever since their wedding: They had married when Werner was 20 and she was just 15. After 13 years of marriage, they divorced in 1977. Soon afterward, Hartmann met his current wife, Debra, whom he married in 1978.

With such a stormy marital past hanging over the Hartmann manor, it was logical for detectives to focus some at-

189

tention on wife number one. She had returned to the house at around nine o'clock on the morning of the discovery of her ex-husband's body. Her absence from the house on that fateful night stirred up a lot of questions in the detectives' investigative brew.

The first questions concerned motive. What would the woman stand to gain by her ex-husband's death? The divorce documents showed that she was receiving $200 a week in child-support payments and alimony. The divorce agreement stipulated that this amount would be paid for 10 years. On top of that, Hartmann was paying his ex-wife a salary for the accounting work she was doing for his company. Would she have jeopardized a steady income for the unsure future she faced if he were dead? Clearly, money would have been no motive for her to order a "hit."

In any case, the first wife had an iron-clad alibi for herself on the night of the murder. Lawmen therefore crossed her out as a viable suspect.

Meanwhile, the autopsy on the victim's remains painted a not-so-pretty picture of his death: about a dozen shots had pierced Hartmann's body from the waist up, leaving an ugly pattern of wounds. Powder burns indicated that the shots had been fired from extreme close range, maybe a foot or less away.

It appeared that Hartmann had taken his shower, wrapped a towel around his waist, and then stepped one foot into the bedroom. Here he was confronted by the gunman. Shots were fired, hitting the victim a few times. Fighting the searing pain and growing weakness, the strongly built man turned around to flee into the bathroom, hoping to save his life. More shots slammed into his back. One of the slugs broke his spine. He collapsed to the floor, his lifeblood seeping from the raw wounds in his body. He bled to death quickly.

The murder bullets were all from a .38-caliber revolver. Only one gun had been used, indicating that at some point during the shooting, the killer had paused to reload. Unloading a full barrel into the victim and then repeating the process smacked of overkill and unbridled hatred. No professional hitman would let his emotions take control, unleashing such a frenzied volley.

Only one detail hinted at a pro: Some of the shell casings were missing, meaning that the gunman had stopped to pick them up before leaving.

Apparently no one outside the house had heard the shooting. This element was not really surprising, since the house was surrounded by shade trees and set off from neighboring houses by wide lawns and streets.

Speculate as they might, the detectives had to admit that they didn't have a firm handle on the case as the first day of investigation drew to an end. A man had been gunned down in his own bathroom and there didn't seem to be any reason why.

As the probe continued, a closer look at Werner Hartmann began to suggest that the motive might have been connected with money, after all. He had the reputation and look of a wealthy playboy — silk shirts, gold chain necklaces, custom-made suits, and, of course, his young wife, a woman who could give Madonna a run for her money in the sex department. But, it turned out, all was not well in the Hartmann castle.

Authorized searches of the slain businessman's papers uncovered long lists of unpaid bills. Hartmann, it appeared, was up to his neck in creditors — and they were howling for payment. Some bills were several months overdue. The line of credit was stretched so thin, in fact, that it was threatening to snap altogether in several places.

Apparently the Hartmanns' lavish lifestyle was a credit-card company's dream. The fancy cars in the driveway and the garage — there was a Lincoln Continental to go along with the Mercedes and the Rolls — really belonged not to Hartmann but to the banks who had issued the credit for them. And soon — very soon — the banks were planning to repossess.

191

Questioned by sleuths about whether she was aware of the state of the family finances, Debra Hartmann admitted that they had been living somewhat beyond their means. She said business had been good, but not good enough to let them buy expensive toys like the $100,000 Rolls. Credit seemed like the best way to go, and once the ball started rolling, it didn't slow down. Then it picked up more speed in a way that frightened her.

Her husband, Debra Hartmann told detectives, had turned to organized crime for quick loans when he'd needed to pay off bills. Unfortunately, business never picked up enough to let him pay off the legitimate bills fast enough so that he could then pay off the mob. It became an expensive vicious circle.

The detectives had little sympathy for the murdered man's financial plight, but here was the first hint of a motive: Had an irate loan shark sent over one of his men to teach the errant borrower a lesson in gang business? Probers knew it was a possibility that needed checking out.

A little checking also showed that both Werner Hartmann and his gorgeous wife were not above hijinks bordering on the edge of the law. The first such escapade had involved Debra and the luxury Rolls-Royce convertible.

The previous September, two patrol officers on foot had spotted the Rolls cruising with its top down along a low-rent cafe and bar area of North Chicago. It was early in the morning, just before 2:00 A.M., and the driver and passengers in the Rolls were having what looked like a merry old time. Then, an empty bottle went twirling into the air from the car, landing carelessly on the head of a passerby in the area. The car and its passengers, apparently heedless of anything, kept rolling along.

The two officers immediately commandeered a taxi waiting nearby and took off in pursuit. When the Rolls speeded up, one of the officers used his portable radio to call for assistance. Three patrol cars responded. Within a few minutes, they surrounded the fleeing auto at a corner and the officers ordered the drunken party into the street.

Another empty bottle on the car floor showed the officers what the deal was. As posh as the "suspects' " clothes and car were, they were still nothing more than some people out on a drunk. But there was something else, too — a .38-caliber automatic pistol was found under the driver's seat, apparently shoved there by the sexy blonde at the wheel just before lawmen pulled her over.

The group was taken to headquarters for booking. It turned out to be a colorful assembly: The blonde gave her name as Debra Hartmann, her place of birth, Hawaii, and her profession, nightclub stripper. She gave a current address in Northbrook, the nearby swanky suburb.

One of the blonde's companions in the Rolls was identified as a suspect involved in trafficking drugs in Florida. The other passengers were known habitues of Chicago's sleazier nightspots. In their extravagant evening clothes, they looked like characters out of the recent Dick Tracy movie.

Police booked them for disorderly conduct. Debra Hartmann got an additional rap for failing to register a firearm. It was nothing major, but the name Hartmann got its first listing on the police ledger.

The second listing came just two months later. Neighbors of the Hartmanns heard the unmistakable sounds of gunshots coming from the Hartmanns' home. Police answering the alert found Werner Hartmann in a virtual state of rage. Debra and he had quarreled, and she'd finally stomped out the front door and hopped into the Rolls parked outside. As she'd pulled away, tires screeching, Werner pumped several bullets from a derringer into the passenger-side door. The volley barely slowed the car down, but passersby would have seen the rather unusual sight of a Rolls-Royce with bullet holes in its chassis.

Werner Hartmann was hauled into court and soon convicted of recklessness with a firearm. The judge placed him on probation.

Although there were no further incidents at the Hartmann home requiring police intervention, the indication was that tempers in the big house were smoldering. Seven months later, Werner Hartmann would be dead. Had the pressure of his business dealings ruined his marriages as well as his professional life? It was food for speculation, but in that department the sleuths were already having a feast.

The investigation into Werner Hartmann's murder continued into a second day, then a third and fourth. Still, not a single lead turned up that might unravel the tight ball of clues that lawmen kept bouncing up and down.

It was a full month before the ball came to rest, if only briefly. The information came from the FBI. Their technicians had finally been able to evaluate some tests that had been made on Debra Hartmann and her stepdaughter at the time the murder had been reported. The tests had been routine, involving paraffin testing of the two women's hands. Debra Hartmann's hands were clean, but the stepdaughter's showed a faint trace of gunpowder.

The lawmen contacted the girl's mother, who'd moved back with her daughter to Florida. When the officers called, the mother informed them that her daughter had not been herself in the last few weeks. She'd been acting highly nervous, especially when anything relating to her father's death was mentioned. At one point, she'd even blurted out a fantastic story about firing a gun at the scene of the crime. It all sounded like the imaginings of an adolescent who'd undergone shock. With the police technicians discovery, however, the story took on new importance.

The stepdaughter and her mother both flew back to Chicago to answer the detectives' questions. Meanwhile, some new technical information added another twist to the mystery pretzel. A pathologist discovered that the victim had been shot at *two* distinct times of the day. The first volley had occurred at about 10 o'clock on the evening of June

194

8th. The bullets had killed Hartmann outright. But then a second volley from the same gun had been discharged at his dead body several hours later, on the morning of June 9th.

In an attempt to find an answer to the puzzling series of events, lawmen turned to the services of a certified hypnotist, who succeeded in putting the victim's daughter into a trance. Although any information obtained in this way is not recognized in court, it can nevertheless prove useful in opening up paths that otherwise might remain forever blocked.

So it was in this case. The girl recalled seeing a third person in the house at the time she and her stepmother discovered her father's body. It was an acquaintance of Debra's named John Korabik. An identification check on Korabik showed him to be a 25-year-old professional tennis player who worked at a club on Chicago's North Side. He had no criminal record. However, he did have a close connection to Debra Hartmann.

According to what the investigators learned from certain sources, the young tennis pro had been Debra's lover for some time. Putting two and two together, the sleuths came up with a possible scenario: Werner and Debra had quarreled over her lover two months earlier, with Debra storming out of the house and Werner firing shots at her. Then, when Werner suggested that his ex-wife come back to help with the books, Debra eagerly invited the woman to live with them in the same house, perhaps figuring that Werner would return to his former spouse and permit Debra to pursue her own lover in peace.

The triangle aspect — or perhaps it was even a quadrangle — now surfaced as a fruitful avenue of investigation. With the new information, the detectives went back to question Debra Hartmann. They found the widow not-so-grieving and currently living with her boyfriend, John Korabik. Demurely, she insisted she had engaged in her romance only following her husband's death.

Detectives are not born yesterday. They knew that Debra

195

Hartmann had been cheating on her husband. They also now strongly suspected that John Korabik had been in the death house. Why had Debra tried to cover up his presence?

Delving into Werner Hartmann's affairs further, the detectives discovered that he had two insurance policies on his life. Like the man himself, the policies oozed wealth—one bore a face value of $250,000, the other weighed in at $150,000, and both included double-indemnity clauses. With Werner Hartmann's death, the beneficiary stood to gain close to $1 million. And the beneficiary—the detectives learned, to no surprise—was Debra Hartmann.

The money was motive enough. The apparent souring of the Hartmanns' marriage also added incentive. It looked like the lawmen were onto something hot.

Unfortunately, the investigative sizzle suddenly went into a deep freeze. The sleuths just didn't have the hard evidence needed to go ahead with arrests and indictments. They needed some link to the crime or some testimony that would finger Debra Hartmann and John Korabik. But as much as the detectives tried, they couldn't quite come up with anything.

The case remained stymied for the next five years. To all intents and purposes, it appeared as though the murder of Werner Hartmann would remain not unsolved—lawmen were sure they had some solid suspects—but unprosecuted.

The breakthrough came from the mouth of a small-time criminal serving a prison term for car theft and illegally selling guns. His name was Ken Kaenel. With nothing to lose and maybe a reduced prison stretch to gain, Kaenel told lawmen of one day in 1982 when a tennis pro had offered him 50 grand to do away with a Chicago businessman by the name of Werner Hartmann. Kaenel admitted he was interested, so the tennis pro—John Korabik—gave him a .38-caliber automatic to do the job. But when Kaenel tested the weapon in his basement and the gun kept misfiring, he balked. He returned the .38 to Korabik with a "no thanks."

Lawmen verified Kaenel's story the hard way: They went to the basement of his former lodgings and extracted several bullets still stuck in the wall from the test-firing. Technicians compared them with the slugs removed from Warner Hartmann's body. They matched like peas from the same pod.

Finally, here was a link between the murder weapon and John Korabik.

Police requested Kaenel's cooperation in collecting further evidence. Kaenel agreed. He was already in his 50s, and he was desperate to spend his remaining years a free man.

Wearing a police wire to record their conversation, Ken Kaenel paid a courtesy call on Debra Hartmann, now living alone in an apartment in the community of Deerfield. Her affair with John Korabik had long been over. They had stayed together for little more than a year. Again, the split had come with the discharge of firearms: Korabik had been wounded in the legs by a gun blast while at his home. The police report stated the discharge was accidental, but shortly afterward, Debra Hartmann moved out of the house.

During the chat between Debra and Kaenel, the blonde ex-stripper casually followed the other's train of conversation. Kaenel talked of Hartmann and of how he himself might have been the one who could have blown him away. Then Debra let loose with the information that she'd promised her boyfriend more than $200,000 to do away with her husband. The money was to have been used in an investment scheme that she, too, could profit from, but that was not to be. Korabik, she said, screwed her royally.

A federal grand jury indicted Debra Hartmann, John Korabik, and Ken Kaenel on January 20, 1989, charging them with conspiracy to commit murder in order to collect life insurance. The life insurance policies, it turned out, had been falsified with the forged name of Debra Hartmann.

197

The prosecution was put in the hands of Steven Miller and John Farrel, two state attorneys who'd worked closely with the police in gathering the evidence that led to the indictment. No charges or suspicions were leveled against Werner Hartmann's daughter. It appeared to the investigators that the 14-year-old had been nothing but an innocent dupe in the hands of the plotters. Perhaps she had been brought to the house, forced to fire some rounds from the murder gun into the cold corpse, and then told to keep her mouth shut. The probers figured that if she had talked, the others would no doubt have put the blame for the murder entirely on her, pointing to the evidence of her fingerprints on the murder gun. It was a smart scheme, and, but for the testimony of Ken Kaenel, it would undoubtedly have worked.

On March 12, 1990, the trio of suspects heard themselves found guilty of federal mail and wire fraud—not murder, which was never actually charged. With tears flowing from her pretty eyes, Debra Hartmann denied having anything to do with her husband's shooting. "I've been punished for eight years," she sobbed. "I have nightmares . . . I haven't murdered anybody."

Prosecutor Miller stood unmoved, at one point describing the blonde as "a narcissistic parasite who lived for parties, fine clothing, and luxury automobiles."

She was sentenced to 22 years.

Her codefendants got slightly lighter terms: 16 years for Korabik and 20 years for Kaenel, a surprised defendant, since he'd been banking on his testimony getting him off with a slap on the wrist of one or two years.

With her conviction and sentencing brought to pass, it will be a long time before sexy Debra Hartmann will be seen club-hopping in a luxury Rolls and waving champagne bottles at the gaping crowd.

"THEIR GRAND SCHEME CLIMAXED IN TRIPLE-MURDER!"

by Benison Murray

They are known as Georgia's "Golden Isles"—Jekyll, St. Simons, and Sea Island. At first glance, they seem an unlikely place for murder and mayhem, the living is so gracious. But they were being discussed by two individuals in July, 1983, who were not only intent on robbery, but murder.

From the beginning of the Jekyll Island club in 1886 until World War II, this island, of the trio, was the remote winter retreat of such people as the Morgans, the Vanderbilts, the Fricks, and the Goulds. People of wealth.

Little St. Simons was founded by one family as a private hunting lodge. Today there is a luxurious playground which contains a golf course, two tennis courts, and a crown jewel of a hotel. If you play, you pay, but the people who do so aren't concerned about money.

Sea Island is home to The Cloister, and basks in the reflected glory of this internationally known resort. It is frequented by notables from all over the world.

Money attracts predators like a crippled calf lures the hunting leopard. Small wonder, then, that these enclaves of wealth and status were the topic of conversation between two men intent on what they considered a more equal distribution of that lovely green stuff.

199

They were lacking a couple of essentials necessary for their undertaking. One was a car; the other a gun. After further discussion, it was decided this could be remedied. A cab driver had a car. Most cabbies carried guns for protection. The two went in search of a taxi driver as a first step in the right direction.

George Francis, 57 years old, drove a cab for a living. He had seen everything twice, and because he was an honest man he carried a gun. He didn't want to help anybody become a criminal — especially if it meant taking his money or his life.

He had been around the block of life two or three times, and while he wanted to believe in the milk of human kindness, no one had ever treated him like a bottle baby. That was why he prided himself on being a judge of people. He felt he could spot some guy on the make quicker than you could flag his cab.

But whatever it was that George Francis depended on to separate the sheep from the goats, it wasn't working on the last week in July. That Tuesday, he picked up the two men who were to be his last passengers. The destination they gave was only a ploy. George Francis, his luck run out, was left dead in a pond off Interstate 95. He had been shot once in the back with his own gun.

Now in possession of the two articles necessary to implement their plan, the two men moved toward Sea Island. Their goal would be the $600,000 house of the Roberts couple. It was located just 100 yards from the Atlantic ocean. There was only one entrance, and special security arrangements, but they had figured that out, too.

The island was noted for its parties. Given by friends for other friends, any excuse will do. Someone buy a boat? Let's celebrate. Barbecue and beer. Quiche and chilled white wine. The two men had seen in Sunday supplements the extent of the marvelous events that took place on Sea Island. The people there could afford to have parties just to launch a season.

And this was the basis of their plan to enter the posh island. With one man hidden in the cab, and the other driving, who would think it was other than transportation called by some party guest who wanted an early bedtime?

The unsuspecting Roberts couple, when confronted by the two men, were taken totally by surprise. A short unequal battle with William Roberts left blood on the carpet, but the outcome was a foregone conclusion.

It was but the work of a moment before the furious man and his terrified wife were trussed like chickens for the market. Nude, each tightly bound, they were placed in the bathtubs in separate bathrooms, their heads wound in towels and bound with tape also.

Unable to move or free themselves, each endured a dirty death — stifled, and finally suffocated in porcelain prisons.

Upstairs and down, the beautiful house was totally ransacked. The two men were intent on whatever goodies they could find. The bathrooms were gone over, in a hunt for drugs. Bedroom closets were carelessly opened, the clothes shoved aside, and shoe boxes emptied. Merill Roberts' purses were turned upside down, then tossed on the floor.

Bureau drawers were yanked out, their contents tossed like a salad, then discarded onto the carpet. Pictures and paintings were pulled from the walls — the rich had wall safes, didn't they?

Who knew what bonanza could be found?

All of these laborious efforts were accompanied by beer drinking — their first find, and the cans, when emptied, joined the strewn belongings of the Roberts' on the floor.

Somehow, credit cards, even cash were overlooked in the manic rush of greed.

Replete with brew and surfeited by their murder and robbery spree, the two men thought to locate the keys to the Roberts' 1977 BMW. Then, with one man driving the cab and the other in the BMW, the two killers disappeared into the night.

Four days later, on a Friday night, a popular party was held by a hostess known for parties. Her guests arrived eager to see and talk with other friends. The Roberts were late, and, as time passed, it seemed they were not coming. The oil executive and his wife hadn't even sent their regrets. One woman, a neighbor of the missing couple, determined to go to their house the next day to see what was wrong. It was so unlike them.

On Saturday, bright and early, the worried neighbor went to the Roberts' house, wondering if one or both of them were too ill to even phone for help.

With the familiarity of a friend she knocked, then pushed open the door and peeked in. The house was eerily quiet. But the lack of response was not the worst thing.

The whole house had been overturned. Chairs lay on their sides, their legs in the air like so many dead dogs. The woman withdrew hastily and made good time to her own phone and called the department of Glynn County Police Chief Jeffrey Hesser.

A phalanx of patrolcars was immediately dispatched to the posh address. Officers sent to the scene radioed back for a homicide team. They had what they knew was a particularly brutal double murder.

Preliminary questioning of the neighbor who had sounded the alarm gave officers the information that the couple had not attended a party given the night before.

Other officers set about securing the crime scene and keeping away huddled residents in the area attracted by the unusual sight of police cars. Horrified, these neighbors gathered in frightened groups waiting with that odd intensity of people at a tragedy.

Homicide arrived neck-in-neck with the lab technicians and coroner. A perfunctory examination of both bodies gave homicide detectives the information that the couple had been dead for about four days. The cause? Probably suffocation, but more than this he was not prepared to say. Rape? Sexual molestation? All of this, the coroner said,

202

putting away his gear, would have to wait on the official autopsy.

Detectives working the case weaved their way through overturned chairs and a carpet of beer cans. The general havoc wreaked figured it to be a robbery with intentions from the first to commit murder. The murders may have been agreed upon to prevent identification.

While detectives mulled over the ramifications of the case, lab technicians busily checked doors and windows for illegal entry. They dusted for latent prints, a long and laborious process. Every doorknob, picture frame, beer can, and bureau drawer in the house would be just the beginning. A first step.

Blood scrapings were taken from blood found on the carpet. It was thought that Roberts had fought with the intruder. With luck, the victim may not have been the only one who had bled. Perhaps his assailant had also left a tell-tale sample. One that, when tested, could be used as evidence against him, if and when the case came to trial.

The nylon cord binding the victims was carefully saved, as were the coverings found around their heads. The make and year of the missing Roberts vehicle was sent out over the air in a BOLO advising lawmen to be on the lookout for the BMW and the suspected killer in it.

Police Chief Jeffrey Hesser, facing avid newsmen, stated, "It is difficult to determine if anything is missing. Before or after the deaths, the persons responsible, it seemed, apparently went through (the house) pulling out drawers and throwing things all over the floor."

But from the chief's statement it could be assumed that the police were entertaining the idea that there had been more than one intruder.

In the meantime, the autopsy had been scheduled for Saturday night. The results showed that the deaths had resulted from suffocation and that there had been no sexual molestation of Mrs. Roberts. It was determined that the murdered pair had been dead since the previous Tuesday, the 26th of July.

Information given to the police furnished a lead in the case. It was said a cab had been seen in the area of the Roberts house on that Tuesday night. Detectives legged it to the cab companies found one cabby missing. They also learned he carried a .38-caliber gun for his protection. One had been recovered at the Roberts' house. Could there be a connection? And where was George Francis, the cab driver?

The question was answered the next day. That was Sunday, when the lifeless body of the hapless cabbie was found in his watery grave, in a pond just off Interstate 95. He had been shot once in the back, possibly by his own gun. Now the hope was that ballistics tests would prove that the recovered .38 would be the same gun that shot its owner. This would link the death of Francis with those of the Sea Island residents.

The residents were terrified at this new twist to the case. With the certain knowledge of wealth and status, they had considered themselves well-protected against outrage of the kind that had blitzed the Roberts couple.

Extra security measures were taken. Guns were brought out from drawers where they had reposed since their purchase. Some people hired extra guards to patrol their homes. Other bought big dogs, an asset that increased in value the more vicious they could be proved. Sea Islanders had learned they were not immune to sudden death from vicious killers, violent, rampaging outlaws.

Lawmen were taking their own precautions. They were aware that three-time killers had little to lose in a confrontation. Forewarned was forearmed. They stressed to one another the need to approach the BMW with caution when sighted. They had to assume the driver was armed, even though the .38 had been found at the death house. Nothing said he couldn't have more than one gun.

When the BMW was seen by an alert patrolcar, it was being driven brazenly right under lawmen's noses.

Sheer bravado or innate stupidity, the officers thought, led the suspect to be out in a car which, after the discovery of the bodies, would be sure to be looked for. Now, the stupidity was compounded when the suspect, finally aware he had been seen, took off in a high-speed chase.

The patrolcar whipped into action. Red light sweeping the road in front of it and the tail of the BMW, an alert was broadcast to all police in the vicinity.

The BMW turned a corner on two wheels and seemed about to do a 360 turn as the determined officers followed it. Other patrolcars joined the chase, the BMW leading, through three coastal counties before lawmen were able to cut off their quarry and force the car to a screeching halt.

The suspect leaped from the BMW, hands raised. He shouted to the converging officers that he had taken poison. While one cop ran to radio for an ambulance, the others surrounded the suspect, now gasping and gagging, and took him into custody.

An ambulance, arriving within minutes, loaded the seriously ill man aboard the emergency vehicle, then sirens howling, rushed him to the Glynn Memorial Hospital, where doctors began a race against time to try and save their patient.

Identified as Theodore Woodard, the 25-year-old man managed to tell doctors he had taken Paraquat, a deadly weed-killer. Doctors knew the herbicide ingested by the patient gave them little chance to save his life.

Woodard was listed in critical condition. Lawmen were told it would be the greatest of luck if their suspect survived to face formal charges now being prepared against him.

Moribund or no, a guard was put outside the man's door, stationed to watch the fatally ill suspect. Cops, being pragmatic creatures, *believed* the doctors, as much as they believed anyone. It was just that they had little faith in finalities, for the suspect had feet, didn't he?

In spite of the chase, the rush to the hospital, and the

hasty ministrations of the doctors, some information had been given to detectives by Theodore Woodard.

The cops now knew they had been right when they thought there was more than one killer. Woodard had a partner in the horrendous killings of the Sea Island couple and the shooting death of George Francis. This was a College Park youth by the name of Kenneth Bernard Blanks. GBI spokesman Jim Hallman told the media that a nationwide lookout had been put out for Blanks, an 18-year-old.

The following Tuesday, justice was thwarted or perhaps meted out to the Brunswick landscaper, Theodore Woodard. The potent weed-killer he had taken just before his capture caused massive and fatal "respiratory, renal and liver failure" according to hospital authorities. It was exactly a week since the Sea Island couple had been murdered.

That same night, GBI agents stationed in Atlanta followed leads they'd been after, looking for Blanks. Staked out in an Atlanta bus station, they had a tip Blanks would be arriving on the 9:15 bus from Savannah.

Leads had been found in the Queen City that provided names for lawmen. These had been followed up with people interviewed in the Metro area. Information was developed from one of those questioned when this person contacted Metro police, who in turn got hold of GBI agents. Blanks had phoned him and was expected to arrive by bus. He would be waiting for transportation. Blanks would phone when he got in.

Armed GBI agents, bolstered by local Metro cops, placed themselves strategically about the downtown bus station to await the bus from Savannah. When their quarry alighted from the night bus he was allowed to get into a phone booth, then surrendered.

Kenneth Blanks offered no resistance to officers and listened stoically as he was arrested and read his rights. He was then taken to the Fulton County Jail to wait for Glynn

County authorities who were to pick him up as soon as they arrived.

On August 3, 1983, Blanks was transported to the seaside county where he was formally charged with the bizarre slayings of the Roberts couple and the shooting death of George Francis.

Relieved to have one *live* fish on their forensic hook, lawmen set about questioning Kenneth Blanks. The tape that resulted would be used in his trial for the slaying of the Sea Island couple.

The teenager, a dropout from the job corps, seemed anxious to give his version of events that led to the slayings of the three people.

"It was all a mistake," Blanks said. "I didn't know anybody was going to get killed."

How about the gun that had killed George Francis, he was asked. Didn't he think it would be used at the Sea Island house?

If he hadn't gone along with it, Woodard would have killed him, Blanks told the skeptical lawmen. It was all a terrible mistake.

Not one officer present believed this. They suggested to the sullen Blanks that the whole scheme had been well-conceived. A plot from beginning to end. They suggested to Blanks that the deaths had been not only planned, but from the manner of the deaths, enjoyed.

Still protesting his essential innocence, Blanks was returned to his cell to await his arraignment.

Charged with the July slaying of the Sea Island couple and the cab driver, Kenneth Blanks appeared in court in September, 1983 to hear why the state intended to seek the death penalty in his case.

A pre-arraignment conference was required under Georgia's unified appeals procedure which governs the handling of death penalty cases. In it, attorneys for both sides discuss possible motions they plan to file before trial.

The youthful defendant sat quietly in court. He appeared impassive as he listened to prosecutors and his own defense. He was dressed in blue jeans and a white turtle-neck sweater and played with a pencil on the table in front of him.

Superior Court Judge Blenn Taylor Jr. read aloud the aggravating circumstances upon which the state based its death penalty request.

It was Blanks' first court proceeding since the month before, when he had been arrested.

According to state prosecutors, each of the killings was "outrageously vile, horrible and inhumane" because in each was involved torture, depravity of mind . . . aggravated battery."

Besides the charges of murder in the first degree for the deaths of the Roberts couple and George Francis, the cab driver, Blanks was charged with theft, burglary and armed robbery.

At the end of the hearing it was decided that the man would be arraigned on October 3, 1983.

No trial date was set.

Kenneth Blanks' trial for the murders of William and Merill Roberts didn't take place until February, 1984. It was to last seven days while the state and the defense fought over the fate of the defendant.

The jury, composed of eleven white women and one black man, after an interminable process of *voir dire,* were sworn in and when complete, settled to hear the evidence that would be put before them.

Blanks' defense was that he had taken part in the killings of the Roberts couple to save his own life. He had feared the fury of his friend, the self-poisoned Theodore Woodard.

The defense lawyer assigned to Blanks argued that Woodard was the "mastermind" behind the slayings and that Blanks had never intended to kill the Roberts couple.

The state described the defendant as a cold-blooded killer with "an abandoned and malignant heart . . . he doesn't mind robbing and killing so he can party and be a big-timer."

The jury deliberated an hour, then asked to hear a replay of the tape the defense had said Blanks gave because "he believed it was the right thing to do."

But it was not to be an easy decision for the jury. After hearing the tape, they recessed for the night and finished hearing the two-hour tape the next morning. After a further 15 minutes they returned with their verdict.

Kenneth Blanks was found guilty of all counts against him and sentenced to die in Georgia's electric chair.

Superior Court Judge A. Blenn Taylor set an execution date and added consecutive 20-year sentences for the other convictions of burglary and theft by taking.

But the state of Georgia is not through with Kenneth Blanks. He must yet come to trial for the first-degree murder charge levied against him in the death of George Francis. This is expected to take place sometime in 1985, and until such time he must be considered innocent of the charge against him.

"HE BURNED HIS VICTIMS ALIVE!"

by Brian Marriner

Burgate House is a large mansion standing on its own grounds in the county of Hampshire, England. It is situated on the outskirts of the small town of Fordingbridge, which is eleven miles from Salisbury. But this is no ancient manor house dating back down through the centuries. Burgate House was built during World War II when wood was in short supply in Britain; in fact, timber was rationed and was reserved exclusively for essential war work, being used in the construction of certain boats and aircraft—the Mosquito fighter-bomber was built entirely of wood, for example. And so the mansion was constructed of concrete.

That simple fact was to bring three vicious and homicidal punks to speedy justice.

On the morning of Tuesday, September 2, 1986, Mrs. Hillary Carpenter, part-time housekeeper for the wealthy Cleaver family, went to work as usual to Burgate House. As she walked up the gravelled drive she noticed smoke coming from an upstairs bedroom window. Slightly puzzled, she continued on to the house, finding the servant's door unlocked. Once inside the house she was even more puzzled to discover that all the curtains were still closed, keeping out the morning sunlight. She drew them back to allow light to flood into the gloomy downstairs of the house and as she

210

walked from room to room her eyes took in various disturbing facts. A gun cabinet belonging to her employer was open, its weapons missing. Strewn across the floor was what looked like fire-lighters.

In the kitchen someone had left the fridge door open, and empty milk bottles littered a table-top. Most puzzling of all was the fact that in the ornate dining room the long and highly-polished table was still set for dinner the previous evening, and the meal remained on the table half-eaten.

Still not seriously alarmed—but becoming increasingly worried—Mrs. Carpenter went upstairs, where she heard the family dogs, two dachshunds, going frantic. They were barking and acting in an excited manner outside one of the smaller bedrooms. Opening the door partially, and peering through the gap, Mrs. Carpenter saw the body of a woman on the bed. She could not tell who it was for the body was too badly burned.

Stifling her screams of horror, the housekeeper hurried downstairs to telephone for the police—only to discover that the lines had been cut. She then ran outside and alerted the family gardener and together they went to the local police station to report their grim discovery.

Hampshire police officers were quickly on the scene and even the most experienced and hardened detectives were sickened by what they found. Five people lay dead in the house—the entire family had been massacred during the night.

Four of the victims were in the master bedroom: Joseph Cleaver, 82, the owner of Burgate House; his invalid wife Hilda, also 82, still strapped into her wheelchair; their son Thomas, 50, and Mrs. Cleaver's 70-year-old nurse, Margaret Murphy. The fifth victim, Wendy Cleaver, 45, wife of Thomas, had been taken to a smaller bedroom and raped repeatedly before being strangled.

All the victims had been bound and gagged. But the four in the master bedroom had not been granted the doubtful mercy of being strangled. For the revolting fact was that they had been liberally sprinkled with gasoline and then set alight. They had been burned alive. As a result, the post-mortem features included the typical curled and twisted foetal position and sinews, the flesh puffy and blackened, almost baked in parts. One of the corpses was still smoldering.

It was apparent that the killer, or killers, had hoped to burn the house to the ground and thus destroy all evidence of their terrible deeds. But the concrete house simply would not burn, and its unique construction meant that vital forensic clues were preserved. These clues were initially all the police had to go on — but they proved to be enough.

Crime officers went over the house, dusting for finger-prints and taking photographs of the victims and other clues. Trying to ignore the chilling scene which had greeted them, they moved quietly around the house sifting for clues. It was apparent from the start that there had been a burglary of some kind after the killings. A desk in the study had been ransacked, bottles of milk had been drunk by the thirsty killers, and the trail of fire-lighters indicated that they had come to the house with the intention to commit arson. In the tasteful dining room of Burgate House the half-eaten meal on the table was mute testimony of a quiet family night shattered by sudden violence.

One of the first tasks for detectives investigating this gruesome mass murder was to build up a picture of the victims' background. Somewhere in the background of their lives lay clues to their deaths — and their killers.

Joseph Cleaver was a retired millionaire who had built up a publishing business which employed 500 people, and had retired after undergoing heart bypass surgery some ten years previously. At about the same time, his wife Hilda had suffered a stroke, which left her unable to speak or walk. Cleaver had devoted his declining years to looking after his wife and fortunately he was wealthy enough to be able to afford to keep a household staff to help look after the house and its grounds. He was also able to afford a private nurse.

Detective Chief Superintendent Alan Wheeler soon made a crucial breakthrough in the case. A former handyman employed by the Cleavers had been fired a month previously for being drunk and violent. He and his wife had occupied a cottage in the grounds, the wife helping out in the house. Both had been evicted from the cottage, and the handyman, George Stephenson, 35, was known to harbor a grudge. He had a long record of criminal convictions. It became a matter of urgency to trace him and Chief Superintendent Wheeler, heading the murder hunt team, briefed his detectives on the possible suspect.

The housekeeper was able to confirm that several items of value were missing from the house, presumably having been stolen following the murders. They included the contents of the gun cabinet — three shotguns and a rifle with ammunition — and a television set and video recorder. On the day that he had been fired, Stephenson had played squash with a friend in Bournemouth, then returned to the Cleaver house late in the evening in a state of drunkenness. He had a violent brawl with his wife, beat her up, and the resulting row woke up the entire household.

Cleaver had fired him on the spot, telling him to leave the cottage quickly. That had been on August 7th. His wife had run away from him that same day and it was known that Stephenson had lived in the Bournemouth area for some time after being fired.

Stephenson's background was investigated in depth. He had worked as a croupier in a Bournemouth club from 1976 to 1978 and before that had worked in the construction industry in London. He had many convictions for petty crime and had served at least two prison sentences. He was known as a "ladies' man," having been married twice and known for keeping a string of girlfriends. His second wife, the one who had split from him on the night he was fired by the Cleavers, told police about his past and the women in his life.

The murders themselves were brutal but straightforward from an investigative point of view. A pathologist's report indicated that Wendy Cleaver had been raped and strangled, but attempts had been made to set fire to all five bodies. Wendy had been spread-eagled on the bed, and some of her clothing ripped from her. The degree of bruises to her body indicated the ferocity of the rape. One bizarre fact was that her husband, Thomas, had an artificial leg in which he kept over $700. It was still there—the killers had missed it.

Chief Superintendent Alan Wheeler held a press conference in the murder house shortly after the crimes had been discovered, and told reporters: "We are seeking George Stephenson in connection with the five murders. He was born in September 1951 in Bishop Auckland, County Durham. His description is medium build, height five feet nine inches, blue eyes, brown hair and moustache. He is armed and dangerous. I want to stress to the public that this man is dangerous and violent and should not be approached under any circumstances." The detective also revealed that an all-points red-alert bulletin had been sent to all ports as well as airports and train stations.

The police had recovered a book from the house—saved from the fire because of the concrete construction—which recorded the names of people Stephenson had given as references when he had first applied for the job of handyman. One couple named lived in Bournemouth. When police raided their house, they found the television set and video recorder missing from Burgate House. They explained that they had been friendly with Stephenson, having put him up for a few days after he was fired from his job. Noticing that their television and video equipment was not working, Stephenson said he could get them cheap replacements.

On the morning following the murders they had found the equipment on their doorstep and assumed Stephenson had left it for them. In fact, he had later telephoned to ask them if they had received it and said he would stop by within days to collect the cash for the items. The couple had no idea that the items were stolen and had become innocently involved in the police manhunt.

The book recovered also revealed how Stephenson, a petty crook, had been able to get himself a position of trust inside a wealthy household. In July 1985 he had replied to a newspaper advertisement for a live-in cook and handyman at Burgate House, and went to an interview for the position with his second wife—whom he had married eight months earlier—after knowing her for just three weeks. It was she who had impressed the Cleaver family and had influenced them to offer Stephenson the job. But when Stephenson began drinking and beating his wife he had to be fired. The murders stemmed from that fact.

Stephenson hated the Cleavers for daring to fire him and envied them their wealth. He also wanted that mini-arsenal of weapons for a major armed robbery he was planning with two other men. But revenge had been the driving motive.

After Stephenson's picture was flashed on television screens throughout Britain with a "wanted" warning, a car-hire company in Coventry got in touch with the police. A man resembling the photograph had hired a red Rover (an English automobile) from them two days before the murders, showing his driving license in the name of Stephenson as proof of identity. But one of the two men accompanying him had actually paid for the rental, writing a check and giving his real name and address. Both men, brothers, lived in Coventry.

Coventry police raided the address given for George Daly in the city, and arrested both brothers there, less than two days after the murders. George Daly, 25, had first met Stephenson in a bar in Coventry in 1984, and both men were later arrested for handling stolen goods and received a two-year jail term for this offense. Their friendship had developed while in prison, and they had kept in touch afterwards. After he was fired from his job at Burgate House, Stephenson went to live with Daly and his common-law wife in Coventry, sharing their modest home. The younger brother, John Daly, 21, was a single man, and he too had a record of petty crime.

Both brothers quickly began talking under police questioning, each blaming Stephenson for the murders. He had instigated the burglary-arson attack. The younger brother was full of remorse and made a detailed confession. But incriminating as these confessions were, they were useless as evidence against Stephenson by themselves. Further corroborative evidence needed to be found.

Stephenson, meanwhile, had been alerted by seeing his picture on television and went on the run. During this period as a fugitive he used the time to construct an alibi for himself, and concocted a story which cleared him of any involvement in the murders. He telephoned Hampshire police to say that he was innocent of any murders—it was all the work of these two Hell's Angels—and he intended to give himself up to clear his name. But he took a train south and spent Wednesday night at a campsite on the edge of the New Forest with two attractive young nurses he had met in a bar. Later, in a tent, he invited them to smoke a cannabis (marijuana) cigarette with him, then revealed that he was the most wanted killer in Britain. He played a grim guessing game with them. He said he was wanted by the police, and asked them to guess if it was for robbery, rape, or murder. They guessed wrong. Stephenson showed them his photograph on the front page of a newspaper and said "It's me they want, but I'm innocent. It was two Hell's Angels who did it." He autographed his picture for the girls.

Later, he allowed himself to be "persuaded" to surrender to the police. In reality, he had provided himself with a cunning alibi; two witnesses who would confirm that he had spoken of the two mystery Hell's Angels before police even questioned him.

At 2:00 A.M. on Thursday, September 4, 1986, Stephen-

216

son phoned the police from a call-box near the camp-site and waited by the kiosk for police to arrive. Once in custody he was cocky and confident, denying all knowledge of the murders. At first he claimed to have given two Hell's Angels a lift to a spot close to Burgate House, and he supposed they must have committed the crimes. When told that the Daly brothers had both confessed and named him as being the ringleader, he replied, "So, you have your culprits."

Later, he changed his story. He admitted having driven the Daly brothers to Burgate House, but insisted that he had sat outside the house in the car while the two masked brothers had burgled the premises. He had known nothing of any rapes or murders until he saw the television news and he was shocked.

Despite hours of intense questioning by detectives, Stephenson refused to crack. Detective Chief Inspector Luty, who headed the team which questioned Stephenson, said he had never known such a callous and arrogant killer. "He enjoyed being questioned, and the notoriety. He would ask how big the case was in the newspapers and was it going to be the worst murder of all time?"

The evidence of both Daly brothers was crucial in the resulting trial. In their confessions they told how Stephenson had approached them with the idea of robbing Burgate House. While living with George Daly, Stephenson had been planning a big payroll robbery at a nearby factory, but after discovering that the premises were heavily guarded Stephenson had decided that they needed guns to carry out the robbery successfully. And he knew where there were guns — at Burgate House. He said the Cleavers also kept a substantial amount of cash at the house and that he knew there was a safe somewhere.

It was the inducement of ready cash as well as the fact that the victims were old which caused both Daly brothers to fall for the bait which Stephenson dangled too temptingly. They agreed to hire a car and drive with Stephenson

217

to Hampshire, there to burglarize Burgate House. At this point neither brother had murder or rape on their minds. They were criminals and knew violence as a common currency, but even they had certain standards and limits, things they would not do, and murder figured high on that list.

But the Daly brothers were relatively dumb criminals and it was easy for Stephenson to arrange a scenario which would make both brothers into killers against their will and almost without knowing it. They might have realized that Stephenson had more than plain burglary in mind, however, when he insisted that they arm themselves with pickaxe handles, fire-lighters, and two cans of gasoline. They drove to Burgate House on the night of September 1, 1986, arriving at around 8:00 P.M. when the family usually had dinner. What Stephenson could not have anticipated was that there would be five people for dinner that night, the son, Thomas, and his wife, having driven from Surrey to keep the old folks company.

The family had just finished the main course when the three men, wearing stocking masks and carrying pickaxe handles, burst into the dining room. Stephenson was wielding a shotgun he had taken from the gun cabinet. Trying to disguise his voice, he ordered the women to remove their jewelry and the men to hand over their wallets. The family pleaded not to be hurt, saying they would cooperate with the robbers fully.

All five of them were then forced upstairs and were bound hand and foot. Hilda Cleaver, in her wheelchair to which she had been confined for the past ten years, needed no restraint. Stephenson then dragged Wendy Cleaver into a smaller bedroom and tore off her clothes before savagely raping her. The Daly brothers said that Stephenson insisted that all three of them rape or sexually assault her to bind them in complicity. It was John Daly who, after raping an almost unconscious victim, strangled her with a piece of ribbon.

The three men then searched the house for money and valuables. They did not discover the wall-safe, hidden behind a painting on the wall of the master bedroom, and they could not have known that Thomas Cleaver kept a cache of money hidden in his artificial leg. They made off with just $90.

Although wearing a mask and still attempting to disguise his voice, Stephenson was secretly determined that no one should be left alive who might identify him. The four remaining victims, bound and helpless in the master bedroom, were doused with gasoline and then set alight while still alive. Fire-lighters were then thrown into the blazing room in the hope that the resulting fire would gut the entire house. "It went up with a swoosh," George Daly told police. But that concrete house foiled the murderers and the fire was confined largely to the master bedroom.

After the murders, the three killers drove back to Coventry via Bournemouth, stopping only to drop off the television set and video recorder. Near the village of Weyhill in Hampshire, the trio came across a police road-block set up after a traffic accident. Stephenson, thinking it had been set up for them, told the Dalys to be prepared to shoot the policemen manning the road-block using the shotguns stolen from Burgate House. But a young policeman waved them through. There can be no doubt that if any attempt had been made to apprehend them at this point, they would have shot to kill.

"I don't think they would have given themselves up," said Chief Inspector Dennis Luty of Hampshire CID.

The gang arrived back at George Daly's home in Coventry in the early hours of Tuesday, September 2nd. They ate a curry meal, then sat drinking liquor stolen from the Cleavers. Coventry police raided the house at dawn on Thursday and arrested the Dalys without a struggle.

The trial of the killers began on Monday, 5 October 1987 at Winchester Crown Court. Outlining the prosecution case, David Elfer, QC, warned the jury of four men and eight women that they would have to face facts "that are gruesome in the extreme" in the course of the trial. Describing the life-style at Burgate House, situated on the banks of the River Avon, Mr. Elfer said the household routine at the luxury country mansion was run with regimental strictness. Dinner was always served at 8:00 P.M. sharp, and guests were expected to dress formally—the men in jacket and tie, the women in evening gowns and expensive jewelry. The front room was left unlocked until 9:00 P.M.

On the night of September 1st, George Stephenson, who had been fired from his job at the house just weeks earlier, returned to the mansion with the Daly brothers to carry out his grisly revenge. Describing how one victim had been raped, and the other doused in gasoline and set ablaze, Mr. Elfer said, "These people were burned alive." The gang, wearing rubber gloves and carrying pickaxe handles, were there to rob the house, but got just $90.

As they went about their evil work the telephone rang. It was the 21-year-old son who wanted to talk to his father. Joseph Cleaver was freed from his bonds and forced to answer the telephone. He was ordered to talk normally and pretend that everything was fine. He did that, the prosecutor saying he had been a "very brave man" during this time.

The prosecutor, after telling of the rape of Wendy Cleaver, described how the other four had been burned alive. Thomas Cleaver, his legs bound with twine, tried desperately to escape from the flames. He broke through his burning bonds and left a trail of flesh across the floor as he crawled to the bathroom. In the bathroom he butted the window with his head in vain attempt to break the glass and get fresh air before he too was overcome with fumes. The prosecutor said: "He was in that inferno, but because one of his legs was false he was able to break his bonds and get away. We know that this man moved after the fire had started because his skin was left on the carpet following his trail. In other words, these people were burned alive." After setting fire to their victims, the gang spent some three hours ransacking the house.

The jury were shown photographs of Wendy Cleaver as she had been found by police. "Her hands were tied and her clothes had been unceremoniously torn from her private parts," the prosecutor said. "One by one these men raped her. Gasoline had been poured on her too, although she was dead by the time that happened. She too had to go into the conflagration—otherwise too many clues would have been available."

The prosecutor declared "The plan of these men was to rob the Cleaver household. They were there for money. They were also there for guns and ammunition. They were to steal a TV and video, and any jewelry or other valuable items they could find. But the plan went further. No one was going to live to tell the tale and that house was then to be burned to the ground, concealing all clues . . ."

The prosecutor told how, after the murders, Stephenson and the Dalys drove back to Coventry where they celebrated by drinking some of the twenty bottles of spirits stolen from Burgate House. The following day the news of the murders was featured on national television news, and it was then that Stephenson phoned the police saying he was ready to give himself up. That was to buy him time to bury the guns and throw the stolen jewelry into the nearby river.

"He prepared a lying account," said the prosecutor. "He would say that he had gone to Bournemouth, but on the way had picked up two Hell's Angels who must have then robbed the Cleavers." George Daly had told the police that he had joined in the robbery on the spur of the moment, without any intention of hurting anyone. "But the fact that Wendy Cleaver was raped in such a disgusting and violent fashion and then strangled shows that no one was going to come out of there alive. That is why they could toy with human beings in such a way."

The younger brother, John Daly, at first tried to cover-up for his two accomplices, but when he was asked by detectives: "Did you kill anyone?" he replied "One." He was then asked "Which one" and he replied "The daughter." He told police that as he was raping Wendy, Stephenson came into the room and brought a knife and cord, placing them on the next bed. When he had finished, John Daly tied the cord around the victim's neck, turned her onto her face, "and pulled the cord tight until her face turned blue."

When questioned by police, Stephenson had told them what charming people the Cleavers were, how kind they had been to him, and how he would never wish them any harm. But all this was pure hypocrisy, the prosecutor declared. Stephenson had been the ringleader of all that happened at Burgate House.

Stephenson and George Daly pleaded not guilty of all the charges of rape, robbery, and murder. John Daly pleaded not guilty of murder, but guilty of robbery and rape.

The following day detectives went into the witness box to tell of finding five bodies, four badly-burned and one still smoldering, at Burgate House. Relatives of the dead, present in court, held back tears as they listened to the evidence.

The common-law wife of George Daly, a widow with three children—one of them to George Daly—testified that Daly, his brother, and Stephenson, arrived at dawn at her home in Coventry on the morning of September 2nd the previous year. It was the morning after the murders. They had had a drinking session. She saw five guns and ammunition being carried into her house.

She said she had first met George Daly in August 1985 and he had lived with her ever since. He had never worked, but used to do odd jobs on cars in the garage. A year later he introduced her to Stephenson, who lived with them until the murders. On that day—September 1st—the men said they were driving to Bournemouth in a hired car on business and might not be back until the early hours. After they had returned home, and had been drinking for a while, George Daly seemed to be in a depressed mood, and she said to him, "You seem quiet. Is anything the matter?" He replied grimly, "If only you knew what I have been doing . . ."

Asked how long she had been widowed when she first met George Daly and took him into her home, the witness broke down in tears, asking for a glass of water. Then she sobbed: "I can't go on. I can't." The judge excused her from giving any further testimony.

One of the nurses who had camped out with George Stephenson while he was on the run told the court how she and her friend drank wine and smoked a cannabis cigarette with Stephenson. He seemed a nice man, quite normal. He later confessed that he was wanted for the Burgate House murders, showing them a photograph of himself on the front page of a newspaper. He denied any guilt, saying he had been set up by two Hell's Angels. He autographed the newspaper photograph for them and commented that the Cleavers had been "nice harmless people."

The police interviews with the three men on trial had been recorded on tape and later in the trial these tapes were played for the jury. Stephenson's voice echoed around the wood-panelled courtroom as he was heard saying: "I have no blood on my hands." He was denying rape, burglary, or murder. "I had nothing to do with the atrocities which happened to these people," he said. Members of the jury were handed transcripts of the tapes so they could follow the evidence. Detective Chief Inspector Dennis Luty told of how Stephenson had, in his first interview, denied any knowledge of any murders, but the Daly brothers had told a very different story of events, and when he told Stephenson that the Dalys had admitted fully their parts in the murders at Burgate House, Stephenson had replied cockily, "So, you have your culprits."

223

Later in the interview he said, "I am denying everything. If the Dalys have admitted to doing something like this, I don't know why they are involving me in it. I have done nothing. I can swear to God I have got no blood on my hands. I have killed, burnt nobody. I have got no evil in me whatsoever."

John Daly, in his taped interview, admitted that the mansion robbery had been planned four days in advance. He said Stephenson had suggested the burglary. He said it was Stephenson who had dragged Wendy Cleaver to a separate bedroom and raped her. He had then forced the others to do the same.

George Daly was heard sniffing, apparently in tears, in the course of his interview. He said that after the five people in the house were taken upstairs he noticed that one of them, and Stephenson, was missing. He went in search of them and found Stephenson with the younger woman. Asked what Stephenson was doing, Daly sighed and said "You know what he was doing."

Asked if he had been aware that the woman was being raped, he replied "Yeah" and started sobbing. He said he left the room but Stephenson came after him and said all of them had to do the deed. Daly went back into the room and got on the bed. He went on, "I was going to do it, but I felt sick, as if I was going to throw up. I got off." Asked if he had had intercourse with the woman, he replied, "Yes and no." Relatives of the dead wept openly at this point.

George Stephenson went into the witness box on Friday, October 16, to give a confident and even arrogant account of his innocence. He said he had been shocked to see his picture on television as a wanted man. He had indeed driven the Daly brothers to the scene of the crime, but he claimed he had never left the car, and had no idea that the occupants of the house had been murdered. He said that after the robbery, when the Dalys returned to the car, he

224

asked about the Cleavers. Daly said they had been left tied up but unharmed. Stephenson looked the jury in the eye and went on. "I suggested to George Daly that we should make a telephone call to the police so that they could release the Cleavers, but he assured me he had not tied them very tightly, and they could get free of their own accord." He went on to describe George Daly as being a "Rambo terrorist."

Cross-examined by defense counsel for George Daly, Mr. Anthony Palmer, QC, described Stephenson as a habitual criminal. He told the man in the dock: "The only way out for you is now to blame the Dalys to save your own wretched skin." He went on: "I believe you have forty-six different recorded offenses of dishonesty in your name?"

"I would have to agree with you," Stephenson replied drily. But he went on to insist vehemently that he had never been inside Burgate House on the night of the murders.

George Daly went into the witness box and told the jury frankly that he expected life imprisonment. "I am going to be found guilty and get life anyway because of my involvement. I am not stupid enough to think I am going to walk away from this court."

Asked by his counsel to describe in his own words what happened on the night of the murders, Daly said he had seen Stephenson, shotgun in hand, raping Wendy Cleaver. "At that stage I was numbed and disgusted with what had happened," he said. He denied having raped Wendy Cleaver himself, saying he had merely lain on top of the bound and gagged woman for a few seconds. He had been persuaded to sexually assault her by Stephenson, who had said, "One has done it, we have all got to do it now."

When his brother came out of the same room he was deeply upset, crying and banging the wall with his fist. Daly admitted throwing a fire-lighter into the room where four of the victims were trapped and soaked with gasoline, claiming that Stephenson had said to him, "They are all dead. We have got to burn the house to get rid of the evi-

225

dence." Describing Stephenson as the ringleader, Daly told the jury, "He refuses to acknowledge that he went into the house because he has more to hide. The crime was committed by all three of us . . . I caused those people deaths by throwing the fire-lighter, but I thought they was dead."

Addressing the jury, towards the end of the trial, the lawyer representing George Daly said his client should be found guilty of four cases of manslaughter. Stephenson had been the ringleader—"a man with a smooth, persuasive tongue who was cunning and much more clever than the Daly brothers. Stephenson programmed the monstrous happening at the country house and misled George Daly into believing that the victims were all dead. When Daly set fire to the house it was not to cause death—because he honestly believed that the occupants were already dead—but to destroy evidence. He could not therefore be regarded as a murderer." It was one of those circular and peculiar statements of logic which lawyers are prone to deliver.

On October 26th, the judge summed up the evidence to the jury, following the 18-day trial. Mr. Justice Hobhouse said, "Here there have been horrific crimes committed, the details of which you have had to listen to. It must have been quite horrifying and disturbing to you, but without forgetting the nature of the crimes involved, you must approach the matter in the completely dispassionate manner." He said that the fact that all three defendants were members of the criminal class did not automatically mean that they were guilty and it was for the prosecution to prove their guilt. The defense did not have to prove anything.

The judge said there had been what was colloquially known as a "cut-throat defense," with the defendants trying to place the blame on each other. George Daly had given evidence which was strongly prejudicial to Stephenson; likewise, Stephenson had given evidence strongly to adverse to both George and John Daly.

The judge said, "You must be very careful in evaluating such evidence. It is not safe for you to convict anyone on

Franklin James Bradshaw, Utah millionaire, was shot to death by his own grandson.

Frances Bernice Schreuder, heiress to milions, coaxed her son to kill her father to prevent him from cutting her out of his will.

Marc Francis Schreuder shot his grandfather at the instigation of his own mother, Frances.

George Alec Robinson was convicted of murdering successful Virginia real estate developers George Lewinski and Elizabeth Elliot.

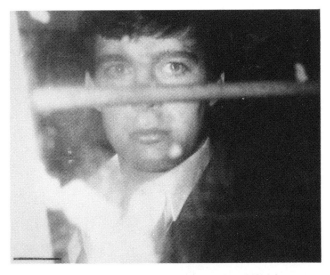

Jeremy Bamber was driven by greed to kill his entire family.

Model Sheila Bamber
called herself
"Bambi." Her half
brother shot her to
death in her bed.

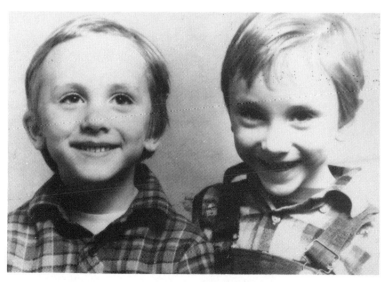

Sheila's six-year-old twin boys, Daniel and Nicholas, were
brutally shot to death by their Uncle Jeremy, the same night
their mother and grandparents were killed.

Artist renderings of millionaires Neville and June Bamber
before they were murdered by their stepson.

The body of Mississippi millionaire Annie Laurie Hearin was never found.

Werner Hartmann, Chicago playboy, was shot a dozen times at point-blank range emerging from a shower.

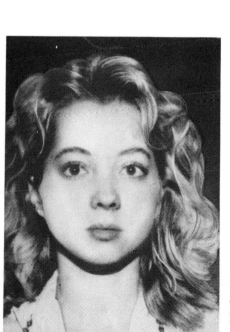

Debra Hartmann was convicted of murdering her husband to get his money.

The Roberts' luxurious home in Sea Island, Georgia.

William Britt Roberts and his wife, Merrill, were murdered at their exclusive mansion in Sea Island, Georgia.

Kenneth Blanks was
convicted of killing
William and Merril
Roberts.

Joseph and Hilda Cleaver were drenched with gasoline and lit on fire in their country mansion.

Margaret Murphy, Hilda Cleaver's private nurse, was a victim in the brutal country killing.

George Stephenson, the disgruntled employee, together with two other men, tortured and killed the Cleavers, his former employers.

John Daly, above, and his brother, George, were part of the team that helped Stephenson take five innocent lives.

The million-dollar mansion at Seabrook, Texas were deviant millionaire William List was murdered.

Elbert Homan was sentenced to forty years in prison for the savage murder of William List.

Jeffrey Stratton was convicted of robbery in connection with List's murder.

Eunice Edwards was shot to death at her home in Palm Valley, Florida.

Lee Myers murdered Eunice Edwards to impress his girlfriend.

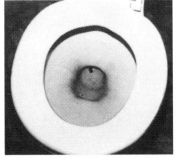

Myers tried to flush away the casing of the fatal bullet in Edwards' toilet but was unsuccessful.

the word of either George Stephenson or George Daly." He said they were both to some extent admitted liars and both had the very strongest motive and incentive to give against the other. The jury must not draw any adverse inference from the fact that John Daly had elected not to go into the witness box.

The jury retired to consider their verdicts. It was October 27th and after some six and a half hours deliberation they returned to the court to tell the judge that they had not yet reached verdicts on the five murder charges. However, they had found George Stephenson and George Daly guilty of rape and robbery. The jury was sequestered.

The following day the panel finally returned its verdicts on the murder charges. Stephenson was found guilty of four of the murders but was acquitted of the murder of Wendy Cleaver. George Daly was acquitted of all five murders but found guilty of manslaughter. John Daly had admitted all five murders from the start.

George Stephenson was sentenced to four life sentences for murder, and one each for robbery and rape. He smirked as the judge told him, "These killings were committed in circumstances of indescribable bestiality and cruelty. You showed no mercy—you deserve none." He made no recommendation that Stephenson should serve a minimum of 25 years. George Daly was sentenced to 22 years imprisonment, and John Daly was given seven life sentences but without any recommendation. The judge said he was showing mercy to John Daly because he was the youngest and had to some extent been led astray.

Stephenson made a mocking remark to the Dalys in the dock, and George Daly lunged at him in fury, having to be restrained by warders.

After the case, Chief Inspector Luty said of Stephenson, "He has been arrogant since day one, always willing to put everyone else down in order to get out of trouble. He is without remorse or conscience. He's a very hard and evil and vicious criminal. It was always his intention that whoever was in the house would be killed."

All three men had criminal records stretching back to their early school days. Stephenson was first caught housebreaking at age 16 and had been in trouble with the police ever since. The women in his life spoke of his violence towards them. From prison he had written to his second wife apologizing for his violence towards her, but his letters expressed no remorse for the murders. However, proof of his twisted mind was given in letters he had sent to a friend, saying he had been sent mad during a two-year prison sentence when he had been shunned by friends and relatives, who never wrote to him or visited. Stephenson had warned in one letter, "They will pay for what they are doing." But like all criminals, Stephenson had made five innocent people pay for the imagined "offense."

George Daly was aged 14 when he was first caught stealing, and later was to go to prison with Stephenson for a joint offense. The prison friendship which developed as a result was evil. John Daly was first in trouble with the police at age twelve. At thirteen he was convicted of burglary and arson.

Relatives of the victims expressed satisfaction at the sentences, although one declared that they should have been given the same sentence as they gave their victims—they should be burned alive.

This particular case is one of the worst in Britain in recent years, illustrating as it does that terrible modern tendency for criminals to treat their victims as being "disposable," a basic throw-away attitude towards other human beings that is truly frightening.

"RICH COUPLE SLASHED WITH A PAIR OF SCISSORS!"

by Krist Boardman

The Old Town district in Alexandria, Virginia is well known for its historical structures dating back from before the Civil War. Many of the streets are still cobblestoned, giving tourists the flavor of the old days when people travelled the roads in horse and buggy.

One of the famous buildings in Old Town is located at 413 Prince Street. The four-story brick structure was built in 1805 as one of Virginia's first banks.

During the Civil War, the Union forces used it as Virginia's state capitol and governor's mansion. Over the years, additions have been erected onto the magnificent building which has been renovated by one of the community's most respected and loved real estate investors, Elizabeth Elliott.

Elliott had the shrewd business sense to realize the historical importance of many of the buildings in the Old Town district. She bought many of them and aided in the renovation of others.

And as the property values in the area soared, so did Miss Elliott's fortune. By 1984, the property she owned and managed was worth well into the millions. Her riches, however, had virtually no effect on the way she lived her life. Although she could have hired a manager to care for her many properties, she wanted to keep her hand in the everyday business affairs. Elizabeth would walk through the community and collect the rents from her tenants, keep the books, and make certain all repairs on her buildings were taken care of promptly and efficiently. Her apartment, which she also used as her office, was in the annex to the huge brick mansion that had once been used as the state capitol, and it was there that tenants would drop by and pay the rent and where Elizabeth kept all her real estate files.

She lived in the apartment with her long-time friend and business associate Karl von Lewinski, 71. Lewinski himself was a realtor with an interesting background. In his heyday, Lewinski had worked on the *Washington Post* as a news reporter. Many in the community often referred to him as the Baron, which was in keeping with his imposing physique.

The barrel-chested Lewinski stood at least 6 feet tall and weighed about 240 lbs. His German-style handlebar mustache only lent further effect to his grandiose stature. Oddly enough, Lewinski was the son of a German diplomat, and his lineage did in fact include the title of Baron.

Both Elizabeth Elliott and Karl von Lewinski were known throughout the community of Old Town as cultured and sociable. They hadn't an enemy in the world . . .

On February 9, 1984, sometimes between 7:30 and 8:00 P.M., Oliver Pendil heard rumbling sounds from his landlord's apartment just below him. Only a few minutes later, he heard a distinct low moaning sound. The thought that something grave could have happened downstairs did occur to him, but it seemed more likely that Lewinski had tripped over something and hurt himself.

The following day, Friday, February 10th, Pendil passed by Elizabeth Elliott's apartment and noticed the daily newspaper lying on the floor outside the door, and all was silent inside. This was unusual because Pendil knew Elliott and Lewinski were always up and about early in the morning. Pendil remembered the moaning sounds of the night before and felt a pang of guilt. What if something terrible actually did happen last night? he thought. That would explain the reason for the moaning sounds and for the eery silence inside the apartment now.

Pendil, however, continued on his way to work, believing that his fears were getting the better of him. Probably nothing had happened, he decided, and there was no reason to fret.

Later in the day, while still at work, Pendil decided to phone Elliott just to make sure everything was all right, but there was no answer. When he returned from work, he passed by her apartment again. The newspaper as well as a parcel of mail were lying outside the door.

Now Pendil realized something was definitely wrong. He walked around the outside of the house; and, peering through an apartment window, he could see an overturned wooden chair and a large mirror lying on the floor but no sign of either Karl von Lewinski or Elizabeth Elliott.

Pendil now strongly suspected foul play. He immediately rushed up the stairs to his flat and phoned Elliott's relative, who lived only a block away.

The relative was soon at the apartment where Pendil was waiting for him. The relative took out a set of keys from his coat pocket, searched among them and, within moments, opened the door. It was approximately 8:00 P.M. by now, and the apartment was only half lit by rays of moonlight shining through the livingroom window.

Upon entering, Miss Elliott's relative could see Lewinski's silhouetted form sitting on the armchair in the living room.

"Karl," he called out. But there was no response. All was silence. The shadowy form on the armchair remained still. Elliott's relative then advised Pendil to call the police while he stayed in the apartment.

Only minutes later, homicide detectives were on the scene, led by Alexandria Police Sergeant Ronald T. Graves. When Graves first entered the apartment, he checked the body sitting on the chair for any signs of life. There was no

231

pulse. Blood was spattered on the floor beside the victim, and his shirt front appeared soaked with dried blood. Graves continued on through the apartment, cautiously avoiding papers strewn on the floor, in order not to contaminate the evidence. When he passed the grand piano and entered the bedroom, he found the second body lying on the floor. Elizabeth Elliott was fully clothed; she, too, was dead.

A cursory examination of the victims revealed some significant facts about the murders. The evidence already indicated the two victims were definitely murdered. It wasn't a suicide pact or the kind of slaying in which one of the victims kills the other and then himself. Both victims displayed defense wounds. There were deep gash marks on their hands, as though they had been warding off an attack. As for a probable murder weapon, there were several deep holes on either side of Karl von Lewinski's throat, apparently caused by a gun blast. Elizabeth Elliott's wounds were hidden by her clothing, so a determination in her case would have to wait.

After quickly surveying the remainder of the scene, Sergeant Graves had the apartment sealed off from onlookers. A crime lab crew soon arrived, and police photographers snapped pictures for almost a half hour.

During these preliminaries, Oliver Pendil told Sgt. Graves about the moaning he'd heard the night before. "They were unusual sounds," he explained. "They weren't enough to alarm me in the present tense, but I never heard those sounds before."

Elizabeth Elliott's relative then told the sergeant about Pendil's emergency phone call and how they both entered the dark apartment: "Karl von Lewinski's body was sitting in the living room in a large chair in an upright position, as if he just sat down. I said 'Karl' and there was no response."

Graves jotted this information down, then returned to the apartment and asked the crime lab supervisor for a progress report.

232

"We haven't found a gun or knife or anything that would cause those kinds of wounds," the supervisor said pointing to the body of Lewinski. "We did find a wallet in the man's trouser pocket with a lot of cash in it. So far, we're just marking things into evidence," he concluded.

Graves soon left the scene to confer with two other homicide detectives, Jerry McHugh and Derrill Scott.

"This is what we've got so far," Graves told them. "There's a desk drawer in the living room that's wide open. Papers lying all over. Some dresser drawers in the bedroom are open. And I noticed a mark on the woman's index finger. It looks like a ring was removed. So it seems like a robbery-turned-murder, right?" he asked rhetorically. "There's just a few problems with this: The male victim, Karl von Lewinski, had a wallet full of cash on him. If somebody came to rob the place, why the hell didn't he take the cash? A couple of other things: We found some jewelry and silver inside the apartment. Why didn't the robber take any of these?"

The detectives discussed these curiosities but for the present time, they could come up with no viable solution.

After the city's medical examiner, Dr. James C. Beyer, finished examining the body, he walked over to Detective Graves and gave him his present findings. "I'm not sure exactly what kind of instrument was used as the murder weapon, but the wounds were certainly not caused by a gun. Both victims were stabbed to death. The male victim suffered at least 10 stab wounds, the woman probably more. The man was stabbed in the chest, throat, face and back. I don't know if you saw it, but whoever did this is a very powerful person. Did you notice the victim's hand?" Dr. Beyer asked the detective.

"Yes," Sergeant Graves responded. "Defense wounds."

"Right. But one of the wounds is on both sides of the hand. Whatever instrument was used, it was thrust right through his palm and came out on the back of the hand. Cause of death seems to be hemorrhage. Exactly which wounds were fatal, I can't say right now. Give me a few days, after an autopsy. I should know everything by then. As for time of death, all I can say right now is at least 12 hours ago. No signs of rigor mortis."

The medical examiner soon left, followed by attendants carrying the victims on a stretcher to the morgue wagon.

Investigators, meanwhile, canvassed the building and neighborhood for witnesses. The possibility that the victims had enemies was soon quashed as witness after witness described the couple in the most glowing terms.

"I feel like I have lost my surrogate grandmother," said one of Elliott's tenants.

"They were wonderful people," another remarked.

A neighbor, who had once been a tenant of the victim's, recalled Elliott as a "very trusting, very giving and a very forgiving person." The woman also added something else, which would later prove significant to the investigation.

According to her, Elliott always collected rent money from the first of the month to the tenth. "I know that a lot of her tenants paid her in cash," the witness said. "She would take the money and put it in her desk drawer and let it pile up. I once told her she should put it in the bank right away, but I guess she liked to do things her way, and she was very trusting."

The ransacked desk drawer in the victim's apartment now made detectives believe that robbery was the motive. A check with Elliott's relative also backed up this theory. According to the relative, Elliott did in fact have a habit of letting the rent money collect in her desk drawer until about the tenth of the month when she would deposit it.

The evidence which conflicted with a robbery motive had an explanation: The robber had probably gotten away with enough valuables and just decided to leave the other items behind. Of course the robbery motive wasn't yet definite, but sleuths knew it was a worthy line of investigation to follow.

In an attempt to ascertain what valuables, if any, had

been taken, probers asked Elliott's relative to examine all items recovered at the murder scene, including the victim's jewelry, silverware, and clothing. After studying the contents, the relative said he remembered several items that appeared to be missing, among them a diamond ring and two mink coats.

Detective Graves jotted down a description of the missing jewelry and obtained several photos of the victim wearing rings. He had blow-ups made of these photos and assigned an investigative detail to check with pawnshops throughout Alexandria. Other investigators checked with known fences, who usually bought stolen items and sold them on the black market. A records check of all known convicted burglars in the area was also made. These suspects were all questioned but nothing came of it.

While investigators were getting nowhere on this aspect of the probe, publicity surrounding the case produced immediate benefits. Only hours after the public learned of the murders, a woman phoned the Alexandria Police Department and told a detective she might have some very important information about the murder of her friend.

"I was just talking to her on the phone this Thursday at around six at night. We were talking, and all of a sudden she said to hold a minute. I waited and she came back on the phone after a couple of minutes. 'It was one of my tenants at the door,' she told me. She said he had to use the bathroom. We talked, I guess, ten more minutes."

"While you were talking to her, did she ever mention the name of the tenant?" she was asked.

"No. She just mentioned that the tenant dropped by and had to use the bathroom. It was just a mention."

The woman gave her name, phone number and address and an investigator was assigned to check out her statement.

Over the next several days, the police were out in force interviewing every known tenant of the victim. Detectives also attempted to check through the victim's real estate files, several of which had been strewn on the floor and dresser at the murder scene. Special attention was given to interviewing tenants whose names appeared on these files.

Detectives had a difficult time making sense of the organization of the files. Although the victim was a shrewd businesswoman, her files were a mess. Records at landlord tenant court were easier to work with. Detectives paid special attention to Elliott's tenants who were late with rent or who were in the process of being evicted.

While lawmen were busy questioning these tenants, Medical Examiner James Beyer reported his findings to Sergeant Graves. According to Beyer, Elizabeth Elliott had been stabbed 18 times with a blunt-pointed instrument.

"Two of the wounds were fatal," he pointed out. One was located in the upper chest and the other under her armpit. In both cases, the murder weapon had punctured the aorta, the major artery of the heart. As for Lewinski, the coroner revealed that he had been stabbed a total of 12 times, the most damaging wounds being in the throat and lungs.

According to the pathologist, the amount of blood loss indicated that both victims were alive at least several minutes after being attacked; it was even possible they were both conscious.

As for the time of death, Beyer estimated that both had died between the hours of 7:30 and 10:00 P.M. on Thursday, February 9th.

After the coroner concluded his report and left, Graves contacted the crime laboratory to ascertain if they, too, had uncovered any interesting clues. According to the lab supervisor, however, most items appeared to be only ordinary evidence. There were several blood smears on the floor of Elliott's apartment, but the blood type was consistent with both victims'. There was, however, one interesting find. Some of the papers strewn about on the floor contained fingerprints which did not match either Elliott's or Karl von Lewinski's. Since both victims were friendly, outgoing people, the prints were likely of a friend, who had handled some of the files, or perhaps an accountant or lawyer. Graves, nevertheless, made a note of it just in case a suspect developed whose prints matched the prints that they found.

Questioning of Elliott's tenants as a way of ferreting out a suspect became a futile uphill climb. There were several tenants with criminal records of burglary and/or violence, but there was not a stitch of evidence to link them to the crime and their alibis for the hours between 7:30 and 10:00 P.M. all panned out. Each day, investigators returned to headquarters weary, frustrated and annoyed after being harassed by many indignant tenants who were outraged at the lawmen's probing questions.

Investigators focused most of their attention on Elliott's tenants who lived in the immediate vicinity of Old Town. Elliott, however, owned and managed buildings far from her own home, but the investigators hadn't yet gotten to these tenants when there was a sudden break in the case.

A call came from the Bethesda, Maryland Police Department that a man had found a pillowcase with some curious items inside, including a bloodstained pair of scissors as well as reams of paper with identification in the names of Elizabeth Elliott and Karl von Lewinski.

In short order, two detectives from the Alexandria Police Department drove down to Bethesda and interviewed the witness who appeared nervous and apprehensive during questioning. He identified himself as Abel Miller and told detectives he was rummaging through some trash when he picked up the half full pillowcase.

"What were you doing looking through garbage?" he was asked.

"I usually go through trash," he answered. "Lots of interesting things you end up finding. I was working at this house, putting in a lock—I'm a locksmith—and after work, I thought maybe I'd find something interesting. Well, I find this pillowcase. Lots of things inside. I figured I'd take it home with me and see maybe

237

there was something in there I could use."

"Did you touch anything?" a detective asked.

"Well, I was going through it, like I said," he explained. "But after I picked up the scissors and saw the blood, I just pulled back. Didn't touch nothing after that except the papers. I was just looking through them."

The lawmen noticed while questioning Miller that there were what appeared to be splotches of blood on his shirt. Asked about it, Miller explained that he'd cut himself working, and he offered no resistance to having the stains analyzed at a crime lab. The witness also agreed to take a polygraph.

The results of the test were shocking. During the exam, Miller was asked if he felt he could possibly murder someone, and, although he replied in the negative, the polygraph showed he was being deceptive.

When detectives confronted Miller with the results, the witness admitted that he had been seeing a psychiatrist for what he called a very quick and violent temper. He claimed that he knew he had violent tendencies and wanted to control them but, deep down, he felt that his temper might some day explode and he would end up killing someone. That's why when he said he couldn't kill someone, the polygraph showed he was lying.

Miller's psychiatric records checked out accurately with his testimony as did the crime lab report on his blood-stained shirt.

During continued questioning, however, another suspicious item turned up. Detectives asked him a theoretical question. Just suppose he had been in the apartment where the victim had been slain. How could he reasonably explain Lewinski's huge 240-lb. body ending up in the armchair seat?

Miller replied that Lewinski was probably dragged from behind the bedroom area where he had been cut down. He went on to explain how the body would have to be twisted through a narrow doorway to get it into the living room.

These details seemed to imply not only a reasonable method of transporting the body to the armchair but an accurate knowledge of the apartment's physical layout.

The detectives' hearts began thumping wildly when it became apparent that this man knew a little too much about the murder scene to be just an innocent bystander. They confronted him with this fact, but he shrugged it off in a congenial manner, explaining that, of course he knew exactly what the apartment looked like because he saw the entire layout among the papers in the pillowcase. The detectives searched and found several items with an accurate diagram of Elizabeth Elliott's apartment.

As questioning continued late into the night, it became obvious that Abel Miller was just who he claimed to be – a garbage picker who stumbled onto some very heavy evidence.

Detectives brought the evidence back to the Alexandria Police Crime Lab where it was processed for fingerprints and other possible clues. Several sets of fingerprints were recovered among the various articles, some matching the victims' and others matching Abel Miller's. There were also a few unmatched sets.

Relatives and friends of the victims who were shown the evidence identified the scissors as Elliott's but claimed they had never seen the torn black glove.

Dr. Beyer examined the 12-inch scissors and said he believed it could have caused the kind of tissue damage he observed on the victims, but he couldn't definitely say it was the actual murder weapon.

Tests run on the scissors, however, revealed traces of human hair which matched Karl von Lewinski's, and bloodstains which were the same type as Elizabeth Elliott's.

Sgt. Graves also checked pictures taken of the crime scene and smiled grimly when he observed a photo of the victim's bed. Lying on top of it were two pillows, one of which was missing a cover.

The pillowcase find gave detectives more incentive in

239

their probe and, although they still had no solid lead on a suspect, they continued interviewing tenants without letup.

Then, on February 22nd, a call came into the crime-solvers section of the Alexandria Police Department. A Washington, D.C. pawnshop owner who had been sent photos of Elizabeth Elliott's jewelry claimed that several of the items pictured were similar to those he had bought from a man on February 10th, the day after the murder.

"I have the receipt in my hand right now," he said.

Detectives obtained his address and raced down to his shop. The man offered them the jewelry as well as the receipt, which had a signature in the name of George Robinson. They carefully placed the item in a plastic bag and obtained a description of the man who had pawned the jewelry.

"I remember him very well," the owner told them. "He seemed to be a nice man, a little nervous though."

"Do you remember what he looked like, any identifying features?" he was asked.

"Yes. A tall, black fellow. Thin. Not too thin, though. He had a slight mustache, and his hair was cut short."

Detectives noted down this information and returned to police headquarters to decide on a plan of action. On the way, they dropped off the pawnshop receipt at the crime laboratory for processing.

When they reached headquarters and began discussing the case, one lawman jerked forward at the mention of the name George Robinson. "We just questioned a guy by that name a few days ago," he said. "Nothing to do with the Elliott-Lewinski case. Grand larceny, I think."

A lawman went through several open files and came up with a document naming George Robinson as one of the witnesses questioned during a burglary investigation in the vicinity of North Payne Street.

"Mrs. Elliott owns a couple of houses there," one of the sleuths noted. "If Robinson's one of her tenants, it's a good bet he's our man."

Several investigators checked with Elliott's law firm and the county clerk's office and things began to fall into place. Elliott did in fact own the building in which Robinson lived. Even more to the point, court records indicated that on December 1, 1983, Elliott had started eviction proceedings against Robinson for failure to pay three months rent of $750. By January 6th of 1984, however, the case was dropped.

In their attempt to uncarth links between Robinson and the victim, investigators also searched through the bundle of papers found with the bloody scissors in Elliott's pillowcase. Again they struck paydirt. There were rent receipts in the name of George Robinson and some bank receipts in the name of several of his relatives. In addition, fingerprints lifted from these receipts were now compared with latents recovered from the pawnshop ticket. The prints were the same. Checking further, detectives learned that Robinson had been charged with forgery and grand larceny the year before in Arlington. His fingerprints taken from that arrest were compared with those already recovered. They were a perfect match.

It was time to give Mr. Robinson a visit.

On February 23rd, Detectives Jerry McHugh, Derrill Scott and Steven Coffman arrived at Robinson's home and interviewed him. They informed him from the start about how his name came up in the investigation. The pawnshop ticket was one item that needed explaining, they told him. Then there were the fingerprints and the eyewitnesses' description.

"If we have to, we could put you in a line-up. Do we really have to do it?"

Robinson said he'd like to help them, but he didn't know what they were talking about. After approximately an hour of aimless questioning, McHugh and Scott decided to take Robinson down to headquarters, a slightly more potent atmosphere for interrogating the suspect.

At the homicide office, interrogation continued. Playing

241

a mind game with the suspect, the police told him they were his friends and if he told them all he knew, it would be much better for him in the long run. They'd look out for him.

By nine o'clock that evening, after a gruelling eight-hour grilling session, the suspect admitted that he had murdered Elliott and Lewinski after being discovered burglarizing the apartment.

After obtaining this confession, detectives charged Robinson with the murders of Elizabeth Elliott and Karl von Lewinski.

News of the arrest spread throughout the community like a shockwave, friends, relatives and co-workers of the suspect were stunned. He just couldn't have done it, they said. "All I know from his babyhood on up is he was a perfect child," said a close relative. "I've never seen him angry in my life . . . They got the wrong man."

One of Robinson's former co-workers knew the suspect as a "leader." A lot of the employees looked up to him. He took an interest in people."

Friends admitted that Robinson had money problems. He had quit his job four months before and hadn't been able to find another one. "Being unemployed bothered him," said a neighbor. "He had three kids, and he wasn't working and his wife wasn't working." Friends claimed, however, that Robinson just wasn't the kind of person who would hurt anyone.

Detectives, though, knew that, despite Robinson's reputation as a kind, loving, gentle family man, the robbery motive as well as evidence and his confession proved something quite the opposite, that Robinson was, indeed capable of, and had in fact committed a ferociously violent act.

But only shortly after Robinson's arrest, there was a new twist to the investigation. When detectives questioned the suspect again to obtain a more complete account of his crime, he proposed a brand new version of events and insisted that he, in fact, was not the murderer.

According to Robinson, the day before the slaying, he had been in Washington, D.C. and was introduced to two men named Bomber and Jimmy who were driving towards Alexandria. They offered him a ride and, on the way, got to talking about their money troubles. Robinson told them about quitting his job several months before. Bomber was in a similar situation. Then Robinson got an idea and suggested burglarizing his rich landlady's home. It was easy meat since she kept her rent money in a desk drawer.

"All you'd have to do is go there," Robinson recalled saying to his partners. "We'd say, 'Mr. Robinson' and she'd open the door. (The two of you) would just run in and grab the money."

But, as Robinson continued, their plans went awry. His two partners went inside while he waited. Then he heard a horrible scream.

"I didn't even go in there until I heard her scream."

He saw both men standing over the fallen Elliott and Lewinski. Bomber was holding a pair of bloody scissors.

At this point, according to Robinson, something snapped inside his head. He snatched the scissors out of Bomber's hand, bent down over the stricken Lewinski and stabbed him in the neck.

"I felt like if I didn't stab Karl I was gonna . . . he was gonna . . . I'm all mixed up. I wasn't even supposed to go in. It wasn't supposed to happen that way."

A check was made in the D.C. police department records for a man going by the name Bomber. As it turned out, there was, in fact, a man arrested for heroin possession in D.C. who used the nickname Bomber. Investigators went to his home and questioned him.

He admitted that he had met Robinson but flatly denied being involved in the murder. According to Bomber, he had spent the entire evening of February 9th in a local bar with some pals. He gave detectives their names as well as the name of the pub where he'd spent the evening.

The bartender remembered him being there all night, and

his friends vouched for him. Since the only name Robinson gave detectives for the other suspect was Jimmy, investigators had no way of learning his identity or address.

Alexandria Police Captain Andre G. Salvas conceded his doubt regarding Robinson's alleged accomplices: "We're not totally convinced there was a third subject, but we're not ruling it out."

On March 8, 1984, Investigator Jerry McHugh interviewed Robinson again, explaining how Bomber and the other accomplice had been checked out.

"Be honest with me," McHugh pleaded. "Did they have anything to do with the crimes?"

"No," Robinson finally admitted. "They didn't have anything to do with it."

Police were now convinced he was the only person involved in the murder; and, with Robinson's confessions and the evidence compiled against him, Commonwealth Attorney John Kloch also felt there was enough to bring him to trial on capital murder charges.

The trial was held in Alexandria Circuit Court, Judge Albert H. Grenadier presiding.

Attorneys George West and James Clark were appointed by the court to defend Robinson. Their salary amounted to a meager $573, yet their intense effort to defend their client was far in excess of their payment.

They fought the prosecution every step of the way. First, they argued for a private detective to wade through the evidence and investigate any witnesses who could help their client. Judge Grenadier okayed this request. Later during the trial, Clark argued that detectives did not thoroughly investigate the witness who found the pillowcase containing bloodstained scissors, implying that their defendant might not actually be the killer.

Clark and West also pushed to have Robinson's statements to police sealed from the jury because, they claimed, the defendant had not been adequately warned about the dire consequences involved in speaking with the police.

Again, the judge agreed with Clark and West, sealing all but one of Robinson's confessions.

But for Prosecutor Koch, the defense attorneys needed a lot more ammunition than defensive strategies. Kloch called over 70 witnesses to give evidence linking Robinson to the crime. As for physical evidence, there was Robinson's fingerprints on papers found in the pillowcase with the bloodstained scissors. Kloch also introduced the pawnshop receipt with Robinson's signature and fingerprints as well as the jewelry pawned, which was positively identified as being Elizabeth Elliott's.

As for witnesses, there was the pawnshop owner who easily identified Robinson as the man pawning the jewelry.

But the most damning evidence of all was provided by the defendant himself. In the one taped question and answer confession allowed during the trial, George Robinson's voice told the court the bloody, detailed account of his crimes:

Detectives: Did you go down (to Elizabeth Elliott's apartment) around 6 or 6:30?

Robinson: Yes.

Detectives: What happened?

Robinson: I was there for a while, about 30 or 40 minutes.

Detectives: Who was in the house?

Robinson: Karl, and Ms. Elliot. I did not even know Karl was there. I asked Ms. Elliott for a drink of water. She went in the kitchen. I started to go in the desk . . . Karl caught me.

Detectives: What were you going to get out of that desk?

Robinson: I thought some money, 'cause when I gave her the check (earlier that day) she put the check in the desk.

Detectives: What happened when Karl found you?

Robinson: We rassled for awhile.

Detectives: Where was Ms. Elliott?

Robinson: She was still back there somewhere. I don't know where.

245

Detectives: And what happened when you and Karl were wrestling?

Robinson: I grabbed some scissors from the desk. I stabbed him. He started to run.

Detectives: How many times did you stab him?

Robinson: About three times . . . He just started to run towards the back of the house. Then he fell.

Detectives: Was he still in the living room?

Robinson: Sort of. I guess he was in between the hallway . . . Then Ms. Elliott came.

Detectives: Were you still standing in the hallway?

Robinson: I was bent down over him (Lewinski), and she asked what was wrong, and he hollered . . . She looked and she saw blood, and she screamed.

Detectives: What did she say?

Robinson: 'Oh, No!' Something like that.

Detectives: What did you do then?

Robinson: I just stabbed her.

Detectives: How many times did you stab her?

Robinson: About twice I guess.

Detectives: Then what happened?

Robinson: Karl was getting up off the floor again, and he was coming right back towards this way . . . He fell across the chair.

Detectives: Then what did you do?

Robinson: Panicked . . .

This testimony from the defendant's own mouth was, undoubtedly, the most crucial weapon in the prosecutor's arsenal.

Kloch's major problem in the case, however, was in convincing the jury that Robinson not only went to Elliott's home to rob them but that he had also planned their murders. Kloch contended that all details of the case could not be known because "two of the probably three people who know what happened are dead."

He did, however, point out that Robinson's actions after murdering the couple showed a sort of sick practical rationale. If the murder was something that occurred in a panic, why then did Robinson patiently ransack the apartment after having murdered the two victims?

Defense Attorney Clark argued that there was no premeditation on the part of his client because his client wasn't the killer. Clark implied that two other men killed the victims, contending it was just physically impossible for Robinson to have carried out the crime.

"The commonwealth would have you believe," he argued, "that George Robinson was able to enter the apartment and subdue Mr. von Lewinski with a pair of scissors without Mrs. Elliott being able to call out for help on the number of telephones in the apartment . . . . or running into the street."

Prosecutor Kloch dismissed the defense's contention that two other men had committed these crimes as mere "hypothetical possibilities" and "red herrings."

Defense Attorney George West lashed back in his closing statement, referring to Kloch's term "red herring" as "an interesting way of characterizing doubt."

On June 14, 1984, the seven-woman, five-man jury began deliberation on the case. Once they returned to the courtroom to ask several questions. All told, they spent 11 hours sequestered. Then on June 15, 1984, they returned with a verdict finding Robinson guilty of the two capital murders and two robbery charges lodged against him. The maximum sentence for capital murder charges in Virginia is death. But the jury came in with the maximum verdict short of death for each of his crimes: life in prison for each robbery and murder conviction.

According to Virginia law, a person sentenced to two or more consecutive life prison terms is eligible for parole after 20 years. If sentencing runs concurrently, eligibility is in 15 years.

At Robinson's sentencing hearing on July 26, 1984, Defense Attorney George West pleaded for leniency, contending that Robinson's violent act was an aberration of his character which would never occur again.

"Mr. Robinson went there without the intention of hurting anybody," he asserted. "He went there only with the intention of sneaking some money. When he was caught, there was an individual born who had not existed before and who has not existed since."

D.A. Kloch, however, saw the murder in a different light, calling it "a horrible and sickening crime for a few bucks."

When it was time for sentencing, Robinson went before Judge Grenadier and, with tear-filled eyes and choking voice, said, "It's been hard for me to accept that I've committed this act. I've hurt so many people in this — my family and the community. I'm truly sorry that I've caused so much grief and pain."

Judge Grenadier also found it hard to accept what Robinson did. "The court cannot articulate the absolute horror of what you did," he told Robinson before imposing sentence. "It was completely unwarranted."

Judge Grenadier then sentenced the defendant to the maximum, four consecutive life terms.

EDITOR'S NOTE:
Oliver Pendil, Abel Miller, Jimmy and Bomber are not the real names of the persons so named in the foregoing story. Fictitious names have been used because there is no reason for public interest in the identities of these persons.

"WHO AMBUSHED THE KINKY MILLIONAIRE?"

by Clarence Walker

Seabrook, Texas, is a quiet coastal village of 5,000 inhabitants, situated 30 miles east of Houston. Local citizens and Vietnamese immigrants have given the town its reputation as a "seafood heaven" by fetching shrimp and oysters from the Gulf of Mexico.

With the exception of an ongoing war between the Vietnamese immigrants and the local shrimpers over fishing rights, crimes are rare. To visitors, Seabrook seems to be a peaceful fishing village. Violence, however, can turn the most peaceful locale into a living hell.

On Wednesday, October 17, 1984, while most citizens in Seabrook carried on everyday living, evil lurked inside the mansion of millionaire William List on Todville Road. Armed with a 16-gauge shotgun, a deranged male paced erratically around the house as if he were a warrior commanded to kill anyone on sight.

"I need some heroin," the gunman demanded of his companions.

An injection of the powerful drug caused his body to tremble; a stream of blood rushed to his brain. He tripped out. His mind drifted between fantasy and reality. Glancing at the clock, the gunman pronounced, "Our guest is on the way." Carefully, he inspected the slug in the gun's chamber.

249

At 5:45 P.M., Bill List pulled his vehicle into the garage. As usual, he honked the horn, but on this day he received no response. He exited his car and silently entered the door that led into the house.

"Get ready! He's coming," a voice whispered.

Once inside the front room, List froze in his tracks. It appeared that someone had ransacked his mansion. His red face was contorted with anger and confusion. Gritting his teeth, List headed upstairs when a voice yelled, "Hey, Bill!"

Before List had a chance to respond, a shotgun blast struck him in the head. Reeling backwards, he gripped his head and tumbled to the floor. There he lay kicking, trying to fight the horror of death that would soon overtake him.

The executioner walked over to the man. He pointed the gun and prepared to shoot again. But the body had stopped twitching.

Within the next few minutes, while the gunman continued to stand over the body, his two associates took a VCR, cassette tapes, and a stereo and loaded them into List's vehicle.

"Let's get the hell out of here," one of the men said.

"Go ahead, I'll be right with you." Apparently the gunman had something else on his mind. He unzipped his trousers and murmured, "No more pain." Then he urinated on the dead man.

As the four men drove away in the car, the killer flipped on a song by Tina Turner, "What's Love Got To Do With It?"

When List failed to report for work the following morning, his supervisor became worried. List was the owner of a nationwide company that built oil-rig trailers. He usually arrived well ahead of his 8:30 A.M. schedule. After several calls went unanswered, the supervisor notified police. When Seabrook officers arrived at the multimillionaire's mansion, they detected no signs of a forced entry, nor anything out of the ordinary. All the burglar bars were intact except for an obviously cracked window on the west side of

250

the mansion. Walking around to the garage, one of the officers paused; his eyes focused on what appeared to be blood seeping from beneath the door. When he twisted the knob, the door was locked.

Alarmed, the officer rushed to the south side of the building and peered through a window. In view lay the body of Bill List. Backing away from the window, the officer advised his partner to stand guard while he radioed for assistance.

Chief Bill Kerber arrived on the scene promptly, followed by Officer Broussard and a team of crime technicians.

"We're almost certain he's dead," the officer said to Chief Kerber, who had known List for many years. Before the officers could enter the house, a city maintenance crew had to use a blowtorch to break the burglar bars. Because the mansion had three levels and 30 rooms, the investigators were in for a long, hard search for evidence. The crime-scene search lasted until midnight. Apparently, someone had intentionally and randomly destroyed the first floor to the house. Expensive chandeliers were broken. A large planter had been hurled with such force that it protruded from the wall. Furniture and food were strewn on the floor. A gold set of china plate had been thrown into the pool. There was acid in the Jacuzzi, and a glass water fountain valued at $50,000 had been broken.

"From the looks of things, there was no struggle. Whoever committed the murder wrecked the house on purpose," one of the officers at the scene noted.

"I would say they tore the house up out of anger," added another officer.

The officers were startled by words scrawled on the wall. In red, the words said, "No more pain. Bill List is a sick man. No more fist for List. Have a nice day."

"Sounds like something weird has been going on here," Chief Kerber reflected.

A search of the residence yielded no significant evidence, but, to their surprise, the police discovered a wooden platform rigged with ropes and chains.

"Well, I'll be holy! It's a torture chamber," an officer remarked.

In the master bedroom, officers discovered boxes of pornographic material and sex toys.

"I've always wondered what was going on in this place. Now I have the answer," Chief Kerber said in disgust.

A Harris County coroner made a preliminary examination of the body and confirmed that List had died from a shotgun wound to the head. His pockets had been turned inside out; no wallet was found.

The body lay at the bottom of the staircase near the patio area. Most of the blood was in that area. The victim was clad in a white shirt, blue slacks, and brown loafers. His skull was totally destroyed. Photographs were taken from every angle, and diagrams were made to record the destruction to the house. The body was then removed to the morgue for an autopsy. Meanwhile, a special bulletin was aired to local police to be on the lookout for List's stolen 1984 Pontiac, license number 344-FRZ.

While the crime-scene search continued, Chief Kerber and Lieutenant Harris questioned List's employees and business associates. They stated that List might have been slain by a jilted lover or, maybe, because of a business dispute. List was very secretive about his homosexual lifestyle, an employee pointed out. But the deceased's lifestyle was no secret to Chief Kerber because List had admitted to him privately that he was gay.

"List's being a homosexual did not bother us as long as he did not break the law," Kerber stated.

From the beginning of the investigation, police suspected that List had brought someone home with him and, for whatever reason, that person had murdered him.

The month of October, 1984, was an evil month for the deceased's family. At the time of his death, List was deeply concerned about the outcome of a trial in which a 35-year-old man was on trial for murdering List's daughter, Debra

Thornton. The notorious case had been dubbed the Pickax Murder. List's murder was also highly publicized in the news media. Unfortunately, with his death, the surviving family was left to witness justice in both cases.

Neighbors described Bill List as a hardworking man who mostly kept to himself.

"He lived a strange life," a neighbor commented. "I often wondered why a man would live alone in a mansion."

What kind of background did List have? Overall, he was no stranger to the criminal justice system. Born in Ohio in August of 1927, List served prison time in 1959 for molesting juveniles. He told a psychologist in prison that he learned about homosexuality when he was only eight. Though he was married and had two children, his wife filed for divorce before his parole.

When he was paroled in 1962, List took his two children and moved to Houston. He started a trailer business and became a multimillionaire. Despite his homosexual lifestyle. List was regarded as a shrewd businessman. He bought a brick company for a reasonable price and made his own bricks for the mansion. When he poured the slab for the 34,000-square-foot home, his neighbors feared that he was building an apartment complex. By the time he died, List's fortune was estimated at over 10 million dollars. The mansion itself was valued at 1.3 million dollars.

In the early stages of the investigation, detectives spent their time running down false leads. Then one phone call broke the case. An officer from the Houston Police Department informed the Seabrook cops that three suspects who might be responsible for the murder had been taken into custody. One of the suspects had tried to cash a $300 check—made out to List's payroll department—at an inn on Telephone Road. The clerk became suspicious and notified employees at List's business place. A supervisor there, who knew the check had not been authorized, told the clerk to call the police because List had been found murdered in his home. The suspects were arrested with evidence to prove they had been in List's mansion. They were identified as 16-year-old Tom Sanders, 23-year-old Jeffrey Stratton, and 19-year-old Elbert Ervin Homan, who went by a nickname, Smiley. The three identified a fourth suspect, 19-year-old Michael Boyler, who undoubtedly had left Texas. While making these arrests, the police recovered List's stolen Pontiac. Tom Sanders had List's driver's license in his wallet. Holman had the car keys and List's wallet in his back pocket. Jeffrey Stratton had the credit cards in his possession.

After being advised of their legal rights, the suspects were transferred to the Seabrook Police Department, where they were interrogated separately. The suspects were frightened.

Homan began to shake. It appeared he was ready to spill his guts.

In a lengthy confession, Homan revealed the evil scheme that led to murder. Officer Nana Holleman typed the statement, as follows:

"I was down on my luck, drifting around on Westheimer Boulevard, sleeping in alleys or anywhere I could lay my head. I was using drugs heavily and turning tricks to survive. My life was one big fantasy. I used to dream about a rich man taking me away from the streets and giving me whatever I wanted. And then it happened: A rich man came along. On Saturday, October 13, 1984, I was standing in front of a grocery store on Westheimer when Martin Boyle and Bill List drove up in a white car. Martin asked me if I wanted to go riding and I agreed. When I was inside the car, Bill looked at me and said, 'You are charming, young man. You have a beautiful smile. Would you like to live with me?' "

Homan said he agreed to live with List as long as Martin stayed with him.

Homan continued, "List said we could live at his house but insisted that we would have to do our share of the housework. Then he started asking about the kind of sex we liked. When we arrived in Seabrook, List drove off on a deserted road that led to his mansion. It was the largest place I had ever seen. There were bright lights everywhere. I said to myself, 'My dream has come true.' "

The mansion reminded Homan of a castle. This magnificent environment and List's millionaire status were something Homan always craved for; he intended to please this sugar daddy to get the best things out of life. At least, he thought he would.

"There were two other guys living there. Tom Sanders and Jeffrey Stratton. Bill gave me a bedroom and said to make myself at home. He had plenty of drugs and I used some and passed out. Later that night, Bill woke me up and told me to extend my hand. He wrapped a tape measure around my wrist and said, 'You are going to sexually assault me with your hand.' "

At this point in his confession, Homan paused and began sobbing. The investigators waited patiently until he regained his composure. In a quivering voice, Homan related a tale of sex horror.

"List had the weirdest sex preference of any human alive. On the first encounter, Bill lubricated my hand with shaving cream. Then he made me shove it into his anus. While I massaged his anus, he masturbated. The filthy ordeal lasted for hours. The following morning we ate breakfast, but before Bill went to work he told us to clean the house. Jeff Stratton was his favorite houseboy. Tom Sanders was Jeff's lover, so they laid back and had fun. I thought I had found a real sugar daddy in Bill List, but I lost all confidence when I learned how perverted he was.

"Bill was a braggart with a hot temper, very hard to please. He was always fussing about his house. If he found cigarettes in the ashtrays or if the plants hadn't been watered, he would get angry and demand we get the baseball bats and sexually assault him to relieve his anger. I was tired of doing all those sick things to him. Once he got angry and threatened to take us back to Westheimer.

255

"Sometimes he would torture me. I felt my body had been used for perversion. My dreams were shattered. It was time for the pervert to die. For different reasons, all the boys had agreed to murder Bill. On the fateful day, he was in a joyful mood at breakfast. He gave us all money and acted as if he wanted us to stay. I guess it was his special day—a day for dying—because Bill was so happy."

Continuing his confession, Homan said that he and his accomplices had trashed the mansion by hurling furniture and other expensive items all over the place. During the wild commotion, they took turns using shaving cream to write on the walls. Martin Boyle wrote: "Have a nice day." Tom used red ink to write: "The problem lies in your head." Homan wrote: "Bill List is a very sick man. He is going to die. Thank God, no more pain." And he added the ultimate: "No more fist for List."

Homan further confessed that they argued over who would actually kill the "S.O.B."

"Say, man," he told Martin, "we don't need no pain tonight."

Homan agreed to be the killer. After shooting heroin, Homan paced around the house, waving the shotgun around until it was time for Bill to come home. He sat in a chair atop the staircase, waiting for his prey. Martin was to allow Bill to ascend halfway upstairs before yelling at him to direct his attention to the perfectly aimed shotgun.

"That's when I pulled the trigger."

After completing his confession, Homan signed it and became hysterical. For Homan, the horror of Bill was over.

Jeff Stratton repeated practically everything Homan related. He stated that Bill had been forcing his lover, Tom Sanders, to engage in kinky sex.

"Sometimes the pervert would force us to strip nude and torture our private parts with sex objects. We did not enjoy submitting our bodies to Bill's perverted lust, but we had no decent place to live, and he threatened to throw us out— back to Westheimer. We would not tolerate going back there so we decided to live as stable brothers at the mansion."

Jeff also admitted that, after the murder, they had burglarized Bill's office and stolen his checkbooks. From there they visited some friends' house and told them about the murder. The next morning they cashed several checks and purchased some new clothes to wear. At this point they wanted to leave the state, but were undecided where to go.

Tom Sanders, the youngest of the four, related a similar story. But he added more bizarre details about his sexual relationship with Bill.

"One night I was playing pool at the Midnight Sun on Westheimer when Bill came in and challenged me to a game. After I won the first game he said, 'Let's play again for $100.' To his surprise, I won the second game. He handed me a crisp $100 bill. Then he asked me if I needed a place to stay and I said yes. A deal was made that I would have sex with him and clean his house for $100 a week. From then on, I began living at the mansion and that's how I met Jeffrey Stratton. My first night there, Jeffrey pleaded that we sleep together to prevent Bill from torturing him."

Lieutenant Harris gently interrupted the suspect by asking, "Why didn't you leave the house?"

"I don't know," the suspect replied. "Bill manipulated us to the point that we were undecided whether to leave or to stay. Sometimes he injected us with drugs that made us crave more. The drugs made us feel excited and even more vulnerable for sex. One morning before sunrise, Bill handed me a baseball bat covered with shaving cream. I said, 'What is this for?' He said that I should massage his anus with the bat. It was the worst experience I ever had, but for several hours I used the bat to sexually stimulate and assault Bill."

In between sobbing and laughing, the clean-shaven teenager said Bill also had a torture chamber. He described it as a wooden table outfitted with ropes and chains. "Bill used the chamber to torture his lovers. Every day, Bill said, 'If you want to live here, you have to assault me with your fist, let me sit on your face, or submit your soul for torture.' Finally we decided we couldn't take it any more and we made plans to kill him. We had to rid ourselves of our suffering and pain."

The completion of the confession was transcribed and read by the investigators. They determined that the bizarre story they had heard about Bill List was beyond anyone's imagination. Finally, the big secret about the mansion had been answered.

From information provided by the suspects, investigators learned that Martin Boyle had fled to Belleville, Illinois, to live with his parents or a homosexual identified as a local lawman. An arrest warrant was teletyped to Belleville authorities, and Boyle was taken into custody pending extradition procedures.

Under Texas law, when a suspect confesses to a crime, investigators need corroborative evidence to prove that he actually committed the crime. And if the suspect identifies his accomplices, evidence is required to prove that the accomplices participated in the crime, as well. Following the confessions by the suspects, investigators made the necessary moves to track down the corroborative evidence. The suspects led the police to the I-10 freeway to locate the murder weapon where Homan claimed he had tossed it from the car. After a fruitless search, investigators returned to headquarters.

Now they wanted substantial information to prove Boyle's participation in the murder. A manager at the Starlite Motel on Westheimer stated that Boyle had rented a room on October 12, 1984, and had checked out on October 14th. The manager said he saw Boyle, on the 14th, get in a white Pontiac car, formerly owned by Bill List. Detective Wilbur Hendricks from the St. Clair Sheriff's Department contacted the Seabrook Police Department indicating that Boyle had admitted to his homosexual lover that he had participated in the murder.

Elbert Homan told police that people on the street called him "Smiley" because they said his face was charming. He said he could manipulate people with his charm. A homosexual once told him, "Someday your charm is going to be fatal." Seemingly, the prediction turned out to be true.

The life of Elbert Ervin Homan was like a roller-coaster ride. If he wasn't high on drugs, he was down struggling to survive. What caused Homan to become a tough street kid, even though he was handsome and very talented? Where did it all begin? He was born on Christmas Eve in 1965, but his parents divorced when he was a toddler. He vaguely remembered his father. Homan had attended a number of schools; his fellow students regarded him as a troublemaker.

"He had so many fights at school I thought he would become a boxer," his mother said. "To get whatever he wanted and maintain control over people, he used his charm, which made you want to trust him. His devilish eyes spelled trouble."

At 17, after living with girlfriends and relatives, Homan, on the advice of a relative, moved into the Covenant House, a non-profit home for runaways and street kids. The House is located in Westheimer near the Montrose area.

"The idea sounded great," he claimed. The Covenant House would provide shelter, find him a job, and ultimately make him independent. "My plans were to quit drugs and start a new life," Homan told his friends. "All my life I've wanted to be something great—a judge, a lawyer, or a policeman." But his cockiness and wayward ways caused him to be evicted from the Covenant House.

He ended up back on Westheimer, roaming the streets. The thought of getting a job and becoming that special person was soon forgotten. His mind focused on the glamour of Westheimer, something he conceived of as the good life. Using drugs, turning tricks with men, and hanging out with kids who were lonely and had no future—these were the only activities he could turn to. The hard street life was a way to understand himself.

Westheimer Boulevard is a home for juvenile runaways, prostitutes, and hustlers. A 10-block stretch of Westheimer consists of gay clubs, massage parlors, strip joints, X-rated arcades, and sleazy motels. It is a place where winos are rolled for cigarettes and elderly people robbed for pennies. When the sun goes down, Westheimer is jammed with heavy traffic and kids start hustling. If they fail to make a dollar, it means dumpster-diving for food and a day without a high.

Despite the viciousness of this environment, Elbert Homan had convinced himself that he could survive. Even in the midst of these sordid circles, he still had dreams of some day becoming wealthy or at least of breaking away from it all and building a new life. But after he was arrested on charges of aggravated robbery and attempted murder, Homan could not break away from the street life. Though a judge had placed him on 10 years of probation for the robbery conviction, almost immediately when he left Harris County Jail, Homan headed back to Westheimer. By then he was using every dime to buy heroin. On his right shoulder, Homan had a tattoo, "F.T.W." The letters stood for "F"—The World." Somehow the devil had caught hold of Elbert Homan, and there was no turning back. He was like a walking time bomb and, in due time, he would finally explode. For Bill List, his life of wealth and fame would succumb to the fatal charm of Elbert Homan.

On July 11, 1985, Homan had his final day in court. He pleaded guilty to murder. Judge Pat Lykos sentenced him to 45 years in prison. Additionally, Judge Jon Hughes sentenced Homan to life in prison after revoking his 10-year probation for a 1983 robbery conviction. Both sentences will be served concurrently. He will be eligible for parole in 2005.

On July 18, 1985, Jeffrey Stratton was sentenced to 15 years in prison for robbery and credit-card abuse stemming from the murder. A juvenile court judge placed Tom Sanders on probation. After many court hassles, charges against Martin Boyle were dismissed on May 30, 1986.

EDITOR'S NOTE:
Tom Sanders and Martin Boyle are not the real names of the persons so named in the foregoing story. Fictitious names have been used because there is no reason for public interest in the identities of these persons.

"WANTON MURDER OF THE WEALTHY SOCIALITE"

by Barbara Geehr

Palm Valley, FL
December 14, 1989

On the early afternoon of Thursday, May 11, 1989, Captain Robert Porter of the St. Johns County Sheriff's Office in St. Augustine, Florida, fielded two telephone calls which aroused his suspicion that something was wrong at the home of 84-year-old Eunice Edwards, a wealthy widow living alone in a big house in nearby Palm Valley.

The first call came from one of Mrs. Edwards' neighbors. She said that the socialite, ordinarily seen several times a day, had not been seen in a few days and that her 1988 white Cadillac was missing from her garage. Minutes later, the second call—this one from Police Detective Dan Archer of Atlantic Beach—followed. Archer wanted to know if, by any chance, Mrs. Edwards had filed a theft report with the county sheriff's office.

"We're a little concerned at not being able to reach Mrs. Edwards," Archer said. "We have a little problem over here about some checks returned by her bank. We believe they may have a forged signature."

Though no such report had been filed, Captain Porter sent Detective Mary Levek, along with some uniformed deputies, to Mrs. Edwards' house to check on the woman's well-being. Upon arrival there, the investigators got no answer to their bell ringing. They found all doors and windows tightly locked and were unable to detect any signs of forced entry.

Through questioning neighbors, the sleuths learned that not a single one had seen Mrs. Edwards during the past few days. All the neighbors thought that was rather strange, since they usually saw Eunice puttering around in her garden every day.

Returning to the house, Detective Levek and Deputies Randy Capo and Jeff Nolan managed to pry a back patio door open. Entering through a room used as a den, they made their way through widely scattered broken glass to a hallway which had openings to a bathroom and bedroom. There they found Mrs. Edwards — or, rather, the body of Mrs. Edwards. Fully clothed and face up, she was sprawled out on the floor near the bathroom door. Her head, with a gaping bullet wound in the left side, was resting in a pool of blood. Next to her lay a crumpled jacket and a pair of gold earrings.

With the help of Deputies Capo and Nolan, Detective Levek secured the house and then called Captain Porter to report the findings.

"Stay where you are," Porter directed. "I'll pull a few people together and we'll get over there right away."

With Palm Valley less than 20 miles north of St. Augustine, it did not take long for the captain, Sergeant Chuck West and evidence technician Marcia Touvet to reach the Edwards house.

Following a brief organizational discussion, Porter officially assigned Touvet to the processing of the crime scene. "Since Deputy Jeff Nolan has already been inside and seen the body, he'll go along with you and give you any assistance you need," Captain Porter said.

He then told Mary Levek to get in touch with Detective Dan Archer and make arrangements to meet with him in Atlantic Beach. "He's one of the two people who asked us to check on Mrs. Edwards' well-being. Get the specifics on what prompted his concern," Porter directed the investigator.

"I'm on my way," Levek said.

"Okay. And everyone just remember that Sergeant West and I will remain on call for any help anyone needs." With that, Captain Porter ended the meeting.

Detective Levek left the Edwards property and evidence technician Touvet wasted no time getting the processing of the crime scene under way. "Okay, Jeff," she said to the deputy assigned to help her, "I noticed a tire track in the driveway as we came in. Let's put something over it to mark it. I'll do a plastic casting later."

As Nolan located the tire track and put his hat over it to mark it, Touvet got out her video equipment from her car. "Before we go inside for a walk-through," she explained to the now-hatless deputy, "I have to video the scene from the outside. Just hold tight until I do that." The evidence technician then methodically videoed the front of the Edwards property, the surroundings, the garage, both sides of the house and the back, ending at the patio door which had been pried open by the first investigators at the scene. "Now," Touvet said to Nolan, "show me the body, and then we'll do the walk-through. When we get to that, keep your eyes open for anything that looks as though it might have evidentiary value. I'll do close-up photos on the second trip through the house. For right now, though, I'll just be more or less panning the rooms with the video camera."

The sight of Eunice Edwards' body brought a strong reaction from Marcia Touvet. "Oh, my God!" she exclaimed. "I can't believe somebody would do this to this wonderful woman! Where is her sister? Is her sister okay?"

A surprised Nolan responded, "I didn't know you knew Mrs. Edwards. As for her sister, we learned during our neighborhood canvass that she died many months ago and that Mrs. Edwards has been living here alone ever since."

Touvet explained her initial shock at the sight of the body. "Though I haven't seen Mrs. Edwards for a couple of years, I once knew her very well," she said. "After her husband died several years ago, her sister came to live with her. They were two absolutely adorable people; they ran around everywhere together. When I was on road patrol and covering this area, I used to stop in regularly to check and make sure they were all right. This is a big house, and I was always concerned about two little old ladies being in it alone. They did have a tiny dog named Duffy, but I doubt he would have been of much help had anyone broken in."

"Well, so much for that," the evidence technician said, abruptly ending her moment of reminiscence. "Let's get to the walk-through. We'll start at the den, as though we'd just come through the back patio door."

The two returned there. Touvet, panning the room with her video camera and observing the shattered glass strewn across the floor, the couch and nearby chair, commented, "It's a heck of a lot of glass. You have to wonder whether there was a struggle here before Mrs. Edwards got to the hallway."

In the den also, Touvet noted the tiny bone fragments on the carpeting. "Probably blown here as the fatal bullet passed through the victim's head," she said. "Better put some pieces of paper over each one. We don't want to miss any when we get to photographing and collecting the evidence. They're so tiny, we'll probably have to use tweezers to pick them up."

From the den, the two went to the east bedroom, the only downstairs bedroom in the two-story house. They made special notations of the expensive jewelry in this room. It filled a two-and-a-half-foot-tall jewelry box on top of the dresser and practically overflowed from the top dresser drawers when the scene processors pulled them open. On the dresser also, they noted four jars filled with coins. Neither the jewelry nor the coins appeared to have been touched.

Deputy Nolan commented, "It doesn't look much like robbery was the motive for this murder."

Touvet and Nolan next went to the kitchen. Finding nothing there in the line of evidence at that time, they walked upstairs, noting the pictures on the wall along the way. Among them was a framed love letter from Mrs. Edwards' husband. It had been written during a time when he was in the armed services and away from home.

At the top of the stairs, they entered a loft-type bedroom where a four-poster bed with a lace bedspread and pillow sham dominated the room. The evidence technician pointed out to the deputy the body imprint across the spread and the facial tissue tucked part way under one of the pillows. "Mrs. Edwards used to lie on the bed and read a lot," she said. "She told me that she enrolled in literature classes at the University of Florida after her husband died. She said she was known as the oldest student the university ever had. You know, I can't help smiling at the tissue tucked part way under the pillow. Every time I saw Mrs. Edwards, she had a tissue in her hand."

A typewriter on a marble-topped table not far from the bed caught Deputy Nolan's interest. He asked if Mrs. Edwards had been a writer.

"Not that I know of," Touvet answered. "I believe she did work at a Beaches radio station for awhile and, of course, she's been active in Palm Valley and Ponte Vedra community affairs for twenty or more years. That's what keeps bugging me as we walk through her house. With robbery out as a probable motive for the murder, I can't find an answer to the question: Why would anyone want to murder such a sweet and caring person as Mrs. Edwards?"

Deputy Nolan replied, "As you well know, there are probably as many different motives for murder as there are different kinds of people. But I do agree with you that this one may be hard to come up with—as well as surprising."

The investigators, finding no tangible evidence in either the loft bedroom or the adjoining bathroom, went back downstairs and into the lower-floor bathroom. Nolan expressed surprise at seeing coats, jackets, sweaters and gardening clothes hanging on a heavy rod over the tub in the bathroom.

"Mrs. Edwards was a pack rat; she never threw anything away," Touvet explained. "She didn't have room in closets to hang up bulky or little-used things; so whenever she came in from the outside, the first thing she did was head for this bathroom to hang up whatever jacket or sweater or coat she happened to be wearing. I may not be able at this point to figure out a motive for her murder, but I can tell you one thing. Whoever killed Mrs. Edwards had to know her well. Whoever it was had to know how to get into her house and had to know she had this habit. The location of the body and the jacket indicate Mrs. Edward had just entered the house and was on her way to this bathroom, jacket in hand, when she was shot."

"What you're theorizing then is that the killer stood in this bathroom, gun in hand, ready to fire the fatal shot into Mrs. Edwards' head when she entered her home and walked down the hallway to hang her jacket up in the bathroom?"

"I believe we'll find sufficient evidence to support that theory. For example, note the tieback thrown into this wash basin after being ripped from the curtain at the window. Why was it ripped from the curtain at the window? Obviously to keep anyone on the outside to see what was going on inside. Well, let's see what else we can come up with in here."

In the continuing search, Touvet did find substantial evidence to support her theory on how Mrs. Edwards had been killed in cold blood. First, there were the gunpowder burns on the hinged edge of the bathroom door and on the molding of the wall the door was attached to. They were about as high up from the floor as Mrs. Edwards was tall.

"These powder burns indicate that the killer hid behind the open bathroom door and fired the fatal shot through the crack between the edge of the door and the wall," Touvet explained to Deputy Nolan. "We'll have to take this door down and get it to the lab to have the gunpowder burns processed."

Then there was the strand of hair found on the lid of the toilet. It was brown and four-to-five inches long. "Obviously not from a white-haired little old lady," Touvet commented, as she pointed the strand of hair out to Nolan. "We'll have to send this for microanalysis."

Finally, upon raising the toilet lid, Touvet spotted a bullet casing lying at the bottom of the bowl. "I can't believe this!" she exclaimed, motioning Nolan to come take a look. "Surely the killer wouldn't just drop the casing into the toilet and not flush it down." She thought about it a moment and then said, "Let's see. We found the lid of the toilet closed when we got here. What the killer probably did was drop the casing into the toilet, close the lid and then push the flush handle, assuming the casing would just flush away. But it obviously didn't. The toilet gives us three good pieces of evidence: the strand of hair from the lid, the bullet casing from the bottom of the bowl and the latent we're going to get from the flush handle, assuming the killer pushed it down and the bullet just didn't flush away."

The evidence technician completed the video part of the investigation around Mrs. Edwards' body. Starting at the head area, she videoed the victim all the way down to the foot area, then shot the body from the back side, the front side and the bathroom side. Finally, Touvet taped it from a position in the middle of the stairway, so she would even have a shot of the body from a downward angle.

She then took the video camera back to her van, got her photograph equipment, returned to the house and repeated with the still camera the same process she'd been through with the video camera. This time, however, she did closeups of each item of evidence discovered on the first trip through the house, as well as of Mrs. Edwards and the various parts of the victim's body.

During this phase of the investigation, Touvet realized as she was photographing the glass on the couch in the den that there was something askew about one of the pillows.

268

"Something looks funny here," she commented to Nolan.

She picked up the pillow, discovered a bullet had been shot through it, knocking some of the stuffing out of its back. Tracing the bullet's course, she found it had continued on through the back of the couch and exited through the wall behind it. "Let's go outside and look for the bullet," she said to Nolan.

They did and, with comparative ease, found it had hit a brick wall, ricocheted and landed in a nearby plant bed. They had far more difficulty tracing the path of the bullet which had been shot through Mrs. Edwards' head. Eventually, however, they found it had traveled nearly 15 feet through the hallway to ricochet off a window between the den and the living room and then continued on another seven feet east to come to a stop atop a dresser.

Touvet added photos of both bullets and their respective paths to her collection of evidence photos. After that, she and Deputy Nolan processed all the rooms in the house for fingerprints. As anticipated, the best latent came from the flush handle of the toilet in the downstairs bathroom.

Touvet commented, "I can tell from the size of the latent that it was left by a man. It certainly was not left by Mrs. Edwards. She had small and delicate hands and fingers."

With the first basic steps of the crime-scene investigation completed, Touvet decided to leave charting, measurement-taking and the physical gathering of evidence for the next day. She called Captain Porter to advise him that the body could now be transported to the medical examiner's office for an autopsy.

"I'll get in touch with Dr. McConaghie right away," Porter said.

When Detective Mary Levek left Mrs. Edwards' home, following the organizational meeting on that Thursday afternoon of May 11th, she contacted Dan Archer, as Captain Porter had instructed. After identifying herself and relating how Mrs. Edwards had been found dead in the hallway of her home, she asked the Atlantic Beach police detective if she could meet with him to talk about the forged checks he'd mentioned to Captain Porter, as well as about any other reasons he'd had for becoming concerned about Mrs. Edwards' well-being.

"Certainly," Archer replied. "And you should probably also meet with Betty Drake, the manager of a condominium here in Atlantic Beach. She's the one who contacted this department about the return by Mrs. Edwards' bank of a couple of rather large checks bearing Mrs. Edwards' signature and payable to the condominium. I believe I can save you some time. I'll get in touch with Betty Drake and arrange for the three of us to meet in her office at the condominium."

At the ensuing meeting, Betty Drake told how a man she judged to be around 20 years old had come into her office three weeks earlier to inquire about renting one of the condominium units on a weekly basis. "Weekly rentals are common in this area, because so many people come here to vacation for a couple of weeks or a couple of months," the condominium manager explained. "If we happen to have an empty unit, we'll take a weekly rental. We happened to have one, so I showed it to this man and he decided to take it."

Upon signing a three-week rental agreement, Drake continued, the lessee made out a check for $1,200 to cover the first two weeks.

"When he handed the check to me, I saw it had been pre-signed with the name Eunice Edwards. He had signed the rental agreement as Lee Seymour Myers, so I naturally asked who Eunice Edwards was. He told me she was his grandmother and that she'd given him the check to take the apartment. I simply assumed he was on a vacation which his grandmother was paying for. Consequently, when I requested his driver's license for identification and made a photocopy of it, I was surprised to see the man's address was a local one. Mr. Myers then explained that he lived with his mother and stepfather and was taking the apartment for some people who were coming in from out of town for a friend's graduation."

Levek said, "Detective Archer mentioned that the bank returned more than one check bearing Mrs. Edwards' signature. How many others were there?"

"Just one," the condominium manager answered. "That was in the amount of six hundred dollars and was to cover the rent for the last week of the three-week lease. Mr. Myers was to have vacated the apartment by noon today."

In answer to Detective Levek's question about the people who were supposed to be coming in from out of town, Betty Drake replied that she'd never seen anyone but Mr. Myers go in or out of the unit he'd rented.

Drake then told how she'd received both of Mrs. Edwards' checks back in the morning mail. "The woman's bank wouldn't honor them," she explained. "The checks weren't returned for insufficient funds or anything like that, so I called the bank manager to find out the reason. He said that officials there suspected that Mrs. Edwards had not endorsed either one of the checks. They knew Mrs. Edwards well, knew she'd owned the Palm Valley home in which she lived for more than twenty years and just could not believe she would be renting a condominium only ten miles from her residence.

"The bank manager had telephoned Mrs. Edwards to inquire about the checks," the condominium manager continued, "and Mrs. Edwards told him she definitely had not signed any such checks. He said I should probably call the Atlantic Beach Police Department."

Drake added that before doing that, she tried to reach Mr. Myers by phone at the home of his mother and stepfather. "I had the address from the photocopy I'd made of his license at the time he signed the rental agreement," she explained.

Getting no answer to her call, Drake said she then took it upon herself to check Myers' apartment. "It was on the way there that I observed a white Cadillac parked in the space reserved for Mr. Myers' unit. I'd not seen any other car parked there except the red Mazda Excel Mr. Myers drove. Anyway, when I entered the apartment, I saw Mr. Myers' belongings stacked by the door, indicating he was going to be leaving.

"Oddly enough, my attention was caught by a woman's white purse among his belongings. I was curious about a woman's purse being there. I looked inside it and found identification for Eunice Edwards. I just didn't feel right about what was going on. That's when I called the Atlantic Beach Police Department. Detective Archer can tell you what happened following that."

Archer, after explaining that the Atlantic Beach Police Department didn't usually handle bad-check complaints, said, "I discussed the situation with my superior officer and we decided we'd do a little check, strictly as a courtesy. I came over here, talked with Ms. Drake and got Lee Myers' home address from the photocopy she'd made of his license."

The Atlantic Beach detective related how he went to that address, found no one home, returned to the condominium and, with Betty Drake, entered Mr. Myers' apartment. In this superficial look-through, he told Detective Levek, "We found other checks belonging to Mrs. Edwards. They hadn't yet been signed. When Betty told me about the white Cadillac standing in the parking space reserved for the unit which had been rented by Mr. Myers, I ran a check on the tag and learned the vehicle was registered to Eunice Edwards of Palm Valley. I tried to reach Mrs. Edwards by phone several times but never got an answer. That's when I called the St. Johns County Sheriff's Office to ask that someone check on the woman's well-being."

Detective Levek asked to see the apartment rented by Myers. The condominium manager and the Atlantic Beach police detective took her there and, on the way, noted that the white Cadillac was now gone and Myers' red Mazda Excel now stood in the parking space reserved for his unit.

Inside the apartment, Betty Drake observed that the white purse and some of the other articles she'd seen on her previous visit were now missing. Levek, taking it upon herself to search through the trash, found several receipts with Mrs. Edwards' name on them. She said, "I believe I need to have a little talk with this Lee Myers."

Upon return of the three to the condominium office, she obtained Myers' address and the tag number of Mrs. Edwards' Cadillac. Then after thanking Betty Drake and Detective Archer for their cooperation, Levek left to call Chuck West to ask him to meet her in Atlantic Beach. "We may have a lead in the Edwards case," she told the sergeant. "We need to talk to a Lee Seymour Meyers who lives with his mother and stepfather here in Atlantic Beach."

"Be right over," West said.

Night had moved in by the time Detective Levek and West got to the residence of Myers' parents. Finding only Mrs. Myers at home, the detectives introduced themselves and explained the purpose of their visit. Sergeant West said, "We were hoping to find Lee here. We wanted to ask him a few questions about some checks he gave to a local condominium for rental of an apartment. The checks carried the signature of Eunice Edwards. Mrs. Edwards is now deceased. We believe she was a victim of foul play and would like to find out how Lee happened to know Mrs. Edwards and how he happened to be in possession of some of her checks."

After expressing shock at the news of Mrs. Edwards' death and Lee's possession of some of her checks, Mrs. Myers said, "Well, come in. I can tell you what I know, but it isn't much."

Once the investigators were comfortably seated inside, Mrs. Myers explained her son's relationship with Mrs. Edwards. "Lee, who is twenty-one, has been doing odd jobs for Mrs. Edwards for the past several months — actually since the death of Mrs. Edwards' sister who'd been living with her for some time. That left Mrs. Edwards

273

alone in a big house. Being well up in years, she found there were many things she couldn't — or didn't want to — handle by herself. She hired Lee to do odd jobs around the house, drive her to and from the doctor or dentist's office and things like that. Since the Edwards house is only a short distance from here, the arrangement worked out pretty well. Mrs. Edwards would telephone Lee when she wanted him for something and he could get there in a matter of minutes."

Concerning checks, Mrs. Myers said the only thing she knew was that Mrs. Edwards had telephoned early the previous morning to ask for a meeting. "She didn't give a reason for wanting the meeting other than it had something to do with checks. When I later asked Lee what she was talking about, he said he had no idea."

Mrs. Myers, asked by Detective Levek if she'd set up the requested meeting, answered, "No. I told Mrs. Edwards I would just stop at her house on my way home from work that evening."

"That was yesterday evening?"

"Yes. And I was surprised to see that her car was not in the garage, because the last thing she said on the phone was that she would be expecting me. I knocked on her door, anyway; I got no answer. I knocked on all her windows and again got no answer. I figured she must have had to go somewhere and would telephone again if she really wanted to talk to me."

Mrs. Myers further said that as she went to get into her car to drive the rest of the way home, she happened to see lights on in the trailer across the street from the Edwards house. "I knew Mrs. Edwards owned the trailer and the five acres of land it sits on and that it had been empty for a long time. I was surprised to see there was someone in it. I walked over there and asked the man who answered the door if he knew where Mrs. Edwards was. He answered that he hadn't seen her. I asked him what he was doing there. He identified himself as Mrs. Edwards' preacher for

274

the past eighteen years and explained he had rented the trailer from Mrs. Edwards and had just moved in an hour or so ago.

"I had observed two cars parked in his driveway," Mrs. Myers continued, "and I asked if both belonged to him. He said he owned one of them but didn't know who owned the red Mazda Excel he'd found parked there when he was moving in. Before I left the property, I looked inside the red car and saw a toolbox that looked like my son Lee's toolbox in the backseat. I got some bad feelings. Lee had stolen a couple of cars in the past and had abandoned them on those five acres belonging to Mrs. Edwards. I was afraid he might be up to something again."

Sergeant West asked if Mrs. Myers had taken the tag number on the red car.

She replied that she hadn't and, in fact, had momentarily forgotten about the red car when she reached home and saw Mrs. Edwards' Cadillac in the driveway. "At first, I thought she'd come to my house for the talk she'd asked to have. But when I got inside, Lee told me he'd driven the Cadillac home after taking Mrs. Edwards to a dentist's appointment that afternoon. He said Mrs. Edwards needed him again early the next morning and told him to take her car so she would be sure he'd get there on time."

"Did you ever confront Lee about the Mazda Excel?" Levek asked.

"Yes. We had a big argument about it last night. He finally admitted he'd rented it with my American Express card and left it parked across the street in the trailer's driveway when Mrs. Edwards told him he could use her car to drive home. I told him to get the car and return it to the rental agency right away."

Sergeant West commented that it sounded as though Mrs. Myers had had a few problems with her 21-year-old son.

"You can say that again," Mrs. Myers sighed. "Actually, Lee is on probation."

275

"For what?" West asked.

Mrs. Myers related an incident involving Lee and another family member. "Lee was only seventeen at the time," she recalled. The family member cared very much for this boyfriend who dropped her cold when she refused to have sex with him. She was so absolutely devastated that Lee decided he was going to teach this kid a lesson. He went over to the boyfriend's house and, with a clipboard and box in hand, told the kid he was a UPS delivery man and had a package which had to be signed for.

"Being the only one in the house at the time, the boyfriend took the clipboard inside to do the signing. Lee followed, pulled out a sawed-off shotgun, threatened the kid with it and then tied him up. Lee got five years on charges of assault and kidnapping, but was released on probation and in my custody last August after serving two years."

"Does the probation carry the stipulation that Lee has to be home every night?" West asked.

"Yes."

"So if he doesn't come home tonight, he will be violating his probation?"

"That's right. But I have no reason to believe that he won't be coming home tonight. So far, he always has," Mrs. Myers said.

"When did you last see him?"

"This morning. I followed in my car when he drove Mrs. Edwards' Cadillac back to her house. I thought she would be there and I would be able to meet with her, as she had requested. I knocked on her door and again got no answer. I had to go to work so I left a note on her door to that effect. Lee thought Mrs. Edwards had probably spent the night at a friend's house and was simply late getting back. He was going to wait for her; I went on to work."

"Is there anything else you can tell us that might be of help in the investigation?" Detective Levek asked.

"Not that I can think of," the woman answered the investigator.

276

"Then we'll be on our way. Thanks for your cooperation. When Lee gets home, please tell him we'd like to talk with him. We'll check later to find out if he's here."

As Mrs. Myers escorted Detective Levek and Sergeant West to the door, she said, "I do have one more thing to say."

"What's that?" Levek asked.

Mrs. Myers replied, "Instead of talking to my son and possibly thinking of him as a suspect in Mrs. Edwards' death, you better talk to that guy who moved into Mrs. Edwards' trailer."

The two investigators returned to the Edwards house to talk with evidence technician Marcia Touvet, to check on any further developments at the crime scene and to interview the preacher who had moved into the trailer owned by Mrs. Edwards. Taking things one step at a time, they advised Touvet that since Lee Seymour Myers had an arrest record she would be able to get a set of fingerprints from his arrest file to compare with the latents picked up inside the Edwards house.

Except for an interview Detective Frank Welborn had had, nothing of additional significance had developed at the crime scene. Welborn, unaware that Levek and West already knew Mrs. Edwards' previously empty trailer was now occupied, told about observing a man pull his car into the trailer's driveway that afternoon.

"I went over to talk to him, find out who he was and what was going on there," Welborn related. "The guy became real belligerent and said he was the one who should be finding out what was going on. He said he was tired of being asked who he was and what he was doing there. Apparently some woman went over there last evening just as he was starting to cook dinner and asked a lot of questions. There was a mix-up of some kind about a red car that was parked in the driveway, he said. The woman seemed to think it was her son's car and he had left it there. A little later, he said he saw a young guy walk up the driveway, get

277

into the car and drive it off."

Getting no comment from either Levek or West, Welborn continued, "I had a hard time calming this guy down. I told him Mrs. Edwards was deceased, that we suspected foul play and simply wanted to find out if there was anything he could tell us that might help in the investigation. At first, he refused to give a statement and that gave me momentary cause for suspicion. In the end, however, he did give a statement in which he identified himself as Mrs. Edwards' preacher for the past eighteen years, stated he'd rented the trailer from her three days before and had moved in yesterday afternoon. I believe the guy is legitimate."

"Good!" Levek commented. "You've just save us an interview we were about to do." Turning to Sergeant West, she said, "We might as well go back to the Myers house and find out if Lee has come home. "I've a gut feeling that he's not going to."

"It's probably well founded," West commented.

It was heading toward midnight by the time Levek and West reached the home of Lee Myers' mother and stepfather for the second time. Both parents were still up and both were highly upset because Lee had not come home. Mr. Myers was obviously annoyed by the return of the investigators and, in a demanding voice, wanted to know why they had come back.

Sergeant West, unfazed, replied, "Because we suspect foul play in the death of Mrs. Edwards and believe Lee may be able to give us information that would help in the investigation."

The stepfather, in a somewhat more civil tone, asked, "How was Mrs. Edwards killed?"

"We're not allowed to tell you that," the sergeant answered.

"Well, can I ask you something?"

"Sure. What?"

"Was she shot?"

"Why do you ask me that?"

"Because my three-fifty-seven Dan Wesson Magnum is missing."

"The answer to your question is yes," West said.

Mr. Myers did an about-face and became cooperative to the point that he gave the sergeant some cartridges he kept in supply for his gun.

"These will be most helpful," West said. "Our evidence technician can take them to the lab and find out if they match the cartridges recovered at the crime scene."

When Levek and West left the Myers residence for the second time, Thursday, May 11th, had become another filled page on the calendar of time, and the page for Friday, May 12th, lay clean before them. Despite the embryonic hour, they decided to go back to headquarters. They left the cartridges given to them by Mr. Myers for Marcia Touvet to take to the lab and to kick fact and fancy around until they came up with a direction to pursue in the investigation of Mrs. Edwards' murder.

They could not dismiss Lee Seymour Myers as a suspect. "However," West pointed out to Levek, "whatever evidence we have against him at this point is purely circumstantial. It is not sufficient to get a warrant for his arrest on a first-degree murder charge.

"On the other hand," the sergeant continued, "we do know it's likely that Lee, wherever he is, is in Mrs. Edwards' car. His mother told us she left him sitting in the white Cadillac in the driveway of Mrs. Edwards' house on Thursday morning. The Cadillac was later seen at Lee's condominium by the condominium manager and Detective Archer of the Atlantic Beach Police Department. The Cadillac was gone a short time after that, along with some of Lee's belongings, and the Mazda Excel—the car rented by Lee—was back in the parking space reserved for Lee's condominium."

"I thought Mrs. Myers said Lee took that red car back to the rental agency," Levek interrupted.

"No," West pointed out. "What Mrs. Myers said was she

told Lee to go get the car from the trailer driveway and return it to the rental agency. That doesn't mean he did it. As a matter of fact, we know he didn't do it because after he retrieved the car from Mrs. Edwards' trailer on Wednesday evening, it was seen back at the condominium the next morning."

"You have to be right," Levek commented to Sergeant West.

Sergeant West continued thinking aloud. "Anyway," he said, "we can put out a BOLO on Mrs. Edwards' Cadillac; but even if or when that car is picked up, we have nothing to have Myers held on so we can get to him and ask him some questions pertaining to the homicide. However, his probation officer could have him held on a warrant for violation of probation."

"That sounds like a good idea," Levek agreed.

"Unfortunately, we can't get to the probation officer at two o'clock in the morning," West said. "We'll have to take care of that sometime later today."

"Let's at least get the BOLO out on Mrs. Edwards' Cadillac before we leave," Levek suggested. "The sooner we get people watching for it, the better. Isn't it fortunate I had the foresight to get the tag number from Detective Archer?"

West entered the BOLO into the system, noting in addition to the information on the Cadillac that the vehicle may be driven by 21-year-old Lee Seymour Myers, a suspect in a murder case and that Myers may be carrying a gun.

Before going to their respective homes to catch a few hours of sleep, the investigators left a note for Marcia Touvet. In it, they asked that cartridges given to them by Lee Myers' stepfather be taken out of evidence custody and sent to the lab for comparison with the cartridge recovered at the crime scene.

When the evidence technician reported to work that morning and found the note, she figured it had to be her lucky day. Touvet had already planned to obtain a set of

Myers' fingerprints from his arrest file and take it to the Florida Department of Law Enforcement (FDLE) crime lab in Jacksonville for comparison with the latents she'd lifted at Mrs. Edwards' house. She could now have both items of evidence processed at the same time. She lost no time in picking up the cartridges and getting on her way.

Sergeant West and Detective Levek, somewhat refreshed after a few hours of sleep, were at their desks at the St. Johns County Sheriff's Office by 10:00 A.M. As their first order of business, they went to talk with Lee Myers' probation officer about Myers' situation.

That officer, after listening to their story, cooperated by agreeing to obtain the warrant. "It's no big deal," he said. "I'd be getting a warrant out on Myers, anyway, once I learned he didn't report home last night."

As soon as the probation officer went through the necessary procedures and obtained the warrant, West entered the information into the national computer system. "Someone is bound to spot that white Cadillac," he commented to Levek with confidence. "When they do, they'll hold Myers on this violation of probation warrant and we'll finally get to talk to him about the homicide."

"I like your confidence," Levek said.

The medical examiner now officially reported that Mrs. Edwards had been killed by a single bullet which had entered the left side of her head and had exited the right side. He estimated that death had taken place at approximately one or two o'clock on the afternoon of Wednesday, May 10th.

Marcia Touvet, returning from the FDLE crime lab late that afternoon, advised Levek and West of the results of the evidence processing. She said a ballistics expert, after examination of the two bullets recovered at the crime scene, determined that both had been fired from a .357-caliber Magnum revolver and that the casing recovered from the toilet bowl matched the cartridges given to the investigators by Lee Myers' stepfather. Additionally, Touvet said, a fin-

281

gerprint expert found that the latent lifted from the flush handle of the toilet in Mrs. Edwards' downstairs bathroom matched one of the prints in Myers' arrest file. "We've finally placed Lee Myers at the scene of the murder!" Touvet said excitedly.

More excitement was to follow. Just before midnight, the St. Johns County Sheriff's Office received a teletype from the Louisiana Highway Patrol (LHP) in Lake Providence, advising that Mrs. Edwards' Cadillac had been recovered and that the driver, Lee Seymour Myers, had been taken into custody. Captain Porter immediately telephoned the LHP in Lake Providence and spoke with Senior Trooper Aaron R. Britton who had made the arrest.

Britton reported that at 10 o'clock that night, he'd stopped a Cadillac on US 65, four miles south of Lake Providence, on a speeding violation. "The guy was doing seventy-six in a fifty-five," the trooper said. "I asked him where in the hell he thought he was going. He answered that he was going to his sister's house which was now only about ten miles farther down the road. I told him he was going to take a little detour with me first.

"When I got him to the patrol office," Britton continued, "I ran a computer check on the Cadillac and on the guy's driver's license. When the reports came back showing the car stolen and Myers with a St. Johns County warrant out on him for violation of probation, I arrested him."

"Where is Myers now?" Captain Porter asked.

"I took him to the East Carroll Parish Jail here in Lake Providence," Britton replied.

Porter asked if Myers had resisted arrest or tried to flee.

"No, none of that stuff," the trooper answered. "Okay," Porter said. "I'll get things together here and be back in touch shortly."

The captain telephoned Sergeant West to advise him that Lee Myers had been arrested by a highway patrol officer in Lake Providence, Louisiana, and that Mrs. Edwards' car was at the highway patrol station.

"You better call back and get that Cadillac impounded right away," West advised. "Give orders that no one is to touch it. We're hoping to find a major item of evidence in that car, which will help in our investigation of Mrs. Edwards' murder."

"Okay, I'll do that," Porter said. "What are your thoughts on our next move?"

"I believe it would be beneficial for us to go ahead and go out there," the sergeant suggested. "Not only do we need to search the Cadillac for the murder weapon, but the quicker we can talk to Myers, the better are our chances of getting a confession."

"I think you're right. How soon can you get things together and be on your way?"

"I'll call Levek and Welborn right now and tell them to be ready to leave in the morning. There's no need for us to charter a flight. I have my pilot's license; I'll just go ahead and rent a little four-seater."

"Okay," Porter said. "I'll call the highway patrol office back, get Mrs. Edwards' Cadillac impounded and advise that our investigators will be leaving here by plane in the morning. Good luck!"

West, Levek and Welborn left St. Augustine in the small rented plane at 10:00 A.M. on Saturday, May 13th. Despite bad weather all the way, they arrived at the airport in Monroe, Louisiana, at four o'clock that afternoon. They registered at a local hotel, freshened up, got something to eat and rented a car to drive directly to where Mrs. Edwards' Cadillac was impounded.

In checking the car, they started with the trunk. The first things they found upon opening it were the white purse belonging to Mrs. Edwards and a real estate brochure with the name Lee Myers written across the front. There were also several filled plastic garbage bags in the trunk. Some were stuffed with clothes obviously belonging to Myers; others contained fast-food remains and trash. Sergeant West, in opening one of the bags containing Myers' cloth-

283

ing, found what he had hoped to find; the obvious murder weapon — the .357-caliber Magnum revolver stolen from Lee Myers' stepfather. The bag also contained 20-to-30 rounds of ammunition.

Though it was past the midnight of Saturday, May 13th and into the beginning of Sunday, May 14th, the St. Johns County sheriff's investigators headed for the East Carroll Parish Jail where the county sheriff's office was located and where Lee Seymour Myers was being held. The jail and the sheriff's department were a part of the courthouse, which was located in the bayous for which Louisiana is well known. They found the sheriff and five deputies waiting there to welcome them.

It had been decided that Levek and Welborn would make the first attempt to get a confession from Myers, while Sergeant West would remain with the sheriff, establishing good relations and being available if needed.

"Our interview room isn't the best," the Louisiana sheriff explained to Levek and Welborn. "The heater in there keeps kicking on and off, we have to keep the copy machine running day and night and the dispatch office is right next door so you can hear the phones every time they ring."

Levek commented that it really would be better if they could do the interview in a room where there were no distractions. "Isn't there some other room we could use?" she asked.

The sheriff, making every effort to be hospitable, opened up a little-used small room in the back of the tax collector's office.

Levek, realizing the room was undoubtedly the best in the courthouse, exclaimed enthusiastically, "Oh, this will be perfect!"

"Good, then," the sheriff said. "You and Detective Welborn just make yourselves as comfortable as you can. I'll get Mr. Myers brought in from his holding cell."

Once Lee Myers entered the room in which the interview was to be conducted, the investigators introduced themselves and explained they were there to find out what Myers could tell them about Eunice Edwards' murder. Levek had barely finished reading the suspect his Miranda rights and he not only agreed to talk but started doing so before either Levek or Welborn could ask him the first question.

Myers said he didn't know anything about Mrs. Edwards being murdered but would like to explain how he happened to be driving her car. He then related that a friend who worked on shrimp boats in Jacksonville came to his house on Thursday morning, May 11th, and told him he was going to Texas for a few days. "He said Eunice was letting him use her car and he asked if I would ride along with him," Myers said. "I wasn't doing anything special and I figured I could stop and see my sister along the way. So I said sure, I would go along. I threw a few clothes together and we took off."

Myers further stated that after the two got to Louisiana, his friend told him he'd decided he would stay in Texas, once he got there. "Because he wasn't going to be coming back, he said he'd hitchhike the rest of the way and I could drive Eunice's car back to Palm Valley after stopping at my sister's. I dropped him off and was on my way to my sister's when I got stopped for speeding."

Levek and Welborn were so surprised by Myers' trumped-up tale that they were momentarily speechless.

"Well, that's my story," Myers said. "I have nothing else to say."

When Detective Levek found her voice, she said, "Now, Lee, you know that story doesn't add up. We know about the checks you wrote to the condominium on Mrs. Edwards' account and we know about Mrs. Edwards calling your mother and asking for a meeting. We know you're on probation and were probably terrified. We also know about your stealing your stepfather's gun and we believe we have sufficient evidence to convince a jury that you are guilty of first-degree murder.

"However, we also believe there are two sides of every

285

story and we'd like you to tell your side. When we're called to testify before the jury, we don't want to make it sound like you're a cold-blooded murderer."

Lee Myers gave up his thin facade of bravado with a deep sigh.

Levek said, "Just go ahead and tell us in your own words how this whole thing happened."

According to Myers' statements, he'd met a girl in Atlantic Beach, with whom he'd become instantly smitten. The girl came from a well-to-do family and was a student at a nearby Florida college. He wanted to impress her, to make her think that he, too, had money and was smart. The girl's parents were coming in from California to attend her upcoming graduation and she was worried about finding a proper place for them to stay, since they didn't like staying at hotels.

Myers said, "So I told her I had a condominium and her parents could stay there. She thought that was a great idea. Of course, I didn't have a condominium so I had to get one. I'd been doing odd jobs for Eunice Edwards and knew she had a lot of money. I didn't want to lose this girl, so I took some checks out of Eunice's purse, signed her name to them and got a condominium. I also rented a Mazda Excel, but I used my mother's American Express card for that. I got it out of her wallet."

Myers said he thought everything was going okay until Eunice Edwards telephoned him on Wednesday morning, May 10th, and told him she'd learned he'd been writing checks on her account. "She said she didn't want me using her checks and was going to ask my mother to stop by on her way home from work to get the situation straightened out. I panicked. I didn't want my mother knowing about the checks; I didn't want everything blown way out of proportion and I didn't want this girl finding out that I wasn't really rich, wasn't really a big deal.

"During Eunice's phone call to me, she said she had an appointment with the dentist that afternoon and wanted me to drive her. I told her I couldn't. I knew I had to figure to do something with Eunice before she got to talk to my mother that night. I wasn't sure what I was going to do, just that I had to do something to keep her quiet."

"So what did you decide?" Detective Welborn asked.

"I didn't really decide anything," Myers replied. "I just got my stepfather's gun, loaded it and, a little past noontime, went down to Eunice's house and waited there until she got home from the dentist. I met her in the driveway when she pulled in and walked inside the house with her. She said she had to go back out because she forgot to bring in the mail from her car.

"I didn't know how the gun was going to sound; so while she was outside getting the mail, I put one of the pillows from the couch over it and fired a shot into the back of the couch. After I did that, I went into the bathroom, stood behind the bathroom door and waited for Eunice to come down the hall. I knew she would be coming to the bathroom to hang her jacket up. That was her pattern; she always did that. I just waited and as she came down the hall and got to where I was standing behind the door, I shot her through the crack between the door edge and the wall."

Detective Levek asked, "Did you try to flush the spent cartridge down the toilet?"

"Yes. But it wouldn't go down. I wanted to get out of there so I didn't fool around with trying to recover it. I took one live round and one spent round out of the gun and hid them behind some stuff on the kitchen counter. I don't understand why I did that. I don't understand why I did anything."

Lee Myers waived extradition, was subsequently returned to St. Augustine by transport and locked up in the St. Johns County Jail. State Attorney Tom Cushman advised serving only the warrant for violation of probation on the afternoon of Myers' arrival.

"Myers is bound to be held without bond on that warrant at his first appearance, so he's not going to be going any-

287

where," Cushman said. "I believe we'll have a more solid warrant on the murder if we wait to obtain it until after we get an indictment."

The investigators followed the state attorney's advice. Myers was held without bond at his first appearance on the violation of probation warrant.

In the days that followed, Marcia Touvet, the evidence technician, recovered the rounds of ammunition Myers had mentioned hiding behind "some stuff" on the kitchen counter in Mrs. Edwards' home. Detective Levek obtained handwriting and hair samples from the prisoner. A handwriting analyst determined that Myers had signed Mrs. Edwards' name to her checks. Another expert found that the hair sample from Myers' head matched the stand of hair lifted from the toilet lid in Mrs. Edwards' downstairs bathroom. The tire tracks found in the driveway of the victim's home proved to have no evidentiary value.

On May 25, 1989, a St. Johns County grand jury based on evidence presented by Levek and Touvet, handed down a five-count indictment against Lee Seymour Myers, 21, in the fatal shooting of 84-year-old Eunice Edwards with a .357-caliber Magnum on May 10th in her Palm Valley home. After only five minutes of deliberation, the jurors unanimously indicted Myers for first-degree murder, armed robbery with a firearm, use of a firearm in the commission of a felony, forgery and uttering a forged instrument. It was the first time two female officers ever presented testimony alone before the St. Johns County grand jury; the unanimous decision and the briefness of time in which it was reached gave Levek and Touvet great satisfaction.

In June, Howard B. Pearl, the assistant public defender named to represent Myers, requested a competency evaluation for his client. He said Myers "experienced mood variations within a short time frame" and was "unable to communicate adequately" with his counsel.

Circuit Judge Richard O. Watson granted the request and Myers was subsequently examined by a clinical psychologist and psychiatrist. The clinical psychologist was of the opinion that Myers "was not suffering from a mental infirmity or disease at the time of the alleged offenses" and was "competent to stand trial."

The psychiatrist also found Myers competent to stand trial. He stated, "Mr. Myers does not demonstrate psychopathology which could interfere with his competency to stand trial."

Judge Watson set a pretrial hearing for December 4th and scheduled December 11th for the starting date of the trial.

Before those dates rolled around, Myers tried to escape from his cell on three separate occasions. In the first try, which took place in July, he attempted to remove a block from his cell with part of a mop brace. Deputies said had Myers been successful, he still would have had a long way to go before he could have gotten out of the facility. "He would have had to find a way through stainless steel mesh and another wall before getting outside and then would have had to scale a ten-foot fence topped with barbed wire," they said.

In another, in late October, deputies got a tip that Myers would again try to escape. This time, he and an accomplice apparently tried to saw through a metal wall fixture with a hacksaw blade. Officers found half of a hacksaw blade buried near a fence on the jail recreation grounds. They did not find the other half in a search of Myers' cell and suspected he had flushed it down the toilet.

On December 11th, Myers went to trial on the five counts for which he'd been indicted. State Attorney John Tanner, planning to seek the death penalty on the first-degree murder charge, presented 20 witnesses and 66 exhibits during the testimony.

Assistant Public Defender Howard Pearl rested his case without presenting a defense. During almost two hours of closing arguments, however, he used jury members to consider a verdict of second-degree murder, based on the actions of the defendant who, he said, had not developed emotionally past the age of eight. "You can't look at the course of conduct presented here and say it's normal," he said.

On Thursday, December 14, 1989, a St. Johns County jury took only one hour and 45 minutes to find Lee Seymour Myers guilty of first-degree murder in the shooting death of 84-year-old Eunice Edwards. Jurors also returned guilty verdicts against Myers on the other four counts of his indictment.

At the sentencing hearing the following day, the clinical psychologist who, a month earlier, found Myers competent to stand trial, now stated that the murder of Mrs. Edwards "didn't make sense, in part because the killer had average or above average intelligence." He further said that when he asked Myers why he shot Mrs. Edwards, Myers replied, "I just felt like it."

The psychologist also testified that he found Myers one of the most emotionally constricted individuals he'd ever met and very difficult to read. "His personality had to be shaped by the events in his background. He was five years old when his father died."

Jurors, after 45 minutes of deliberations, recommended that Circuit Judge Richard Watson sentence Myers to life in prison for the May 10th shooting of Eunice Edwards. Life sentences in Florida carry no possibility of parole before 25 years have been served.

EDITOR'S NOTE:

Betty Drake is not the real name of the person so named in the foregoing story. A fictitious name has been used because there is no reason for public interest in the identity of this person.

"THE ALL-IN-THE-FAMILY MILLION DOLLAR MURDER"
by Jerry D. Spangler

It was March 17, 1982, and Frances Bernice Schreuder was enjoying the evening watching her 10-year-old daughter perform in a ballet at the Lincoln Center in New York. But unbeknownst to Mrs. Schreuder, investigators with the New York District Attorney's office were at that same time trying to gain access to her apartment at #10 Gracie Square.

It had been a cold day on New York City streets as Investigator Stephen Klein, armed with an arrest warrant, waited impatiently outside the posh Manhattan apartment to catch sight of the Schreuder woman, a prominent arts socialite and board member of the prestigious New York Ballet. Building security had earlier refused him access to the apartment and Klein had resigned himself to waiting outside the building for Frances to return.

Klein gave up his surveillance about 10 P.M. and decided to return the next morning. When he did return, he found someone had inadvertently left the main door to the building open. Klein and another investigator quietly slipped inside and promptly went up to the sixth floor and knocked on Frances Schreuder's door. They were greeted by the voice of a maid who refused to open the door and refused to say if Frances was at home.

When attempts at negotiation failed, Klein called for back-up men from the 19th Precinct. Five uniformed officers then forced their way into the apartment as a hysterical Frances Schreuder screamed epithets at the officers. A female officer finally calmed the woman down and explained the Miranda warning to her. She also explained to Frances that she had been charged in Salt Lake City with first-degree murder in the death of her own father.

The officers allowed Frances to go into a bedroom to change out of her night clothes, but within minutes they heard screaming from the bedroom. The officers rushed into the room and found Frances' 10-year-old daughter tugging on her mother's leg as her mother hung precariously from the sixth floor window. As the girl begged her mother not to jump, officers assisted her in pulling Frances from a certain suicide. Taking no more chances, they promptly handcuffed the woman and took her to the 19th Precinct for booking.

The arrest of Frances Schreuder—the epitome of New York wealth and affluence—climaxed four years of intense investigation into what investigators have labeled one of the most classic "murder for inheritance" cases ever. The case involved at least two attempts to hire professional hit men, an attempt to poison the victim's oatmeal and finally, a cold-blooded killing by the victim's own grandson acting on orders from the victim's daughter. According to prosecutors, Frances Schreuder feared being cut out of her father's $20 million estate and ordered her 17-year-old son, Francis Schreuder, to kill Frances' wealthy father before he could change his will.

"This is not your usual kind of case," said one defense attorney. "We are dealing with consanguinity in the highest degree. It's a scenario a playwright would be proud of . . . but the consequences are so drastic, so deadly."

Charlie Simms was the first person to arrive at Bradshaw Auto Parts about 8:45 A.M. on July 23, 1978. It was a Sunday, but Simms, a former employee of Bradshaw, knew that

Franklin James Bradshaw, 76, the founder of the auto parts chain, traditionally opened the warehouse on Sundays to assist stranded travelers and others with desperately needed auto parts on a day when all other parts stores were closed.

Though the front door was open, it appeared to Simms that no one was minding the store. He became uncomfortable after a few minutes when no one appeared to assist him. Bradshaw himself was usually on hand to help early-morning customers, but the store was deathly quiet.

After a few minutes, Simms was joined by a second customer, and he too thought it was odd that the store appeared to be vacant. Bradshaw had always prided himself on customer relations, and it was highly unlikely he would leave two customers unattended in his store. Simms and the customer began looking around, and it did not take them long to determine why the elderly proprietor had not assisted them.

As the two men peered over a tall counter on which the cash register and several parts catalogues rested, they saw Franklin James Bradshaw sprawled face up in a large pool of uncoagulated blood, his wallet out on the ground and his pockets turned inside out.

"He was lying there on his back in a big pool of blood and the stuff from his wallet and his pockets was lying out on the ground," Simms would later tell police. "It didn't appear that there was a struggle, at least there were no signs of a struggle; nothing was tipped over. I told the other guy in there that it looked like he had been murdered and I called the 911 emergency number."

While Simms was still on the phone with police dispatchers, the first police officer arrived on the scene. Simms and the other customer then went outside the building and directed the officer to the crime scene. The officer instructed the men to wait outside while he went inside and verified the victim had died of most unnatural causes.

Patrol Sgt. Larry Stott had been cruising the warehouse-commercial district just west of downtown Salt Lake City before 9:00 A.M. when dispatchers relayed a 911 emergency call of a dead body at an auto-parts warehouse at 337 E. Pierpont Avenue. Violent crime was not uncommon in this area of the city often frequented by transients and hobos. When Stott first got the call, he thought it may have been a mugging in which a victim had tried to resist, or maybe even a hobo who had died of alcoholism or exposure, or may even have died in a fight over a wine bottle. "There is an awful lot of crime in this area," he later told the court.

Sgt. Stott arrived at Bradshaw Auto Parts at 8:58 A.M. and was met outside by two men who claimed to have discovered the body of the owner behind a counter in the building. When Stott went to investigate, he didn't find a transient as he had originally thought. Instead, he found one of Salt Lake City's most prominent citizens: Franklin James Bradshaw, a wealthy auto-parts magnate who parlayed a single parts store into a sizeable chain of stores scattered throughout the western United States.

"The wound was obvious," noted Stott. "The back of his head was gone, and I couldn't tell at that time if it had been done with an ax or a gun. It was obviously no accident and he was obviously dead." Stott also noticed the store did not appear to be ransacked and nothing seemed to be missing or out of place.

Upon verifying the apparent homicide, Stott called for back-up officers and detectives. He also requested paramedics just in case there may have been a faint spark of life left in the victim's body. Bradshaw, however, had long been dead. Stott then checked the doors and windows, and with gun drawn, searched the building just in case the killer was still inside. When two other officers arrived, a second search was conducted with the same results: there was no one hiding in the building.

A check of all points of entry indicated that all except the front door were secure. There were no broken windows and there were no signs of forced entry on any of the doors or windows. "We determined that whoever committed the

294

crime would have to have entered and left by the front door," Stott said. Because of no signs of forced entry, police could only speculate about whether the assailant had been hiding inside the building when Bradshaw arrived to open the business at 7:00 A.M.

Detectives who arrived on the scene also noted the position of Bradshaw's body and his wallet. The wallet appeared to have been forcibly pulled from his back pocket, and items from the wallet, including credit cards, were strewn about the body. Bradshaw always carried about $50 in cash with him, family members later told police, but the wallet was empty of any cash. On first appearance, the motive appeared to have been robbery.

But detectives then discovered about $150 lying on the counter by the cash register. It was obvious Bradshaw had been preparing to put the money in the cash register when he was shot. But if robbery was the motive, probers reasoned, why kill Bradshaw for the $50 in his wallet and then leave $150 lying on the counter in plain sight?

Officers also looked for signs of ransacking or signs that Bradshaw resisted his attacker. There were none. "We purposely looked for anything that would indicate a struggle or ransacking, but there was nothing," Stott would later tell the court. "Nothing seemed to be missing."

The crime scene was then sealed for detectives who took photographs and tried to lift fingerprints. No useful prints could be raised, and officers failed to find the murder weapon at the scene. Despite painstaking searches of the building and outside grounds, detectives could find no physical evidence.

The killing shocked, but did not surprise, those who knew Bradshaw and his habits. "This (the killing) is terrible," Simms later told the press. "I am not surprised something like this happened."

Bradshaw typically worked seven days a week, and was the first to arrive in the morning and the last to leave at night. Employees had become concerned about Bradshaw's and their own safety. Over the past few years, the area around the warehouse deteriorated and became home to transients and other assorted riffraff. But despite the warnings from friends and employees, Bradshaw continued his regular business practices. "The customer always came first with him," remarked one employee. "He would open early for anyone."

It may have been that regular practice that led to Bradshaw's death, police speculated. "Bradshaw was the first in every morning and the last out every night," commented Lt. John D. Moessler. "It appears someone knew his schedule and figured he would be alone."

The first promising clue came when police questioned employees about anything unusual that may have happened at the store. The lawmen were told that a young man had been caught stealing a box of tools earlier that month. The incident was not reported to police when employees decided to let the man go with a stern warning. The next morning, however, the toolbox was missing.

Police believed the young man may have had an accomplice hiding in the store, and that when the young man was released and the store closed, the second man made off with the tool box. Detectives speculated that maybe that same thief had returned to the store and had been caught pilfering supplies and had decided to kill Bradshaw rather than be turned over to police. It wasn't much of a theory, but it was all police had to work with.

An autopsy was conducted the next day by the state medical examiner who reported that Bradshaw had been killed by one shot to the back of the head and one to the small of the back. Either shot would have been fatal, he explained. The two slugs — both .38 caliber "dum-dum" slugs — were determined to have been fired at very close range. There were powder burns near both wounds.

Both slugs were subsequently determined to have been fired from a .357 Magnum, and were later matched against bullets of similar caliber on file with the Salt Lake City Police Department. The slugs could not be tied to any known weapon or other crime scene from which slugs had been taken into evidence. The slugs, which were in surprisingly good shape, were the only pieces of hard evidence in the case and would enable a positive ballistics test if the murder weapon could be located. That evidence, however, would be useless without a weapon.

Police, meanwhile, had been pursuing the theory that a cornered thief may have resorted to violence, but the theory did not last long. The thief, who was later located, denied any involvement in the homicide and had an adequate alibi, with witnesses to back him up. He also claimed there was never an accomplice who had remained behind in the auto-parts store.

Fifteen investigators were assigned to the Bradshaw homicide and they worked the case around the clock, trying to unravel the mystery. The most popular theory, though detectives openly admitted it had holes, was the killing had been a random act of violence by a trigger-happy or trigger-nervous bandit.

If it was a robbery, it had been very well planned and executed. The killer knew exactly when the elderly man would open the store and that he would be in the store alone before the regular employees arrived. The killer also had to have known the store would be open on a Sunday and that the area of the city is always deserted on Sunday mornings. No one would be around to interrupt the crime.

Evidence at the scene indicated Bradshaw did not resist his assailant and may not even have known of the robbery until the slugs crashed into his back and skull. Bradshaw's wallet was wrenched from his pocket, indicating it was taken after Bradshaw was killed. Valuable credit cards were pulled from the wallet, but none were taken from the scene.

Family members, many of whom arrived out of state for the victim's funeral, were each questioned about the homicide, but were unable to shed additional light on the investigation. As the leads began to dwindle, police were convinced the killing must have been done by a trigger-happy bandit.

Police pursuit of that angle was also fruitless. Street snitches were each questioned and known bandits were pulled off the streets and interrogated. No one knew who had killed Bradshaw, nor was any known holdup man mysteriously missing from the city after the killing. If it was a local gunman, he was doing an extraordinary job of keeping the incident a secret.

Eventually, all leads were exhausted and police were ready to admit failure. Even a $10,000 reward by Bradshaw's family failed to provide new clues or evidence in the case. For the next two years, the case was filed as an unsolved homicide, probable motive: robbery.

In the meantime, sleuths would learn that Franklin James Bradshaw, 76, was somewhat of a folk hero in Utah because of his incarnation of the American work ethic. People saw in Bradshaw the fulfillment of economic promises that anyone can become a millionaire. Having started in the working world as a copper miner and later a clerk in an auto-parts warehouse, within 50 years, he had amassed a fortune worth $20 million.

Even as a youngster in the early 1900s, Bradshaw had an uncanny business sense. During yearly trips with his father to their Canadian sheep ranch, Bradshaw would sell his sleeping berth on the train to other people unable to get a berth. In doing so, he would always add a couple of dollars to the original price, pocketing the profit and returning the original amount to his father.

Bradshaw was born on April 3, 1902, in Lehi, Utah, where he spent the majority of his youth. He was popular in the local high school and was active in athletics. He later went to the University of Utah on a football scholarship. As a teenager in Lehi, Bradshaw had an inclination toward mechanics.

"He was constantly tinkering with the family car, and in exchange for working on the car, his father would let him drive," said a female relative in a newspaper interview.

While at the university, Bradshaw married Bernice H. Jewett on Oct. 31, 1924. Two things happened that year that changed Bradshaw's life forever: first his mother, who had a great deal of influence over him, died; and second, a disabling football injury eventually resulted in his quitting school.

The newlyweds spent the first years of their marriage traveling from one job to another. Bradshaw first went to Butte, Mont., where he worked in a mine, but left shortly thereafter because women were not welcome in mining camps. The couple then packed their things and headed to Portland, Ore., where Bradshaw landed a job with Ford Motor Company. He managed to work himself into management, but because the couple did not want to live in Portland, they again packed their bags and headed for Los Angeles.

After a short stint as a bookkeeper, Bradshaw told his wife, "I know now where I want to live and know what I want to do. I'm going back to Utah and establish a business there."

After returning to Utah, Bradshaw landed a job in a machine shop, but he wasn't happy. In a letter later written to his employees, he said, "The pay was good and the hours favorable, but I wasn't learning new things or doing the work I completely enjoyed. I started to watch the want ads in the paper and one day I saw an ad, 'Employee wanted to work in parts store, chance for advancement,' so I immediately drove to Salt Lake City and put my application in at the Auto Parts Co."

The owner of the business told Bradshaw he wasn't looking for just an employee, but for someone who could help him build up the business. "To my surprise, he hired me and didn't even bother to look over or study the other applications," Bradshaw wrote.

While employed at the parts company, Bradshaw continually devised ways to improve the business and his own work habits. Despite the fact that he was ineligible for overtime, he worked long hours trying to build up the business. Within a year, he had worked himself into a position where he was writing the majority of the store's invoices and became an invaluable employee.

One day, the owner sent Bradshaw to Provo, about 60 miles to the south of Salt Lake City, on a business trip. While there, Bradshaw noted the growing city did not have an auto-parts store, and "I saw the opportunity to start a business of my own and at the same time help (my current employer) by being his franchise jobber," Bradshaw said.

In 1929, Bradshaw opened his first parts store in Provo. Bradshaw, his wife Bernice, and their 2-year-old son, Robert, moved into a stuffy apartment above the store. The situation became even more crowded when two daughters were born within a two-year period.

The Depression instilled in Bradshaw and his three children the work ethic of those hard times. His belief in honesty, frugality and hard work was conveyed to his children. But Bradshaw also had a business sense "second to none," and in 1937, in the heart of the Depression, he opened his second parts store in Salt Lake City and moved his family to a three-bedroom home on the east side of the city. A year later, a fourth child, Frances, was born.

With the auto-parts business booming and making the Bradshaw family a small fortune, Bradshaw had time for his first love — geology. Though he continued to work weekends and long hours at the store, he found time for geology correspondence courses and trips to the library. His insatiable appetite for knowledge in the field of geology enabled him to become one of the largest holders of federal oil and gas leases in the United States. The once small-town businessman became a multi-millionaire within the span of only a few years.

The added cash flow also enabled Bradshaw to expand the auto-parts business, and at the time of his death in 1978, he had 31 stores throughout the West. He also helped found the Wasatch Chemical Company for no other reason than that there was at that time no raw chemical outlet in Utah.

But the impact of this wealth was lost on Bradshaw, who was described as a "very frugal man . . . who did not believe in extravagance." He always brought a brown bag lunch to work with him each day, he drove a company truck, and he always bought his clothes at discount stores. "Material things didn't mean a damn to Frank," one of his store managers told police. "They didn't captivate him. Usually when a guy makes it big, he spends it big. But not Frank. He didn't know he had won the battle because he never enjoyed the fruits of that victory."

He also disagreed with employees who encouraged him to take time off from work, something he would always refuse to do. The disagreements were always in good nature, and his employees viewed Bradshaw more as a grandfather than an employer. "He was a person concerned about his employees—each one of us individually was somebody special to him," said one former secretary.

While Bradshaw never spent the fortune—estimated at about $20 million at the time of his death—he had spent a lifetime attaining, he did enjoy the prestige of being well known. "Dad was never impressed by money," said one daughter. "He liked being important though. He liked the fact that people knew his name when he went to conventions. But he didn't become a millionaire because he liked money. He liked to think the little guy had a chance. He always considered himself the little guy who made it big."

Bradshaw's life was not without tragedy, however. In 1967, his only son, Robert, died after a lengthy illness. The death was particularly hard on Bradshaw who had personally groomed his son to take the helm of his growing business.

At the time of Bradshaw's death, his daughter Frances was divorced and living in New York City with her own 10-year-old daughter. Bernice Bradshaw, meanwhile, still lived

in the three-bedroom home that she and Franklin had purchased in 1937.

When investigators began checking the family history of
the Bradshaw fortune, they reached the same conclusion as
Bradshaw's own family and associates: the fortune had
been obtained honestly through hard work and relentless
perseverance. Detectives could come up with nothing that
would indicate a family member had done the killing out of
anger or out of a desire to get his or her hands on the family fortune which Bradshaw guarded vehemently.

Detective Joel Campbell, who was assigned to head the
investigation, reported he interviewed each of the family
members. He dutifully recorded that he had interviewed
Frances three days after the funeral for her father and that
she believed Franklin Bradshaw had left all of his money to
the three daughters and their mother. She then indicated
her father may have changed his will prior to his death.
Frances seemed confused about Bradshaw's estate, and
Campbell saw nothing unusual about her comments at the
time.

The case eventually became ice cold, and Det. Campbell
and the other detectives were left waiting for something to
happen or someone to come forward with information.

It was Oct. 16, 1980—more than two years after Bradshaw had been murdered—when detectives got their first
break: a long-distance phone call from a close relative of
the victim's. She told Detective Campbell she had just had
a conversation with an individual who wished to remain
anonymous and that the informant had told her he had had
a conversation with Marc Schreuder, the son of Frances.

According to the relative, Marc told the man, a long-time
family friend of the Schreuder's, that he (Marc) had committed the homicide, and that Marc had given the informant a .357 Magnum he claimed was the murder weapon and
had asked the informant to hide the weapon for him. The
female relative told detectives she had negotiated with the
informant and they had reached an agreement in which the

302

informant would turn the gun over to her for investigative purposes. She, in return, had promised not to reveal his identity at that particular time.

Detective Campbell and Michael George, an investigator with the Salt Lake County Attorney's Office who had been assisting Campbell, finally had the break they knew would come. They embarked on an arduous process of constructing a case out of two-year-old bits and pieces of evidence, imperfect memories and reluctant witnesses.

On Oct. 17, 1980, Campbell received a teletype from New York City Detective Edward Reagan of the 20th Precinct who said the suspected murder weapon had been turned over to him by the female relative who had called Campbell. Reagan told Campbell that the .357 Magnum Smith & Wesson Highway Patrol Special, serial number N281919, had come out negative on an NCIC check.

Utah investigators were ecstatic about the discovery of the murder weapon, and on Oct. 27th, Campbell and fellow Homicide Detective John Johnson traveled to New York City to question the female relative and to test fire the weapon to confirm whether or not it was indeed the gun that had killed Bradshaw.

Upon questioning, the relative told the detectives the informant had told her Marc had purchased the weapon in Midland, Texas, and that Marc had stayed in Texas with a Dr. Marek. The informant also told her the weapon may have been purchased from a police officer with a hobby for collecting guns.

The next day, Campbell and Johnson met with New York City Detective Frank Nicolosi of the Ballistics Squad. Nicolosi test fired the weapon turned over by the relative and gave the Utah detectives four expended slugs. The slugs were later taken back to Salt Lake City and mailed by certified letter to the Bureau of Alcohol, Tobacco and Firearms regional laboratory in Treasure Island, Calif. Detectives also included in the parcel the two slugs extracted from Bradshaw's body.

303

ATF Investigator Ed Peterson conducted ballistics tests on the slugs and obtained a "positive match," indicating the weapon turned over to New York authorities was in fact the same gun that had fired the fatal slugs into Bradshaw's body.

While waiting for the ballistics tests, Campbell also requested an ATF weapons check to see who had originally purchased the gun. Campbell learned from the ATF Gun Trace Detail in Washington, D.C. that the pistol had been sold by a police officer in Grand Prairie, Texas, to a Sgt. Jerry Banks of the Colorado City, Police Department.

Campbell then contacted the Colorado City Police Department and was informed that Sgt. Banks had resigned from the department, and he was now chief of police in Stenton, Texas, a short distance away. Campbell then called Banks in Stenton and interviewed him by telephone.

Banks told Campbell that he had made arrangements to sell the gun in 1978 and that he and his wife had gone together to a Midland, Texas, bank where they met a male Caucasian in his late teens or early 20s and the gun was sold for $175. Banks told Campbell the gun sale had been arranged through a third party, but he could not remember the details of the transaction. He suggested Campbell contact his now ex-wife who might remember more of the transaction than he did.

Upon calling the woman, detectives learned that she and Jerry Banks had had a conversation with a local carpet store manager to whom they mentioned they were interested in selling a .357 Magnum. The store manager later mentioned that fact to a friend who worked at a Midland bank. The bank employee had later called Banks' ex-wife asking about the price of the gun. He then called back a day later telling her he had a buyer for it. He instructed her to take the gun to the bank where he worked the coming Saturday morning at 10:00 A.M., and she would be met there by the buyer.

Banks' ex-wife then told detectives that she and Jerry

went to the bank and were met by a young man in his late teens or early 20s. Her husband made the transaction with the youth, but neither she nor Jerry ever knew the buyer's name. She said she thought the name of the bank employee was Raines.

Campbell and Detective Ron Nelson, another homicide detective assigned to the case, then traveled to Midland to interview the witnesses in person and to try to track down the bank employee who had arranged the sale. After checking the bank, detectives learned that there was indeed an employee there named Raines who worked as a security guard. Upon interviewing the guard, the investigators learned that a friend, John Malcolm, had indicated to him (Raines) that he knew someone who wanted a gun and that Raines had recently heard of a gun for sale. Raines said it was Malcolm who had assisted a young man in the purchase of the gun.

Campbell and Nelson then went to interview Malcolm who remembered little about the gun sale. The detectives, confident they were not getting the whole story from Malcolm, questioned two young men who worked for Malcolm. They not only remembered the gun sale, but identified a photograph of Marc Schreuder as the young man who had stayed in Midland in 1978 with a friend named John Marek, the son of a local doctor.

Neither of the employees witnessed the gun sale, but they said it was John Marek who had contacted Malcolm about buying a gun and that the transaction would have occurred about the same time Schreuder was staying with the Marek family. They placed the time of the gun transaction in the summer of 1978.

On Oct. 29th, after returning to Salt Lake City from Texas, Campbell and Johnson again boarded a plane, this time for Hartford, Conn., where Marc Schreuder was a student at Trinity College. After reading Marc the Miranda warning, the officers asked to interview him about the homicide. Schreuder told the officers he would not talk to

305

them without his attorney present and then made the comment, "You'll have to prove these allegations in court."

The detectives returned to Salt Lake City and began the tedious process of tracking down numerous leads and verifying much of the information they had already gathered. The once-cold trail was now red hot and the detectives, once stymied by a lack of clues, were now overwhelmed with new evidence and enthusiasm.

The victim's relative again called Campbell, this time to reveal the name of the informant who had given her the murder weapon. She added that he had not cooperated with her pleas to go to police with what he knew about the Bradshaw killing.

On Dec. 3rd, 1980, Detectives Campbell and Nelson again returned to Texas to interview John Marek. Upon questioning the young man, Marek indicated he did indeed know Marc Schreuder and that they had been classmates at Kent University in Kent, Conn. Marek told the detectives that a few weeks prior to his own July 24, 1978 birthday, Marc Schreuder had called him from New York City and told him he was planning to travel to Salt Lake City to visit his grandfather and that while he was there he wanted to do some camping and hiking for which he wanted a handgun. He asked Marek to find him a gun and indicated he might be stopping in Midland, Texas, in the near future.

Marek told Schreuder he could probably find a gun, and the telephone conversation ended without Marek knowing for certain if Schreuder was coming to Texas. Several weeks later, just prior to Marek's July birthday, Schreuder showed up at the Marek residence unexpectedly. Marek entertained Schreuder for several days, after which Schreuder again asked Marek if he knew where he could get a gun. Marek called Malcolm who told Marek that he had heard of a gun for sale.

The transaction took place the next Saturday morning, July 22nd, at a Midland bank, Marek told the detectives. He said Malcolm, Schreuder and himself had all gone to the bank to purchase the gun. That same day, Schreuder left Midland by commercial airliner, telling the Marek family he was on his way to Salt Lake City to visit his grandfather.

The detectives confirmed with other members of the Marek family the story given by John Marek, and they all agreed it was July 1978 when Marc Schreuder had come to visit them and had stayed in their home. One Marek relative also told detectives she remembered Marc had a book with him and had told her it was his favorite. The book was Agatha Christie's "Death on the Nile." Marc was seen boarding the airplane with the novel (about murder for inheritance) tucked under his arm.

After interviewing the Marek family, Detectives Campbell and Nelson flew on to New York City to interview the key informant. He told officers that Marc Schreuder had come to him in the summer of 1978 and had given him a pistol, stating, "I have shot my grandfather in Salt Lake City at the warehouse where he works." Schreuder then gave the gun to the trusted family friend and asked him to keep the gun in the event police ever searched the Schreuder residence.

The man agreed to store the weapon and hid it in his apartment, he told detectives. After about two weeks, Marc returned to the man's apartment with his mother, Frances Schreuder, who asked the family friend to take them to a gun store where they could buy a leather cover for the pistol. After buying the gun cover, the pistol was again left with the family friend for safe keeping. He kept the gun until Oct. 16, 1980, when he gave the gun to Frances' relative.

The informant then told the investigators he knew Frances Schreuder had attempted to hire someone to kill her father. He said he had met a tough-talking printer for the *New York Daily News*. When Frances later approached the informant about hiring a hit man, he put her in contact with the stocky printer.

307

"She (Frances Schreuder) was very, very distressed," said the informant, a New York school teacher and long-time friend of the Schreuder family. "She had had it with her father and wanted to do him in, kill him, whatever you want to call it."

Acting on the informant's leads, detectives later tracked down the printer where he still worked for the *New York Daily News* and the printer confirmed what the informant had told probers. He said he met Frances at one time in her apartment where she gave him details, including photographs and addresses. One photograph was of Bradshaw. She told the printer her father was going to leave her out of his will. Frances then took out an envelope containing $5,000 in small bills.

The printer said he took the money and left. He used most of the cash for booze, and some to pay off old debts. He said he checked into a New York YMCA on Oct. 29, 1979, to avoid Frances for awhile. He said he later met her at her apartment and told her he had gone to Salt Lake City and had failed in his mission. Frances was upset and yelled at him that she would have to go on welfare and take her children out of school. He shrugged and walked out.

The detectives then returned to Salt Lake City with innumerable clues and the murder weapon, the key piece of evidence that had broken the case wide open. On Dec. 5, 1980, a juvenile order of detention was issued for Marc Francis Schreuder. Utah prosecutors also began instigating proceedings in juvenile court to have Marc certified to stand trial as an adult (he was only 17 at the time of the killing). Later that same day, Detective Bob Beltrandi of the Hartford, Conn. Police Department arrested Schreuder and booked him into a Connecticut jail pending his extradition to Utah.

But the investigation into the Bradshaw homicide did not end with Marc's arrest. Detectives worked doggedly to verify that Marc had left Midland bound for Salt Lake City the day before the homicide. Only two airliners had Midland flights to Salt Lake City that day, and both said their records for 1978 had been destroyed.

The detectives kept trying to get passenger lists and hounded airline officials in national and regional offices. Finally they found the passenger lists, but Marc's name was not on the lists for either airline. It was then that Investigator Michael George thought of looking under a different name, one under which Marc had been born. He had changed his named to Schreuder when his mother had remarried.

When George checked the passenger lists under this different name, he found a ticket had been issued. George also found a passenger list for flights leaving Salt Lake City the day of the homicide and found a passenger by the name of Schreuder.

Detectives also spent hundreds of hours checking with cab and car rental companies for any record of someone who had rented Schreuder a car or had given him a ride to the parts warehouse. Too much time had elapsed, however, and records of such rentals or cab fares had long since been destroyed.

Sleuths also contacted Bradshaw's neighbors about the habits of Marc Schreuder, but none of the neighbors were acquainted with Marc Schreuder. Investigators also sifted through 20,000 receipts from the New York YMCA and confirmed the printer had indeed stayed there.

Months began to pass as the detectives followed up every clue and then reconfirmed their findings. In May 1981, the slugs from the murder weapon were hand carried by Investigator Michael George and Detective Joel Campbell to the ATF laboratories near San Francisco where they were again tested and the results were the same as before. Ballistics tests confirmed beyond doubt that the handgun which had fired the four test slugs was the same gun that had fired the two slugs into Bradshaw's body.

While investigators were diligently following leads, prosecutors and defense attorneys were haggling over details of the arrest. Numerous appeals were filed in the case, and the 90-day extradition period expired before many of the legal issues were resolved. Connecticut authorities dismissed charges against Marc Schreuder and released him. Marc then promptly disappeared.

Much of the investigation during 1981 centered around the Bradshaw family and the possible motives family members would have to kill Franklin Bradshaw. What they found was a family torn apart by greed and jealousy.

Frances had attended public schools in Salt Lake City and had graduated from East High School. In 1956, she left home to attend Bryn Mawr, a prestigious college in Pennsylvania. While there, she became involved in an incident in which she was accused of theft.

In 1959, Frances married an Italian merchant who imported pearls for a Fifth Avenue business in New York. They had two children and four turbulent years of marriage. Frances later filed for divorce.

In testimony that would later become critical in Marc's trial, a Salt Lake psychiatrist said Marc had told him when his mother remarried, life became a living hell. After bearing a third child, Frances divorced again in 1975.

With three children, no husband and an expensive New York lifestyle, Frances turned to her parents for financial support. The clashes between a strict father and an extravagant daughter soon became frequent. "She had no income of her own and was dependent on her parents," said one relative. "One of the main frictions was money for Frances."

Bradshaw cut back the money flow to Frances and tried to lure her back to Salt Lake City with a promise of financial support. Frances refused and decided to take another course of action. She instructed both of her older children to return to Salt Lake City during the summer of 1977 and work for their grandfather in his parts warehouse.

A business manager of the auto-parts warehouse recalled that cash shortages began almost immediately upon the arrival of the two teenagers. "From the day they came in we had cash shortages," he said. "It was a hell of a mess. We were short $1,400 the first day."

Franklin Bradshaw couldn't figure what was happening to the money and tried to implement tighter cash controls. But the shortages continued. Bradshaw even tried hiding the cash in parts storage bins, but the money still disappeared. Before the summer was out the business was reportedly missing more than $200,000. When the teens returned to New York after the summer, the cash shortages stopped.

Franklin Bradshaw finally caught on to what was happening when a secretary discovered several checks made out to cash and deposited in a N.Y. bank account. There were two $10,000 checks with Bradshaw's forged signature. "Frank was in a state of shock," the secretary recalled. "He started yelling, 'Oh my God!' and then he started to cry."

According to letters and statements to his employees, Bradshaw was extremely angry with Frances and began formulating plans to disinherit her. He even drafted a new will cutting Frances out of the inheritance. A copy of the draft, which was not an official will, was turned over to police.

Frances and Marc settled back into their routines after the homicide, secure in the assumption that Bradshaw's will would take care of them forever. Marc had taken a college aptitude test a few months before the homicide, and shortly after the homicide he took the test again and scored even higher. It was then that he enrolled in Trinity College.

Frances began receiving a $3,000 a month allowance from her father's estate. That amount later increased to $5,000 a month. A year after the murder, she moved from the middle-class apartment where she had been living to a high-class co-op near the mansion of the New York mayor. The posh living quarters consisted of the top two levels of the seven-story structure. One estimate put the value of Frances' new home at $1 million.

Frances also became a large donor to the New York City

311

Ballet. Those donations eventually landed her a seat on the company's board of directors. In July 1983, Frances donated $400,000 to the ballet to establish a scholarship in honor of the founder of the New York Ballet.

In early 1981, the biggest concern of detectives was finding Marc Schreuder. The legal problems had been rectified and the arrest warrant was still active, but Marc could not be found. It was Oct. 26, 1981 — just over a year after detectives received their first major break in the case — when Manhattan police tracked Marc down and arrested him at a post office letter drop.

With Marc in custody, detectives proceeded full steam ahead on their case against Frances, and on March 18, 1982, capital murder charges were filed against the New York socialite, accusing her of ordering her son to kill Bradshaw out of fear she would be cut out of the millionaire's will. The aggravating circumstances constituting a capital offense was "murder for pecuniary gain."

Detectives spent the rest of 1982 reconfirming their case. They had proof Marc Schreuder was in Midland, Texas days before the homicide; that he purchased a gun later used in the homicide, and that he departed Texas bound for Salt Lake City the day before the homicide. They also had evidence Marc had been stealing from Bradshaw the previous summer, apparently to support his mother.

The case against Frances was not as strong, however. The case was based primarily on circumstantial evidence and on the testimony of two witnesses who were not considered the most reliable, especially under an intense cross-examination by a court-wise defense attorney.

In June 1982, Marc Schreuder's capital homicide case went to trial. Marc chose to have the case heard by Judge James S. Sawaya rather than a jury. After several days of challenging the admissibility of the evidence and the credibility of the witnesses, defense attorneys shocked everyone, including the judge, by admitting that Marc had killed his grandfather. They argued, however, that Marc should be guilty of only manslaughter because he acted under extreme emotional pressure from his mother and was not responsible for the crime.

Defense Attorneys Paul Van Dam and Joe Tesch, admitting the overwhelming circumstantial evidence against Marc, called a psychiatrist who had examined Marc to testify on why Marc was not responsible for the crime. He testified that Marc had no friends but his mother, and that the mother-son relationship had reached a point that it was very, very sick.

The psychiatrist concluded that Marc was not mentally ill, but maintained that he suffered from a pathological Oedipus situation, a complex in which a child has lascivious desires for a parent of the opposite sex. He said Frances Schreuder appeared to suffer from a narcissistic personality disorder, and had been extremely abusive to her children.

Judge Sawaya agreed in part with the defense argument and found Marc guilty of second-degree murder, a lesser offense. He told Marc, "These were a bizarre and unusual set of facts, but there was no excuse or justification for what took place. I have not seen a great deal of evidence of remorse. This was a cruel, heinous crime. Besides the fact that Mr. Schreuder killed another human being, the victim was his own grandfather.

Defense attorneys argued that Marc lived his entire life in an emotional hurricane. "There is a person upon whom the full weight of the law should fall," said Tesch, "but she is not here." That full weight of the law was to fall on Frances Schreuder about a year and a half later.

Frances' defense attorneys argued that Marc's testimony was that of a desperate man trying to avoid the death penalty, and they went into Frances' September 1983 trial confident they would discredit the prosecution witnesses. The witness they failed to discredit, however, was Marc Schreuder who surprised both defense attorneys and prosecutors by agreeing to testify against his mother.

In an obvious illustration to everyone, Marc demonstrated he had finally cut the apron strings with his mother and that he had matured during his first year in prison. He testified in a calm decisive voice that his mother had ordered him to kill Bradshaw and said she had been plotting to kill him since 1977.

Marc testified his mother had ordered him to steal from his grandfather and to kill him if the opportunity presented itself. He related that his mother had suggested putting amphetamines in Franklin Bradshaw's oatmeal so he would have a heart attack. She also suggested knocking Bradshaw out and then burning down the parts warehouse with Bradshaw inside. Another plan was to drop an electrical appliance into Bradshaw's bathtub, Marc testified.

Marc told jurors that he arrived in Salt Lake City on July 22, 1978, and had stayed in a Salt Lake hotel. The first thing he did was call his mother and beg her to reconsider. "I told mother I just didn't want to go through with it," Marc testified. "She said a lot of things. One thing she said, 'If you don't do it, just don't come home again.' "

The threat of being locked out of his own home terrified Marc, and he pleaded with his mother for about 90 minutes to let him abandon the terrible assignment. "I just didn't want to do it," he said.

The next morning, July 23, 1978, Marc took a cab from the hotel to the auto-parts warehouse and hid behind a loading dock. He watched his elderly grandfather arrive for work and open the warehouse. It was then about 7:20 and Marc waited a few more minutes before going in. If his grandfather was surprised to see him, he didn't show it. They talked for about 15 minutes and Marc tried to convince Franklin to send more money to Frances. When Bradshaw turned his back, Marc pulled out the revolver and fired. "I just remember two shots," he told the jurors. "I don't remember a whole lot. I couldn't shoot him with his face to me."

Following his mother's instructions, Marc then took his

314

grandfather's wallet from his pocket and scattered credit cards and change over the floor to make it appear like a robbery. Within an hour, he was on a plane headed back for New York City. That evening he told his mother the grisly deed had been done, and Frances told him, "Thank God," and ran over and hugged and kissed Marc.

Marc then told an obviously angry and disturbed jury that he had committed the crime only because of his mother's threats to commit suicide. "It was difficult to say no to her," he explained. "She keeps harping on you and harping. You just can't say no. If you'd say no, she'd scream and go into hysterics. It was like that all the time."

The jurors rejected the arguments of New York Defense Attorney Michael Rosen and Salt Lake Defense Attorney Kevin Kurumada that the killing was Marc's idea. After only three hours of deliberations, the jury convicted Frances Schreuder of first-degree murder. Judge Ernest F. Baldwin sentenced her on Oct. 31st to a life prison term at the Utah State Prison after jurors could not unanimously agree on the death penalty.

The injustice of the entire affair, contended Prosecutor Ernie Jones, was that Franklin James Bradshaw's fortune was used to defend both Marc and Frances Schreuder. The legal fees alone are expected to exceed $1 million, perhaps twice that amount once appeals are exhausted.

EDITOR'S NOTE:

Dr. Marek, John Marek, Charlie Simms, Jerry Banks, Raines and John Malcolm are not the real names of the persons so named in the foregoing story. Fictitious names have been used because there is no reason for public interest in the identities of these persons.

315

"HORROR OF BRITAIN'S 'BAMBI' MURDERS!"

by George Carpozi Jr.

The White House Farm is a stately agricultural compound, nestled in the charming, rolling-hill English countryside of Tolleshunt D'Arcy in Essex. It's not too distant from the white sandy beaches lapped by the waters of the North Sea, yet far enough a way to escape the raucous city noises of neighboring London just to the southwest.

The centerpiece of this verdant landscape is a stately Georgian-styled red-brick farmhouse that on today's real-estate market would surely command a $350,000 American pricetag — provided the buyer would be willing to ignore the tangled web of three past tragedies that have left the property to bear the title of "The Cursed Mansion."

Sometime before the end of World War II, when German bombers were dropping their blockbusters on England, the then-owner of White House Farm hanged himself. In 1946, the new proprietor was found drowned in a horse trough.

It was then that the farm passed on to the wealthy Bamber family. Neville, a handsome, blond-haired man of 6-foot-3-inch height, had finally settled down to farm life after a career as a magistrate and wartime fighter pilot. For some dozen years Neville and June Bamber tried, but could not have children. Then they decided to adopt.

In 1957, they were given a tiny girl at birth and named

her Sheila. Three years later, they adopted a boy they christened Jeremy. Each of the youngsters' roots were planted in pitiful paste that one day in the distant future would take an ugly bloodstained stance on the tapestry of one of Great Britain's most heinous crimes — "The Bambi Murders," as they would be labelled.

This is largely a tale of two illegitimate children born to parents close to the highest of British circles, and who ultimately figured most prominently in the murders most cruel.

First, let's dwell on Sheila, who was born in London's Paddington section in July, 1957, to the 19-year-old unmarried daughter of the senior chaplain to the Archbishop of Canterbury. The chaplain was a curate in the Archbishop's office — and played a leading part in the procession of clergymen in Westminster Abbey when Queen Elizabeth was crowned by Archbishop Geoffrey Fisher.

When the archbishop was told of his canon's affair, he commanded that Sheila be put up for adoption through the Church of England. And ordered the banishment of his canon.

Looking for a good home for his daughter, the canon remembered Neville Bamber, his Essex neighbor and pilot, whom he'd met during wartime service in the Royal Air Force.

He was cognizant of how desperately the Bambers wanted to have children and couldn't. He prevailed upon them to adopt his illegitimate daughter. Thus, on February 6, 1958, Sheila was registered at Maldon County Court as the adopted child of Neville and June Bamber.

To escape further flack from his irreligious encounter in the sack, the curate quietly took his wife and children off to a new life in Canada, where he became principal of the Montreal Theological College and later a university professor.

Unencumbered any more by the stigma of giving birth to an illegitimate daughter, Sheila's mother herself went

317

off to live in Canada and married a dentist there.

Back in Britain, Sheila grew up unaware of her background. Yet, after the private hell into which she was born and her reincarnation as the Bambers' adopted daughter, she was destined to receive more of fate's low blows.

Sheila's life since her adoption had been far from smooth. From earliest days at private school she exhibited wild streaks of rebelliousness.

Her adoptive brother Jeremy was no different . . .

Let's dwell on Jeremy's origins now.

With daughter Sheila a toddler at this junction and June still infertile, the Bambers decided to adopt a son, and did so in January, 1961, through the Church of England Children's Society.

The child they brought to their home and named Jeremy was born of an illicit liaison between an ex-nurse, now running a bakery in Kensington, and a London stockbroker who tossed in the towel to run a wildlife preserve in Scotland.

After the adoption, Jeremy was christened by the millionaire head of a renowned jam company.

Like his stepsister, Jeremy was exposed to the best of educational centers. He started at Gresham's School in Norfolk, where tuition and board in the early 1960s ran $9,000 a year.

At school, Jeremy was branded an arrogant bully and reported more than once for mistreating younger boys.

When at home, Jeremy—like his stepsister—was constantly hounded by his stepmother, a Bible-spouting fanatic who'd constantly quote moralistic passages—especially when the children went into their teens and dated. Outings with the opposite sex were always surreptitious for the Bamber kids, because both despised the preachments. To June, sex before marriage was a sin in God's eyes.

Her religious obsession led twice to mental illness so serious that doctors were compelled to treat Mrs. Bamber with electro-convulsive therapy.

To the outside world, June was the very epitome of upstanding righteousness. Virtually all of the 900 residents of the village knew the Bamber family as "The Archers of D'Arcy" because of their resemblance to the British Broadcasting Company's popular radio show featuring a farming family.

Mrs. Bamber was also an active social director at the 14th century St. Nicholas Church, where she organized breakfasts for the congregation and sent meals out to the elderly.

Her husband Neville, besides being a full-time farmer, also tended to church duties and served as a justice of the peace. Moreover, for 24 years he had sat once a week on the bench at Witham Magistrates Court.

Bamber had a big heart, too. His generosity was reflected in his designation of a portion of his land as a campsite for deprived London children during summers. Further, he exhibited his beneficence when he failed to interest Jeremy to go with him on sports he liked, particularly shooting and salmon fishing.

Knowing of his stepson's growing wanderlust, Bamber financed vacation trips for Jeremy to Australia, the Far East, and the Continent.

His stepfather was well aware of Jeremy's growing bad habits at home—spending late hours in neighborhood pubs, womanizing, and being a general pain-in-the-neck on the farm. Bamber prayed that the excursions to distant lands would tame his stepson.

But they didn't. While in New Zealand, Jeremy became involved in the smuggling and distribution of heroin with a close friend. He was destined to get into deeper hot water at a later time back home . . .

Meanwhile, Stepsister Sheila was herself going in no better direction than Jeremy. That aforementioned streak of rebelliousness that surfaced in her early adolescence continued to reflect Sheila's deportment into her later years.

319

Like Jeremy, she came to loathe the comfortable rural life and yearned for the bright lights, where she could pursue her ambition to be a model, far from gritty farm soil and the noxious odors of tractor exhaust, as well as endless boredom.

Sheila's encounters with her stepmother about going with boys were just as unnerving as Jeremy's. Yet, whereas Jeremy could vent his frustrations at Mrs. Bamber by screaming at her to shut up, Sheila could not go one-on-one against her stepmother when being berated for harboring teenage sexual yearnings.

In one incredible incident in which Sheila was reprimanded for showing immoral and ungodly attitudes toward sex, her stepmother screamed at her: "You're the Devil's Child!"

Mrs. Bamber had caught Sheila sunbathing topless in a field and in heavy petting with a boyfriend, a young man she'd later marry.

That chilling accusation sowed the seeds of paranoia that were to leave Sheila seriously disturbed—she would actually begin to believe that she was possessed by Satan and had the powers of a witch. But that nightmare was still to come.

By the time she was 17, Sheila had had it up to here with life at the homestead. She said goodbye to her folks and younger stepbrother and moved to London.

Again, however, her stepfather's magnanimousness reared its head. He endowed upon Sheila a $30,000-a-year allowance to live in a West London flat.

Once installed there, Sheila adopted a professional nickname, Bambi, and with her slim figure and wide, almond-shaped eyes, she soon made the books of the top model agencies.

Not long after arriving in London, Sheila hooked up with the beau her mom caught making love to her topless in the pasture. Reggie Smythe was 23 and an artistic potter. In 1977, when she was 20 and three months pregnant, they married. Six weeks later, she lost her baby.

In June, 1979—after a second miscarriage—she gave birth to twin sons, Nicholas and Daniel.

But happiness was short-lived. When the twins were only four months old, Sheila and her husband split up—and in 1982 they were divorced.

Her "ex" would remember Sheila as "a beautiful, tragic woman," one who, having reached London after her departure from home, relied heavily on marijuana and cocaine for surcease from the madness into which she was slipping.

The drugs only deepened Sheila's twisted thoughts, which soon became peopled by enemies—the CIA, doctors and nurses at St. Andrew's Hospital in Northampton (where she was treated twice for mental condition, as her mother had been), and her new boyfriend.

A time would come in the not-too-distant-future when Reggie Smythe would mount the witness box in London's famed Old Bailey Courthouse and testify at one of England's most sensational murder trials: "Sheila had bizarre delusions about possession by the Devil and complex ideas about having sex with her twin sons. She thought the boys would seduce her and saw evil in both of them. In particular she thought Nicholas was the woman-hater."

Smythe was describing his wife's condition that led to her second hospitalization at St. Andrew's. After a five-week confinement the second time around, Sheila was discharged and was now barely able to cope with the twins. A concerned Reggie Smythe took the lion's share of looking after Nickie and Danny while Sheila sought new modeling assignments.

Religion was just one of two obsessions that devastated Sheila. The other one was a search for her roots. She wanted to find her natural mother. She began checking and counter-checking through adoption agencies and ultimately tracked down her natural brother.

Finally, in 1982, she arranged a meeting with her mother at Heathrow. Three years later, there was a long reunion between daughter and mother after the latter came from Canada to Britain for a lengthy visit with Sheila.

That was five months before that horrific August day of 1985 when Great Britain would be rocked by news of one of the nation's bloodiest mass murders.

During this disturbing period of his sister's life, Jeremy continued to wallow in his outrageous conduct — and at the same time become beneficiary again to his father's willingness to favor his stepson's lot.

Around Easter of 1984, Neville Bamber gave Jeremy a rent-free cottage at Goldhanger, five miles from Toleshunt D'Arcy. There, his troubled stepson took up farming and performed chores on the land similar to those he attended to on his parents' farm.

But despite all the more-than-generous gifts bestowed on him, Jeremy's hatred of his family grew increasingly.

He despised his fashion-model sister for being given $30,000 a year to live on in London.

He abhorred his mother for interfering in his relationships with women and for her overzealous proselytizing.

He thought of his father as old and spent.

And he viewed his stepsister's twin sons — his nephews — as spoiled and as obstacles to his inheritance . . .

This, too, was a time when he was desperate for money.

Wealth had cascaded on the Bamber family. And Jeremy stood at this point in time in 1985 to inherit a third of the family's $1.25 million estate. At the moment, however, he was receiving a mere $12,000 a year as salary for his toils on the farm. He dreaded the drudgery of farm life.

Away from the farm, Jeremy Bamber found relief in drink and dames. And when he finally decided to break off from the rigors of farming and seek an easier pursuit at making a living, he got a job as a cocktail barman in an American-style eatery in Colchester, a joint fitted with a 1960's jukebox and the cut-off back of a Chevrolet outfitted as a refrigerated salad bar.

Working there as a waitress during the Christmas holiday

322

was 21-year-old Alyce Pratt—attractive, vivacious, sexy, and vulnerable to the attractive Jeremy. It was romance at first sight.

By now, Jeremy was living in the cottage, away from home. But he'd visit his parents frequently to perpetuate the family ties.

His earliest encounter with Alyce was sexual. He seduced her after they split a bottle of champagne in the honeymoon suite of a local hotel.

Bamber continued to see other women, yet Alyce remained his No. 1 sweetheart and bedmate.

Alyce, an education student at Goldsmith's College, was waiting tables mainly to pay the freight at school. Somehow, she had won Jeremy's trust and he confided in her as—so far as is known—in no other woman before her.

He told Alyce about his hatred of his parents, sister, and her "spoiled" twin sons. He dwelled at length on how much he despised farm work, and on his penchant to go out into the world and earn big bucks.

"It's important to have money when you're young," he droned on endlessly. "I want to live in London, to have money to spend on drinks, to take people out to dinner, even go abroad. I hate to run to my parents every time I need some extra cash."

Jeremy was earning about $110 a week in the restaurant—a salary that was hardly adequate for the lifestyle he craved. He wanted to be out on the London scene, but his limited income restricted him to the precincts of Essex.

He came to regard nearby Colchester, an Army garrison town, as a substitute—a poor one, at most—to swinging London. Nevertheless, he tried to make the most of it there by joining the fastest of the fast sets around.

"I'm a provincial laborer," he would chide acquaintances with mock cynicism when patronizing the clubs—flamboyantly dressed in Chinese slippers, skin-tight trousers, and eye-liner heightening his dark gypsy looks.

In one of Colchester's fairest pubs, Jeremy Bamber formed another relationship—with Marie LaSalle, a striking French-born blonde and mother of two.

When Marie was bedding down with Jeremy, her unsuspecting husband baby sat with the children—until he found out about his wife's liaison. Then he ditched her, leaving Marie to live together with Jeremy for a time—even as he continued courting Alyce Pratt!

One overt thought constantly crossed Bamber's mind—what would happen if his parents learned about his romance with a married woman and mother who was 12 years older than he.

"Most certainly they would disinherit me," he confessed to Alyce and to a close friend of hers, after she pointed out to Jeremy the dozen years' age gap between him and Marie.

Over the weeks and months of their relationship, Alyce Pratt perceived a rising corrosion of hatred on the part of Jeremy Bamber toward his parents. His dialogue was filled with hatred for his stepparents and stepsister, as well as her twin sons.

The first real manifestation of Jeremy Bamber's psychotic tendency surfaced when he told Alyce of how he strangled rats with his bare hands on the farm to prove to himself that he was capable of murder. This followed his conversations with her about how much he hated his family and wished they were all dead—and then came the horrors of his plotting to kill his parents. He advanced a sequence of bizarre murder scenarios.

In one of his earliest diagrams to do away with his family, Jeremy planned to sedate his parents, then burn the house down and let police assume that his father had fallen asleep and dropped a cigarette.

Alyce was horrified. "I told him," she would relate at a later time, "that they were vile and foul things to say, and I would rather he did not say things like that to me . . . They were horrible thoughts."

Later, he came upon the idea of shooting his parents

324

himself and then pinning the murders on Sheila.

"I remember him saying," Alyce would relate, "that Sheila would be a good scapegoat because she had been admitted to a mental hospital and wasn't in control of her senses."

Then Alyce was to be given another insight into her boyfriend, on a weekend before the dread time when the multiple murder spree would occur.

"He had taken the twins up to bed and read them a bedtime story," Alyce would say . . .

It was 3:26 A.M. on August 7, 1985 a Wednesday, and the desk officer at the Chelmsford police station was listening to a caller relate how his sister had gone berserk with a gun and slain their parents, her two children, and then turned the gun on herself.

The man who phoned police identified himself as Jeremy Bamber and gave authorities his parents' farm's location.

When authorities arrived at the White House Farm mansion, no one was there to receive them. So they burst into the house and found a scene of unspeakable horror. As it was established later, this is the sequence in which one murder after another wiped out the Bamber family . . .

Neville Bamber was sitting in a kitchen chair when the killer struck and bludgeoned the old soldier to his knees — before shooting him eight times, with seven bullets lodging in his head and neck.

The 6-year-old twins, Nicholas and Daniel, huddled on makeshift mattresses in another room, were also shot — repeatedly. Nicholas received three bullets in the head — one right between the eyes. And Daniel, still asleep and sucking his thumb, was shot five times in the back of his head.

In an adjoining upstairs bedroom lay June Bamber and her stepdaughter Sheila — apparently there to discuss her marital dissensions with Mrs. Bamber's son. If any such conversation actually ensued, it most certainly ended in the rocketing bark of gunfire.

When police found her, June Bamber had apparently

staggered out of bed—after taking seven bullets in the head, one between the eyes—and was now lying very dead on the bedroom floor.

Sheila was still on the bed. Obviously she'd been unable to scramble to the safety that her stepmother had tried to reach in vain. She had two gunshot wounds to the throat. The rifle lay across her body, muzzle pointing upward—as though she had pulled the trigger! By her side was a blue-covered Bible, one of dozens that Mrs. Bamber had scattered around the house.

This was a dreadful tragedy and the London tabloids screamed about it in their biggest, boldest, blackest Page One headlines.

At the outset, the Essex police believed Jeremy Bamber's story—that he "discovered" the bodies on returning home and that "my crazy sister killed my family." It certainly looked that way—at first blush.

It certainly looked that way, too, when Jeremy attended the mass funeral two days later and broke into convulsive sobs, at the gravesite. So much so, he had to be supported by other mourners.

What police then were not aware of was Jeremy's behavior prior to the funeral. Not more than 15 hours after the murders, he exhibited an extraordinary callousness and arrogance. He went on spending sprees, entertained groups of friends to $75-a-head champagne and lobster dinners, whooped it up with a wild drug orgy.

The night before the funeral, a friend told Jeremy to put white make-up on his face to make him look more tragic. And he did.

Then he also went on a shopping spree after a chum told him, "Buy yourself some really slick stuff . . . you're now inheriting all this money . . ." So Jeremy bought a fantastic Hugo Bosch suit and, during the wake that followed the funeral, he went around showing off the label.

He even joked openly at the funeral about his girlfriend Alyce Pratt's protruding tummy—a suggestion that Jeremy had made her pregnant. In front of all the relatives, he patted her on the bulge and quipped, "It's about time you told everyone you're pregnant, darling."

The relatives didn't appear shocked at this weird deportment at such a solemn occasion, which prompted Jeremy to whisper to Alyce: "The only reason they are being so bloody pleasant to me is because they're like a pack of vultures, all waiting to see what they're going to get out of it."

Then he laughed and sneered: "If they think they are going to get a bloody thing, they're joking."

Finally young Bamber glanced at his watch and snapped, "Come on, let's get out of here. Time's up!"

And two days after the August 16th funeral, young Bamber threw caution to the winds and flew to Amsterdam to buy a large amount of drugs.

When he returned, he surrounded himself with friends once more and continued to wine, dine, and have a rollicking good time with them.

If the police were aware of Jeremy Bamber's total lack of grief for his family's murders, they certainly never let on. As far as they were visibly concerned, Jeremy's mentally disturbed half-sister was the killer—now beyond the reach of the law, since she was dead. And as far as the constabulary was concerned, she'd taken her own life after murdering her family.

This despite the fact that Jeremy's cousin went to the police at the very outset and made it clear that he and other members of the family didn't believe Sheila was the killer.

"Let's see the forensic evidence," the cousin demanded. "I want you to show me her fingerprints on the cartridges . . ."

But they didn't take him seriously, he was to say at a later time. "They remained convinced that Sheila did it."

The relative was so certain that Sheila couldn't have committed the crime and spoke of it so openly that the press took a second look. The London tabloids sent their top crime reporters to probe along with the cousin and a niece of the slain Neville Bamber's.

From that moment on, police became the prime targets of criticism from the press. Reporters on the case were appalled by the conclusions the cops reached—that Sheila Bamber, Jeremy's half-sister, had committed the mass murders, then turned the gun on herself in a suicide.

The first and foremost clue in the investigation was Sheila's actual death. She'd been shot *twice*. One bullet split her brain, the other severed her jugular vein. Either would have been fatal.

Had authorities pursued their suspicions about this incredible "suicide," they would have found that one wound was inflicted by a bullet fired through a conventional gun barrel, the other through a silencer.

How could she have removed—or fitted—the silencer between fatal shots?

When Sheila's body was found, she was barefooted. Her soles and heels as clean "as though she had just stepped out of a bath." Yet she was supposed to have run around the house, from room to room, in a murderous rampage and not have stepped on a single drop of blood—which was spattered everywhere like wall-to-wall carpeting.

Although she was also said to have unlimbered 25 shots from her gun, the autopsy failed to detect any gunpowder or oil on Sheila's hands. Nor a broken fingernail after all that pumping on the bolt-action rifle.

Her stepfather, Neville Bamber, a healthy, stocky 6 feet 4 inches tall, was savagely beaten and suffered a fractured skull and black eyes. How could a slim 5-foot-7-inch woman have inflicted that kind of punishment on her stepfather—before pumping him full of lead?

Authorities also accepted Jeremy Bamber's claim that he had received a distressed call from his father crying: "Sheila's gone crazy . . . she's got a gun." How could he have phoned the police when he was still connected to the farmhouse, where the receiver was off the hook?"

About 40 officers—including experienced crime-scene

operatives—were at the farm. Yet they apparently did not detect suspicious marks on the kitchen windows—later to be determined that an entry had been forced into the house by an intruder. And they didn't find a cartridge case under a wardrobe until two days after the killing.

Frustrated by the authorities' view of the case, the Bambers' relatives took it upon themselves to give the police some "outside" help. Their incentive to do what they were about to do was the absolute belief that Sheila Bamber had no capacity to commit such a heinous crime.

They were very cognizant of the fact that she loved her father, had no experience with guns, suffered from poor hand-eye coordination and, although mentally ill, had never shown violence to her children.

The Bambers' kin turned amateur detectives. They conducted a thorough search of White House Farm and uncovered the silencer—one of the most crucial pieces of evidence—on the first floor.

This find was to prove that Sheila couldn't possibly have shot herself with the first bullet, hidden the silencer in a downstairs cupboard, walked back to her bedroom, and fired another bullet into herself! Therefore, she couldn't possibly have committed the murders.

In the meantime, the one person among all others who could have brought out the truth about the massacre—Alyce Pratt—was keeping a discreet, indeed terrified, silence. She knew who the killer was—did she ever know!

She'd already heard all of the gory details of how Jeremy wanted to sedate the family, then burn the house down, and how at another time he spoke of shooting them and setting up Sheila as the killer because of the time she spent in the mental hospital.

Of course, Alyce didn't take Jeremy too seriously about his intentions to wipe out his family—yet she had reservations about what her lover was capable of doing.

Even on the night before the massacre, and in the knowledge of the detailed planning Bamber had made known to

329

her, Alyce still refused to believe that Jeremy would ever carry out such a horrendous crime.

"He called me just before the killings and said that it was going to be tonight or never," she remembers. "I told him not to be so stupid and disregarded what he said."

But by 3:00 A.M. Alyce's subconscious was all at once confronted by her worst fears. That was when Jeremy phoned again and rasped, "Everything went well. Something is wrong at the farm. I have not had any sleep all night. I love you lots."

By then, all five members of the Bamber family had been slaughtered.

In the days and weeks that followed, Alyce Pratt was haunted by the murders and of how Jeremy had finally confided to her — just before the killings were committed — that he had contracted a mercenary to wipe out his family for $2,500. The guilt of her knowledge and her troubled conscience were beginning to prove an immense strain on her.

At the same time, Jeremy Bamber's paranoia was growing as well. It certainly seemed so. How could he not wonder how many people knew about his confessions to Alyce?

That likelihood became most apparent at Alyce's 21st birthday party when he was teased by her roommate. In a rage, he picked up the cream birthday cake and slammed it in the young woman's face.

Alyce Pratt knew that Jeremy was a psychopath, without conscience. Indeed, he confessed to her that he knew he was sick and couldn't help having evil thoughts.

Yet she couldn't give him up despite the many stormy rows they were having. At one point when they were at it, Alyce wailed at him: "I can't live with the fact you've done this. I don't want you to go to prison. But you need help." Yet Jeremy wasn't even vaguely remorseful. His coldness and indifference to her admonitions ruptured her heart. In a flood of tears, Alyce dialed her best friend.

"She was hysterical," said Alyce's confidante, who had been kept posted on virtually every step of Jeremy Bamber's plans to do away with his family.

"I told Alyce that she had to go to the police because he was a psychopath who could murder again and it would be forever on her conscience. It was a big game for Jeremy. He enjoyed it," she said.

Then with a shrug, Alyce's friend went on to express the bottom line—fear. "I was terrified. I was in a state of terror. We locked all the doors because I feared he'd come back and kill us."

Unable any longer to live with the horrible secret of the massacre, Alyce Pratt went to the police on September 7th. She was accompanied by her friend and both women gave lengthy statements.

Even then, the police appeared to be reluctanat to go after Jeremy Bamber—at least not until the discovery of the silencer.

It now became plain how the murders were committed . . .

After midnight, hoping to find everyone home asleep, Jeremy bicycled to his parents' home, pried open a basement window with a screwdriver, entered, went to the cupboard where the rifle and ammunition were stored, loaded the weapon with a magazine—then went on his murderous tear.

At long last, Jeremy Bamber was taken in custody and charged with the five murders. He was held without bail and confined to Brixton Prison until his trial in October in London's famed Old Bailey Courthouse. Public and press turned out en mass.

It was an electrifying trial and, after all the evidence was delivered, Jeremy Bamber—"The money-crazed monster," as the British journals had labelled him—was found guilty by majority verdicts on all five counts of murder.

Dressed in a double-breasted, pin-striped suit, Bamber

stared at the jury foreman as the catalogue of guilty verdicts was read out. Jeremy looked pale—and his mask of innocent defiance seemed to slip for a moment as he cleared his eyes and visibly swallowed.

He was now condemned to prison for life five times over. And he must spend at least 25 years behind bars for a crime that the court described as "evil beyond belief."

The judge, "Mr. Justice Drake," as the British prefer to identify him, castigated Jeremy with the harshest words ever spoken from a bench in England—but rightly so. There had not been a mass murder of this magnitude in the land of John Bull since the end of World War II.

Certainly there were many horrific crimes committed, such as those of the London Strangler, among others. Yet this one had many more heinous elements. Avarice was one. Greed another. Hatred fit in there, too. And one could conjure up still more elements to make this a crime like few others in Britain's history.

"You have a warped and callous and evil mind, concealed by an outwardly presentable and civilized appearance and manner," intoned the judge after receiving the jury's verdict.

"I find it difficult to foresee if it will ever be possible to release a person who could plan and kill five members of his own family, including two little boys," the judge continued.

Mr. Justice Drake was only warming up. Now he was beginning to be full-blown as he bellowed: "I don't doubt that you thought your sister's illness would be such that it would be difficult for people to be aware of your guilt.

"It is clear from what we heard of Sheila being a prime suspect that your ideas and plans came somewhere near to success."

The judge told Bamber he believed he killed partly out of impatient greed for the family fortune, which he would have inherited anyway.

"And you also killed out of arrogance," the judge thundered. "I believe you resented any parental restriction or control.

"Your conduct in planning and carrying out the killing of five members of your family was evil beyond belief."

As the judge castigated him, Jeremy took it all in stoically. He betrayed not a sign of emotion as Mr. Justice Drake went on: "If you had planned to kill your mother alone, or your father, or even your sister, each would have been a dreadful crime.

"But you killed them all. You fired shot after shot into them—and also into the two little boys, aged six. You murdered in cold blood as they were asleep in their beds."

Mr. Justice Drake had spoken his piece. Now it was time for the sentencing—none of the weeks and months that we must wait for commitment after conviction in the USA.

"I recommend that you serve a minimum—and I mean a *minimum*—of 25 years . . ."

Those were the judge's last words. In the next moment, Jeremy Bamber was shuffled off to the cells to serve the term imposed.

By the time he's sprung—if he can manage it with good behavior and all that—Jeremy Bamber will be at least 50 and the year will be 2011.

And by then, the fortune he had planned to gain by killing his parents will have long before gone to the closest surviving relatives, whose efforts turned the case around.

And that's the bottom line on England's "Bambi Massacre Case."

EDITOR'S NOTE:
Reggie Smythe, Alyce Pratt and Marie LaSalle are not the real names of the persons so named in the foregoing story. Fictitious names have been used in order to comply with British police regulations.

"HIGHWAY HORROR
FOR HANNA"

by Loretta Linser

For the long-distance trucker, driving can become an almost somnambulistic endeavor. When enough miles and enough hours have passed, when the view becomes little more than an endless smear of asphalt and roadside greenery, the senses of the driver are attuned to but two things: getting where he's going, or stopping somewhere to fuel his truck with gas and himself with coffee so he can continue getting where he's going.

Jim Gilroy was no doubt focused on one of those two goals as he piloted his truck down the westbound lane of Highway 402, near London, Ontario, at 7:15 P.M. on July 5, 1984. But whatever roadrunner reveries he may have been entertaining, he was soon jolted out of them. The scenery that summer evening was not so tranquil, the landscape no longer a mind-lulling blur. On this night, the still-life composition of the roadside was animated by two frantic figures.

Slowing down to get a better look, Gilroy saw that they were two men—one young, the other middle-aged. He also saw, from the desperate way they were signaling for help, that something was very wrong.

Gilroy decided to find out just what was going on. He brought his truck to a full stop on the shoulder of the highway and asked the two men what the problem was. They explained that the older man's wife had been shot by two men in a blue car. Police and medical assistance were needed — and fast. Did Gilroy have a CB radio they could use?

Jim Gilroy's initial concern was replaced by wariness. He saw no body, no signs that the violent assault the two men described had taken place here. It crossed his mind that these people might not be crime victims at all, but criminals — that they had concocted this story to get someone to stop in order to mug him. Such things did happen, but Gilroy was determined that it wouldn't happen to him. He decided to investigate the situation before offering the men any assistance.

Swinging down from the cab of his truck, Gilroy asked the pair where the injured woman was. They gestured toward the ditch beyond the guard rail. Keeping one watchful eye on the men in case they tried to jump him, Gilroy went over to the ditch and glanced down. As he did so, his distrust was washed away on a wave of horror.

Lying face down in an ever-widening puddle of blood was a dark-haired, middle-aged woman. She was motionless except for the barely perceptible breathing with which she clung to her ebbing life. Gilroy thought that maybe, if he could help her breathe, he could help her live. Scrambling down into the ditch, he gently turned the woman over to take her weight off her laboring lungs. That was when he saw the gaping gunshot wound in her left temple.

Realizing that immediate medical attention was the woman's only hope of survival, Jim Gilroy leaped over the guard rail and ran back to the road. Unfortunately, he told the two men, he didn't have a CB radio in his truck; they would have to flag down another motorist.

Crossing over to the eastbound lane, the trio managed to wave down two other drivers. The first, another trucker, used his CB to contact the Ontario Provincial Police, while the second used a first-aid kit in a valiant effort to keep the victim alive until the ambulance arrived.

But the ministrations of this Good Samaritan, however noble, were too little and much, much too late for 48-year-old Hanna Buxbaum. When she was finally brought into London, Ontario's Victoria Hospital at 8:01 P.M., she was, in the words of the head of emergency services, "essentially dead." And, despite efforts to resuscitate her, less than one hour later she was officially dead.

Sergeant Roger Aisladie of the Strathroy, Ontario, Police Department was the first officer to arrive at the scene. He approached the victim's husband, 45-year-old Helmuth Buxbaum, and asked him what had happened.

Buxbaum explained to Sergeant Aisladie that he and his wife Hanna had been en route to their home in Komoka, Ontario, after having picked up a relative—the young man who, along with Mr. Buxbaum, flagged down Jim Gilroy—at the airport in Toronto. They were traveling down Highway 402 and were less than one and a half miles from Komoka when they stopped to offer help to a motorist who seemed to be having car trouble.

Buxbaum, who'd been behind the wheel of the family station wagon, said he'd stopped when he saw a man waving his arms as he stood beside his vehicle, which was parked on the shoulder. As the Buxbaums' car came to a halt, the man who'd been signaling approached the driver's side—while a second man, his face enshrouded by a ski mask and his hand clenching a revolver, emerged from behind a nearby pillar and approached the passenger side of the station wagon.

Then, Buxbaum continued, the armed assailant flung open the passenger-side door. His free hand, as unyielding as a manacle, clamped onto Hanna Buxbaum's arm, and he dragged the defenseless mother of six out of the station wagon, over the guard rail, and into a ditch.

Hanna screamed. She sobbed. She begged the two marauders to spare her life, if only for the sake of her children. But her pleas inspired no pity, stirred no mercy in the hearts of her assailants. First, they tore her purse out of her hands. Then, as her husband and young relative watched helplessly, transfixed with fear, the masked gunman pumped two bullets into Hanna's head and upper body.

As the gravely wounded Hanna Buxbaum crumpled to the ground, the two men ran back to their vehicle — Helmuth thought it was an older-model blue Nova — and made their getaway down the westbound lane of Highway 402.

Helmuth and the youth had been fortunate enough to escape the grisly assault unscathed. Now it was imperative that they get help — and right away — for the less fortunate Hanna. And that was what they were trying to do — standing at the roadside, waving their arms at passing motorists in a desperate semaphore of distress — when Jim Gilroy spotted them and decided to stop.

From that point, the events that unfolded on that lethal summer night were fairly clear-cut. But the events that preceded them remained murky. Who, police wondered, were these mysterious assailants? And why had they targeted Mrs. Buxbaum, leaving her husband and relative unharmed?

Detective Inspector Ron Piers of Toronto's Criminal Investigation Bureau, who headed the murder probe, was anxious for answers. While he asked for information from anyone who had been in the vicinity of the crime scene between 6:45 and 7:15 P.M. that night, other investigators embarked on an all-out search for the getaway car and its occupants.

The lawmen's diligence paid off. Some weeks passed, but eventually some arrests were made — seven in all. Not two, but seven.

Four of the seven London-area residents originally charged in the slaying pleaded guilty to lesser charges and received sentences ranging from 15 months to life imprisonment. Of the unholy triumvirate that remained, one agreed to talk in exchange for a reduced sentence. And, as his squalid story unfolded, it was revealed that the slaying of

337

Hanna Buxbaum was not merely the tragic outcome of a roadside robbery. It was an execution, borne of a conspiracy that included sex-for-sale and rampant drug abuse among its evil underpinnings.

Paul Llewellyn, a small-time cocaine dealer, claimed to have met Helmuth Buxbaum at a London strip joint in December 1983. He said that Buxbaum, the multimillionaire owner of a dozen nursing homes and private hospitals, sought to squander his hard-earned wealth by indulging two expensive tastes—drugs and prostitutes. Llewellyn was more than happy to oblige him by supplying both—in copious quantities.

Buxbaum wasn't unfettered in his enjoyment of these excesses, however. There was something that threatened to spoil his fun—and he enlisted Paul Llewellyn's aid in eliminating this threat.

In his testimony at Helmuth Buxbaum's trial before the Supreme Court of Ontario on October 21, 1985, Llewellyn implied that Buxbaum spent almost as much time complaining about his wife as he did injecting cocaine and carousing with hookers.

"Almost immediately, he said that his wife was a pain in the ass," Llewellyn related, and it wasn't long before "he came right out and asked me if I could get [her] killed.

"The only excuse he gave me," Llewellyn continued, "was that he couldn't divorce her because she would fight for the children."

The "excuse" may have been poor, but Helmuth Buxbaum certainly wasn't—so Llewellyn agreed to lend a helping hand. In exchange for $25,000—with Buxbaum offering a $10,000 bonus if Hanna's body remained missing for a year—Llewellyn said he would recruit a killer for him.

Paul Llewellyn may not have had the killer instinct required to carry out the murder himself, but he did have a bad cocaine habit—an addiction that was costing him up to $700 a day to satisfy. So, while he dawdled over finding a hitman for Buxbaum, he accepted the millionaire's money with great alacrity. "It was at this time more or less of a scam to make some money," he admitted.

So, when Buxbaum gave him $5,000 in June 1984, along with a photo of Hanna to aid the assassin in identifying his target, Llewellyn used the money to finance a trip to Orlando, Florida. He told Buxbaum that he ". . . wanted to be out of the country when [the murder] happened."

Except the murder wasn't imminent. At this point, Paul Llewellyn had done little but take Buxbaum's money — and he wasn't shy about asking for more. While still in Florida that June, he called Buxbaum to complain that his funds were running out. He requested, and received, an additional $3,500.

But Helmuth Buxbaum's subsidies couldn't keep pace with Llewellyn's spending. He'd received $8,500 in less than one month — yet when Llewellyn returned to Ontario on June 27th, he was flat broke. He was also in deep trouble with one of his cocaine connections.

Continuing his testimony, Paul Llewellyn said that he owed a man $1,000 for cocaine. The disgruntled supplier had warned Llewellyn that if he failed to come up with the cash within a week, he'd break his legs. Llewellyn knew his only hope was Helmuth Buxbaum — and that Buxbaum would soon slam shut the till if Llewellyn didn't follow through on his part of their deadly bargain.

"I was getting telephone calls. He was getting pretty insistent," Llewellyn told the court.

It also occurred to the debt-ridden dope fiend that a couple of broken legs might well be the least of his worries. By soliciting Llewellyn's services in arranging the contract hit, Buxbaum had already made clear that he had murder on his mind. Who knew what he would do if Llewellyn continued to procrastinate?

"I was scared that if I didn't do anything about it, I would be killed myself," he asserted.

So, the very next day, Llewellyn contacted an acquain-

339

tance, Jesse Buck, and asked him if he would kill Hanna Buxbaum. Buck agreed to participate. He then recruited another accomplice, Gary Foshay, who in turn brought a man named Terry Armes into the lethal conspiracy.

On July 4th, the day before Hanna Buxbaum was ruthlessly gunned down, Paul Llewellyn met with Helmuth Buxbaum in the parking lot of a fast-food restaurant. Buxbaum handed Llewellyn another $5,000; to ensure that the killers recognized their intended victim, he also provided additional photos of Hanna and of the family station wagon.

The two conspirators then got into Buxbaum's car and started away. With Jesse Buck following them in a blue Nova rented for the killing, Buxbaum and Llewellyn cruised along Highway 402, looking for a suitable location where they could perform their vicious task.

"We were going to pick a spot where Hanna Buxbaum was to be abducted," Llewellyn explained to the court. "The bottom line was, she was supposed to be murdered, but it was supposed to look like she was taken away on the highway, like she was kidnapped." He added that Buxbaum also instructed the killers to take Hanna's jewelry and mail it, with a ransom note, from the United States. That, Buxbaum reasoned, would lend credence to a kidnapping theory and would dissuade police from focusing on him as a suspect. After all, the Buxbaums were an exceedingly affluent family; one of them being abducted for ransom wasn't so farfetched an idea.

But it turned out that the nursing-home mogul was much more adept at making millions than at plotting the perfect crime.

In the original plan, Hanna was to have been killed on the way *to* the Toronto airport — an easterly route — not on the way back. Therefore, the site Buxbaum and his cohorts eventually chose was along the eastbound lane of Highway 402. When the appointed time arrived, the assassins took their positions in the designated area, waiting to flag down

Helmuth Buxbaum and his unsuspecting spouse as they headed for the airport to pick up their young relative.

It didn't come off as planned, however. A police cruiser on routine patrol, noticing the killers' blue Nova parked on the shoulder, stopped to check on the condition of the vehicle. Helmuth Buxbaum had no choice but to keep driving — and to arrange for his hitmen to commit the murder on the return trip from the airport.

Evidently, the change of plan gave Jesse Buck a change of heart. After the police cruiser departed, he told the others they could count him out. Unfortunately for Hanna Buxbaum, Terry Armes and Gary Foshay had no such second thoughts.

The day after the murder, Paul Llewellyn said, he met with Helmuth Buxbaum and was given an envelope containing $13,000. He kept $3,000 for himself, then gave $5,000 to Gary Foshay and $3,500 to Terry Armes. The remaining cash was divided up between two minor players who participated in the murder scheme.

True to form, Llewellyn spent the bounty of his avarice on vice. He acknowledged that he immediately used $1,550 of his blood money to make a quick cocaine score. The remainder was spent on booze, porno movies, and, of course, more drugs.

Helmuth Buxbaum's defense attorney, Edward Greenspan, would have none of it. In his combative three-day cross-examination of the prosecution's star witness, Paul Llewellyn, he accused the self-confessed thief, pimp, and pusher of having two ulterior motives for fingering Helmuth Buxbaum. The first was that, by agreeing to testify for the crown, Llewellyn avoided having to stand trial on charges of first-degree murder — and, if convicted, having to serve a life sentence.

The second motive? That Llewellyn himself had reasons for wanting Hanna Buxbaum dead, Greenspan asserted. It was all his idea, not Helmuth's.

Brandishing an affidavit from a jailhouse buddy of

341

Llewellyn's, Greenspan told the 10-man, 2-woman jury, "What in fact happened was that Buxbaum's wife had found out that [Llewellyn] was supplying cocaine to Buxbaum and had threatened to report [Llewellyn] to the police."

Earlier testimony had established that in May 1984, Llewellyn had done landscaping work at one of the Buxbaums' nursing homes and their residence to pay off a fine for a drug conviction. His brief stint as the couple's employee ended when Hanna, learning that her husband was obtaining drugs from Llewellyn, fired him.

Helmuth Buxbaum's only crime, according to Defense Attorney Greenspan, was to have had the misfortune of meeting up with a dope-peddling predator like Paul Llewellyn.

In one of the many heated exchanges that took place during the marathon cross-examination, Greenspan repeatedly contended that Llewellyn, having pegged Helmuth Buxbaum for "the sucker of all time," sought to control Buxbaum by making an addict of him.

"He was the answer to your dreams, wasn't he?" Greenspan asked sardonically. "For the first time, you were able to get your claws into a very rich man. . . . [So you] badgered him, pulled out a needle, and for the first time in his life injected him with a needle of cocaine. . . .

"Helmuth Buxbaum was a man that you saw had these unusual appetites for sex and for drugs . . . and you were going to use that weakness to get closer to him and make him more dependent on you."

Paul Llewellyn, playing cobra to Greenspan's mongoose, trained a sub-zero gaze on the defense attorney. Then he struck. "I think you're dreaming, Mr. Greenspan," Llewellyn said through the slightest of sneers.

Llewellyn went on to allege that Helmuth Buxbaum was hardly the beleaguered innocent the defense attorney was attempting to portray.

"There's two people in Helmuth Buxbaum. You don't

even know the other side of Helmuth Buxbaum, Mr. Greenspan," Llewellyn argued. "There's no possible way you'd even know him."

He also disputed the defense's allegation that he was angry with Mrs. Buxbaum for terminating his employment at the nursing home. "Being fired is something that's not very important to me," he shrugged.

By his own admission, Paul Llewellyn was not the most honest and upstanding of citizens. It is conceivable that, when he first told his story, the jury was skeptical. Following the defense's devastating cross-examination, perhaps they were more skeptical still. But after the prosecution presented its case, all doubt was eradicated. Yes, Paul Llewellyn was a self-admitted liar—but when he spoke of Helmuth Buxbaum's dark side, he spoke the truth.

As the trial wore on through the winter of 1985, crown attorneys called dozens of witnesses. They all verified that Helmuth Buxbaum had talked frequently of killing his wife and had behaved strangely around the time of the slaying.

According to one witness, a prostitute whom Buxbaum had visited once or twice a week since February 1984, the nursing-home magnate had contemplated everything from staging a boating accident to using poisonous herbs before he decided on the kidnapping-murder scheme. She said Buxbaum had complained to her that Hanna, a deeply religious woman, had "badgered" and "pressured him" to seek professional help to overcome his drug addiction.

"He was talking about how his wife was depressing him, and he was thinking about getting rid of her," the witness elaborated.

Another witness, after confirming that Buxbaum "was sick and tired of his wife pestering him about his drug use and wanting him to go into drug treatment programs," added that Buxbaum found his wife sexually undesirable and preferred to consort with teenage hookers.

That Helmuth Buxbaum had little regard for his wife Hanna was underscored by his behavior on the night she

343

was murdered.

"I found that he was cool, calm," reported Sergeant Roger Aisladie, the first police officer to speak with Helmuth Buxbaum at the crime scene—or rather, near the crime scene. For when the lawman arrived, Buxbaum was about a half-mile down the road from where Hanna lay dying. He seemed reluctant to return to her, and he never requested that Aisladie see how she was.

Jim Gilroy, the trucker whom Buxbaum and his relative had flagged down soon after the shooting, was equally baffled by Helmuth Buxbaum's lack of emotion. "I couldn't understand the calmness," he said. Like Sergeant Aisladie, he testified that Buxbaum showed little inclination to approach his wife, remaining on the other side of the guard rail while Gilroy assessed her condition.

But as damaging as these witnesses' testimony was to the defendant's case, they were still the small guns in the prosecution's armament. On November 21, 1985, the crown attorneys broke out the heavy artillery.

Like Paul Llewellyn, 36-year-old Terry Armes had originally been charged with first-degree murder in the roadside slaying of Hanna Buxbaum. In September 1985, he pleaded guilty to second-degree murder, which, although it too carried a sentence of life imprisonment, also offered the possibility of parole after 10 years. Now, before a spellbound courtroom on a chilly winter afternoon, he detailed the gruesome events that occurred on that balmy summer night.

A longtime abuser of drugs and alcohol, Terry Armes admitted he was "in a fog" on the day of the murder. Nonetheless, he did recall meeting with Jesse Buck and Gary Foshay the night before. They had two guns, Armes testified, and they were discussing their plans to kill a woman from Komoka.

The next thing Armes knew, it was early morning. He, Buck, and Foshay were sitting in a blue Chevrolet Nova at the side of Highway 402. Although he continued to swim in and out of consciousness, he did remember Jesse Buck standing at the front of the car, talking to Helmuth Buxbaum, when an Ontario Provincial Police cruiser pulled up. The patrolmen had assumed that the murderous quartet were motorists in distress, so they'd stopped to offer assistance.

Their plan temporarily thwarted by the unexpected arrival of the law, Buck and Buxbaum agreed to speak later through Paul Llewellyn, who had departed for Toronto to establish an alibi for himself. Shortly thereafter, Armes once again lapsed into an alcoholic haze.

On his next foray into consciousness, Terry Armes found that he was still seated in the blue Nova. The painful glare of the morning sun had now been replaced by the muted glow of twilight. Gary Foshay, a revolver tucked into his waistband, was driving the car west on Highway 402. Jesse Buck was no longer in the car.

Armes said he was then struck by the realization that the lethal plan was going to be carried out—and that he no longer wanted any part of it.

Knowing that they were expected to lie in wait at a site preceding the County Road 14 exit—the off-ramp that Buxbaum would use to go to Komoka—Armes tried to persuade Foshay to drive beyond the exit, hoping that a faulty location would foil the plan.

He was somewhat relieved when Foshay brought the car to a halt under a railroad trestle just past the Buxbaums' exit. And he was very relieved when he spotted the Buxbaums' station wagon pulling off the County Road 14 exit ramp further up the highway.

"I just thought, 'Thank God, he is gone, maybe I can get Gary to get the hell out of here,'" Armes recalled.

But then he spotted the station wagon again—only this time, it was coming down the on-ramp.

Buxbaum stopped the station wagon behind the blue Nova, Armes said. Then Gary Foshay walked up to the car. He opened Mrs. Buxbaum's door, pressed the gun to her head, and screamed at the terrified woman, "I want your money and your jewelry!"

Tragically, if Terry Armes' testimony was accurate, it would appear that Hanna Buxbaum saw through this robbery ruse—and saw who was behind it. For, as Helmuth Buxbaum stepped out of the car and stood at the roadside, watching Hanna struggle to free herself from Foshay's clutches, she looked pleadingly at Helmuth and said, "No, honey, please, not this way."

The stunned court then heard Terry Armes describe how Foshay dragged Mrs. Buxbaum over the guard rail and into the ditch. Armes was unwilling to witness the execution, so he remained at the roadside and instead watched Helmuth Buxbaum. As they heard three shots ring out, he noted that Buxbaum "didn't even flinch."

After the shooting, Armes continued, he and Foshay jumped into the blue Nova and drove back to London. They stopped once along the way to remove and discard a cover they'd used to conceal their license plate. Later that night, they threw the murder weapon, some shells, and Mrs. Buxbaum's purse into the Thames River.

The following morning, Terry Armes concluded, he, Gary Foshay, and Jesse Buck took a train to Toronto. They met there with Paul Llewellyn, who gave them their share of the $13,000 Buxbaum had provided to pay for the hit.

Confronted with Terry Armes' shocking eyewitness testimony, as well as that of some 60 other prosecution witnesses; the defendant chose to break his silence. On January 15, 1986, determined to counter these accusations, Helmuth Buxbaum took the stand.

After chronicling the details of his early life, the Austrian immigrant spoke at length about his relationship with Hanna. "She was the best friend I had," he declared. Although Buxbaum conceded that he had been unfaithful to his wife for much of their marriage, he claimed that he had told her of his affairs and that she had forgiven him.

It was only after he suffered a stroke on April 17, 1982,

Buxbaum said, that he became sexually indifferent toward his wife. In an effort to cure his impotence, he went to a prostitute and found he could perform sexually with her. As a result, he began to seek out prostitutes — and only prostitutes — to satisfy his carnal needs.

In earlier defense testimony, a psychiatrist had substantiated Buxbaum's story. He testified that Buxbaum's stroke had produced a brain disorder that caused personality changes, impotence, and hypersexuality, a condition in which mental functioning regresses and the patient loses the ability to repress "hedonistic desires." This loss of inhibition, the doctor postulated, would also account for Helmuth Buxbaum's cocaine abuse and his inability to overcome his addiction.

Continuing his testimony on January 17th, Buxbaum flatly denied that he'd discussed murdering his wife with any of the prostitutes he'd been seeing. He also disputed Paul Llewellyn's story, claiming that the substantial amounts of money he'd given the young drug dealer were intended only to set up a steady cocaine connection.

As for the night of the murder, Buxbaum claimed that he'd gotten back on the on-ramp to Highway 402 only because he'd spotted the blue Nova by the railroad trestle and had mistaken it for a neighbor's car. When he saw that it was not their neighbor having car trouble, Buxbaum said, but a strange man with a gun, he was "perplexed and confused and didn't know what to do."

He and Hanna jumped from their car, Buxbaum continued, and he tried to flag down a passing truck. It was then, he said, that "I heard three shots . . . I saw a white cloud and I saw the gunman with Hanna's purse."

After the gunman fled, Buxbaum went on, he backed the station wagon to where his injured wife lay to make it easier to get her into the car and take her to the hospital. He and the young relative they'd picked up at the airport then went to the roadside and flagged down Jim Gilroy.

After giving their statements at the police station, Bux-

347

baum and the youth were taken to the hospital where the mortally wounded Hanna Buxbaum was undergoing emergency treatment. When he was told that Hanna had died, Buxbaum said, "I didn't believe it; I couldn't believe it." He was too upset to look at the body, he claimed, adding indignantly, "They didn't have the decency to wash her face before they showed it to me."

Shortly after Helmuth Buxbaum left the stand, his attorney, Edward Greenspan, delivered a valiant closing address in a last-ditch effort to rescue his client from a first-degree murder conviction. Calling Helmuth Buxbaum a pathetic "wimp" who was exploited and manipulated by Paul Llewellyn and the others, he argued that the self-made millionaire had no motive to kill his wife and that the prosecution had failed to prove otherwise.

"People don't kill because they're unhappy with their sex life," Greenspan contended. He suggested, however, that people *do* kill when they see their gravy train about to be derailed. Once again, Greenspan targeted Paul Llewellyn as the mastermind behind the murder plot, alleging that he had Mrs. Buxbaum killed because she was jeopardizing his lucrative arrangement with Helmuth.

When Hanna Buxbaum fired him from his landscaping job because he was supplying drugs to her husband, she became "a dangerous woman to [Paul Llewellyn]," Greenspan charged.

In a masterly performance, Greenspan dissected Llewellyn's account of his trip to Orlando and subsequent events with the precision of a microsurgeon. Using hotel receipts and phone records as evidence, he argued that at least one preliminary murder plan would have involved the killer coming to Ontario while Hanna was away on vacation.

"The proposed victim of the murder is in Europe . . . does that make any sense to you?" Greenspan asked the jury.

Telephone company records also showed, the defense attorney said, that Paul Llewellyn had not, as he had testified, called Helmuth Buxbaum from Toronto, where Llewellyn had gone to establish an alibi for the murder. The reason he did not call Buxbaum from his hotel, Greenspan contended, was that had he done so, other people in the room would have overheard his conversation — and would therefore know that the $13,000 Buxbaum planned to give Llewellyn was not blood money, but drug money.

Edward Greenspan's powers of persuasion, however, were insufficient to sway the jury. On February 13, 1986 — more than one and a half years since he had stood on that desolate roadside, signaling for help to passing motorists in an eerie reenactment of the prelude to his wife's savage slaying — Helmuth Buxbaum was found guilty of first-degree murder. He received a life sentence and will not be eligible for parole until he has served 25 years.

Gary Foshay, the triggerman in the murder-for-hire scheme, stood trial in September 1986. On October 10th, he was found guilty of second-degree murder. He was sentenced to life in prison and is required to serve at least 18 of that sentence before he can be considered for parole.

EDITOR'S NOTE:

Jim Gilroy, Paul Llewellyn, and Jesse Buck are not the real names of the persons so named in the foregoing story. Fictitious names have been used because there is no reason for public interest in the identities of these persons.

"FIEND SUCKED SUSAN'S FINGERS DRY!"

by Bill G. Cox

Everything about the scene on the morning of Monday, March 19, 1990, spoke of upper middle-class success. Dana K. McIntosh drove his silver Mercedes away from his $218,000 four-bedroom home on Sunny Land Lane in the Lakewood section of Dallas, Texas, headed for his computer software company. The 43-year-old McIntosh was president of the firm, which was a bright star on the Dallas metroplex business horizon.

The handsome, bespectacled executive was also a respected family man. The attractive 42-year-old wife Dana usually kissed before leaving home was Susan Kidd McIntosh, the daughter of a wealthy Tyler, Texas, dairyman who left a sizable estate when he died in 1976. Susan and Dana were high school sweethearts in their hometown of Tyler and had been married on August 8, 1970. McIntosh was an Army lieutenant at the time. Friends said the couple had been overwhelmingly in love, and the years that followed proved the excellence of the romantic match.

Now the well-liked and respected couple had two lovely daughters, 8 and 12 years old. The McIntoshes were active in church and community affairs and could have been a model family for an American family magazine.

On this day, the two daughters were with their grandmother in Tyler, where the McIntoshes had visited and attended church on Sunday. The children had stayed on for a visit during spring break from school, so Susan and Dana had their spacious home—located only a mile from beautiful White Rock Lake and the large city park encircling its shores—to themselves Sunday night.

That such bliss could be interrupted by unimaginable horror was a possibility far from the minds of Lakewood's residents as they started the work week.

Some two hours after arriving at his company offices on Dallas' North Central Expressway, McIntosh said he needed help getting one of his cars to a mechanic. He asked a co-worker to accompany him to the Lakewood address to drive one of the vehicles while he drove the other.

At the house, McIntosh asked his co-worker to accompany him inside to pick up the other car keys. The co-worker followed McIntosh into the house and then into the garage. There a terrible sight greeted them. Susan McIntosh, fully clothed, was sprawled on the garage floor in a large pool of blood, her body partly slumped against a freezer.

After the initial shock abated, the co-worker rushed back into the house and dialed 911. When he returned to the garage, he found the sobbing and distraught McIntosh tugging at his wife's prone form and crying for the other man to help him load her body into his own car. He didn't want to wait for the ambulance, he said.

The employee complied, although in his opinion, the blood-covered woman was already beyond any medical help.

At the hospital, doctors immediately noticed the large gash across Susan McIntosh's throat. When she was undressed, the full horror of the slashing and stabbing attack became evident. Her body had been mutilated with 20 to 30 wounds, mostly in the torso. The frenzied knifer had hit every major organ, the examination showed.

There was an especially long gash across the victim's

lower abdomen, near the pubic area.

Susan McIntosh had apparently been dead when she was found, but she was not pronounced dead until her arrival at the hospital emergency room. Semen was found in her body, but apparently there were no signs of forcible rape. It was assumed she could have had marital intercourse the previous night. The victim had fought fiercely with her killer, which was evident from several defensive wounds on her hands, it was reported.

Although Susan had been completely dressed when discovered and the slash and stab wounds appeared to have cut through her clothing, it was discovered when she was undressed that her hair and underclothing were damp— another bizarre element in the strange case.

While friends tried to comfort the distraught husband, those present, including police officers summoned by hospital attendants when the body was brought in, noticed that Dana McIntosh had what appeared to be fresh scratches on his face and neck.

When police asked how he had been scratched, the computer company executive, perhaps in a state of shock, denied that he was scratched. Later, when pressed about the scratches, he said that he must have received them while playing with the family's pet dog. He wasn't sure just when.

The co-worker who had accompanied Dana McIntosh recalled that he'd noticed the scratches when McIntosh arrived at the office that morning.

Another weird circumstance was reported to the police by hospital nurses. One nurse said that she noticed McIntosh sucking his dead wife's fingers as she lay on the emergency room table. When she stopped him from doing this with one finger, he started sucking on other fingers.

Asked about this strange behavior, the husband explained that he had been kissing his wife's fingertips. But the nurses were quite certain that McIntosh had been sucking them.

The fresh scratches on the husband's face and neck and

his apparent sucking at his wife's fingers — which detectives thought could have been an attempt to remove his own blood and tissue from under his wife's fingernails — struck the sleuths as highly suspicious. Dana McIntosh was taken in for additional questioning.

Later, in a taped interview with Dallas Detective Donald Ortega, McIntosh said that he had received one or two scratches from the family collie at an earlier time but had no explanation as to how he had suffered more than a dozen others.

"I don't know about the scratches on my nose and all that type of stuff," he told Detective Ortega. "I know that I did not have these scratches this morning. I don't know how these scratches got here. I wish you all would tell me."

During the 23-minute interview, Detective Ortega asked McIntosh if he had any problems with his wife that would have caused him to harm her.

McIntosh replied emphatically, "I haven't had no problems, and I did no harm to Susan K. McIntosh . . . or anybody else, and you guys need to get out of here and find out who the hell did!"

The executive said he last saw Susan alive when he kissed and hugged her before leaving for work.

Still later, McIntosh speculated to investigators that his wife might have scratched him accidentally when hospital personnel tried to pry her loose from his grip, but the medics recalled that the woman had been dead on arrival.

Dana McIntosh continued to hotly deny that he had harmed his wife in any way and stubbornly refused to allow police to enter and search his residence. However, detectives obtained a search warrant from the courts. Crime scene technicians and detectives carefully processed the large residence on Sunny Land Lane for clues. They could find no evidence of forced entry into the home or the garage.

Meanwhile, teams of investigators went door to door in the high-class residential area. No one reported having seen or heard anything unusual that morning or the night before. No strangers had been seen lurking around the neighborhood, nor were any unknown vehicles seen prowling along the streets.

The absence of forced entry into the victim's home seemed to rule out a burglar as the attacker. This theory was enhanced by information from a neighbor, who told police the family had a security system that was always in operation.

The shocked neighbor told a detective, "When I needed to borrow some eggs or something—Susan was the kind of person you turned to if you needed eggs or syrup for waffles—I'd phone her; and she'd say that one of her daughters would meet me at the door, but she had to cut the security system off first."

The search warrant authorized the investigators to collect evidence "such as blood, hair, skin tissue, and the toenails of the family collie dog, Bitsy." The ensuing search took more than two hours, with much of it concentrated in the area of the McIntoshes' master bedroom.

The technicians discovered what was thought to be blood in the bathroom. In the garage where Susan's body was found, the investigators observed blood on a cardboard box, on the freezer, and on the license plate of a station wagon in addition to the large pool of blood in which her body was sprawled.

Using a chemical solution, technicians found evidence of blood in the master bedroom sink, on the sink faucets, and on a towel rack. Tests also showed positive signs of blood on the shower handle and along a foot-wide area at the bottom of the shower stall.

Police and forensic medical experts who analyzed the blood locations, recalling that the victim's underclothing and hair were wet, theorized that the woman's body might have been taken into the shower and washed off after she was stabbed in the garage.

During the search, the investigators took possession of a

steak knife and a carving knife for analysis, but neither could be immediately identified as the murder weapon. One highly interesting item did surface as detectives combed the rooms of the fashionable home: an insurance policy in the amount of $250,000 on Susan McIntosh's life with her husband named as the beneficiary.

"A quarter of a million bucks could be a motive," one detective said as he thumbed through the insurance papers. But this theory didn't make much sense, considering what friends and relatives said about the apparently close, loving, and happily married couple.

Meanwhile, after preliminary questioning by detectives, Dana McIntosh was released without any charge being filed against him. Police said they had no evidence to identify Susan's brutal killer. It was speculated that even more than one person might be involved—though no reason was given for this idea.

The absence of any signs of a struggle or forced entry at the home baffled investigators. Much about the case was baffling. About the only thing it was safe to assume was that the victim had been stabbed to death between 8:00 and 10:00 A.M. on the morning she was found by her husband and his co-worker.

Later, after obtaining a court order to take body samples from Dana McIntosh, the slain woman and the family's pet collie, detectives escorted the obviously nervous McIntosh to the Southwest Institute of Forensic Sciences.

Blood, hair, and saliva samples were taken from Dana McIntosh. Detectives told reporters that the samples would be compared with physical evidence obtained in the initial stages of the probe.

In the meantime, friends and fellow church members rallied behind Dana McIntosh and said they refused to believe that he had slain his wife.

At his wife's funeral, McIntosh sobbed loudly at the final graveside interment ceremony, clutching one of his young daughters to him. The bright red scratches on him were something that didn't go unnoticed by other mourners.

As one relative of the slain woman told reporters: "He was sitting right there in the middle of a crowd, and he had those scratches on his face. It just worried the hell out of me." Still, the same relative could not help but recall the last time he had seen Susan McIntosh alive at a church service.

"They just looked like the ideal family. He sat with his arm around her all during the church service, with those beautiful kids on each side."

As friends recalled, the couple was approaching their 20th wedding anniversary. The McIntoshes were frequently referred to as "the perfect Christian couple."

Since moving to Dallas some 10 years earlier, the McIntoshes had become known as an energetic couple in the Methodist church they attended. They helped start the church's highly successful day care center, worked together on numerous committees and programs, and took part in adult Sunday school classes in addition to regular Sunday attendance at worship services.

The charming couple was also socially active in the community, attending parties and other gatherings. Taken all together, the impression that people had of the McIntoshes—and particularly of Dana McIntosh—was far from one that could conceive of him as a savage slasher who'd killed his wife.

"The phrase 'beyond a reasonable doubt' has taken on a new meaning for me," said one friend. ". . . I've known him since 1986 and worked closely with him and just can't believe that he did this."

As police intensified their efforts to collect evidence, a startling development strengthened the belief of McIntosh's friends that he wasn't responsible for the stabbing death of his wife. Officers were sent to McIntosh's computer firm when Dana McIntosh called police to report that his office had been burglarized and ransacked! The break-in was found out by McIntosh and another company official when they arrived shortly after 9:00 A.M. on a Saturday. McIntosh told detectives that the burglar had taken financial records and had also spread pictures of Susan McIntosh and their children across his desk.

McIntosh's attorney told reporters that the burglary puzzled him because no money or valuables were kept in the office. He suggested that police might have broken in and searched the office for evidence linking his client to the murder. "Sometimes if they have a warrant they will bust in someplace if it's locked. I'm not accusing the cops, but I know that they are desperately searching for evidence and a motive."

Dallas Deputy Police Chief Ray Hawkins, obviously angry at the insinuations of McIntosh's lawyer, responded, "When the facts are sorted out, we'll see who is desperate." He said that no search warrant was executed at the high-rise office of the computer firm.

Police also learned that McIntosh and the other official had waited three hours before reporting the burglary to police. They had evidently called the attorney first, according to the police report on the matter.

The attorney told reporters, "There's not a burglar in the world who would be interested in anything in [McIntosh's] office, unless it's computer related. I don't understand why anyone would break in here. The burglary may be coincidental." But he added that the burglary worried him because he thought McIntosh might be in danger.

"The burglar could be somebody out there who killed [McIntosh's] wife and may do something to him now."

Homicide Detective Cathy Harding, who was leading the murder investigation, told newsmen, "We find the burglary interesting." She did not elaborate or discuss possible links to the slaying.

The company officials told investigators they did not recall whether the McIntosh office door was locked when the burglary was discovered. But the officials said the main of-

357

fice doors were secured by a dead bolt. They also said the only way to get into the building after hours and on weekends was by using a magnetic card at the back door. All doors to the office building were always locked at 9:30 P.M., and security guards made continual rounds of all the offices, the firm officials told police. Each individual office door was locked and could only be opened with a key, they added.

McIntosh had returned to the job only the day before the break-in, he said. He had worked until about 7:45 P.M. when he left with two business associates.

Before the burglary occurred, police had previously acknowledged that the investigation was turning up questions about Dana McIntosh's finances. The finding of the quarter-million-dollar life insurance policy on which McIntosh was the beneficiary had intensified this phase of the probe.

In fact, as detectives concentrated their investigation on Dana McIntosh's family life and business interests, a few holes were appearing in the untarnished reputation that had made the computer executive seem such a pillar of the community at first.

One official told police that the computer firm was in sound financial shape. Its product, a software package that enabled users to create a database, was especially useful for insurance and medical billings, police learned. The company had established a network of vendors across the nation who sold the software and furnished a training program for purchasers.

But a former executive of the company gave police a different story about the firm's financial condition. He said that the company, like others before it in which McIntosh held an interest, was chronically cash-poor and badly managed. The former official, who had been in charge of sales, said McIntosh was "terrible at paying bills.

"If I bought anything, I bought it when I knew we had some funds that had just come in," said the former official.

"I'd know that there was money, and I'd ask for a check right then."

Checking Dallas County court records, investigators learned that during the 1980s, McIntosh and companies with which he had been affiliated were sued more than a dozen times by banks, suppliers, business associates, and others. The suits alleged failure to pay debts and keep leases or contractual terms.

Another former employee of the computer company revealed that Susan McIntosh had taken an "active role" in overseeing the firm's books during the past year. "The company was having financial problems," the witness said. "I know that Susan's money frequently funded the deficits in the organization."

The bad fortune had started several years before, said the ex-employee, when Susan was forced to dip into her family's money to finance an ill-starred computer venture of her husband's. The former official estimated that Susan McIntosh had lost more than $200,000 in that undertaking.

The financial troubles appeared at times to have caused a stressful relationship between the McIntoshes, police were told. The witness said, "I have seen them when they were not wonderfully loving to one another. I walked in on them one day, and they were having words over the checkbook or something having to do with office finances. It was like two cold warriors sitting and glaring at one another. Susan was a very stubborn individual. Dana is a very stubborn individual."

But a high official of the computer company still insisted the firm was on solid financial foundations, saying, "There is nothing about our financial position that we did not completely anticipate."

He explained there had been only a temporary financial downturn in the past two years as the firm changed from selling costly software packages to a less-expensive product line.

An attorney who represented Dana McIntosh said, "He's

359

out there wheeling and dealing as much today as he ever was. He's got plenty of money."

Police and reporters checking the court records found that in 1981, Susan had agreed to mortgage part of her substantial inheritance to help her husband buy a computer company in the Dallas area. The land included some that had been in the family for generations, according to reports. The original $150,000 loan was refinanced several times, but in 1985, the records disclosed, the McIntoshes had defaulted. As a result, Susan lost her interest in 594 acres as well as stock in several banks that had been left to her by her wealthy dairyman father at his death.

A close friend said that Susan had been devastated by the losses. In fact, only two weeks before her violent death, she had confided to the friend that she had just learned her husband's business was faced with possible bankruptcy.

"She was shocked," said the friend. "At that point, she was not sure what she was going to do."

Susan still had a large amount of holdings, including a $38,000 gasoline station in Tyler, it was reported.

Further examination of records revealed that the Internal Revenue Service several months earlier had filed a personal tax lien against Dana McIntosh on a debt of $13,287.

Detective-Sergeant Gary Kilpatrick confirmed that the McIntosh marriage wasn't always as smooth as friends had reported. They had sought marital counseling several years earlier. Still, the detectives found no evidence of infidelity or recent marital problems, the detective-sergeant said. In fact, police learned that Susan had planned to fly with her husband to Washington, D.C., on Monday night—the day of the murder—presumably on business.

One acquaintance of Dana McIntosh told detectives that the businessman struck him "as a guy who always was trying to put forth a certain impression: successful businessman, a Christian—that sort of thing."

Digging into the suspect's background, the sleuths raised questions about McIntosh's oft-repeated claims of courageous service as a Vietnam veteran. Friends of the computer executive had said that McIntosh, as a rifle platoon leader in 1969, was a war hero who received several decorations for valor, including two Silver Stars, two Bronze Stars, and an Army Commendation Medal. These recognitions for valiant service were reflected in records of the U.S. Army Reserve Personnel Center in St. Louis, Missouri.

However, a retired Army colonel who commanded the battalion in which McIntosh had served, said he had no recollections of the young Army lieutenant, one of about 30 officers under his command. He described the recorded medals as "rather remarkable, given the fact that he was only there for three months."

On August 14, 1990, about five months after the slaying of Susan McIntosh, her husband was indicted on a charge of murder by a Dallas County grand jury to which police presented all their findings and evidence.

With the murder trial set to begin in a state District Court in Dallas on April 8, 1991, a reporter for the *Dallas News* wrote that the enigmatic case was either one of "searing public scrutiny added to crushing personal tragedy" for McIntosh, or "one of middle America gone haywire."

The state raised the curtain on its circumstantial case against the defendant. After police photos of the scratches on McIntosh were introduced, a forensic medical specialist testified about what he found when he examined Dana McIntosh at the request of police.

"On the left side, he had scratches on the neck and cheek coming from three different directions. . . . He had in excess of twenty [scratches] on his face." McIntosh also had a red mark in the center of his chest, the witness said.

The witness testified under cross-examination, however, that none of the blood evidence found in the McIntosh master bathroom or elsewhere identified Dana McIntosh as the killer.

McIntosh, who had claimed that he'd gotten the scratches from the family's pet collie, was not linked to the

361

slaying by blood samples taken from the victim's finger-nails, another witness testified. The blood specialist said DNA tests revealed a piece of tissue taken from the victim's fingernails belonged to the victim, not her husband.

The specialist said that blood found on all of the victim's fingernails and hairlike tissue on two of them could not be compared. It was also revealed that no tests were made on the nails of the pet collie because they would have been worthless; the dog had walked through the victim's blood before the nails could be clipped. However, only one of the eight nail clippings taken from the dog had blood on it, according to the specialist.

The pathologist who performed the autopsy on Susan McIntosh told the jury that the body had more than 20 stab wounds, 2 to 5 inches deep, and also multiple cuts. There were several cuts on her hands, indicating that she fought with her attacker and sustained defensive wounds, he related. The doctor said he believed the wounds were inflicted by someone she knew, basing his opinion, on vast experience with victims of so-called crimes of passion and multiple stabbing.

Though nothing he had seen conclusively linked the husband to the slaying, the pathologist said, the evidence didn't conflict with the prosecution's theory of the murder.

Assistant District Attorney Mike Gillett asked the witness, "Your examination and findings are consistent with Dana McIntosh having had a knife in his hand in his garage and having fought with and stabbed to death Susan McIntosh, while she fought him off as best she could with her hands, having scratched Dana McIntosh on his face, marking him as her killer for time eternal?"

"Yes," the pathologist replied.

The prosecution called to the stand the co-worker who had been with Dana McIntosh on the morning Susan's body was found. The witness recounted a chilling conversation with McIntosh that occurred a few weeks after her death.

362

"He told me his attorney had asked him, if he had been the one to kill Susan McIntosh, how would he have done it."

Continuing, the witness quoted McIntosh as having said, "First of all, I wouldn't have used a kitchen knife. It's too flimsy and it would break."

The witness added, "He told me he would have used a hunting knife, that he would take it and go in under her sternum and rip it straight up. I told him to stop. I couldn't take it."

Other employees of the firm testified that they observed scratches on McIntosh's face on the morning before his wife's body was found, scratches not there the previous day, and that McIntosh uncharacteristically lost his temper two times. He had apologized, saying he had lots on his mind.

Two nurses took the stand to tell about Dana McIntosh's actions in the hospital emergency room. They said he removed his wife's fingers from under a sheet and sucked on them. The nurses said he told friends he was kissing her hands, but that he took each finger into his mouth — one by one — until they forced him to stop.

"Was this kissing hands or sucking fingers?" asked the assistant prosecutor.

"Sucking fingers," one nurse testified. "As I would take one hand away, he would take the other."

A relative of Susan McIntosh said that he was sickened by what he overheard McIntosh tell his two young daughters about their mother's death. The witness said that McIntosh told the girls, ages 8 and 12, that he was trying to pick her up in the garage but kept slipping in her blood. He also told his daughters that he didn't know how he got the scratches on his face but guessed that their mom had scratched him in the emergency room.

The witness said the 8-year-old had responded, "How could that be? She was dead."

After the prosecution closed its case without linking the defendant to the murder by physical evidence, the defense

363

called Dana McIntosh to the stand. He denied that his wife had made the facial scratches, which the state contended to be the key to its case. He kept to his story that the collie had made some of the scratches and that he didn't know how he got the others. It was apparently this weak explanation of the livid scratches that played a part in the jury's verdict.

After deliberating for only 45 minutes, the jury found Dana McIntosh guilty of murder. The jury recommended a sentence of 75 years in prison.

Although a murder weapon was never identified, the jury found that McIntosh used a deadly weapon when he killed his wife. Texas law requires that a defendant who receives more than 60 years for murder in which a deadly weapon is used must serve a minimum of 15 years before parole is possible.

McIntosh would probably be denied by law the $250,000 life insurance benefits as well as his wife's estate, which was also estimated at $250,000.

"CUNNING BRUNETTE'S MONEY & MURDER SCHEMES!"

by Joseph L. Koenig

In 1962, teenage Ana Lou Weltey, in the dusty panhandle town of Quannah, Texas, took as her husband one James Edgar Goodyear, a career man in the United States Air Force. To her marriage Anna brought her dark good looks and an infant son, Michael, born ten months earlier in Roswell, New Mexico. Goodyear, an expansive, warm-hearted man, adopted the boy as his own in 1965.

"Michael was a warm and loving child," a family friend would recall, "but he wasn't right, not like the other kids. For one thing, he was accident prone and ungainly, always falling down and hurting himself. For another, he had a large, sloping forehead, sunken cheeks and a jutting jaw. Because his eyesight wasn't real good he always wore thick glasses with heavy black frames. Worst of all, the poor kid suffered from pica eating, which meant he was always gobbling up stuff which wasn't at all fit to eat, things like dirt and paint right off the wall."

In 1966, Anna Goodyear, who was then 22 years of age, presented her husband Jim with a son of his own. A daughter was born the year after. From all accounts, Jim Goodyear was a doting father who opened up his heart and his home equally to all his children, home being in a comfortable middle class neighborhood of Orlando, Florida.

365

In the summer of 1971, just back from a tour of duty in Vietnam, 37-year-old Jim Goodyear—who was never known to have a sick day in his life—fell grievously ill without warning. At the hospital where he was brought seemingly on the brink of death a diagnosis was made of kidney failure. Within three days he developed pneumonia and had to be placed on a respirator. One day later, on September 16th, his circulatory system gave out and he died.

James Goodyear was laid to rest in Orlando, where he had spent the last few years of his life. His grieving widow filed a claim with the company that had insured his life and was rewarded with the sum of $70,000.

A few years later, in the mid-1970s, Anna Lou Weltey Goodyear met and fell in love with one Bobby Joe Morris who ran a construction company in Pensacola, Florida. When Morris moved his business to Trinidad, Colorado in 1977, because of better business prospects there, Anna and the kids went along.

In Trinidad, a city of 10,000 in the southeastern part of the state, hard by the New Mexico border, Morris operated the municipal water treatment plant while Anna enrolled as a nursing student at a junior college. The couple led a quiet and uneventful existence until January 4, 1978, when Morris was brought to a hospital emergency room suffering from a high fever and shock after complaining of severe abdominal pains. It was no secret that Bobby Joe Morris was a heavy drinker. To the doctors treating him, it seemed obvious that the cause of the excruciating pain wracking his body was an inflamed pancreas.

On January 21st, after nearly three weeks of hospitalization, Morris went home. Just two days later, suffering from a severe bout of nausea, he returned to the hospital. In the emergency room doctors recorded a pulse beat of 140. Each time the patient attempted to raise his head in response to a question, he lost consciousness.

The next 24 hours were a critical time for Morris. When that first day passed, there was a distinct improvement in his condition, but on the second he became "agitated" and had to be restrained. A short while later, he slipped into a coma complicated by wildly fluctuating blood pressure—pointing to circulatory difficulties—and decreased urine output—pointing to kidney failure. It came as no surprise to his doctors when his heart began defibrillating and he ceased breathing on January 28th.

Puzzled by the strange symptoms of his fatal illness and unsure of its actual cause, doctors ordered an autopsy. By that time, however, the 37-year-old contractor was resting in his casket inside a funeral home. The pathologist, reluctant to disturb the body, merely unbuttoned Morris' shirt, took a few small tissue samples and rebuttoned the shirt. As might have been expected, such a post-mortem shed little light on the case of Bobby Joe Morris' death.

His common-law widow's grief was assuaged, somewhat, by a check for $77,000 which she received from the company with which she had insured Morris' life six months before his death.

That same year, Anna Lou Weltey Goodyear Morris legally changed her name to Judi Buenoano, which in Spanish is a rough translation of Goodyear. Although the woman never spelled out the reasons for the change, a friend suggested that it was because new acquaintances too often asked if she were part of the multimillionaire tire family. Later, the police would speculate that the woman had more venal reasons—that she already cashed in several life insurance policies under the name of Goodyear, and it was time to evade the prying eyes of insurance investigators.

In June of 1979, with his mother's blessing, Michael Goodyear, who was now 18 years old, enlisted in the United States Army. Early in the autumn, given his first extended leave, he hurried to his mother's Pensacola home. On October 27th, his first night back, he was brought to a hospital complaining of nausea and dizziness.

Michael Goodyear left the hospital a day or so later with

367

little improvement in his condition. Back home, he deteriorated rapidly. On November 1st, he complained for the first time of a tingling sensation in his fingers and toes, the onset of a fast-spreading paralysis which would leave him permanently crippled. By the middle of December, Michael had been fitted with a prosthetic device for his right arm and heavy metal braces for his legs.

Unable to come up with a satisfactory diagnosis, Army doctors sent Michael to Walter Reed Army Hospital in Washington, D.C. From there he was moved to the Tampa Veterans Administration Hospital where he remained until May 12, 1980, when his mother drove down to the Gulf Coast metropolis to pick him up and drive him back home.

Just one day later, on May 13th, Judi Buenoano took Michael and his brother and sister for a canoe ride on the East River in Santa Rosa County north of Pensacola. The outing barely had gotten underway when a fisherman spotted the 37-year-old woman and her younger son struggling in the water.

"At first, I thought they were playing," he would recall. "But then I spotted the canoe."

After he pulled the pair into his boat, he went on, Judi "told me there wasn't any use trying to save the other boy because he was already gone."

When he brought his craft to a boat ramp a few yards downriver with Judi seated beside him in her waterlogged clothing, and with her younger son unconscious over a gunwale, he noticed Mrs. Buenoano's daughter sitting on the ramp. Her mother, he recalled, said "really nothing" to the girl to indicate that her brother had drowned.

"The most she talked about was that the other boy had been hurt pretty bad," he said.

A brief investigation by police ended in a ruling that Michael Goodyear's death had come as the result of a tragic accident. His mother's pain was salved, in part, by a $180,000 payment from the company that had insured the young soldier's life.

368

Michael's loss was not the only one Judi had suffered that year. Barely three months earlier, on February 4, 1980, her 48-year-old boyfriend had died suddenly in Fort Walton Beach, Florida.

In August of 1982, Judi Buenoano, then 39 years of age, made a novel suggestion to her new boyfriend, 37-year-old Melvin Carson of Pensacola. Because marriage appeared inevitable, why not insure each other's life for half a million dollars? Carson, whose own life already was insured for $50,000, said that he was satisfied with his coverage. Eventually, however, Judi had her way.

"We had originally started talking about a $100,000 policy," he would remember, "and Judi wanted to go for a half million. I couldn't afford a half million, and I told Judi that. But we ended up getting a half million dollars' worth."

Four months later, in December, Melvin Carson came down with a bad cold which just wouldn't go away. When he told Judi that he believed that years of heavy smoking might have left him with a vitamin deficiency, he would say later, his live-in girlfriend had just the answer—multivitamin Vicon C tablets, which she provided herself.

"Each night, after we finally retired to the bedroom," he would say, "she kept the pills on the nightstand on her side. She would reach over and give them to me."

Not long after, Carson became gravely ill. Unable to keep his food down, crippled by agonizing abdominal pains, he checked into Sacred Heart Hospital in Pensacola for two weeks. There, doctors diagnosed his ailment as high blood pressure.

"When I got out of the hospital," he would remember, "Judi was somewhat distant . . . We didn't argue or anything like that. We were just not the lovey-dovey couple we were before."

Judi, he recalled, gave him more of the Vicon-C tablets. He noticed that when he took one of the pills, he inevitably felt terrible the next day. If he skipped a pill, he felt fine.

369

"After a couple of times of getting sick," Carson said, "I decided to wise up and not take the pills any more."

Some six months after that, Melvin Carson purchased a set of speakers for his automobile and on Saturday morning, June 25, 1983, he asked Judi to install them for him. After she finished work on the car, the couple went shopping.

"Judi had told me she was pregnant," Carson would remember. "I was ecstatic. I had always hoped for something like this."

During the shopping expedition, the couple discussed the possibility of marriage and whether or not Judi should have an abortion. That evening, Carson and his girlfriend went to a going away party for an employee of Judi's beauty salon. Before entering a downtown restaurant, Carson said, Judi gave him instructions about where to park the car.

Late that night Carson left the restaurant to pick up the vehicle at the intersection of Baylen and Garden Streets. When he switched on his lights, two sticks of dynamite which had been hidden in the trunk and hooked up to the taillights exploded.

For an instant, Melvin Carson didn't know what hit him. Because it was dark inside the vehicle, he thought the car battery had exploded. Then, feeling a twinge of pain in his back, he placed his hand there and brought it away red with blood. Looking down, he saw that one of his shoes was missing.

Carson struggled out of the smoldering wreckage and tried to walk away. A friend came up and told him that he was badly hurt and should lie down. When Carson told the friend to go away, that he was going back to the restaurant, the friend wrestled him to the ground. Soon an ambulance came and took him away.

Melvin Carson spent the next ten weeks in a Pensacola hospital where doctors repaired his injured stomach, kidneys and liver and both his large and small intestines. Later,

370

he returned to the hospital for surgery.

Pensacola police were puzzled by the powerful blast which came so narrowly to claiming Carson's life. A routine background check revealed that Carson had no links to organized crime or extremist political groups, members of which were often the target of such blasts.

While he was still hospitalized, Carson submitted to a series of interviews with Pensacola Police Officer now Detective Ted Chamberlain. When Carson mentioned the vitamin capsules he had taken six months earlier and which had made him deathly sick, Chamberlain asked if any of the pills were left. Carson told Chamberlain where to find them and the officer sent them to the state crime lab. Chemists soon determined that the capsules had been emptied of vitamin C and refilled with paraformaldehyde, a lethal poison.

Late in July, Judi Buenoano was taken into custody by Pensacola police and charged with the attempted poison murder of Melvin Carson. Subsequently, she was also charged with the murder by drowning of her son Michael and the theft of $20,000 from the company which insured his life.

In Okaloosa County, Florida, meanwhile, authorities announced that they were conducting an "unofficial" investigation into the death of a 48-year-old man who had dated Judi Buenoano early in 1980. The probe was dropped, however, when an exhumation of his body indicated that he had died of natural causes.

In the final week of January, 1984, exactly six years after his puzzling death, Bobby Joe Morris' body was exhumed from a small graveyard in Brewton, Alabama. Tests on the dead man's liver pointed to a lethal dose of arsenic as a possible cause of death.

A little less than two months later, in mid-March, investigators journeyed to the Orlando cemetery where James Goodyear had rested since 1971 and exhumed his body. Organ samples and hair and fingernail specimens were sent to a crime lab, where—according to Dusty Rhodes, an investigator with the state attorney's office in Orlando—they were tested for the presence of arsenic and other poisons.

"The body," Rhodes noted, "was very well preserved."

At Judi Buenoano's trial for the murder of her son, Michael, which got underway in the Pensacola suburb of Milton, Florida in late March, Assistant State Attorney Russell Edgar told the jury that the death of the young GI was planned by his mother so that she could collect on his life insurance policy. Together with Officer Chamberlain, Edgar had put in 1,000 to 1,500 hours of legwork to build a case against Buenoano for the murder of her son.

The defense saw things differently, maintaining that the young man's death was an accident, the result of panic in the canoe when a fishing line snagged in a tree causing a branch with a snake resting on it to fall into the boat.

Among the prosecution's first witnesses was the Santa Rosa County Sheriff's Department paramedic who had brought up Michael Goodyear's body from the bottom of the East River. The witness told the court that when he discovered him floating face down in about 15 feet of water, the boy was wearing leg and arm braces weighing about 50 pounds.

On Saturday, March 24th, a Dover, Delaware woman who had lived with the defendant in Orlando and in Pensacola told the jury that Judi Buenoano was "ashamed" of her son, Michael, and hid him from visitors. Judi, she claimed, "was very distant" from her son, whom she sent to a school in Miami for emotionally handicapped children. Michael, she noted, was allowed to come home only on vacations. When visitors came by the house, she said, Judi would make her take the boy for a drive.

Michael, she said, "was messy, slobbered a lot, was hyper and had trouble with coordination."

On Monday, March 26th, an insurance agent told the court that in October, 1979, he visited the defendant to "discuss her life insurance coverage" and sold her a policy

372

on Michael. Other policies in the amounts of $15,000 and $20,000 had been "taken out several years before."

The witness went on to say that he never met Michael Goodyear and did not see him sign the forms insuring his life. Prosecutors, it was noted, claimed that his mother had forged the boy's signature to the policy.

Another prosecution witness, an investigator for the insurance company, confirmed that Mrs. Buenoano did not say anything about her son's paralysis when he filed the policy.

"I recall talking to her about the medical history of her son, and she said he had always been healthy," the witness testified.

A relative told the court that for several months after Michael's death, Judi did not mention to the family that he was ill or had died. In November, 1980, less than a month after the boy died, the family decided to visit Judi and her children. When the witness phoned to make arrangements for the trip, Judi said nothing about Michael.

"She called me back and told me that Michael had died," the witness testified. "She told me that he was in the Army and he got involved in chemical warfare or something of that nature."

On Saturday, March 31st, after some six hours of deliberation, a jury found Judi Buenoano guilty of the first-degree murder of her son, Michael, and of grand theft for collecting $108,000 in benefits form the company insuring his life.

"I think it was a difficult decision, to decide whether or not the woman took the life of her own child," Assistant State Attorney Edgar said after the verdict was in. "One can't even imagine this crime, yet the evidence was compelling."

But the guilty verdict and possible death sentence that went with it were just the start of Judi Buenoano's troubles. For that afternoon, just hours before the jury announced its verdict, Judi Buenoano was rearrested and charged with attempted murder and grand theft stemming from the 1983 car bombing of Melvin Carson.

During the penalty phase of Judi's murder trial, on Monday, April 2nd, the defendant took the stand to claim that her conviction had come at the hands of a vindictive prosecutor.

"You have witch-hunted me," she told Asst. State Attorney Edgar. "I don't see how I've been convicted of murder when no murder was committed. I love my children. I would never harm any of them. I know what happened. All you have are presumptions."

When Edgar asked the woman about allegations that she had punished Michael severely, Judi responded:

"It's a sad day when we cannot discipline one of our own children."

Testifying on behalf of Judi Buenoano was a young woman who said that the defendant had given her a place to stay when she was broke and homeless. "She's a wonderful person and always loved and cared for me as one of her own," she said.

Edgar, who earlier had termed the defendant "a black widow spider that fed on her young," disagreed.

"She made more than $100,000 off the death of her own child and enjoyed spending every penny of it," he said.

The jury, after just 90 minutes of debate, voted to spare Judi Buenoano's life, recommending to Judge George Lowery that he sentence her to life in prison.

Prosecutor Edgar said that he had no objection to the life sentence.

"I know and am confident she will be executed somewhere else," he said.

Judge Lowery accepted the jury's recommendation, sentencing the dark-haired woman to a life term from which, under Florida law, she would not become eligible for parole until 25 years had passed.

On Friday, August 31st, an Orange County grand jury sitting in Orlando indicted Judi Buenoano for the 1971 poisoning murder of her first husband, James Edgar Goodyear. State Attorney Robert Eagen told newsmen that the March 14th autopsy on Goodyear's body indicated that he had died of arsenic poisoning. Judi Buenoano pleaded innocent to the charge on Friday, October 5th.

Ten days later, in an Escambia County courtroom in Pensacola, Judi Buenoano went on trial for the attempted murder of Melvin Carson.

On Tuesday, October 16th, Carson told the jury about the car bomb which tore up his intestines, cut his head and blew a shoe off his foot.

"Basically," he said, "it turned up my insides and turned them inside out."

Also testifying that day was an employee of Judi Buenoano's cosmetics shops who said that while Carson was in the hospital Judi had painted a grim picture of his health.

"She said that Melvin was very ill, that he had cancer," that witness recalled. "She said it was very bad, and she didn't expect him to live."

Another of Judi Buenoano's employees testified that her boss had told her that she was a "scientific pathologist" affiliated with Eglin Air Force, Pensacola.

The witness went on to say that on two occasions she had gone on cruises with her boss, who picked up the tab. In April, 1983, she remembered, Judi was planning a world cruise which would cost $20,000 per person, and was planning to take along her children, but not Melvin Carson.

The woman said that when Judi was told her boyfriend's car had been bombed she passed out at the restaurant table where they were seated at the time.

"She jumped up and grabbed her heart, and her eyes rolled back in her head."

But, the witness was quick to note, since that night she had seen the defendant fake emotions on numerous occasions and no longer believed the fainting spell was genuine.

Forensic scientists told the court that when they combed Melvin Carson's ruined car for evidence, they turned up

375

"debris all over the place," including the wire used to put the bomb together. When they searched Judi Buenoano's Gulf Breeze home, they found identical wire, wire so unusual that they were unable to find it in any store in Pensacola.

On Wednesday morning, October 17th, Roger Martz of the FBI Crime Lab in Washington, D.C., told the jury that the vitamin capsules which Judi Buenoano allegedly gave her boyfriend contained no vitamins at all. What they did contain was paraformaldehyde, a toxic substance normally found in insecticides and fungicides.

In his closing argument on Thursday, October 18th, defense counsel said that, "There's not enough evidence in this case to convict Judi Goodyear-Buenoano for chicken thievery, much less attempted first-degree murder.

"This whole thing is built around a big guess. The prosecution "wants you to convict this lady on basically a big guess. The state wants you to guess that if she poisoned Mr. Carson, she must also be guilty of the bombing."

Assistant State Attorney Michael Patterson conceded that his case was built upon circumstantial evidence, but maintained that it was good evidence nevertheless.

"Use your common sense," he told the jurors. "Trust your common sense."

The bombing, he maintained, was "a cunning, cold, calculated and cruel attempt to collect an easy half-million dollars."

It took the four-woman, two-man jury barely 40 minutes to find the evidence sufficient for a verdict of guilty of attempted first-degree murder.

Judi Buenoano told newsmen she was not surprised by the verdict and that had felt all along that it was impossible for her to receive a fair trial in Milton, close to Pensacola.

"I just don't really feel in this area I have gotten a fair trial in this or the last case," she said. "I don't think I'll ever get a fair trial because of the publicity."

376

"MURDEROUS MISTRESS!"
by Olga Kogan

For a rural Mississippi boy, David McCoy did quite well for himself. Other youths of his generation in the town of Henley Field took a look around, saw that jobs were scarce, and resigned themselves to lives of menial labor, of routine broken only by the sounds of the Sunday gospel choir or the family banter at a holiday meal.

That wasn't enough for David McCoy. He didn't want rags, he wanted riches. And he found them, only not in Henley Field, Mississippi, but in Chicago, Illinois. The trouble was, David found not just riches, but also an early grave, courtesy of three bullets to the head.

Young and restless as he was, the teenage David McCoy realized that the Bible Belt South was not the place for an entrepreneurial type such as he. No, for him, better a big city, and, in segregation-era 1957, better a big Northern city.

With little more than his kit-bag in tow, young David McCoy made his way to the Land of Lincoln. Before long, the Chicago gusts blew him into the hands of a not-so-scrupulous lawyer who gave the kid five bucks for distributing the shyster's card to shaken accident victims. McCoy didn't mind chasing ambulances—he was young and full of energy.

Working for somebody else wasn't McCoy's style,

though. He stuck with the lawyer just long enough to learn everything he could from him. What he learned, in a nutshell, was that it didn't pay to be too honest.

As soon as he could, McCoy took what few dollars he had in his pockets and put it to work, investing in small-time corner businesses. As young as he was, he had a tough-looking mug—and a quick temper, to boot. His business partners quickly learned not to cross him.

As his assets grew, so did McCoy's ambition. He began investing in more prestigious enterprises—restaurants and nightclubs. And since most of his investments were in the city's rough-and-tumble south-side district, he inevitably came into contact with the criminal element there. Exercising prudence, he began going on his business forays accompanied by new partners named Smith & Wesson.

But McCoy needed more than muscle to keep his ever-growing operation thriving. He needed cohorts, the kind of men who would carry out his orders without question. Fortuitously, he had several cronies of the same easy-money ilk as himself. One by one they joined the McCoy gang, and soon, David McCoy found himself, godfatherlike, at the head of a "family" organization.

He also found himself head of a real family. Mrs. McCoy was a looker, and with Mr. McCoy's sex drive no less formidable than his business acumen, the couple soon had five children. In time, they, too, joined the family business.

McCoy was already flying high by 1968, when he had his first brush with death. As are all wealthy men, he was a target of thieves and burglars. One evening at his home, he investigated some suspicious sounds and came up against a gunman sifting through the silverware. The gunman got off a shot before running away.

The slug didn't kill McCoy, but it did some lasting damage—severed nerves that turned McCoy into a paraplegic for life. No amount of money, he discovered, could make him whole again.

Not one to despair, however, McCoy adapted to a handicapped lifestyle with the help of whatever mechanical devices were available. He even outfitted his car with gadgets that enabled him to drive by himself.

Life went on for the successful businessman—a merry-go-round of wheeling and dealing that turned on real estate and banking, light industry, and even a security-guard agency. The world looked like his entrepreneurial oyster.

Then that oyster coughed up a lump of coal instead of a pearl. State agents began investigating insurance companies' complaints that certain claims being filed were bogus. The claims kept coming back to one source. At its center was an operation headed by David McCoy.

It was 1974. McCoy was taken to court. He was tried and found guilty of masterminding the scam. He was ordered to pay a hefty fine and sentenced to five years' supervision by the courts.

The experience sobered the fast-moving businessman, but it didn't slow his pace. He began concentrating on the world of finance, buying a conrolling interest in the Palos Hills State Bank, a suburban bank in the district where many of his other business concerns were located.

With the bank as his foundation, McCoy could afford to indulge his sympathy for other people who were as down and out as he himself had been in his youth. When a poor but sharp kid came along looking for work, McCoy would find him a job. Hard-up businessmen turned to McCoy to get start-up money for their schemes. Many among them looked upon McCoy as their model for success. And McCoy, despite his severe handicap, found that he could do good in the world and still reap a profit.

Among his properties was a club named Sweet Georgia Brown. Here, he liked to relax at the end of the workday, greeting people from his wheelchair as they walked through the foyer. Club regulars knew him for his easy smile and gracious welcome. For a man with so much on his mind, McCoy seemed as though he didn't have a care in the world.

In fact, it wasn't so. Although his financial empire was holding fast, his marital life was reaching the point of make or break. In 1981, it broke. McCoy moved out of the big house in the fashionable south-shore area where he'd lived with his family.

The new love in his life was a slim-hipped 25-year-old model named Sheila. They set up domestic life in a sprawling luxury home in one of suburban Chicago's fancier areas. The sculpted shrubbery outside the house and the huge satellite dish on the roof were the outward trappings of the McCoy wealth. Inside, besides the designer furniture and professionally-ordered decor, a heavy-duty alarm system paid testimony to McCoy's priorities. Having been burned once, he would not permit another trigger-happy punk to mess with his life.

As it turned out, not all the precautions in the world could have saved David McCoy from his ultimate fate.

In 1986, McCoy again found himself on the short end of the stick following a burglary. He and his girlfriend had gone out of town for the weekend. Before leaving, they'd set the interior and exterior burglar alarms, as they habitually did upon departing. When they returned, McCoy routinely turned off the alarm. Everything looked normal until he got to the bedroom.

The safe in one of the closets had been opened. The hard cash inside—more than $60,000—was gone. What was puzzling was the elegance of the robbery: not a scratch was on the safe and nothing but the money was taken. It definitely looked like an inside job.

Authorities interrogated everybody who'd been in the house during the master's absence. One of McCoy's daughters admitted she'd brought some of her friends over at various times "just to visit." She also admitted that one of the visitors—a man—had spent Saturday night at the house.

The overnight visitor turned out to be a prime suspect. Assault and armed robbery were just two of the entries on his rather lengthy rap sheet. Lawmen brought him into headquarters for a chat.

The young man didn't deny being in the house over the weekend, but he flatly rejected any accusations of being in on a robbery. Loudly, he invited the lawmen to give him a lie-detector test so that he could prove his innocence.

The lawmen willingly obliged. The needle on the lie detector held steady during the test questions, but then it began to waver once the questions got into the rougher waters of the robbery itself. Clearly, the suspect was holding back something.

But lie-detector tests are inadmissible in court. In the absence of further evidence, the police had no choice but to set the suspect free.

David McCoy fumed. He was out $60,000 and the culprit had walked.

Still, for somebody with $15 million to his name, McCoy could afford to take a loss now and again. And, though he didn't know it, he had only a couple more years left to enjoy what he still had.

On the afternoon of November 12, 1988, a resident of South Cornell Avenue on the city's south side began to wonder about the black Cadillac illegally parked at the end of an alley near his home. The big sedan stood in just such a way that no other vehicle could get in or out of the alley, which led to the garages in back of the neighborhood homes.

None of the other neighbors recognized the car. The resident, a self-appointed neighborhood watchman, dialed the local police precinct and reported the illegally positioned sedan.

A uniformed officer soon arrived at the scene. The parked Cadillac looked out of place in this lower-class section of town and his first thought was that it might well be a stolen vehicle.

The car itself was a standout. A late-model Coupe de Ville, it looked as though it had just trolled out of the showroom. In fact, the dealer's number was still on the license plate. A mobile phone antenna suggested that the luxury vehicle came with all the extras. But something wasn't right here, the patrol officer figured.

A glance inside the car revealed an extra feature that hadn't come out of any Detroit factory. On the floor of the backseat section lay the limp body of a man. The area around his head was disfigured and dark in color. All the signs indicated that he was dead.

The officer quickly radioed for the Violent Crimes Squad.

A team led by Lieutenant Phil Cline soon arrived to begin the preliminary on-scene investigation. The detectives found the Cadillac's doors locked, but noticed that the keys were still hanging from the ignition. A special police tool quickly had one of the doors unlocked.

A closer look at the dead man confirmed that somebody had taken pot-shots at his head—and from close range. Blood from his wounds had puddled on the car floor. Significantly, more blood stained the front passenger seat. It appeared that the victim had been sitting there first, and then he'd been moved to the back after the shooting.

In contrast to its newly-minted exterior, the interior of the car was a mess. It looked as though somebody had taken a wastebasket and emptied it there. Was this the way the car normally looked, or did it have something to do with the man's death? Sleuths didn't yet venture to speculate. Besides, they were more interested in another object that lay casually on the rear-seat floor.

The small-caliber semiautomatic Beretta pistol they found was a nifty-looking weapon. A check of its chamber revealed that the gun had been fired three times. A check of the dead man's head wounds revealed what looked like an equal number of bullet holes.

One officer noticed the special driving gear hooked to the steering column and the floorboards. It didn't take much deduction to put the name David McCoy to the dead body in the backseat. When you're one of the richest men in Chicago, you don't need a lot of identification cards.

His wallet and I.D. cards were notably missing from the man's person. On the other hand, he was still wearing no less than three diamond baubles on his fingers and a light gold chain around his neck. That a thief would commit murder yet leave such valuables behind seemed rather weird.

Too many questions were cropping up. The crime scene sleuths ordered the vehicle towed to the police garage, where technicians could begin trying to find some answers.

The victim's body was moved to the medical examiner's officer for an autopsy.

The autopsy confirmed that three shots had been fired into the victim's head. Two of the wounds were in the forehead, so close together that at first they appeared to have been made by the one and the same bullet. The other wound was in the side of the victim's head.

The pathologist speculated that the side wound had been inflicted first, causing death. The forehead wounds had then been added for grisly good measure, perhaps to ensure that the victim was really dead, or to satisfy the gunman's penchant for violence.

The technicians checking the death car interior found conclusive proof of what the pathologist had determined — three shell casings from the small-caliber Beretta left on the car floor.

So, who finally got David McCoy? An armed robber? Was it a gangland vendetta hit? Did McCoy have personal enemies capable of killing him? Given McCoy's background, the probers figured that any of those scenarios could fit the picture.

McCoy's immediate relatives were notified of his violent death. The greatest shock at the news seemed to be experienced by his former wife. She had seen him alive and well only 24 hours earlier, when he'd stopped by her house on a routine visit to see the children. If anything, he'd looked jovial. Nothing in his demeanor suggested that he was a man with only a few hours to live. If McCoy was under a cloud of death, he apparently never knew it.

One of the victim's family members shook his head in disbelief when informed of the murder. David, he said, was a man who knew how to take care of himself. Anyone who thought they might take advantage of his paralysis would have come up against a .38-caliber equalizer. McCoy kept the gun in a hip holster. He could draw and fire five shots within as many seconds. It would have taken a brave man to try to get the drop on him.

The investigators had found no gun other than the Beretta at the crime scene. Apparently the killer had brought one gun — the Beretta — and left with another — the .38. A strange exchange, to say the least.

McCoy's girlfriend Sheila confirmed that he'd taken the big-caliber gun with him when he left the house on the day of the murder. Interviewed at the home they shared in a fashionable Chicago suburb, the former model — still slim and sexy and wearing designer clothes — cried upon hearing the news of the death of the man she'd lived with for the past several years.

"Did you know whether Mr. McCoy had any personal enemies?" one detective asked her.

Yes, the woman replied. He'd recently talked about a real estate deal in which the other party had welched on a payment. Some harsh words had been exchanged and McCoy came home fuming. He was still talking about the "rat" on the day of his murder.

There had also been some employee problems, she went on. Some people had been let go rather abruptly, and not always gently. Any one of them might have borne a grudge and acted on it.

It was more or less the same story told by one of the victim's relatives. Other relatives would repeat the gist of the tale during their own police interviews. The circle of investigation quickly widened beyond the victim's immediate family to take in dozens of friends, acquaintances, present business associates, past business associates, company employees, and the many hangers-on who linger in the shadow of any man of wealth and power.

Two days after the murder, a worker in a restaurant near the crime scene was emptying garbage in the industrial bin behind the eatery when he discovered a man's wallet. It contained no cash or credit cards, but an identification card showed that it belonged to David McCoy.

Although the empty wallet suggested robbery, the discovery didn't jibe with the fact that the so-called thief had left behind jewelry on the victim's body. And the three bullets to the victim's head signalled something more than an armed thief out to make a quick snatch.

The papers found scattered inside the death car provided no clue to the murder motive. The Beretta murder weapon, however, offered the faint hint of a trail.

No fingerprints were found on the gun, but its serial number—still present, and undefaced, remarkably—finally turned up in police records following an exhaustive, painstaking search. Detectives were assigned to check out the ownership.

At this point, public rumors about David McCoy's death strongly centered around a mob- or drug-related slaying. But one West Pullman Area officer working the case discounted the rumors. "There is absolutely no evidence to substantiate any of them," he flatly declared to the media.

He wasn't kidding. The ownership of the murder weapon was traced not to any known criminal, but to an elderly man living in a Chicago old folks' home. The trouble was, he said he hadn't laid eyes on the gun for more than two years. Someone had stolen it from him and he'd reported the theft to police. He was a bit irate with the police, too, since at the time of the theft, he'd strongly suspected that one of the home's contract cleaning men was the culprit.

The office of the home had a record of the worker's address, but it was out of date. The cleaning company that employed him provided a current address.

There, two detectives found and confronted the man with the theft allegation, adding gravely that the gun was implicated in a homicide. The suspect caught their drift and began blowing in the same direction. He'd seen the gun while he'd been cleaning the old man's room and slipped it into his pocket. He said it wasn't the gun that he wanted, but the cash he could get for selling it.

After two years, he still remembered the man who'd bought the gun from him. He gave it to the sleuths. With the buyer's name in their notebooks, they thanked the witness and sought out the next owner of the mysterious Beretta.

This man was no more overjoyed to see the lawmen than had been the former witness. In a way, he'd almost been expecting their visit. No one pays $50 for a Beretta that's not hot, and two years ago, that's what he'd paid.

But if the detectives were thinking to nail owner number two for murder, they soon discovered that it wasn't time to take out the handcuffs just yet. This man hadn't seen the gun for a while, either. A couple of months earlier, he'd sold it.

"Do you remember the guy's name who bought it?" one of the detectives asked the somewhat nervous subject.

"It wasn't a guy," the witness said. "It was a woman. Her name's Sheila Daniels."

The name dropped like a bombshell on the detectives' heads. Sheila Daniels was David McCoy's mistress, the woman he'd been sharing his life — and wealth — with for the last several years.

"No doubt about it," the witness maintained. "I'm willing to swear on the Bible that Daniels bought that gun."

The detectives took this information back to headquarters to mull it over. If the mistress was at the center of it all, what was the motive? The sleuths paid return visits to the McCoy family members, this time putting emphasis on the slain man's relationship with the slim-bodied former model.

387

One relative who had not had a chance to have her say earlier now opened up. The "rosy-daisy" days were over between McCoy and Daniels, she said. About a month or so before his murder, McCoy had started talking about ending his live-in relationship with her. He was thinking about asking Daniels to leave the house. And there was one other thing: McCoy was going to change his will to cut out his mistress completely.

Had Daniels stood to gain only a percentage of McCoy's wealth, she still would have come out a rich woman. Without her name in the will, she'd gain nothing. Although Daniels operated a clothing boutique, the prospect of having to work full-time for a living might not have seemed too attractive to her, certainly not after lolling in the lap of luxury for so long.

Lieutenant Phil Cline personally took charge of interviewing Sheila Daniels at home.

A look of surprise crossed the pretty woman's face when the detectives popped the word Beretta for the first time. What, she asked in return, would she be doing with a weapon? David had kept a Smith & Wesson in the house, but beyond that, there were no other firearms.

The detectives then asked Daniels point-blank whether she had ever bought a gun from the witness who'd claimed he had sold a Beretta. Daniels shook her head negatively. With her doe eyes and fashion-model cheekbones, she had a lot going for her in being persuasive, but in this case, it wasn't charm that the detectives were looking for, but straight answers. And Daniels, they figured, was throwing them a curve.

They shifted the interrogation to headquarters. Finding herself removed from the sanctuary of her own home and placed in the strange and impersonal surroundings of the interrogation room, the suspect's defense slowly crumbled. Yes, Sheila Daniels now recalled buying a gun from a fellow about two years earlier. She hadn't want to say anything about it because someone had stolen the weapon from her a month or two before.

"Why didn't you report the theft?" one of the detectives asked.

Sheila suspected it was taken by one of her relatives, she replied, and she didn't want to get him into trouble. Reluctantly, she now gave his name.

Detectives brought her relative in for questioning. Although the finger of guilt was strongly pointing in his direction, he wouldn't waver. He never stole a gun. He never committed murder. A lie-detector test backed up his story.

So detectives returned to Sheila Daniels. This time, with her permission, they subjected her to a lie-detector test, as well. When it was over, they knew they had their woman.

Daniels admitted that she'd sent the lawmen looking for the wrong person. The real gun thief, she said, was her brother, Tyrone. Still skeptical, but eager to follow up the new lead, the detectives picked up 20-year-old Tyrone Daniels and brought him in for interrogation. He was accompanied by his live-in girlfriend, who became a valuable witness in her own right.

That week, the girlfriend said, she and Tyrone had gone on a surprise spending spree. Just about anything she'd wanted—dresses, shoes, jewelry—he bought for her. It was unheard-of extravagance for them, but he kept telling her not to worry—he had plenty more cash to spend.

"Where'd you get all the money?" the detectives asked Tyrone Daniels. It was almost a rhetorical question.

The jig was up, and Tyrone Daniels was now very well aware of it.

As he described it, he'd gone to see his sister at David McCoy's home on the day of the murder. Sheila and David got into an argument—not their first—and Sheila became angered to the point of fury. They kept arguing even as David went into the garage to get his car.

Tyrone said that David had just positioned himself on the front seat when Sheila pulled out the Beretta and fired a shot into David's head. The slug sealed their romance forever.

Sheila immediately called her brother for help in depositing the body in the backseat. As they were doing this, David appeared to move—he was apparently still alive—so Tyrone himself took the gun and fired off a couple more shots.

Now, Tyrone told the probers, he began thinking about the best way to cover up their crime. He figured that the simplest solution was to stage a mock robbery, so he took the victim's wallet and the gun from his hip holster. David habitually carried a lot of cash on his person, so the blood money was considerable.

With Tyrone at the Cadillac's wheel and sister Sheila trailing behind in her own car, the couple drove to a spot they thought was as good as any and abandoned the vehicle and its grim cargo. In his haste, Tyrone left the keys in the ignition when he got out of the car, and he slammed the door shut, unintentionally locking it. It was only at that point that the couple realized the Beretta was still inside the car—the only solid link between them and the murder.

But it was too late. They couldn't risk jimmying the door because someone might see them.

In September 1990, Sheila Daniels went on trial for the murder of David McCoy in the court of Judge Michael Toomin. The prosecutors declared that they would seek the maximum prison sentence—100 years.

After a four-day trial, the defendant was found guilty of murder in the first degree. The judge described the crime as a "cold-blooded execution." On October 10, 1990, Sheila Daniels was sentenced to 80 years in prison.

On the same day, her brother, Tyrone Daniels, also went on trial. He, too, was found guilty of first-degree murder. He drew a sentence of 60 years. In addition, he got a 20-year sentence for armed robbery and a 5-year term for concealing a homicide. Both brother and sister are now behind bars.

"NAKED CAME
THE SLASHER!"
by Bud Ampolsk

Even among the affluent communities that dot Suffolk
County, Long Island's storied coastline, Belle Terre is considered something special. It is a place of exquisite natural
beauty and storybook opulence. Here, along its gracefully
curving Seaside Drive, almost hidden by the deep woods
surrounding them, stand estates comprising acres of some
of the most prized real estate to be found in the northeast.
Prices for such properties are estimated to begin at the one
million mark and go up from there. Included in the fee is a
breathtaking view of the waters of Long Island Sound
which run below the bluff.

Total population of Belle Terre is placed at approximately 800. As might be expected, crime has never been a
problem here. Evidence of this may be seen in the fact that
the position of town police commissioner is an honorary
one, filled by a leading private citizen rather than by a
hard-bitten professional criminologist.

That's why 911 calls are the exception rather than the
rule in Belle Terre. In most cases, such communications are
for "aided" situations such as cardiac arrests and road acci-
dents.

And that's why there was a feeling of consternation on
the part of the dispatcher who fielded the 911 telephone

391

call that came into police headquarters at 6:14 A.M. on the late-summer morning of Wednesday, September 7, 1988.

The caller was a young man, obviously on the brink of hysteria. He gasped out a bizarre tale of having awakened at 5:30 A.M. to discover his adoptive mother dead on the floor of her bedroom and his adoptive father slumped in a chair in a den on the other side of the house. According to the youth, the father had been severely bludgeoned and stabbed and was unconscious but still breathing.

Desperately, the teenager asked the dispatcher for first aid instructions to use while awaiting the arrival of the first crime scene officers. He was advised to lower his father's head to ease the circulatory problems which had been induced by trauma.

The din caused by sirens from Suffolk County police and advance life support vehicles racing through the gentle curves of Seaside Drive brought out a knot of close-by neighbors. They stood wide-eyed and unbelieving as they watched county homicide officers moving in and out of Seymour and Arlene Tankleff's sprawling waterfront ranch-style home. It was beyond their framework of comprehension that something violent and deadly had invaded their privileged sanctuary, much less that it had claimed Seymour Tankleff and his devoted 54-year-old wife.

Yet there was no denying what they saw. Sixty-two-year-old Seymour Tankleff was even now being placed in an ambulance for the rush journey to Mather Memorial Hospital in Port Jefferson. The semiretired real estate and insurance executive would later be transferred to University Hospital in Stony Brook, where delicate brain surgery would be undertaken in a vain attempt to save his life.

If seeing Arlene Tankleff's covered corpse being carried from the Tankleff's sumptuous home on its way to the county medical examiner's office was a nightmare for onlookers, it was a waking nightmare.

Their feelings would be best expressed by a neighbor who had known the Tankleff family for 16 years. Said the man,

"I'm totally shocked. When I walked out this morning and saw all the police cars out there, I mean, I can't believe it."

The feelings of a second neighbor of the Tankleff family expanded on this theme. He commented, "You always have a tendency to think that when you live in an area like this, you're immune to this sort of thing, but you're really not."

Meanwhile, inside the death house, Suffolk County homicide detectives under the command of Detective Lieutenant John McElhone, commander of the Suffolk County Homicide Squad, were busily sorting out the details of what they had discovered thus far.

The body of Arlene Tankleff, dressed in her nightclothes, had been found on the floor of her bedroom. Her son, Martin Tankleff, claimed he had made the grisly discovery when he had awakened at 5:30 A.M. to dress himself in preparation for attending his first full day of classes at Port Jefferson High School.

Martin Tankleff claimed that he had then gone to his father's den where his 62-year-old father was unconscious and bleeding profusely.

The elder Tankleff had still been fully dressed, evidently having remained awake following a late-hour card game with close friends. The game had broken up some time around 3:00 A.M.

Each parent had been bludgeoned and their throats had been cut.

During the police interview, Martin Tankleff said that he himself had gone to bed at 11:00 P.M. on Tuesday, September 6th, and had not arisen until it was time to get ready for school.

As the interview went forward and more crime scene evidence was collected and tagged, Martin Tankleff agreed to accompany the Suffolk County homicide detectives to headquarters. There, he was questioned until noon. At that time the teenager was booked on charges of murder of his adoptive mother and attempted murder of his adoptive father.

In a cryptic statement concerning the arrest, Lieutenant McElhone said that no motive had been discovered as yet. But the commander of the homicide squad reported that Martin Tankleff had made a statement to police in which the young man allegedly had admitted both crimes.

Said McElhone, "Evidence found at the scene forced him (Martin) to admit the crime." The detective declined to reveal what that evidence was.

The announcement of Martin Tankleff's arrest left the tiny hamlet of Belle Terre thunderstruck. People talked in hushed whispers about what had transpired. They reported that Seymour Tankleff was a multimillionaire. Four years earlier, he had sold his lucrative real estate and insurance business because of ill health. Since then, he had invested in a number of lucrative enterprises.

In addition to his business activities, Seymour Tankleff had given liberally of himself to his community. He had served in various civic posts, including the unpaid post of police commissioner and an earlier one of building commissioner. Both Seymour and Arlene had been active in the Belle Terre Civic Association.

Said one of the town constables who had served under Tankleff, "Seymour was very well respected. He has been police commissioner for four years and all the men liked him."

A close neighbor noted, "I've known them (the Tankleff family) to be nice, quiet and active in the community."

Adults who had watched Martin Tankleff grow into adolescence were equally high in their praise for the accused youth. One woman said she was "floored by the news of the stabbings." She recalled that as a youngster, Marty had played with the children in her house.

The neighbor added, "He's a real nice boy."

Close associates of the gravely wounded elder Tankleff revealed that they had never seen any signs of friction in the Tankleff family. One who had attended the Tuesday evening card game commented, "The family was extremely close. Seymour treated his son like a prince, giving him everything he asked for and some things he didn't even ask for."

A village official recalled having seen Martin earlier in the evening of the card game and had noticed nothing amiss. "We chatted for a moment and he seemed fine," the man reported. He also described Martin as a quiet, well-built boy who did well in school.

Sergeant Robert Doyle of the Suffolk County Homicide Squad said Martin's quick action in applying first aid to his stricken father might have been responsible for having saved the elderly man's life. Added the detective, "The fact that Seymour is still alive is miraculous with the extent of his injuries."

However, Sergeant Doyle questioned why Martin had made the attempt. "Maybe he was trying to cover his tracks," the police officer speculated.

At this point in the probe, police spokesmen limited their theories on the motive behind the murder and the attempted murder to "family frictions" but refused to spell out what troubles had beset the Tankleffs.

However, on the day following the bloodshed on Seaside Drive, additional details were made known by county prosecutors as Martin Tankleff appeared in Suffolk District Court before Judge Edward Green.

As the teenager stood, clad in a prison jumpsuit and barefoot, his wrists manacled, at his arraignment on murder and attempted murder charges, Assistant Suffolk County District Attorney Edward Jablonski said of the crimes, "It was a temper tantrum that turned into violence. He's (Martin) a boy that had everything in life and thought he deserved more."

During the tense arraignment proceedings, Jablonski told a hushed courtroom that Martin Tankleff had planned the attacks carefully to the point that he "purposely was naked when he committed the crime so that he wouldn't get blood on his clothing."

395

Jablonski described how the youth had washed the knife and a barbell used during the assault. "He left the knife on the kitchen table next to a watermelon so that police wouldn't suspect that it was the murder weapon," Jablonski charged.

The prosecutor told Judge Green, "Martin Tankleff was an intelligent person . . . and he committed the crimes for a number of reasons. He was angry at his parents." The assistant district attorney did not elaborate on this line of reasoning while in the courtroom.

However, in an interview which followed the court proceedings, Jablonski stated that Martin Tankleff was angry because they (the teenager's adoptive parents) spoiled his summer, restricted his use of the family's Boston Whaler . . . and made him drive to school in a 1978 Lincoln rather than in a newer automobile owned by the family."

According to the prosecutor, the boy's rage was compounded by the fact that the older Tankleffs had planned a vacation trip that did not include him and had decided to have some adult stay with him during their absence. "He (Martin) thought he could stay by himself," Jablonski declared.

According to the Suffolk lawman, Seymour Tankleff had become angry with Martin on Tuesday evening (the night before the attacks) because the youth had failed to set up a card table for the poker game, and had instead taken off for a shopping mall.

For his part, noted attorney Robert Gottlieb, who had been retained to represent Martin Tankleff, argued that the prosecution did not have a strong case against his client. "There is a great deal more to this case before this issue is finally solved," he told the court. The defense counsel also pleaded with the court to allow the suspect to attend Arlene Tankleff's funeral which was to be held on Friday, September 9th.

Judge Green denied the request and held Martin Tankleff without bail. In so doing, the judge noted the "serious nature of the crime."

Prosecutor Jablonski reported that at first Martin Tankleff had denied his guilt but the suspect had later confessed, telling Suffolk County detectives, "I did it."

The Tankleff case took an unexpected and bizarre twist on Wednesday, September 14th, when a close relative of a 48-year-old business associate of the gravely injured Seymour Tankleff reported the associate missing. The man had attended the September 6th poker game on Seaside Drive. According to police, the man had reportedly received death threats during the period between the assaults and his disappearance.

Several hours after the associate had last been seen at noon on September 14th, his car had been found in a hotel parking lot at Hauppauge, Long Island. When discovered, the vehicle's door was open and the engine was still running.

Despite the timing of the man's disappearance, Lieutenant John McElhone, who was still in charge of the Tankleff case, said, "There is no indication of a connection."

Prosecutors insisted that there was no doubt concerning the guilt of Martin Tankleff. However, Tankleff's lawyer said he would go before the court to seek Tankleff's release. The suspect was still being held without bail.

In a statement covering the case's latest developments, Assistant D.A. Jablonski stated, "The man (who had disappeared) had been receiving death threats since the homicide. The (Tankleff) family and even the defendant had indicated in the beginning that . . . he may have been involved in the death and attempted murder of the Tankleffs."

Continued the prosecutor, "Whether his (the missing man's) leaving or being a missing person as is filed right now has anything to do with this case is too early to tell with any confidence."

Jablonski pointed out that the prosecutors had a strong case against Martin Tankleff. This included the presence of blood on his bare shoulder on the morning of the attacks and his confession to the police.

But Defense Attorney Gottlieb countered with the argument that there was an explanation for the blood and that Martin Tankleff had not confessed. Saying that the mysterious disappearance of the Tankleff business associate should raise new doubts about Martin Tankleff's complicity, Gottlieb stated, "This jumps out at you. The facts are that there are outstanding and dangling questions. The flags and sirens should be blaring here."

Supreme Court Justice James A. Gowan, having heard the arguments, now set Tankleff's bail at $500,000 cash or a bond of one million.

In a news conference concerning the missing man, Lieutenant Steve Seidel, commander of the Suffolk County Missing Persons Squad, revealed that the missing man had not been seen since 10:00 A.M., September 14th. He had spent the previous night with a woman relative at her home. The next morning he had gone to his attorney's office "where he appeared upset."

For his part, Prosecutor Jablonski was holding firm to the accusation against Martin Tankleff. He noted that this was the first time he had gone public with the item of blood on the younger Tankleff's naked shoulder.

Said the prosecutor, "This will confirm the fact that he was not wearing any clothes when the crime was committed."

In the 10 days which followed the revelation about the missing business associate, Suffolk authorities went all out to trace the man. He was finally located at a motel in Redondo Beach, California, where he was interviewed by A.D.A. Jablonski.

After the Wednesday, September 28th meeting between Jablonski and the man, the prosecutor's office reported, "He said he had two million dollars in life insurance which he thought would go to his girlfriend and children."

Declared John Williams of the Suffolk County D.A.'s

Office, "He (the businessman) said they'd be better off with the money and without him in their lives."

Williams described the man as appearing confused.

"He said the bludgeoning had been the last straw in a series of misfortunes which had included his wife's death," Williams said.

The prosecutor's office noted that the man intended to return to Long Island voluntarily.

"He's just a missing person," said Detective Sergeant Doyle, who, with Detective McCready and A.D.A. Jablonski, was in California to interview the man. "He's not wanted for any crime," said Doyle.

Defense Attorney Gottlieb rejected that contention, claiming, "It's clear that they were concerned enough about (the man) and his disappearance that they sent the chief of the homicide bureau out there to question him. Obviously they see the connection. That's why they rushed out there."

According to those close to both Tankleff and the associate, the pair had met at a community center about 10 years earlier. They had shared an interest in several retail bakeries and had been co-owners of two racehorses.

According to Sergeant Doyle, while Seymour Tankleff had held a $500,000 life insurance policy on the man, the man had not been the beneficiary of any such policy on Seymour Tankleff. Doyle also noted that the man had not been in any serious financial straits at the time of his disappearance.

On Friday, October 7th, Seymour Tankleff died of his injuries without ever having regained consciousness.

Despite this, having received the financial backing of family members who had posted bond for him, Martin Tankleff was now free on the high bail set by the court. He left his Suffolk County jail cell at Riverhead, Long Island on Tuesday, October 11th.

Reading a prepared statement to a mob of reporters who were on hand for his release, Martin Tankleff said, "I would like to thank all the people who are behind me. If it wasn't for these people, I wouldn't be as strong. My life will never be the same. Someone has taken my parents away from me in a brutal manner . . . I can't wait until all the truth comes out."

On the same day, the slightly built teenager stood at his adoptive father's oak coffin, choking back tears, as he attended a 20-minute service held at a funeral home in Dix Hills, Long Island. The teenager was comforted by family members and friends. Burial was held at Pine Lawn Memorial Park.

Now there was a new development in the unfolding story. This concerned Martin Tankleff's schooling. Despite the fact that he was now out on bail, the teenager would not be returning to his classes at Port Jefferson High School. Officials of the high school had barred Martin's re-entry because of allegations that he had had a knife encounter with another student there on May 26th of the same year.

On this point, A.D.A. Jablonski said he had met with faculty members and they "informed us if he (Martin Tankleff) chose to come back, they will not permit it, because of the knifing incident last spring . . . coupled with the charges against him."

A police source said that in the May 26th incident, Tankleff had allegedly pulled a switchblade knife on a schoolmate and had said, "I ought to kill you." It was said that Tankleff was angry because the other boy had begun to date a girl Tankleff had taken to the junior prom.

The police had not been called at the time. Tankleff had not been disciplined, other than to have the knife taken away from him and his father called, the police sources revealed. School officials refused to confirm or deny these reports.

However, an attorney representing the other youth said that such an incident had occurred in the spring of 1988 and that his client had been questioned about it by police as late as Tuesday, October 11th. The lawyer added, "My client was not threatened by him (Tankleff) and they felt it was a joke and that essentially it is."

Gottlieb argued that until recently the episode had been considered a joke by all parties involved. "The fact that officials have begun taking the incident seriously does Marty Tankleff a disservice," Gottlieb said. "Let them deal with this case and not throw in a lot of phony smokescreens."

As the teenager's relatives now posted a $25,000 reward for information leading to the arrest and conviction of a suspect in the double Tankleff slayings, the prosecution and defense continued to hurl charges at each other.

The family members, in posting the reward notice, stated, "We are posting this reward simply to encourage anyone who has information to come forward and tell what happened. The family is convinced of Marty's innocence. He would not do such a thing."

On the point of possible new evidence, Defense Attorney Gottlieb said he believed the authorities would uncover additional information about the killings that would prove Martin Tankleff had not murdered his adoptive mother and father. He pointed out that none of the hairs found near Arlene Tankleff's body or in her hands belonged to Martin.

This brought a quick rejoinder from Jablonski. He noted that prosecutors had never made any allegations that hairs found in Arlene's hands belonged to her son. On the other hand, Jablonski charged that a tissue used by Martin did contain samples of his mother's blood.

Thus did things stand until Monday, April 23, 1990. It was on that date that the double-murder trial of Martin Tankleff, now 18, got under way before a Suffolk County jury.

In his opening statement to the court, Prosecutor John Collins, who would be the attorney of record for the state, charged that Tankleff had confessed to the September 1988 knifing of Seymour and Arlene Tankleff in their posh Belle Terre home.

"He beat his parents about the head and sliced their throats as if they were pieces of meat," Collins charged.

Outlining the prosecution case, Collins noted that Tankleff had told Suffolk County Detective James McCready that his parents refused to let him drive their new Lincoln to high school.

"They made me drive in a crummy old Lincoln and I wanted something more sporty," the prosecutor quoted Tankleff as having said to the detective.

"I hit my mother with a dumbbell and cut her throat. She fought me. I sneaked up on my father and hit him with the dumbbell.

"He said, 'Marty, why are you doing this?' I didn't reply. I knocked him silly."

Collins said he would produce testimony that would show that Martin Tankleff had talked about his inheritance and his parents' demise prior to the murders.

Continuing his presentation, Collins charged that young Tankleff had removed all of his own clothing before carrying out the attacks. He had also worn gloves to conceal his fingerprints. Once the attacks had been carried out, according to the prosecutor, the teenager had called 911 and told police that he thought a business partner of his father had committed the double attack.

However, the alibi had fallen apart, Collins noted, when Detective McCready had tricked the suspect into confessing by pretending to receive a telephone call from the hospital saying that Seymour Tankleff had regained consciousness and had accused his son of having killed his mother and assaulted his father.

Defense Attorney Gottlieb stuck to one main point. He continued to attempt to implicate the former Tankleff business associate.

Among the first prosecution witnesses were several teenage girls who knew Martin Tankleff. They testified that he frequently told them how he would be a millionaire if his parents died.

Three law enforcement men took the stand, along with an ambulance driver and a neighbor. Each recounted how the first thing they had been told by Martin when they arrived at the crime scene was that the business associate had killed the elder Tankleffs.

A young woman told of seeing Martin as she drove by his house on the morning of the lethal attacks. The young man was standing by a squad car and the girl asked him what had happened. He blurted out the answer, she said, quoting, "Last night, someone murdered my mother and tried to murder my father and molested me." Martin Tankleff then began to babble and seemed to be in shock, the witness recalled.

A male friend of Tankleff's told the jury how during the summer of 1988, the two had worked at a bagel shop. It was then that Tankleff had told the boy that "if his (Tankleff's) parents weren't around, he could do anything he wanted." The teenager said that the defendant was unhappy that his parents forced him to drive their 1978 old blue Lincoln automobile.

"I remember him saying that it wasn't attractive to girls," the youth noted.

An adult witness who had attended the Tuesday evening poker game reported he had seen the Tankleff associate at the card game and had seen no evidence of any kind of friction between Seymour Tankleff and the man. He said the pair had been having a private conversation as he was leaving the Tankleff home at 3:00 A.M.

A high point of the trial was the testimony of Susan Ryan, a hair and fiber expert for the Suffolk County Criminalistics Laboratory. The forensic expert testified that the dumbbells discovered in Martin Tankleff's bedroom, one of which he allegedly had used to bash in his parents' heads, contained a number of cotton and synthetic fibers.

This took on significance because of the prosecution theory that following the lethal attacks, the teenager had jumped into the shower and washed their blood off the dumbbell, as well as the knife he was accused of using to cut their throats.

Ryan said she had spent 37 days testing the hair and fibers found at the scene. Under cross-examination, she testified she had found violet wool fibers on one of two dumbbells found in Martin Tankleff's bedroom and red, blue and light tan cotton fibers and light tan synthetic fibers on the other dumbbell. She said the fibers had not come from a washcloth found on the floor near the dumbbells or the light tan sweatshirt Martin Tankleff was wearing when he was arrested.

In an all-out attempt to impeach the testimony of the former business associate of the dead Seymour Tankleff, Defense Attorney Gottlieb subjected the witness to a grueling and often contentious three-day cross-examination. Over and over again, the lawyer hit away at why the man fled to the West Coast after the assaults on Seymour and Arlene Tankleff.

Finally the enraged witness snapped back, "I staged a scenario because I did not want to go through what I'm going through here: three days on the witness stand and I didn't do a thing and it's not fair. It's not fair that I'm put through this when Marty Tankleff sitting over three is accused of this and I am not, and I'm sitting here for three days baring my soul to the world and it's not fair.

"And nobody cares, okay? And I'm here. And things are out there. Everybody knows everything about my life."

However, it would be a much more subdued cross-examination which would prove pivotal to the jury. This came when the defendant himself took the stand and steadfastly denied that he had murdered his parents.

The teenager testified that he had been confused and in a state where police could coerce him into confessing to a crime which he did not commit.

Describing his version of what had occurred on the morning of September 7, 1988, young Tankleff said, "I loved my parents. I had absolutely nothing to do with (killing them)."

He went on to describe how he had first found his father

in the den, slumped in a chair.

"I said, 'Dad, dad, dad,' then I called 911," Tankleff testified. He said he found his mother dead in the bedroom. When he was pressed to describe the knife wounds, he answered, "They were similar."

Explaining his confession, the teenager said he made a statement after Detective McCready "said he just got off the phone with a detective in the hospital and my father said I had done the stabbing.

"I couldn't understand why my father should say that. He had never lied to me. I started to believe that I had done it. I thought I was having a bad nightmare and would soon awake.

"I finally said, 'Yes,' (I had done the killings) because that's what they (the police) wanted to hear."

There were those who wondered why the teenager had taken the stand. The answer was given by Defense Attorney Gottlieb at an outside-the-courthouse news conference. He said, "So the jury can hear all the facts."

Tankleff's demeanor on the stand was unemotional and reminiscent of what it had been when police had arrived at the Tankleff home on September 7, 1988. It had been that same calm and controlled facade which had first led detectives to suspect him.

On Thursday, June 12, 1990, some nine weeks after the Tankleff trial had gotten under way, the jury retired behind locked doors to consider the extensive testimony and exhibits which had been paraded before them.

At first, the defense took an optimistic stance. Gottlieb reported that his client was confident of acquittal. But as the hours and days rolled by, the strain began to tell. Although there was no way of knowing what the final outcome would be, there were a few straws in the wind. The first came when an alternate juror, who had been excused by the court once jury deliberations started, reported that she would have found Martin Tankleff guilty of murdering both his father and mother.

The requests made by the jury also were of interest. Among notes passed from the jury foreman to Supreme Court Justice Alfred Tisch, the trial judge, were those which asked for such items as:

— Several readbacks of Martin Tankleff's testimony.

— Readbacks of the testimony of arresting officers.

— A request to visit the crime scene. This was turned down by Judge Tisch. However, he did provide crime scene photographs for the jurors to study.

— Several spellouts of the definition of the second-degree murder charges against Tankleff.

— An examination of a sponge which the prosecution charged had been cut when it was used to clean the blood off the blade of the murder knife.

In all, eight days would go by as the jury continued their deliberations. It marked the third longest time a Suffolk County jury had ever taken to reach a verdict.

Finally, on Thursday afternoon, June 28, 1990, word went out. There was a scurrying to reach Judge Tisch's courtroom. The jury had finally come to a decision. In a moment or two the nearly two-year wait would be over.

Every eye was on the jury foreman as he prepared to answer the first question of the court officer.

"On the count of murder in the second degree of Arlene Tankleff due to intentional murder, how do you find?"

"Not guilty," came the answer.

The finding caused a momentary uproar. Tankleff relatives stood and cheered. Some wept openly. But the relief would not last. There were two more counts of murder two to be heard.

"On murder in the second degree of Arlene Tankleff due to depraved indifference?"

"Guilty."

"On intentional murder in the second degree of Seymour Tankleff?"

"Guilty."

Now the court was filled with the anguished sobs of Martin Tankleff. He sat, head covered by his hands, body shaking, his cries mixing with those of his relatives.

What the verdict meant was that Martin Tankleff now stood convicted of having killed both his mother and father. Since there is no difference in the sentence meted out for murder due to depraved indifference and to intentional murder, the teenager now faced sentences of 25 years to life in each homicide.

What's more, should Judge Tisch follow the prosecutor's demands for a maximum sentence, the 18-year-old could be faced with consecutive terms adding up to 50 years to life.

Even as Martin Tankleff was being handcuffed and led from the courtroom, interest mounted as to how the guilty verdict had come about.

Only 3 of the 12 jurors agreed to talk to reporters. Without giving any specifics, they held that the evidence against the defendant had been overwhelming.

One of the jurors elaborated on this point. He said the jury had been troubled by inconsistencies in Tankleff's story. Also, they didn't believe the youth would confess – as the defense had contended – to something he didn't do.

Said the juror, "Normal people don't crack for something they didn't do. The real Mary didn't do it, like he said. The real Marty was somewhere else. The kid snapped."

Defense Attorney Gottlieb called the verdict "inconsistent" and said he would appeal immediately.

For his part, A.D.A. Collins said he was not surprised by the jury's split on the "depraved indifference" and "intentional murder" findings. Collins suggested that the jury "may well have felt that the situation with Arlene Tankleff occurred first and it had somehow gotten out of hand, and then after having the situation occurred with his mother, he then went on to intentionally kill his father."

The prosecutor held that Tankleff's testimony might have proved the key to the state's case. Taking the stand,

Tankleff had told the jury, "I loved my parents. I had nothing to do with this." But most of his testimony was unemotional and he gave what sounded like rehearsed answers to his attorney's questions.

To make his point, Collins referred to the way the teenager had collapsed sobbing into his seat following the reading of the jury's entire verdict.

"He cried," declared the A.D.A. "That was the first time he did that during this whole affair."

Martin Tankleff was due back in court on August 28th, at which time he would be sentenced by Judge Tisch.

"MASTER FORGER WAS A CON MAN KILLER"

by Jerry D. Spangler

There's a small document on display at the Library of Congress in Washington, D.C. It may not seem like much to the average person, but American historians at one time proudly touted it as the oldest printed document in America. The document, called "Oath of a Freeman," was a pledge of allegiance required of all pilgrim settlers in this country in the early seventeenth century.

For the last couple of years, the document has been up for sale for $1.5 million. It passed a battery of tests to prove its authenticity. The only problem with the document is that most experts are now convinced it is an elaborate forgery. It's also a key element in two bombing deaths in Salt Lake City.

Every morning, James Martini arrived at the Judge Building in Salt Lake City between 6:40 and 6:45 A.M. He was rarely late for work, and October 15, 1985, was no exception. It was about 6:40 A.M. when Martini, who operated a jewelry shop in the building with his father, arrived for work as usual. Only on this day Martini decided to wait in the lobby for his father to arrive.

Moments later, a rather ordinary-looking man entered the building and pushed the button for the elevator. About 20 to 30 seconds later, Martini's father entered the building and together all three men got onto the elevator. Martini noticed the man was carrying a box addressed to Steven F. Christensen, a 31-year-old financial consultant with offices on the sixth floor. Martini thought it odd that the man exited the elevator on the fifth floor, but thought nothing more of it at the time.

At about 8:10 A.M., Steven Christensen arrived for work and picked up a package left outside his door. Seconds later, a booby-trapped shrapnel bomb tucked inside the box exploded, shredding Christensen's chest and sending more than 150 pieces of metal ripping through walls and ceilings on the sixth floor.

Christensen's death stirred a stormy controversy in Salt Lake City and James Martini's testimony was to become a key, but controversial, element in the most puzzling homicide case in the state's history. When it was through, homicide investigators had solved much more than a bizarre bombing death. they had cracked what many believed was the most extensive forgery scheme in modern American history. The scheme involved hundreds of historical documents sold over a six-year period for hundreds of thousands of dollars.

Homicide investigators, led by Detectives Ken Farnsworth and Jim Bell, were on the scene of the killing at the Judge Building within minutes of the first report. They sealed off the entire building to scores of horrified witnesses and curious bystanders.

Hundreds of people had been working in the building at the time of the explosion, and detectives began the painstaking process of questioning each of them. Martini, one of the first questioned, told police about the man on the elevator and the package he had been carrying. Martini described the man as 5 feet 8 inches tall, age 30 to 35, with neatly combed dark brown hair. The man, a Caucasian, weighed about 185 pounds and had a distinct five o'clock shadow. It was hard to tell in the poor lighting of the lobby, but he may also have had a slight mustache, Martini added.

Unfortunately for police, that description could fit thousands of men in Salt Lake City. Even a composite drawing proved to be of little help. It was too nondescript. There was one thing about the description that might be helpful, though. Martini said the man was wearing a green letter jacket with brown sleeves, the kind high school kids wear.

James Martini was not the only one who had seen something unusual that morning. Meg Stewart, who had an office directly across the hall from Steven Christensen, had also noticed something very strange. Arriving for work about 6:50 A.M., she stepped off the elevator onto the sixth floor and noticed a man standing toward the end of a dead-end hallway.

"To see someone on that floor at that time of the morning was very alarming," she told police. "He was definitely not maintenance. The person on the floor definitely did not belong there."

As Stewart approached her office, she noticed a cardboard box had been left in front of Christensen's doorway. That was unusual because maintenance people usually worked at night and would have picked up the package and moved it into the office when they cleaned. This package had been left sometime that morning, which was unusual considering the early hour.

Stewart and Christensen had a practice of accepting and holding packages for each other when either was out of the office. She bent over to pick up the package and noticed it appeared personal. It had no postage or official markings. It was addressed in black felt marker simply, "To Steve Christensen." She reached to pick it up, but changed her mind. As she looked up, she saw the same strange man watching her intently from a stairwell. She quickly entered her office and locked the door.

Unfortunately, Meg Stewart could not provide a detailed description of the strange man, nor could she tell police what he was wearing. Her only description was that he was rather ordinary-looking and had "small eyes and chubby cheeks."

Stewart was getting ready to leave her office shortly after 8:00 A.M. when she heard a deafening explosion. "Parts of the wall came in," she explained, noting plaster fell on her right leg, causing a puncture wound. "I crouched down. I didn't know what was going on."

The woman then heard a strange high-pitched crying sound, "like a little child dying." She left her office and went into the hallway where she found Christensen. He was alive, but barely. His chest was bloody, his breathing shallow. He died moments later, from a piece of metal embedded in his brain.

Police questioned scores of building tenants, but could find no others who had seen the strange man carrying the package.

Bombings are extremely rare in Salt Lake City and only one officer had any real experience in bomb construction or investigation. It had been more than two decades since anyone had been killed by such a device. Salt Lake officers decided to call in experts to help. Within an hour of the explosion, agents from the Bureau of Alcohol, Tobacco and Firearms (ATF) were on the scene. Agents spent most of the next two days gathering thousands of bomb fragments and pieces of shrapnel.

While city and federal investigators were still in the early stages of their investigation, Kathleen Webb Sheets, 50, returned home from a morning walk about 9:30 A.M. and found a cardboard box sitting in the driveway by her garage. It was addressed to her husband. As she cradled it in her left arm, a bomb inside exploded, killing Kathleen instantly. Bits of steel were blown through the home and were found in the kitchen. The garage roof collapsed, burying the victim under plywood, said Salt Lake County Detective Jerry Thompson. Because of the secluded nature of her home, it was two hours before anyone discovered the morbid scene.

While the homicide investigations were still in their very

412

preliminary stages, detectives determined it was extremely unlikely that two fatal bombings on the same morning would be unrelated. Salt Lake City police, Salt Lake County sheriff's deputies and federal investigators from both the FBI and ATF formed a special task force to investigate the killings.

ATF Special Agent Jerry A. Taylor began assembling pieces of evidence recovered from the bombing scenes. There were a number of similarities between the two bombs: Both were pipe bombs with rather common components, but used C-cell battery packs as an ignition source, both used mercury switches as a timing device and both used the same kind of smokeless gunpowder. Unlike the bomb that killed Steven Christensen, the bomb that killed Kathleen Sheets had no shrapnel attached to it. The killer had taped row upon row of concrete nails to the pipe bomb that killed Christensen.

It was Taylor's opinion that both bombs were made by the same person. "These bombs are the unique work of a serial bomber, made with identical components," the agent said, adding they were not the work of a professional killer. "A bomb such as this was never used in any organized crime activity I know of. Organized crime hits are usually five or six sticks of dynamite. It's much more of a sure thing."

The Sheets homicide gave investigators their first real indication of motive. Probers were confident the bomb that killed Mrs. Sheets was intended for her husband, the owner of a large and financially troubled investment firm. The company, CFS Financial, had lost millions of dollars in recent months and was on the verge of bankruptcy. Many people, some rumored to have connections with organized crime, had lost small fortunes.

The organized crime angle certainly had believers early in the investigation. "The way the bomb was made, the way it was handled and detonated, the individual who put it together had to be a professional," said Sheriff Pete Hayward

413

at the time. "And when you have that type of money flowing back and forth, there's always a possibility of organized crime."

CFS's business problems were a logical place to begin the investigation. Not only was Kathleen's husband the owner of the firm, but Steven Christensen had at one time been a vice president of the company. With CFS failing financially, Christensen had left the company a few months before the bombings to start his own financial consulting firm. It was possible, probers theorized, that someone somewhere held Christensen and Kathleen's husband responsible for a bad investment.

Just as police were gearing their entire investigation toward the probability that a disgruntled investor had killed Christensen and Sheets, a third bombing occurred — one that would change the entire direction of the investigation and lead police into a maze of forgeries, frauds and million-dollar deceptions.

It was about 2:00 P.M. October 16th, when Mark W. Hofmann, 30, a nationally renowned dealer in rare historical documents, was blown up by a pipe bomb left in his parked sports car. Only this time the victim wasn't dead.

According to Salt Lake Police Officer James Bryant, who interviewed Hofmann as he lay on a hospital gurney, the documents expert had just entered his car when "something, he didn't know what, started to fall" from the car seat. As Hofmann reached for the package, it exploded, blasting Hofmann into the middle of the street, severing body parts and ripping open his chest.

During a second interview, Hofmann told Bryant a brown pickup had been following him earlier that day. The pickup was damaged on the right front end. He couldn't remember the exact license number, but he said it had a T, a W and two 3s in it. He also pleaded with the officer to warn two friends "to get out of town," because the killer might target them too.

Detective Jim Bell also interviewed Hofmann that same

414

afternoon, but noticed nothing unusual about Hofmann's statements. "At that time, he was totally a victim as far as I was concerned," Bell said.

Bell left the hospital and met agents at the scene of the car bombing. As they began going through evidence there and correlating it to Hofmann's statements, Bell's opinion on Hofmann's involvement "changed right then and there." The bomb had not exploded on the floor of the car. Rather, evidence indicated it had been sitting on the console when it detonated.

Detectives also used computers to run every possible combination of license numbers with letters and numbers Hofmann had provided. None was registered to a brown pickup.

Later that same night, after securing a search warrant, officers searched Mark Hofmann's car. They found pieces of ancient Egyptian papyrus, a few historical documents and a plane ticket to New York. They also found brown wrapping paper, a pair of rubber gloves, a black felt marking pen and a piece of pipe.

At that same time, other detectives were searching Hofmann's home for evidence that he made the bombs. They found no evidence of such construction. But tucked away in a corner of a closet, searchers found a green letter jacket. The evidence was circumstantial, yes, but it changed Mark Hofmann from a simple victim into a prime suspect.

The next morning, Bell returned to the hospital to question Hofmann again. After giving Hofmann a Miranda warning, Bell then asked him if he had set the bombs that killed Steven Christensen and Kathleen Sheets. "He said he didn't do it," recalled Bell.

Bell told Hofmann that he was fairly confident he had set the bombs, that police had recovered the green letter jacket from his home. "That set off the medical alarms," recalled Bell, who was then ushered from the room by some doctors. That was to be Hofmann's last interview with police.

Investigators were increasingly confident they were on the right track, but they needed better evidence that Hofmann set the bombs. They also needed a motive.

Detectives Bell and Farnsworth returned to James Martini's jewelry shop in the Judge Building and showed him a photo spread of eight or nine pictures. "One picture gave me a strong feeling in my stomach. It made me feel uneasy," said Martini. He picked it out and handed it to detectives. It was a photo of Mark Hofmann.

Detectives showed the same photo spread to Meg Stewart, but she was unable to pick out the man she had seen.

There was a serious problem with the green letter jacket. The jacket recovered from Hofmann's house had gray sleeves. Martini had described it as having brown sleeves. It was a significant difference, one defense attorneys were sure to capitalize on. Sleuths took the jacket to the Judge Building lobby, where Martini examined it under the same poor lighting that had existed the morning of the bombings. The sleeves appeared brown.

Detectives later located a woman who knew Hofmann and who had seen him in downtown Salt Lake City a few hours after the bombings. She remembered he was wearing a green letter jacket.

Linking Hofmann to the Sheets killing was proving more difficult. The only real witness was an 11-year-old neighbor boy who had been up late the night before the bombings. He looked out the window of his house and watched a gold mini van pull into the Sheets driveway, turn around and then drive slowly away. Hofmann often drove a gold mini van. Witnesses told police he had been driving the van the night before the bombings.

But why kill Christensen or Kathleen Sheets? Kathleen's husband told police he had never heard of Mark Hofmann before and knew of no reason why Hofmann would want to kill him or his wife. Hofmann had no business dealings with CFS or the Sheets family, he added.

But Hofmann did have business dealings with Steven Christensen, sleuths learned. Christensen was an avid collector of historical documents, particularly documents related to the Mormon Church. He had recently purchased from Hofmann a very controversial letter for $40,000.

Christensen's business associates told police that Hofmann had been negotiating to sell Christensen a collection of historical Mormon papers for $185,000. Christensen was to have taken delivery on the day he was killed.

Maybe something had gone awry in the deal, but why kill Christensen? police wondered. Christensen, a devoted father of four young children, was a very religious man. He served as a lay clergyman in his local Mormon congregation, and he was admired by all for the love and charity he exhibited toward everyone. No one could understand why someone would murder him. He was the last person in the world to have enemies, his friends said.

On the other hand, those who knew Mark Hofmann swore there was no way he could have committed the heinous crimes. Hofmann was himself a devoted Mormon, an active churchgoer, a family man with four young children and had a career that was flourishing. He was nationally respected for his work with documents and was hailed in many circles as a genius in the field of early Mormon history. When police named him their prime suspect in the bombings, those who knew Hofmann scoffed openly at police.

But police were confident the motive to the two murders lay somewhere in the hundreds of documents Hofmann had discovered and sold over the years.

When detectives searched Hofmann's home for evidence of bomb construction, they noticed a number of historical documents, along with information concerning the processing and handling of paper and ink. Armed with a second search warrant, officers confiscated several boxes of personal papers, books and equipment used in the documents trade. One of the books was

Great Forgers and Famous Fakes, a standard text for anyone dealing in documents.

Farnsworth and Bell began a crash course in historical documents, researching every document Hofmann had bought or sold. They got to the point where they could recognize all documents that Hofmann had sold, and also identify how and where Hofmann discovered them.

The first major break in the case came when two detectives were going through a box of Hofmann's personal papers and discovered a used manila envelope. On one side was the name of a Salt Lake engraving company. On the other was the name "Mike Hansen." Also in the box, they found a receipt from a tire store to someone named Mike Hansen.

Uncertain who Mike Hansen was, Farnsworth and Bell went to the engraving shop and questioned employees there. A search of store receipts turned up a receipt to a Mike Hansen for an engraving plate.

When engravers make a plate for printing purposes, they take photographs to ensure the accuracy of their reproductions. On a hunch, detectives began wading through thousands of engraving plate negatives, looking for something they might recognize.

After hours of tedious effort, they found something: a negative for a historic promissory note. But the negative was for a blank note. The notes Hofmann had sold carried the signatures of famous 1800s frontiersman Jim Bridger and a trapping companion. Hofmann had sold 16 Bridger promissory notes for about $5,000 each.

Prior to Hofmann's discovery of the notes, only a couple of Bridger's notes were known to be in existence. Police now had evidence in their hands that the 16 Bridger notes Hofmann had sold had been printed in 1985 and that the signatures had been forged.

The negative linked Hofmann to the Mike Hansen alias in a circumstantial way, but not good enough for court. Deciding Hofmann probably did not use the same engraver for all his work, sleuths began going to every engraver in the state, looking for negatives and receipts to anyone named Mike Hansen or Mark Hofmann.

At one shop, they found another receipt made out to Mike Hansen. Detectives turned the document over to forensic examiners who managed to lift a fingerprint from one corner of the document. It was a fingerprint from Mark Hofmann's left hand.

The fingerprint was the most convincing piece of evidence yet linking Hofmann to the Mike Hansen alias. The final pieces of the Mike Hansen puzzle came together when detectives linked the alias to bomb components.

One ATF investigator recognized the mercury switches, recovered from both murder scenes, as a brand sold at Radio Shack. Dozens of investigators began visiting every Radio Shack in the state, looking for anyone who remembered selling C-cell battery packs or mercury switches.

At a Radio Shack near Hofmann's home, detectives found a receipt, dated six days before the killing, for one mercury switch and two C-cell battery packs. The name on the receipt was Mike Hansen. The address he had given on the receipt was for a vacant field. The store clerk described the buyer only as "average looking."

Before investigators finished their canvass of Radio Shack stores, they found another receipt for a mercury switch. The purchaser's name was M. Hansen and again the home address was for a vacant field.

Detectives were confident they now had the evidence to positively link Hofmann to the bombings. Not only had witnesses placed him at the scene of the Christensen killing, but Hofmann's fingerprint on the Mike Hansen engraving receipt linked him to the Mike Hansen who had purchased items identical to those used in the bombs. It was still circumstantial, yes, but investigators were positive it would convince a jury.

But detectives were still a little puzzled about the motive. Why kill Christensen or Sheets? It appeared more and more obvious that Kathleen Sheets was killed to divert attention away from Hofmann's dealings with Christensen, instead directing the police investigation to her husband's failing business.

But why kill Christensen? Had Christensen discovered something so incriminating that Hofmann panicked? Had Christensen discovered the forgeries?

Detectives knew the forgery element had to be the key. Farnsworth and Bell began visiting every engraving shop in the state, eventually following leads into Missouri and Colorado. At another Salt Lake engraving company, they discovered that on December 5, 1984, a man named Mike Hansen had ordered an engraving plate.

This plate was a reproduction of a signature of famed American novelist Jack London. Mike Hansen had also placed an order for a printing plate with the name and address of a man in California.

During their investigation, detectives had located a local orthodontist who had loaned Hofmann $90,000. For collateral, Hofmann had given the man a first-edition copy of London's classic *Call of the Wild*. On the inside of the book was London's signature, an inscription and an address of the book's owner in California. The signature and inscription made the novel worth at least $9,000, much more than a regular first edition *Call of the Wild*.

Detectives compared the signature and address in the book with the printing plates that Mike Hansen had ordered. They were identical to the last detail. In fact, the engraver remembered that the man who ordered the plates had been very specific: The plates had to be exactly like the copy the customer presented.

There was another negative in the engraver's file that caught the attention of the sleuths. About a year before the bombings, Hofmann had been given a copy of a rare Mormon hymnal more than 150 years old. The Mormon Church had given the hymnal to Hofmann in trade for other historical documents. It was worth a couple of thou-

420

sand dollars. It could have been worth several times that figure, but two pages were missing: the cover page and the last page in the book, which had a song known as "The Spirit of God." Sometime after the church had given the hymnal to Hofmann, he sold an identical hymnal to a Utah collector for more than $10,000. Only the hymnal Hofmann sold was not missing any pages. Police could find no evidence Hofmann ever owned two such treasures.

As detectives waded through thousands of negatives at the engraving shop, they found a negative of the "Spirit of God" page from the hymnal. It was apparent that Hofmann had replaced the missing pages in order to substantially increase the book's value. Unbeknownst to the buyer, though, the replacement pages were really forgeries.

Much of Mark Hofmann's business dealings concerned rare Old West currency. In the early West, standard U.S. currency was rare, prompting different communities to develop entire sets of extremely rare notes, some so obscure that they had never before been seen. Collectors of such early money would pay tens of thousands of dollars for Hofmann's discoveries.

At a Salt Lake rubber stamp company, detectives found a receipt to Mike Hansen for several money symbols. They were not ordinary symbols, rather they were the style used more than a century before. Mike Hansen had been adamant: The rubber stamps must look exactly like the copies he had presented. Detectives compared the symbols ordered by Mike Hansen with some of the early money Hofmann had sold. The symbols were identical down to every last detail.

One prominent Utah coin dealer, a frequent customer of Hofmann's, told investigators that Hofmann had approached him in 1984 with a complete set of "Deseret Currency" scrip, money used to finance an Indian war in 1858. The set was in denominations of $1, $2, $5, $10, $20, $50 and $100. The collector was ecstatic over the find. No such scrip had ever before been discovered in denominations

421

above $5. He paid Hofmann $35,000 for the set.

A few months later, Hofmann returned to the same collector with a set of rare hand-written "white notes," currency issued in Utah in 1849 that carried the signature of Brigham Young.

"The discovery was so rare," the collector said. "It really shook me up. It blew my mind. I had never seen one before." The collector purchased one of the notes for $12,000. "I thought it was a very good bargain," he said.

Detectives now had in their hands the evidence that the "very good bargain" was in fact a forgery done with rubber stamps.

Although the forgeries discovered thus far added up to a total well in excess of $100,000, detectives were not prepared for their next find. Several months before the bombings, Hofmann had been browsing through a file cabinet of a New York documents dealer when he found a document called "Oath of a Freeman," an early pilgrim pledge of loyalty. He bought the document for $25 and then turned around and put it up for sale for $1.5 million. The oath was the oldest printed document in America, experts said.

Hofmann did have a receipt from a New York dealer for $25, but lawmen were certain it was not for a legitimate "Oath of a Freeman." While going through the negatives of one engraving company, detectives found a negative for a printing plate for the same oath Hofmann was trying to sell. Someone named Mike Hansen had ordered the plate 12 days after Hofmann said he purchased "Oath of a Freeman" from the New York dealer.

Experts examined both the oath and the engraver's negative under microscopes. They were identical even down to microscopic flaws in the printing plate. The "oldest" document in America was in fact less than a year old, and it was obvious Hofmann had forged it.

Detectives found other evidence of Hofmann forgeries. At a Denver engraving shop, investigators found receipts to Mike Hansen. The address again given by Hansen was within one digit of a residence where one of Hofmann's relatives lived.

In Kansas City, detectives found an engraving company that had filled orders for Mike Hansen. Only Mike Hansen had paid for the order with a personal check that carried the name Mark Hofmann.

In Salt Lake City, probers found a receipt made out to a Mike Harris. The phone number given by Harris was in fact an unlisted phone number for Mark W. Hofmann.

There was no question that Mark Hofmann was using an alias to order engraving plates and that the subjects of those engraving plates were later showing up as important historical discoveries. But how was Hofmann doing the actual forgeries? How could he fool the nation's best documents experts? Many of his discoveries had been examined in detail and had been authenticated by the best in the business.

Determining the authenticity of historical documents is a highly technical field. It is also beyond the technical ability of Salt Lake detectives. Investigators decided to bring in experts of their own to look at the documents and run chemical tests on them. The man that broke the case was William Flyn, a forensic documents examiner for the Arizona State Crime Lab, one of the nation's foremost documents examiners.

Flyn decided the best way to approach the investigation was to gather together all documents that Mark Hofmann had discovered and compare them to other 19th century documents to see if Hofmann's documents shared characteristics that none of the 19th century documents had. For example, if it could be shown the paper or ink was the same in all of Hofmann's discoveries, it would certainly cast doubt on the authenticity of the documents.

Most of Hofmann's discoveries were of a religious nature. They were letters between early Mormon Church leaders, business contracts, land deeds and other communications. Many of them were highly controversial because they contained historical information that conflicted with orthodox church teachings.

Flyn gathered all the Hofmann documents he could from private collectors, museums and the Mormon Church. All cooperated fully with Flyn's investigation. In all, Flyn studied 461 documents, more than 20 of which were known to have been discovered by Mark Hofmann.

During a court hearing, Flyn testified that many of the documents exhibited a microscopic cracking on the surface of the inks, kind of like skin of an alligator. Also, under ultraviolet examination, Flyn noted a one-directional running of the inks on a few documents, as if they had at one time been wet and then hung up to dry. Some documents showed portions of the ink were not the same as in other sections of the same document. "That is to say that data had been added to the document with a different ink," Flyn explained to the court.

All of the unusual characteristics—the cracking of inks, the adding of different inks, the one-directional running of inks—were found only on documents discovered by Mark Hofmann. None of the other 440 documents, all legitimate documents from the 19th century, exhibited any of those characteristics.

"These anomalies all occurred on documents that had been dealt by Mark Hofmann," Flyn said. "None of the documents not associated with Mark Hofmann exhibited those characteristics."

Recognizing the forgery is one thing. Proving how it was done is another. Flyn read in an old text how to artificially age iron gallotannic ink by exposing it to ammonia or sodium hydroxide.

Said Flyn: "After I read that, I made iron gallotannic inks of various types myself and exposed them to both ammonia and sodium hydroxide, and found that it did indeed artificially age the inks. The sodium hydroxide in particular will immediately take the iron gallotannic inks and turn them a deep rust color on paper."

424

But the artificial aging process didn't crack the inks like they had on the Hofmann documents. Flyn re-examined his ink recipe and noticed that some recipes called for additives, most commonly gums and sugars, to give the ink body and to adjust its thickness.

"When I mixed the iron gallotannic inks and added either the sugars or the gum arabic and then artificially age them with sodium hydroxide, I got exactly the same phenomenon as appeared on the Mark Hofmann documents. The ink both artificially aged and cracked," Flyn testified.

Flyn explained the cracking effect is due to a change in the viscosity of gums and sugars when they change rapidly from an acidic state to an alkaline state. "And it's amazing. Under a microscope you can put a drop of sodium hydroxide on iron gallotannic ink with gums and sugars and watch the ink crack."

Flyn said Hofmann probably artificially aged the documents with chemicals by "simply taping a document inside a tank and letting the fumes attack the ink, or you can spray them with an air gun or you can dip them."

Flyn said it was the gum that probably tripped Hofmann up. The book *Great Forgers and Famous Fakes* recovered from Hofmann's home, gives a recipe for iron gallotannic ink. It called for one ounce of gum arabic.

Flyn did not work alone during the examinations. Also on hand was George Throckmorton, a forensic documents examiner with the Utah Attorney General's Office. Throckmorton also noted the ink cracking phenomenon, but he also noted something else. Many of the documents gave off a curious blue haze when placed under ultraviolet light. Only those documents that had come from Hofmann exhibited the hazing effect.

"The blue hazing effect could have been produced in two different manners," explained Throckmorton. I noticed in my personal tests that on some of the old papers we had for experimental purposes that when dipped or treated with ammonium hydroxide, it did leave a sort of blue hazing effect under ultraviolet light. The blue hazing effect also occurred when we treated the document with a weak solution of sodium hypochloride."

It was apparent from examining Hofmann's documents that all were forgeries. In some cases, the entire document was forged. In other cases, Hofmann appeared to have changed dates or added names. All documents Hofmann dealt with exhibited some signs of forgery.

The forgery scheme was both elaborate and brilliant. Hofmann had been dealing documents for six years and had never been suspected of forgery. Said one East Coast expert: "We're talking about everything from early American history to bank notes to documents and letters of a religious history to American literary first editions. As far as I know, that has never been done before on the kind of scale we're talking about. He could be one of the best forgers ever."

The forgeries were so good, in fact, that many of the nation's foremost documents experts ridiculed investigators' claims that Hofmann was a forger. One expert said, "We're dealing with a Western culture where anything before 1860 is considered awfully old. I seriously doubt Salt Lake police are capable of telling the age of paper. From my experience of the police there, and I have appeared before them many times in connection with this case, they are predetermined to make a case against Mark Hofmann and they'll do anything to that end."

The criticism intensified when Mark Hofmann took and passed a polygraph test.

Defense attorneys were quick to publicize the results of the test, which they said proved that Mark Hofmann was home with his wife at the time of the bombings. His spouse passed a polygraph test as well.

Detectives were not anxious to tip their hand. They knew they had enough evidence on Hofmann to put him in prison for a very long time. It didn't matter what a polygraph examiner said. They knew he was guilty.

In the process of investigating the forgeries, Detectives Bell and Farnsworth uncovered evidence of a major fraud that may have been the real motive behind Steven Christensen's death. On the day Christensen was killed, he was to have taken delivery of a collection of early Mormon documents called the "McLellin Collection." Hofmann had been given $185,000 to purchase the collection and was then to turn it over to Christensen, who was going to arrange for experts to authenticate it.

Not only could police find no evidence Hofmann ever had the McLellin Collection, but they found another Salt Lake man who had given Hofmann $150,000 for the same collection. He was also still waiting for delivery.

In the days prior to the bombings, Hofmann had been trying to sell pieces of Egyptian papyrus to various collectors, claiming they were from the McLellin Collection. The McLellin Collection, which no one associated with Hofmann had seen, was rumored to include such pieces of papyrus.

But as investigators began probing the papyrus Hofmann was trying to sell, they traced it to a world famous antiquities dealer. The dealer had been instrumental in proving the Hitler diaries to be fakes. This dealer had given Hofmann a large piece of papyrus from 1st century A.D. Egypt on consignment for $10,000.

Hofmann apparently cut the papyrus into small pieces and went around selling it as part of the McLellin Collection. The dealer identified the papyrus recovered from Hofmann's car as parts of the bigger piece he had given Hofmann. At no time had that papyrus ever been of the McLellin Collection, he said.

The dealer also provided a key to a possible motive. Christensen knew the dealer very well. In fact, the dealer had done authentication work for Christensen in the past. Christensen also knew about Hofmann's attempts to sell pieces of papyrus. What if Christensen had indicated to Hofmann that he was going to arrange for the dealer to authenticate the McLellin Collection? Christensen would in all likelihood discover from the dealer the true source of the papyrus, that it was not part of the McLellin Collection, and that Hofmann had been perpetrating a fraud.

Detectives were certain Hofmann never had the McLellin Collection, if it ever existed. He claimed to have purchased it from a Texas family, descendants of McLellin himself. But police could find no evidence that Hofmann ever went to Texas or had purchased the collection from anyone. In fact, several weeks after the bombings, a Salt Lake newspaper reporter finally tracked down the long-sought-after McLellin Collection in Texas. The owner had never heard of Mark Hofmann.

Sleuths theorized that Christensen must have found out that Hofmann never had the collection. Investigators found one witness who said he was meeting with Christensen a few days before the bombing when Mark Hofmann entered the office. Christensen excused himself without making formal introductions and the two went into a neighboring office. The witness could hear them arguing, but couldn't make out what was being said until he heard Christensen yell, "You can't hide that." Hofmann left the office moments later with a very somber expression on his face.

Police found other evidence of fraud in the days and weeks leading up to the bombings. One investor had given Hofmann $174,000 to purchase a Charles Dickens manuscript. He never told the investor that others had already put up similar amounts, thinking they alone had purchased the document.

One investor became so angry at Hofmann's failure to deliver as promised that he demanded his money back and then slugged Hofmann. The stunned documents dealer replied, "No one's ever struck me before." Still, the man never got his money back.

What Hofmann did with the money, which totaled well over $1 million, no one is certain. In the days leading up to the bombings, Hofmann was pleading with his creditors to give him more time, that he was losing his house and car. "I've never seen him like that before," said one friend. "Mark said he would sell anything he had to raise the money."

Detectives had what they needed. Criminal charges were filed against Mark Hofmann in January, 1986, charging him with two counts of first-degree murder and more than two dozen counts of forgery and fraud. In April and May of 1986, prosecutors began detailing their case against Mark Hofmann to a circuit court judge. Two months of testimony later, Mark Hofmann had been bound over to stand trial.

He never made it to his trial date, though. In January, 1987, Hofmann pleaded guilty to reduced counts of second-degree murder and one count each of fraud and forgery. He was sentenced to long terms at the Utah State Prison. The sentencing judge deplored the indiscriminate nature of the homicides and said the death penalty would have been appropriate. Having no authority to impose the death sentence for second-degree murder, the judge said he would recommend that Hofmann spend the rest of his life in prison.

The case against Mark Hofmann is not yet concluded. One of the deals of the plea bargain is that Hofmann meet with prosecutors to tell them everything about how he made the bombs, who the third bomb (that accidentally went off and injured Hofmann) was intended for, how exactly he forged the documents, and which documents are forged and which, if any, are legitimate.

Detective Farnsworth warned there was no guarantee that Hofmann would ever tell investigators the truth. He had deceived his family, friends and church.

"Even though he remains behind bars, he is pulling other people's strings by controlling the information others desperately need," said Farnsworth. "Whether he will be truthful and disclose the mysteries behind the murders and documents frauds will ultimately be his decision."

Those who know Hofmann are still puzzled. Hofmann did not seem the kind of person to commit murder. He was warm and soft-spoken. Investigators say behind that image was a pathological criminal who could deceive with impunity and who could kill without remorse.

Said one sheriff's detective: "At the time he placed the bombs, he needed to protect the exposure of his crimes. He didn't care if the Sheets children could have been killed or not. I don't know that it mattered to him who picked the bomb up."

One close friend believes he has the answer to how Hofmann could kill so remorselessly with no regard for who else might be killed or injured. "Mark Hofmann was an atheist. He did not believe in God. If there is no God, a person obviously cannot believe there is life after death. If Mark believed in this philosophy, then he believed there are no morals, no sin if there is no God."

One prosecutor said Hofmann's greatest talent was understanding people's greed. "Hofmann was consistently late, he missed appointments, bounced checks and generally frustrated those he dealt with. But in the end he always gave his customers what they wanted. Mark was masterful at dangling the carrot in front of his susceptible prey."

In the end, it was Hofmann's own over confidence that led to his downfall. Why else would a man commit murder wearing the one piece of clothing everyone associated with Mark Hofmann? Why else would he use an alias but pay for things with personalized checks?

"He combines con man techniques with a scholarly background in history and science," said one prosecutor. "But his over confidence caused him to miss a lot of important details—details that eventually gave him away. He would like to go down in history as the world's best forger."

EDITOR'S NOTE:

James Martini and Meg Stewart are not the real

names of the persons so named in the foregoing story. Fictitious names have been used because there is no reason for public interest in the identities of these persons.

APPENDIX

432

"20 Grand for a Double Murder"
True Detective, December, 1986

"Overkill Murder of the Rich Playboy"
True Detective, March, 1991

"Their Grand Scheme Climaxed in Triple-Murder!"
Master Detective, June, 1985

"He Burned His Victims Alive!"
True Detective, June, 1988

"Rich Couple Slashed with a Pair of Scissors!"
Inside Detective, March, 1985

"Who Ambushed the Kinky Millionaire?"
True Detective, August, 1987

"Wanton Murder of the Wealthy Socialite"
Front Page Detective, July, 1990

"The All-In-The-Family Million Dollar Murder"
Inside Detective, April, 1984

"Horror of Britain's 'Bambi' Murders!"
Master Detective, June, 1987

"Highway Horror for Hanna"
Official Detective, November, 1991

"Fiend Sucked Susan's Fingers Dry!"
Official Detective, April, 1992

"Cunning Brunette's Money & Murder Schemes!"
Inside Detective, May, 1985

"Murderous Mistress!"
Inside Detective, August, 1991

"Naked Came the Slasher!"
True Detective, January, 1991

"Master Forger Was A Con Man Killer"
Inside Detective, July, 1987